Finding the Monk Within

also by Edward C. Sellner
published by Paulist Press

STORIES OF THE CELTIC SOUL FRIENDS

Finding the Monk Within

Great Monastic Values for Today

Edward C. Sellner

HiddenSpring

Cover art by Sr. Mary Charles, OSB
Cover design by Joseph Cannizzaro
Book design by Lynn Else

Library of Congress Cataloging-in-Publication Data

Sellner, Edward Cletus.
Finding the monk within / by Edward C. Sellner.
p. cm.
Includes bibliographical references.
ISBN-13: 978-1-58768-048-9
1. Monastic and religious life. 2. Monastic and religious life—Biography. I. Title.
BX2432.3.S45 2008
271.0092'2—dc22

2007039841

Published by HiddenSpring
an imprint of Paulist Press
997 Macarthur Boulevard
Mahwah, New Jersey 07430

www.hiddenspringbooks.com

Printed and bound in the
United States of America

For Nora Chadwick,
Bernard McGinn,
Jacob Deiss, OSB, and
the Benedictine monks of Assumption Abbey

The term "monastic culture" is beginning to be seriously discussed today. It implies the development of a set of tastes and skills, of openness to certain specifically monastic values in all the arts and disciplines that have relation to the monastic life in all its fullness.

—*Thomas Merton,* Contemplative Prayer

Monasticism has its origin in the hidden places of the heart.

—*Wayne Teasdale,* A Monk in the World

Contents

Introduction

Scattered across the landscape of modern Europe, Russia, and the Middle East are the ruins of ancient Christian monasteries, evoking in sightseers and pilgrims alike a variety of often deeply felt responses. Some are struck by their haunting beauty, eliciting in the viewers nostalgia for what once was or perhaps reminding them of what their present lives now lack: a sense of solitude, silence, simplicity; an ordered, prayerful life. The English poet William Wordsworth in his "Lines Composed a Few Miles Above Tintern Abbey" in Wales, alludes to this response when he speaks of affections felt at Tintern "in the blood, and felt along the heart"; of

> A presence that disturbs me with the joy
> Of elevated thoughts; a sense sublime
> Of something far more deeply interfused....[1]

Others, upon seeing the piles of stones and the crumbling walls where stained-glass windows once lit the interior with transcendent light, are repulsed by what they consider to be a waste of time and money for a lifestyle seemingly so "selfish" and so out of touch with the problems and struggles of ordinary people. Their views are reflected in the caustic remarks of the eighteenth-century historian Edward Gibbon in his monumental work on the decline and fall of the Roman Empire: "The lives of the primitive monks were consumed in penance and solitude, undisturbed by the various occupations which fill the time, and exercise the faculties of reasonable, active, and social beings."[2]

Still other visitors, although perhaps initially drawn to the beauty of monastic sites, simply stare blankly at the ruins and turn away, unable to comprehend or appreciate what they do not understand, reminding us of the principle: A person does not clearly *see* what he or she does not *know*.

Whatever our response—whether joy, contempt, or ambivalence—monasteries elicit our attention. They do so, precisely because, lying deep within each of us and underlying much of contemporary Western and Eastern cultures, there is an ancient memory, a vital archetypal energy related to monasticism and its spirituality. Although largely unrecognized and unappreciated today, even, at times, openly ridiculed when recalled, this memory points to a living tradition that touches all of our lives—regardless of our gender or social-religious upbringing, our occupation or place of residence. In the East, this monastic memory includes Hinduism, Buddhism, Sufism, and Eastern Orthodox Christianity. For Orthodox Christians, monasticism originated with the desert fathers and mothers of late antiquity and grew to fruition in such monasteries as St. Catherine's in the Sinai, Mount Athos in Greece, and the numerous monasteries of ancient Kiev in Russia. This memory is also found in the West with its numerous monastic communities, such as the Celtic, Benedictine, and Cistercian, and other religious orders, all of which nurtured—and continue to foster—a daily life of prayer, work, study, and social outreach. In many ways, Christian monasticism in both East and West is responsible for the rise of institutions that we now take for granted, including schools, hospitals, hospices, orphanages, retreat houses, and centers of prayer. Protestants too have their own monastic past, influenced greatly by such men as Martin Luther and others who were monks long before they became reformers.

In the twentieth century, Thomas Merton referred to this rich heritage when he spoke of the need to rediscover and develop "a set of tastes and skills," "certain specifically monastic values in all the arts and disciplines."[3] He contrasted these monastic values with "the confused pattern of Western life." Though our culture is "woven [with] a certain memory" (one that he especially associated with the practice of contemplation), that memory, he said, is "so vague and so remote that it is hardly understood."[4] Merton, as many people know, spent his adult life as a Trappist monk introducing thousands of his readers to those monastic values, believing that everyone is "called to a deep interior life, perhaps even to mystical prayer, and to pass the fruits of your contemplation on to others. If you cannot do so by word, then by example."[5]

In the twenty-first century, other writers are affirming what Merton knew from his own observations. John S. Dunne, a theologian at the University of Notre Dame, writes eloquently of the importance of silence, reflection, and contemplation in a person's life, including his own, and suggests that without them individual lives and the broader American culture are increasingly "filled with violence."[6] Kathleen Norris, a Protestant laywoman, poet, and author, discusses how, living in a culture in which "time can seem like an enemy," she learned from her association with Benedictine communities in North Dakota and Minnesota, how "the monastic perspective welcomes time as a gift from God, and seeks to put it to good use rather than allowing us to be used up by it."[7]

Social critic Morris Berman is more direct and more vociferous than these others in his analysis of the contemporary scene. In his book, *The Twilight of American Culture,* he describes our culture today as in a state of "spiritual collapse," characterized not only by violence, but by an "increasing inability to relate to one another with a minimum of courtesy or even awareness." We live, he says, in a consumer society where shopping has become a popular form of entertainment, and "the medium works against depth and self-reflection." "We live in a collective adrenaline rush, a world of endless promotional/commercial bullshit that masks a deep systemic emptiness." If our civilization is to be saved, Berman writes, only "the new monastic individual" (NMI) will have the capacity to do so: someone who "sees through his or her own cultural conditioning and refuses to be blindly driven any longer by the heroic program of power and achievement." "Real spirituality," he suggests, "is most often a working *against* the grain." "You can choose a way of life that becomes its own 'monastery,' preserves the treasures of our heritage for yourself, and, hopefully, for future generations.... *You and I* can lead the 'monastic' life, and we can start to do it right now."[8]

Living in a culture that frequently encourages amnesia, illusion, and the avoidance of Reality, where do we start? How can we begin to change our lives, and perhaps in the process have some positive effect on our social, political, and religious institutions? How can we, as Merton recommends, start to incorporate monastic values when many of us are so unaware of the monastic heritage that they reflect? Without necessarily joining monasteries (although that, of course, for some is still a legitimate vocational choice), how can we begin to draw upon this rich monastic spirituality as a resource?

As a pastoral theologian, teacher, and spiritual writer, I would suggest that we start with the history of Christian monasticism itself, allowing it to become our mentor, guiding and teaching us the implications of that spiritual legacy for today. For many people, however, especially those living in a culture that focuses much more on the future than the past, history is a dead thing, lacking in interest, relevance, and vitality. For me, however, history has been, as long as I can remember, stories from the past that shed light on present conflicts and predicaments, and that reflect an awareness that not all that much has changed in us and the human journey. As the American writer William Faulkner has said: "the past isn't over; it isn't even past." That awareness is reflected in the meaning of the Irish word for history, *senchas,* which means simply "old tales," stories of heroes and ordinary people that can transform our lives. History can help us encounter *the living presence of the past,* which is, whether we are conscious of it or not, affecting us in all sorts of ways. My own mentor, Donald Allchin, wrote some time ago, in a book by that name, with a conviction that initially drew me to him: "It is only as we gather up the past in its fullness now, that we can live with real freedom towards the time which is coming. We are not liberated from the past by forgetting it. Rather I would believe the reverse is true....It may be, quite simply, the discovery of a saint, a book, an icon from some other part of the Christian world which suddenly we find to be intimately linked with us; the meeting with someone far away in space and time who yet becomes our friend and our contemporary."[9]

That perspective is one that has named numerous experiences of my own. Since childhood, my inner world has been populated with heroes, most of them called "saints," who have inspired me with their holiness and wisdom. My pilgrimages to numerous holy sites have only reinforced that awareness.[10] Evidently, others share that view. Elizabeth Johnson, for one, rightly observes that millions of people throughout the world "have set about creating meaningful lives for themselves and their families in the company of their saints."[11] From Africa, Asia, Europe, and Russia to North and South America, and in spiritual traditions other than Christianity,[12] people are rediscovering the significance of the saints, reclaiming them as spiritual mentors, exemplars, and partners in their daily struggles. As Thomas Merton himself observed, "The saints not only have life, they give it."[13]

With their daily prayer and often extensive libraries and scriptoria, monasteries have always been communities of memory, and the substance of that memory has been the lives of the saints. Jean Leclercq, in his classic on monastic history and culture, *The Love of Learning and the Desire for God,* posits how medieval monks who studied the early writers of the church considered the past, "not as being definitely over, but as a living reality which continued to animate the present." He goes on to say that "if the great ideas of the past are to remain young and vital, each generation must, in turn, think them through and rediscover them in their pristine newness."[14]

This book is based upon the belief that the past is a living thing, capable of teaching us today much about history's relevance, which hopefully each new generation will discover. It is about Christian leaders from the past, those associated with the beginnings of monasticism in both East and West, whom I consider to be contemporaries. All of them are now called "saints," not at all because they were "perfect" human beings (as numerous critics have pointed out), but because they *endeavored* to live authentic, holy lives. Precisely because of their struggles to do so, they have, I believe, something to teach us about monastic values, and, most of all, about ourselves. Theirs is a heritage, as the poet T. S. Eliot said that is "tongued with fire"; they represent aspects of a monastic tradition that can provide a flaming torch, a candle, a light in the midst of our contemporary darkness.

Despite the declining numbers in monastic and religious communities today, there are increasing numbers of laypeople interested in monasticism, and in being affiliated in some way with monasteries and religious communities, a trend that is considered by some, as "the most significant development in monasticism today."[15] More programs, primarily designed to support laypeople, are being created and made available. Some are loosely structured. In England and the United States, for example, the Order of St. Aidan and St. Hild provides a Rule of Life, spiritual guides, and a supportive community for people who want to follow spiritual practices associated with early Celtic Christianity. Participants agree to a daily rhythm of prayer, work, and rest, regular meetings with a spiritual guide called an *anamchara,* or soul friend, and a life committed to simplicity, care for the poor and powerless, respect for the earth, and "reconciliation of all to God in Christ."[16]

Other formation and spiritual direction programs are more closely linked to established religious communities. One example is that of the Cistercian associates. According to a recent article, these "like-minded men and women," evidently from a great variety of professions, are said to be searching for "a deeper contemplative presence in the world" by attempting to follow the teachings of Christ "while living in a world driven by an entirely different set of values," such as humility, obedience, stability, simplicity, and conversion. These values are personally appropriated through their interaction with specific Cistercian monastic communities, which frequently provide at least monthly meetings in which they can participate. On such days, time is spent in prayer, meditation, *lectio divina,* as well as additional time at the monastery for personal and private retreats.[17]

Like the Cistercian associates, the Oblates of St. Benedict provide similar opportunities. An ecumenical affiliation program that welcomes Christians, lay and ordained, who desire to incorporate and express Benedictine values in their daily lives, oblates are, as one program states, "those who discern that God has called them to more of a life of prayer and study and who have turned (for advice, help and direction) to the experience that monasticism has developed over the centuries. They are those who keep the monastic ideal before their eyes, even though they are not monks."[18]

This book is an attempt to help recover that monastic memory, the living presence of the past, for those who desire to name and incorporate monastic values: values of solitude and silence, faith and compassion, friendship and mentoring, contemplation and leadership itself. Chapter one examines the social and religious dimensions of the fourth century CE, the time when monasticism arose, and the life and leadership of Athanasius, bishop of Alexandria, who, although an ordained member of the hierarchy, promoted monastic values. Chapter two looks at Antony, the "first monk," whose story, as told by Athanasius, created an ecclesial revolution. Chapter three examines the lives of Martin of Tours and Hilary of Poitiers, two saintly heroes from Gaul whose leadership helped clarify Christianity's understanding of God, and what it means to follow Jesus. Chapters four and five cover leaders whose writings and ministry had a lasting effect on all of Christianity, for good and ill: Augustine and Jerome, both of whom valued friendship and mentoring. Chapter six explores John Cassian and what he learned from the desert elders about the importance of self-disclosure and mutuality, while chapter seven turns specifically to Brigit of Kildare and early Celtic monasticism where women's leadership and lay monastic participation were welcomed. In chapter eight, the life and thought of Gregory the Great, the first monastic pope, is discussed, with emphasis on contemplation as the foundation of effective leadership. Chapter nine examines the life of St. Benedict and the monastic spirituality that he created, as well as the notable contribution of his sister, Scholastica. Chapter ten focuses on Bernard of Clairvaux, the great monastic reform leader, who taught succeeding generations about mysticism and the importance, above everything else, of love.

Even though, as Leclerq states, "monasticism is inclined toward patristics"[19] due to the fact that so many writings on monastic origins are about or from the pens of male founders, this book attempts to be more inclusive. Though focusing upon well-known Church fathers because of their acknowledged influence, not to mention that their writings are more available, I try to show the significance of women's contributions, including the influence of Monica upon Augustine; of Marcella, Paula, and Eustochium upon Jerome; and of Scholastica upon Benedict. I also show how monasticism itself has its origins in early communities of women, and especially how much women and their leadership were appreciated in Celtic monasticism.

In many ways, all of these early Christian leaders, men and women alike, from Late Antiquity to the medieval period, are representative figures in the study of Christian spirituality. To study their lives is to encounter monastic traditions that are still very much alive. Like the Polynesian chiefs who were considered carriers of divine light for an entire people, or like the Hawaiian kahunas who were and are bearers of consciousness within each generation,[20] these early spiritual leaders were charismatic individuals whose lives were identified with fire, the sacred energy of God. Bearers of light, they passed on monastic values to generations of people, and they can do so for our own. To study their lives, and to let them become our spiritual mentors, is to discover what the poet T. S. Eliot already knew:

> ...the communication
> Of the dead is tongued with fire beyond the language of
> the living.[21]

Hopefully, by becoming familiar with their stories and their thought, you will begin to incorporate their perspectives and values into your own life, as the desert hermit St. Antony did from his own mentors before becoming a monk himself.

CHAPTER ONE

Light from the East— Athanasius of Alexandria

At every period, monks feel the attraction of the "light which comes from the East," from which they know they have received the ideas and the practices on which their way of life is founded.
—*Jean Leclercq, OSB*

When Athanasius was in exile, he betook himself to the holy and divine homes of contemplation in Egypt, where, secluding themselves from the world, and welcoming the desert, men live for God....He himself wrote the life of the divine Antony, and set forth, in the form of a narrative, the laws of the monastic life.
—Gregory of Nazianzus

Christian monasticism began in the East, flourishing in a region today referred to as "the Middle East," primarily Egypt, Libya, Syria, Israel, and the Sinai. The holy man considered to be monasticism's founder was St. Antony (251–356), identified by later generations as "the first monk" and "Father of Monks." As Jean Leclercq says about him, "He remained truly the Father of all monks; and so in all milieus and in every period of the Western Middle Ages they considered themselves as truly his sons."[1]

Ironically, although monasticism later became associated primarily with life lived *in community*, taking as its inspiration the description from the early church in which all were "united, heart and soul," holding all things in common and distributing everything "according to what each one needed" (cf. Acts 2:44–45;

4:32), Antony is portrayed in his life-story as spending much of his adult life *running away* from social contacts; desiring, above all, to be alone. In fact, the term for monk, *monachus,* means "solitary person." Many of those who followed Antony chose to live, as he had done, in seclusion, committed to simplicity of life, poverty, celibacy, and constant prayer. These monks were called "hermits" or "solitaires." As we will see, this did not mean that they were always isolated and never available to others, for, as the early stories show, they and Antony frequently acted as spiritual guides for those who came into the desert seeking help. (One of the ironies of human history seems to be that those who seek to live outside society have always been the ones most eagerly sought out for advice on how to live within it.) Still, the desert monks highly valued solitude as an opportunity to commune with God as well as to gain a clearer understanding of themselves.

After Antony, however, other forms of monasticism developed. If he represents the hermit or "eremetic life," the second major spiritual leader in the desert was Pachomius (292–346), the role model for those living in desert communities, a way of life called "cenobitic." A contemporary of Antony, and like him, an Egyptian by birth, Pachomius is especially known for his humility with his fellow monks and his teaching more by example than words. His monks saw him, as an early Life says, "laboring alone in the work of the monastery, whether tending the few vegetables or getting their food ready; or if someone knocked at the door of the monastery, it was again he who went to answer it. If any of them was sick, he ministered to him until he got well."[2] On numerous occasions, Pachomius is seen carrying clay on his back when building a monastery, weaving mats, cutting rushes, and even cleaning cisterns. He had no pretensions that spiritual leaders should be exempt from even the most menial of tasks.[3] Due to his example, Pachomian communities of men and women multiplied, especially in upper Egypt where they eventually constituted numerous monastic villages containing thousands of monks and nuns.

A third form of monasticism, communal life in, or in close proximity to, urban settings, was developed by St. Basil (c. 330–79), the brother of Gregory of Nyssa (c. 330–395) and of Macrina (c. 327–79). Basil, along with his brother, Gregory, and their mutual friend, Gregory of Nazianzus (c. 329–390), became known as the "Cappadocian fathers," major theologians who had a hand in fashioning a Trinitarian theology that emphasized both the one nature of God and the three persons of Father, Son, and Holy Spirit. Based upon his journey from Cappadocia in east-central Asia Minor to visit monks in Egypt and Palestine (present-day Israel), Basil eventually established his own monastic community upon his return to Cappadocia that was governed by a set of monastic rules that encouraged liturgical prayer, care for the poor, and the education of young people.[4] Although he became known as "the Great" because of his monastic leadership, it was his sister, Macrina, who evidently taught him about communal living in the first place.[5]

We know about Macrina through the stories written by her brother, Gregory of Nyssa. His manuscript about her is truly amazing, revealing much concerning the influence and leadership of women in the early monastic movement. As a young woman, she is said to have determined to start a "common life" within her home with her mother and her servants, treating the latter as "sisters and equals instead of slaves."[6] Contrary to the cultural expectations of women in Late Antiquity when men were primarily identified with philosophy and teaching, Macrina is also portrayed, like Socrates, acting as a teacher and spiritual guide. According to Kevin Corrigan, Macrina's leadership had a major effect on the development of monasticism, affecting many others besides Basil himself.[7] Hers, however, was not the only example of women creating or participating in monastic communities. We know, for example, that Antony's sister was in charge of a monastery in Egypt, that the sister of Pachomius headed a monastery for women, and, as we will see in a later chapter, that the Roman widow Marcella headed a community of women in her home, while many others acted as spiritual guides in the desert regions. In one city alone in Egypt, there were said to live twenty thousand virgins who outnumbered their male counterparts by two to one.[8]

Separate monasteries for men and for women, frequently existing side by side, as in many Pachomian monasteries, began to flourish in the fourth century. "Double monasteries" for both genders also flourished, and were seen more often in Egypt, headed by a male leader, but not always. Egeria, a Spanish nun who visited there in the late fourth century, reports finding the cells of both genders that formed a single monastery, all of whom were governed by the "holy deaconess Marthana."[9] Another woman, Melania (c. 383–438), along with the church historian Rufinus of Aquileia (c. 345–410), may have been the first to establish a double monastery located in Jerusalem. As a result of such pioneers as Antony, Pachomius, Basil, Macrina, Melania, Marthana, and others, "there were monasteries in the mountains, and the desert was made a city by monks, who left their own people and registered themselves for the citizenship in the heavens."[10] Christian monks throughout the following centuries looked back to this early period of formation, inspired by "the light which comes from the East."[11]

This chapter will briefly examine the historical period of the fourth century in which monasticism was born, and then focus upon the Egyptian leader who was instrumental in popularizing it: Athanasius (c. 296–373), the bishop of Alexandria, who loved monasticism and, through his writings, sermons, and conversations, was the first to introduce knowledge of monasticism to the West. Most importantly, it was his *Life of Antony* that became, according to Derwas Chitty, not only "a classic of the spiritual life," but "the first great manifesto of the monastic ideal."[12]

The Fourth Century: Creative Turmoil

Of all the centuries following the life and ministry of Jesus, the fourth century of the Christian era is surely one of the most momentous, a time of tremendous political and religious changes that had a profound effect upon the emerging Church. First, after years of intermittent persecutions of Christians, the Roman emperor himself, Constantine (c. 285–337), converted to Christianity, declaring in the Edict of Milan of 313 the Roman state's official tolerance of Christians, setting in motion a process that would transform a once marginalized sect to one having increasing prestige and power. Constantine's conversion brought many benefits to the Church, not the least of which was the cessation of persecution and the restoration of Christian property that had been confiscated or destroyed. Christians who had been exiled because of their views or condemned to forced labor or made slaves—all were to have their freedom. As a result, they no longer had to exist in a survival mode, attempting to spread their beliefs and spiritual practices while being persecuted for their "atheistic" views. Now they had the ability to practice their religion as they saw fit, organizing ecclesial structures and expressing their worship and spirituality in new forms.

At the same time, this new freedom brought with it an explosion of theological debates that began to divide Christians, one from another. In the Latin-speaking Western part of the empire, Hilary (315–397), the bishop of Poitiers in Gaul, for one, found it "deplorable and dangerous that there are as many creeds as opinions among men, as many doctrines as inclinations....Every year, nay, every moon, we make new creeds to describe invisible mysteries. We repent what we have done, we defend those who repent, we anathematise those whom we defended..., and, reciprocally tearing one another to pieces, we have been the cause of each other's ruin." In another part of the empire, the Greek-speaking East, Gregory of Nazianzus in Cappadocia, also lamented that "the kingdom of heaven was converted by discord into the image of chaos, of a nocturnal tempest, and of hell itself."[13] It was indeed a time of chaos, of turmoil, that, although dark and destructive, also eventually led to greater clarity in what Christians believed as well as the birth of a new breed of Christians: the monk.

Of course, there had always been theological differences, beginning with the diverse personalities and perspectives of Jesus' original disciples, and later reflected in the content of the four gospels themselves. But by the fourth century, with the freedom to disagree, differences within Christianity itself became openly debated, frequently with more ferocity than Christian charity.

This was the century in which a battle began to form between "orthodoxy" (meaning "correct teaching") and "heresy" ("false paths"). Many leaders and their followers, in their genuine attempts to understand the profound mystery of God, took sometimes widely diverging views. As R. P. C. Hanson rightly points out, these early theological conflicts, at least initially, had not so much to do with *defending* orthodoxy as *defining* it.[14] This is precisely what Constantine attempted to do by calling the Council of Nicea (now the city of Iznik in Turkey) in 325. His hope was that by reaching theological agreements among the bishops, *religious* unity within his empire would bring about greater *political* unity.

The main controversy of the council had to do with basic Christian belief regarding the Trinity: the belief that the *one* God was made up of *three* persons equally divine and of equal status: God "the Father," God "the Son," and God "the Holy Spirit." At Nicea, the debate focused more specifically on the nature of Jesus, especially his relationship to God the Father. (The question of the Holy Spirit would be addressed and developed more fully later, especially in the writings of Athanasius, Basil of Cappadocia, and Hilary of Poitiers.)[15] While orthodox believers at Nicea, supported by Alexander, the then bishop of Alexandria, and his young deacon, Athanasius, stated that Jesus was "consubstantial," of one substance with God, and thus truly divine as well as human, followers of a priest from Alexandria called Arius (c. 250–336) stated that Jesus was "like God"; similar to God but not really divine. Arius's argument was that if the Father begat the Son, then the Son must have had a birth in time; therefore, there was a time when the Son of God did not exist. If the Son had come into existence according to the will of the Father, he was, thus, less than the Father, though greater than man. To make their point, Arian followers frequently chanted the slogan, "there was a time when the Son was not." Athanasius and his supporters said the opposite: Christ is God and coequal with God the Father. Sulpicius Severus (c. 363–420), the church historian and biographer of St. Martin of Tours, explains this difference when he describes the proceedings at Nicea in his book, *The Sacred History:*

> ...they [the Arians] interpreted after their own views the Synod of Nicea, and by the addition of one [Greek] letter to its finding, threw a sort of obscurity over the truth. For where the expression *Homoousion* had been written, which denotes "of one substance," they maintained that it was written *Homoiousion*, which simply means "of like substance." They thus granted a likeness, but took away unity; for likeness is very different from unity; just as, for illustration's sake, a picture of a human body might be like a man, and yet possess nothing of the reality of a man.[16]

The bishops at Nicea overwhelmingly agreed with the orthodox position articulated by Athanasius and others, endorsing the coequality of Father and Son in a new creed. Constantine supported this view, but, unfortunately, in the years following the council the apparent consensus reached at Nicea broke down. Due to numerous court intrigues, Arian believers in the empire, supported for a variety of political reasons by the Roman emperors themselves, frequently outnumbered the orthodox. Though the fury of the debate prompted the British historian Edward Gibbon to comment that never had there been so much energy spent over a single vowel,[17] Christians today, Catholic, Protestant, and Eastern Orthodox, agree with the description of Jesus as *both* human *and* divine. After Nicea, the two men who had the greatest effect on the survival of this understanding were, in the East, Athanasius, the bishop of Alexandria, and in the West, Hilary of Poitiers, pastoral leaders described by Rufinus in his *Church History* as "two great lights in the world, [who] lit up Illyricum, Italy, and Gaul with their brightness, so that all the darkness of heresy was driven from even the most remote and hidden corners."[18]

Besides these passionate theological conflicts, another major debate arose in the years following Constantine's recognition of Christianity, a debate Philip Rousseau identifies as "centred not only on doctrine but also on the structure and organization of the church." As Christians increasingly became more assimilated into Roman culture, building fine churches (or taking over the beautiful temples of the pagan gods), and at the same time adapting their liturgies to those of the emperor's court, many began to long for a return to the original simplicity of the gospels. They also began to question the direction of some of their leaders who were developing a more clerical lifestyle. "Spiritual leaders endowed with charismatic power," Rousseau says, "were gradually taken over by men whose qualifications were almost entirely clerical."[19] Jerome (c. 347–420) addresses this trend with his usual caustic remarks, these directed at bishops who act like "lords," and priests who think only of money and how they are dressed: "they must be nicely scented, and their shoes must fit without a crease; their hair is curled and still shows traces of the tongs, their fingers glisten with rings; and if there is wet on the road they walk across on tiptoe so as not to splash their feet." Rather, Jerome reminds them, "you are priests of a crucified Lord, one who lived in poverty and on the bread of strangers...."[20]

As Jerome's comments reveal, within a generation after Constantine, the Church that Jesus had founded had taken on the trappings and structures of a powerful, organized religion, a move that was not appreciated by many Christian followers. This dissatisfaction, this thirst for something else, something more, was precisely what led to the popularity of monasticism as it arose, a new form of Christianity that espoused a return to many of the values originally associated with Jesus. This new breed of Christians offered a new paradigm of the holy life: the monk, a person in search of solitude and communion with God, reacting against Christianity's new comfortability and power. In many ways, monasticism itself was primarily a lay movement that offered an alternative to the rising clericalism and extravagance that divided leaders from those whom they were called to serve. Early monastics, in fact, discouraged priests from joining their communities and from having bishops visit them. Initially, Pachomius's communities, for example, allowed no priests to enter their ranks since they associated priests with what they called a "love of command." There are also stories about desert elders hiding when a bishop approached, fearing that he might want to ordain them. One monk, Ammonius, even went so far as to cut off his ear in order to avoid being made a bishop.[21]

This tension between the emerging Church hierarchy and the monks would grow in the following decades and centuries, with the clergy increasingly becoming more acculturated, living as they did, within society, often as married priests or bishops, while the monks, living on the margins, developed a more ascetic and frequently celibate lifestyle. Not all bishops or clergy, of course, were tainted with clericalism. Some, in fact, were in the forefront of those incorporating monastic values into their daily lives and work. One of these was Athanasius, who was, as we have seen, so instrumental in defending orthodoxy at the Council of Nicea, a man whom Gregory of Nazianzus described as a leader who showed "that the priesthood is capable of contemplation," and that "the monastic life is characterized by steadfastness of disposition rather than by bodily retirement."[22] This Athanasius, bishop of Alexandria for 46 years (although he spent much of his time in exile for his beliefs), not only lived with desert monks for extended periods, but wrote the life-story of St. Antony that drew countless people to embrace monasticism and monastic values, providing a model of holiness for monks as well as for those desiring to live a faithful, steadfast life *in society.*

Alexandria's Famous Catechetical School

Athanasius, the biographer of Antony, grew up in Alexandria, located in northern Egypt at the mouth of the Nile River, on the coast of the Mediterranean Sea. The city had been founded in 331 BCE by the youthful Alexander the Great (356–323 BCE),[23] and it held the largest and best-equipped libraries, museums, and theaters. A city immersed in Greek culture and philosophy, the church that emerged there was one of the most dynamic in early Christianity, known for its intellectual life, mystical theology, and a method of interpreting scripture focused upon allegory and the *spiritual* meaning of texts. Out of Alexandria came the first great schools of the early Church; from it also came some of the Church's most talented theological and pastoral leaders. Two of the most famous were in charge of a catechetical school that educated not only young men, but also, most likely young women:[24] the Christian apologist Clement (c. 150–215) and Origen (c. 185–254).

Clement, through his writings, set out to explain Christian history and thought in terms that his students and his readers would understand by drawing upon Greek philosophy. "For the first time," Charles Kannengiesser says, "a Christian used the philosophical genre, created by Artistotle in the fourth century B.C." to call for "a conversion of the mind."[25] Clement presented Christianity as the highest fulfillment of all the varied philosophies of the ancient world, and, to substantiate his arguments, quoted over three hundred non-Christian writers, poets, dramatists, and historians, including Homer, Plato, Herodotus, and Philo.[26] While pagan philosophers, especially the Stoics, believed that virtue consisted of living according to the *logos* (the mind or reason), Clement recommended that his contemporaries open themselves to God's *Logos,* his "Word," the term the apostle John uses in the prologue of his gospel to describe Jesus (cf. John 1:1–18). Educated by the Christian Stoic Pantaenus, Clement was the first to make extensive use in his writings of the concept of "divinization," the theological term adopted later by Eastern Orthodox Christians to explain the process in which Christians seek to become, by living a holy life, more like the divine image in which they were created. As Clement expressed this, "the Logos of God [Jesus] became man so that you may learn from man how man may become God." One sign of divinization, according to him, is that of *apatheia,* the attainment of inner serenity. Adapting ideas and language from Stoic philosophers, Clement believed that this state can be acquired through ascetic living, which will help a person gain mastery over his or her desires. Those who do so become "friends of God."[27] Athanasius, as will become evident, adopted these ideas as his own, and expressed them in his writings.

Clement's most famous pupil was Origen, who has been described as "the greatest theologian the Eastern Church has produced."[28] He took over the Alexandrian catechetical school after Clement was forced to flee the city due to a persecution specifically directed against Christian educators. For eighteen years Origen administered programs and taught students before moving to the desert region of Caesarea in Palestine. Considered the most prolific writer of Late Antiquity, he produced an unbelievable amount of volumes. Estimates range from two thousand to six thousand works, which include extensive commentaries on scripture as well as homilies, dialogues, and letters.[29] His writings reveal that Origen's scholarship was profoundly rooted in his spirituality, a personal relationship with, as he says, "my Jesus" in prayer, and a belief that faithful Christians can come to "see" God with the heart. As Stoic philosophers and Clement himself had recommended, Origen lived very ascetically: fasting, limiting his sleep, walking barefoot, abstaining from alcohol in what his biographer, Eusebius of Caesarea, describes as "this philosophic way of life."[30]

Like Clement, Origen too sought to explain the Christian mysteries in the philosophical language of his time. He was the first Christian theologian to reflect on the spiritual meaning of the *Song of Songs* from the Old Testament as an image of the "mystical marriage" between Christ and the Church, and the individual person with Christ—a metaphor that would become extremely popular in numerous medieval mystical writings, including those of Bernard of Clairvaux, as we will see. He was also the first to delineate the mystical "ascent" as having three stages: purgation, illumination, and union. For Origen, this ascent was to a God of fire and flame, a spiritual presence who warms, illuminates, transforms. One of his students, Gregory Thaumaturgos, acknowledges the effect Origen had on him and his peers in those terms: "like some spark lighting upon our inmost soul, love was kindled and burst into flame within us."[31] Numerous writers later identified this community of Origen's, this "school of the inner life," with the origins of Christian monasticism itself. As W. H. C. Frend says, "quite rightly, his [Origen's] ideals have been regarded as an inspiration in the monastic movement, and his works were read eagerly in the monastic settlements."[32]

Athanasius's Spiritual Leadership

One of those who visited the monastic settlements of Egypt and read eagerly the works of Origen was Athanasius, the author of the *Life of Antony* and numerous other theological works.

Little is known of Athanasius's early years, except that he was born about 296 in Egypt of parents who may have been African, since more than one commentator refers to the unusual darkness of his skin. When Athanasius was a youth, Alexander, the bishop of Alexandria, became his patron and mentor, taking him into his house and employing him as a scribe. No one knows with certainty how the two of them met, but Rufinus tells an interesting story in his *Church History.* According to him, Alexander first met Athanasius near the seashore where the older man saw some boys at a distance playing a game "of mimicking a bishop and the things customarily done in church." The child who played the part of the bishop by pretending to baptize some of the boys acting as catechumens was Athanasius. Alexander was impressed, perhaps cognizant of how childhood play often can reveal a future career or vocation, and talked with the youth. Eventually, according to Rufinus, Athanasius's parents gave their son to the bishop to raise and educate, and, "like another Samuel," he "was brought up in the Lord's temple."[33] The young man lived with the older man as a son with a father. This was probably the time when he became a student at the famous catechetical school once led by Clement and Origen. There he received a typical classical education in grammar, logic, and rhetoric, studying the Greek philosophers as well as scripture and other early Christian works. As Kannengiesser says, "That he was well educated is clear from his later writings, impregnated with the Bible and the works of earlier Christian teachers, such as Origen."[34]

Athanasius evidently was a precocious student, demonstrating his talents as a writer at an early age. Before he was twenty years old and preceding the Council of Nicea, he produced an apologetic work that was eventually split into two writings, the first, entitled *Contra Gentes (An Oration Against Pagans)* and, the second, *De Incarnatione Verbi Dei (On the Incarnation of the Word of God)*. Drawing upon the thought of Clement and Origen, he delineates in both writings certain themes that will later appear in his *Life of Antony:* how paganism is based upon the worship of false gods or demons who lead humanity away from its full potential, and how that full potential is revealed in Jesus Christ. Demons "impose on people their deceits," while Christ, "the Word of God Himself," "assumed humanity that we might become God." Reflecting the thought of earlier Stoic philosophers and his own Christian mentors, he says that a sure way to becoming divine is through an ascetic life characterized by virtue and self-control. This is done, he says, by imitating Christ as well as the lives of the saints, "by copying their deeds."[35]

Ordained a deacon, Athanasius accompanied Alexander to the Nicea, as we have seen, "aiding the old man," Rufinus says, "with his assiduous advice."[36] There he made a name for himself, praised by the orthodox and vilified by the supporters of Arius. Within five months of the council's conclusion and their return to Alexandria, the older man died, and Athanasius, not yet even thirty years old, was chosen as his successor. He began his episcopal career with the usual responsibilities of a fourth-century bishop, involved in visitations and synods, pastoral correspondence, guidance, and preaching. During these early years of his episcopacy, before his life was overtaken with theological controversy, Athanasius visited the monks in the desert regions of Egypt, below Alexandria, and in nearby Libya. These experiences obviously affected his evolving theology, for, as already revealed in his earlier writings and now in his first *Festal Letters* (written to his people each year at Easter), Athanasius promoted ascetic ideals, suggesting that *every Christian*—not just the ascetic elite—was called to practice what the desert monks valued. (Even at the time of his election as bishop, he was called "the good, the pious, a Christian, one of the ascetics....")[37] As David Brakke says, "Early in his career...Athanasius already possessed a theology that embraced the values of asceticism, yet made room for ordinary Christians."[38]

This is possibly the time he became friends with the desert hermit Antony, although some scholars contend that Athanasius had spent some time with him as a young man.[39] No one knows precisely when the two spiritual leaders met, but it is clear in Athanasius's writings and in other sources that they developed over time a close friendship, reflected in Antony's interrupting his desert solitude to travel to Alexandria at least once to defend Athanasius's stand against the Arians, and his frequent writing to the emperor to have Athanasius reinstated after his first exile.[40] Their love was obviously mutual, considering Athanasius eventually wrote Antony's life-story, portraying him as a father figure, and the epitome of a faithful Christian, and stating in it that he saw Antony "often" and that Antony left him his sheepskin and cloak at the time of the older man's death.[41]

All of this, of course, came later, after theological controversy had interrupted the happiness of Athanasius's early years as an effective pastoral leader in Alexandria, loved by the people he served. The religious and political unity that Constantine had hoped the Council of Nicea would bring did not happen, especially as Arian supporters continued their attempts at influencing Constantine himself. In 336, so influenced, Constantine wrote to Athanasius, asking him to admit followers of Arius back into communion with the Church. Athanasius refused, saying that there could be no fellowship between the Church and those who denied the divinity of Christ. Athanasius's response did not set well with Constantine, who, not so much interested in theological orthodoxy as in promoting peace within his empire, banished Athanasius to Trier, the capital of Gaul. The bishop spent about a year and a half there, the first of five exiles that would keep him from Alexandria for a total of seventeen and a half years. Three of these years he would spend in Rome, and six in the deserts of upper Egypt, living with the monks.

Following the death of Constantine in May 337 (he had finally been baptized by an Arian bishop no less), his three sons took over the empire: Constans, who was sympathetic to orthodox views, and Constantius, an Arian follower, ruled Italy and the East, while Constantius II, a supporter of orthodoxy, ruled in the West. Athanasius was allowed to return to Alexandria, only to leave again when another bishop, an Arian, was appointed by Constantius to replace him. So Athanasius, accompanied by two of Antony's monks, traveled to Rome, seeking the help and support of the bishop who governed there. In Rome, he received an exceptionally hospitable welcome, greeted everywhere with deep respect as the apostle of orthodoxy and the promoter of monastic values. Supported by Emperor Constans, Athanasius lived in Rome for three years, while, back home, the emperor Constantius (a bit less supportive) sent an order that if Athanasius were caught, he should be beheaded!

While in Rome, Athanasius met with Western bishops and discussed theological issues, eventually receiving their support. It was in Rome, too, where he first began to promote the monasticism that had begun to arise in the desert regions below Alexandria. By telling Roman Christians of Antony and the desert monks, the bishop of Alexandria planted in the Latin Church those seeds of the monastic life that were to flower in St. Benedict and St. Bernard, and the entire spirituality of the West. As Edward Gibbon says, "Athanasius introduced into Rome the knowledge and practice of the monastic life....The senators, and more especially the matrons, transformed their palaces and villas into religious houses; and the narrow institution of *six* Vestals was eclipsed by the frequent monasteries, which were seated on the ruins of ancient temples and in the midst of the Roman forum."[42] Many individuals attest to the effect Athanasius's stories had on their own adoption of that ascetic lifestyle. Jerome, for example, describes in one of his numerous letters how Marcella, a wealthy Roman woman, first learned about desert monks, including Antony and Pachomius, from Athanasius, who had escaped "the persecution of the Arian heretics" and "fled for refuge to Rome."[43] As we will see in the chapter on Jerome and his female friends, Marcella established a community for women in the imperial city as a result of the stories she heard from Athanasius.

After spending time in Rome and then wandering over western Europe, giving sermons, addressing congregations of bishops, and visiting the sick and elderly, Athanasius was allowed to return to Alexandria once more, probably in October of 346. Within ten years, he was sent into exile again, possibly from 356 to 362, when a council in Milan condemned his theology. This is when he moved to Upper Egypt where the desert monks provided him shelter, as Gibbon tells us, serving him "as guards, as secretaries, and as messengers," while moving him on the approach of danger "from one place of concealment to another."[44] Although he sometimes would slip back into Alexandria to see friends, including a young woman who hid him for a while, cared for him, and obtained a "load of books for his use,"[45] he remained in the desert until 362. This period of exile and of forced solitude, although painful, was a highly productive and creative time for Athanasius. He wrote not only a number of important works, above all, *Orations Against the Arians,* considered to be his most important doctrinal exposition, but also his *Life of Antony,* begun shortly after the desert father's death in 356. Archibald Robinson says that this period "of forced abstention from affairs was the most stirring in spiritual and literary activity in the whole life of Athanasius."[46] More than half of all his literary works were written during this time.

Finally allowed to go back to his people in Alexandria, Athanasius was received with open arms, only to be sent packing again in the spring of 365 when a new emperor, an Arian supporter, came to the throne. This last exile was relatively brief, for in 366, the aging bishop was allowed to return to his beloved city, and to enjoy his last years undisturbed. Even then, however, he used his time and energy to stabilize and consolidate the Egyptian Church, while corresponding with Basil in Cappadocia about founding an Egyptian-like monasticism there. On January 18, 373, Athanasius died quietly in his own house, after an extremely long episcopacy, recognized for his writings, his pastoral leadership, and perhaps above all for his courage and persistence. Eulogized by Gregory of Nazianzus as "the pillar of the Church"[47] because of his defense of orthodoxy and his promoting of monastic values, Athanasius's feast day is celebrated on May 2. Besides his courageous leadership and his writings, he is identified as the one who produced in 367 the first list of the twenty-seven New Testament books that are today recognized by both Catholic and Protestant churches as inspired.[48] Of his numerous writings, most of them addressed to monastics, male and female, "long before any other Christian hierarch,"[49] the best known is the one on the life and spiritual leadership of the desert father Antony.

A Monk at Heart

Athanasius was one of the most significant figures in the fourth century, that time of creative turmoil when orthodoxy needed defending even as it was in the process of being defined. Primarily known for his defense of the Trinity, his other great contribution had to do with his promotion of monasticism as it emerged as a powerful, transforming force in the life of the Church. Bishop of the great city of Alexandria rather than a humble monk, he did not hesitate to promote monastic values. He did so with conviction, believing them to reflect the values of Jesus himself. He also did so precisely because of his love and admiration for Antony and other Egyptian monks, and his gratitude for their hospitality toward him when he most needed a place to hide. Ultimately, Athanasius's writings, especially that on Antony, made monasticism more appealing to large numbers of Christians looking for a spirituality that provided an alternative to the one the institutional Church had begun to offer.

Athanasius's love for monasticism characterized his life from early on. According to at least one scholar, the Alexandrian bishop's first writing, *On the Incarnation of the Word of God,* "shows the utter devotion of the monk at heart....His relations with the monks, the spiritual sons of Antony, run through the troubled years like a peaceful current beneath a stormy sea. The monks were unswerving in their loyalty to him; and he was consistent in his support of them...."[50] No wonder that later iconography portrays Athanasius not in bishop's clothes, but in the habit of a monk.[51] Without denying in any way the significance of Antony, "the first monk," the rise of monasticism in the West is largely due to Athanasius. Through his conversations in Rome, through his writings, and while in exile, he made monasticism even more popular. Because of his valuing that spirituality it spread like wild fire. A spiritual leader who, according to Gregory of Nazianzus in his eulogy on Athanasius, combined "both quiet action and active quietness,"[52] he reminds us that a person does not have to be a monk to live monastic values, but merely someone who loves that spiritual way of life.

In the next chapter, we turn directly to Athanasius's *Life of Antony* to see what it teaches about the monastic values of silence and solitude. Obviously based upon Athanasius's friendship with Antony, it reveals the author's own depth, which came "from meditating on every book of the Old and New Testament," as well as the personal suffering he experienced in his numerous exiles "when men," as Gregory of Nazianzus says, "came to hunt the saint like a wild beast."[53]

CHAPTER TWO

Hearts on Fire—Antony of Egypt

Antony persuaded many to take up the solitary life. And so, from then on, there were monasteries in the mountains, and the desert was made a city by monks....A great many monasteries came into being, and like a father he guided them all.

—Athanasius, *The Life of Antony*

Athanasius, as noted earlier, probably began writing his account of the life of the hermit Antony shortly after the desert elder had died in 356. He did so in response, he says, to a request from some unnamed monks for more information about the solitaire's life. He also may have done so as a way of grieving the loss of a dear friend, naming for himself what he had learned about spirituality from someone who in many ways was like a father to him (as Antony had been for so many others).[1] Athanasius certainly alludes to this when he says in the introduction to his book, "For simply to remember Antony is a great profit and assistance for me also."[2] It is also clear that Athanasius wrote for a larger audience than the desert monks. He had come to believe, through his years of church leadership, exile, and his own solitude in the desert, that the values the monks expressed in their daily lives were for everyone; that every Christian life necessarily includes some form of discipline, silence, solitude, and prayer. He thus sought to portray Antony as a model of holiness for all Christians to emulate. Considering his regard for the lives of the saints (as is apparent in his earliest writings), it was natural that instead of writing a monastic Rule as Pachomius, Basil, Benedict, Columban, and others would do, he wrote the biography of a monk whose life was worthy of imitation. As Gregory of Nazianzus said in his eulogy, Athanasius "composed a rule for the monastic life in the form of a narrative."[3] This rule-in-story-form was meant for all Christians—not just monks.

Whatever the motivation and whoever the audience, Athanasius's writing on Antony was the first Christian *vita* or life-story ever composed, part of a genre of ecclesial literature that became known as "hagiography," a term that derives from two Greek words: *graphe,* which means "writing," and *hagioi,* which means "about the saints." Hagiographies were written primarily to edify, to inspire, to invite conversion in the lives of their readers or to reinforce a person's commitment to Christian values and beliefs. As the first creator of such Christian stories, Athanasius very likely was influenced by pagan writers, for there seems to be a close resemblance in structure and style with such pagan Lives as *The Life of Appolonius of Tyana,* written about the middle of the third century, and *The Life of Pythagoras, The Life of Plotinus,* and *The Life of the Sophists,* written early in the fourth century. This form of writing, called "aretology" (i.e., an edifying dissertation), had been popular for centuries in pagan antiquity. All of these works portray pagan leaders and, in particular, philosophers as ideal models to emulate. The latter especially were depicted as effective teachers and even healers who were endowed with attributes of wisdom, devotion to an ascetic lifestyle, and intimacy with the gods or God.[4] Considering his Alexandrian education, Athanasius was probably very well acquainted with at least a few of these writings, including Plato's own highly idealized description of Socrates.

The personality of Antony in Athanasius's hagiography seems to fit that heroic, highly idealized mode: a man, yes, of such virtues as compassion, gentleness, and wisdom, but also someone who emerges after twenty years in solitude wrestling with demons as the paradigm of the divinized person who experiences "utter equilibrium,"[5] certainly similar to the *apatheia* described in the *Life of Pythagoras.*[6] While Athanasius's Life describes more of the mythic dimensions of Antony, Antony's *human* dimensions are probably reflected more in the correspondence that he left behind. These letters, a total of seven that are considered to be authentic,[7] reveal a man who obviously acted as a very effective and compassionate spiritual guide for others—probably not so much because he had finally attained spiritual balance (as the Life presumes), but because he was still struggling to do so (as he admits in the letters).

Unlike the *Life of Antony,* which emphasizes Antony's seeming lack of a formal, classical education, the person who emerges in the letters is no ignorant monk, but someone knowledgeable of Platonic philosophy and of the Alexandrian theology of Clement and Origen. (Contrary to later monastic writings on the desert Christians, which stress their lack of education and poverty, evidently many of the early monks, like Antony, came from the "urban elite," were quite learned, and very capable of theological discourse).[8] Despite some of these differences, what both letters and Life agree upon theologically is the crucial importance of ongoing discernment in the spiritual life. This discernment is nurtured in the soil of solitude and silence, and it can lead to the acquisition of self-knowledge, the discovery and love of one's *true* self. As Antony advises in his letters, "Know yourselves....He who knows himself, knows God....He who knows himself, knows all men....He who can love himself, loves all men...."[9]

Aside from the letters, which are relatively brief and certain wisdom sayings, which appear in various collections of the desert fathers,[10] the *Life of Antony* by Athanasius is our primary source for understanding the personality and spiritual leadership of Antony. One of the most influential writings in the history of Christian spirituality, it became the primary model for countless Lives of the saints that followed. As we shall see, it was also responsible for large numbers of people, including Augustine and Jerome, embracing the ascetic lifestyle, whether in the desert or in their own lands. Let us turn now to Athanasius's *Life of Antony* to explore more fully the monastic values of solitude and silence, and how they can foster discernment and self-knowledge.

Antony's Movement into Greater Solitude

Although dependent for its literary form on pagan writers, Athanasius brings his own deeply reflective theology to the telling of the desert hermit Antony's story. The basic structure is derived from the gospels, especially the temptation stories of Jesus (cf. Matt 4:1–11; Mark 1:12–13; Luke 4:1–13); the life of simplicity that Antony embraces reflects the earliest days of the Christian community, depicted in Acts 2:42ff; and the paradigm of the "man of God" comes from Athanasius's love of the scriptures, especially his admiration for the Hebrew prophets and the Christian apostles, martyrs, and saints. As Tim Vivian suggests, Antony is primarily portrayed as a *homo biblicus* (a biblical person): "Athanasius takes a contemporary figure, Antony, and places him in an egyptian setting, the desert, but clothes him in biblical dress."[11] Antony is also depicted as the *sophos,* the wise man, philosopher, and teacher who was recognized by both pagans and Christians in late antiquity as a model of the true spiritual mentor.[12] Through Athanasius's stories, Antony becomes the prototype of the desert elder who provides guidance to all those who seek him or her out, and, later, among Eastern Orthodox Christians, of the *staretz,*[13] the wise and compassionate spiritual guide. Drawing upon all of these paradigms, Athanasius reveals how one man's struggles in the Egyptian desert led him not only to God, but to a clearer understanding of himself, and thus to an effective ministry as a spiritual guide for others.

The *Life of Antony* is divided into four main sections, each one revealing a stage of his life as a hermit, and, overall, the movement from living alone near a village to ever greater solitude in the desert wilderness: the first section, chapters 1–7, provides a description of his early life, his dramatic decision to live as an ascetic, his apprenticeship with certain elders, and his initial struggles with certain demons; the second, chapters 8–10, describes his living among desert tombs where his struggle with the demonic world intensifies; the third section, chapters 11–48, tells of his leaving the tombs for a mountain region (referred to as his "exterior mountain") where he barricades himself in an abandoned fort, daily confronting demons for twenty years, only to emerge as a spiritual master; and the fourth section, chapters 49–88, describes his ministry as a spiritual guide, teacher, and healer as he tries to find and maintain some semblance of solitude and silence in his "interior mountain," located near the Red Sea.

In the opening pages of Athanasius's story, Antony is said to have been born into an Egyptian family whose parents were both Christian and wealthy. Despite his social advantages, however, even as a child he seems to have a calling to solitude, reflected in his desire to be alone, to avoid "friendship with other children," and his yearning, above all, to live, Athanasius says, as "an unaffected person, in his home." Then Antony's tranquil life is unexpectedly interrupted when, at the age of eighteen or twenty, his father and mother suddenly die, possibly of the plague, leaving him and his younger sister orphans. Six months after his parents' deaths, confused and grieving, Antony hears a scripture passage read in one of the churches that immediately speaks to him: "If you would be perfect, go, sell what you possess and give to the poor, and you will have treasure in heaven" (Matt 19:21). Antony responds immediately, giving away all that he owns, placing his sister in a community of virgins (with or without consulting her, it is not clear), and going to live near an old man in a neighboring village.[14] This elder is the first of many spiritual mentors with whom Antony associates before he travels into the desert alone.

A pattern can be discerned in these early years about how much a person can learn from spiritual mentors, incorporating their values and practices into one's own personality and spirituality. As his hagiography shows, Antony observed "the graciousness of one, the eagerness for prayers in another; he took careful note of one's freedom from anger, and the human concern of another. And he paid attention to one while he lived a watchful life, or one who pursued studies, as also he admired one for patience, and another for fastings and sleeping on the ground. The gentleness of one and the long-suffering of yet another he watched closely. He marked, likewise, the piety toward Christ and the mutual love of them all. And having been filled in this manner, he returned to his own place of discipline...." Like a "wise bee," Antony gathers "the attributes of each in himself," and attempts "to manifest in himself what was best from all." As a result, the villagers and those who knew Antony call him "God-loved," "son," and "brother."[15]

As is apparent from this period of his life, one that lasted approximately fifteen years, Antony was not the first solitaire, the first monk, as later generations described him.[16] There is evidence of "village ascetics" in a number of sources other than Antony's hagiography who lived alone or, as E. A. Judge says, "followed the pattern long set for virgins and widows, and set up houses of their own in town, in which the life of personal renunciation and service in the church would be practiced." The ministry of these men seems to have been that of offering prayers for the villagers and serving "as a source of inspiration" for them, but also acting as guides and reconcilers to the communities when called upon. So, although these village ascetics were probably some of those from whom Antony learned, what was innovative in his own life and ministry was that he withdrew into the desert—rather than continuing to live in or near the villages. This may be, in fact, the reason why so many people later followed Antony into the desert: precisely because he had broken their expectations of a "holy man" being always available.[17] Whatever the circumstances, Athanasius himself says that Antony was "the first hermit" because he went so far into "the great desert," away from the villages where his mentors lived. Antony also, of course, was the first to gain such a large following, thus having a major influence on monastic development.

His Initial Struggle with Demons

After this time of spiritual formation with his mentors in which he learned to work hard, to pray "constantly," and to read scripture, Antony is portrayed as being beset by various temptations, because, according to Athanasius, the devil "despises and envies good."[18] (Carl Jung would express these temptations less in terms of the devil's envy and more in psychological terms, positing the emergence of the "shadow" side as a person seeks to become more integrated. This dynamic follows the principle, according to Jung, that the greater the light that is cast in a person's striving for wholeness, the greater the shadow, a shadow that must be acknowledged, and, if possible, eventually befriended.)[19] Whatever the dynamics, Antony and the desert Christians who followed him frequently are depicted as in combat against the devil, perhaps precisely because they seek to live by such high standards and to lead such solitary lives. (Solitude, for many people, has a way of bringing one's "demons" out, which is why later monastic traditions advised that only those who are properly prepared and spiritually mature should venture into solitary living.)

In the stories about Antony, the devil is certainly the main antagonist who takes on a variety of demonic forms, many of them linked, in Athanasius's theology, with pagan gods, some of them Greek (the god Pan, for example), some Egyptian. Egyptians even before the coming of Christianity had legions of demons as part of their cultural and religious history, including the great god Seth of Upper Egypt (where Athanasius and Antony had been raised), who was associated with the spirit of Evil.[20] Some of these demons or gods in animal shapes may have been painted on the walls of the village or on the tombs where Antony later lived alone, and thus contributed to the demonic forms he saw threatening him when he was fasting and praying. Certainly along with fighting Arianism, paganism was one of Athanasius's primary concerns, especially when we consider that at the time when he wrote (so soon after Constantine's conversion), paganism was still very popular.[21] As Antony's later extensive dialogue with Greek philosophers demonstrates in chapters 72–80 of the *Life of Antony,* such teachers and leaders formed an audience that Athanasius hoped to influence.[22] (It is interesting to note that Antony in Athanasius's stories seems more open to dialogue with pagans than with Arians. Although pagans believed in demons, they seem less objectionable than the Arians whose teaching, Antony says, is "from the demons, and from their father, the devil." Much of Antony's hostility toward Arians may reflect

Athanasius's own sense of betrayal: not only was Arius, like himself, from Alexandria, but Arians were enlisting the emperor and others to outright persecute, imprison, and (as Athanasius personally experienced numerous times) send into exile orthodox believers.[23]

Whatever the origin of the belief in demons, Antony, like Jesus, is tempted by them in this first stage of his life-story. Some of the conflicts Antony faces are from within, especially the temptation to leave his asceticism and to engage in a self-indulgent lifestyle. Many of his conflicts, however, are from without, appearing in visible forms. The first of these tempters, in fact, are a woman and a black youth, both of whom represent, Athanasius says, "the spirit of fornication" (evidently a very popular spirit considering the numerous references to it in other desert stories and Lives). The first figure, the woman, is, unfortunately, a familiar one in later hagiographies of male saints, all of whom seem prone to project their own desires and their own "shadow" upon females—blaming them for what they themselves feel erotically, or for what they may have failed to accept and integrate personally. Antony's second tempter, the black youth, is both a victim of the same projections as well as the recipient of much abuse and hatred in Christian history, not only for his race, but because, according to scholars, he represents a homosexual.[24] This figure, linked with homoerotic behavior, is found in a number of desert texts and numerous other hagiographical writings, demonstrating the prevalence of the attraction older monks evidently had toward younger men, especially when separated from women.[25]

As desert monasticism developed, so did the prohibitions in this area, as can be seen in the later Rules of St. Pachomius, which cautioned against immodest bathing, sitting two together on a mat, carpet, or donkey, or clasping "the hand or anything else of his companion."[26] The black youth, however, was evidently not only an abhorrent figure for desert monks, but a source of great fascination for many in Late Antiquity, considering the large number of wall decorations and other Hellenic forms of art that has survived, picturing black males as hypersexual, with huge penises and prominent erections.[27] Medieval writers eventually associated black men with Saracens or Moslems, who not only were considered "infidels," but also had a fairly tolerant attitude toward homoerotic behavior.[28] Such associations, however, came much later after the written prohibitions of desert monasticism. What is clear, however, is the inherent prejudice in early Christianity against blacks in general when the color white was equated with goodness, and black with evil. This bias or outright bigotry is expressed explicitly in a story about Father Moses, a black Ethiopian monk at Scetis in Egypt, who is confronted by some of the desert elders with the scornful question, "Why does a black man come among us?" When asked by others if this did not affect him, Moses patiently replied, "I was grieved, but I kept silence."[29]

In the *Life of Antony*, Athanasius tells us that Antony was able to resist both tempters, the woman and the black youth, because of God's grace, *and* because of what Antony does by calling out, "Who are you?," forcing the devil to identify himself. This is a key step in the discernment process outlined in Antony's hagiography, and one of its major themes. If someone wants to vanquish the devil, one must ask his name, and, in doing so, he will lose all power over that person. According to this theology, the devil or demons have only as much power as we give them. This is demonstrated in the way Antony instructs his followers, all of whom (Christians *and* pagans) lived in a world believed to be populated by spirits, good and bad:

> Whenever some apparition occurs, do not collapse in terror, but whatever it may be, ask first, bravely, "Who are you and where do you come from?" And if it is a vision of holy ones, they will give you full assurance and transform your fear into joy. But if it is someone diabolical, it immediately is weakened, finding your spirit formidable. For simply by asking, "Who are you and where do you come from?" you give evidence of your calmness.[30]

In spiritual direction, this is the principle of "naming, claiming, and taming" one's demons or shadow side in order to be set free of their destructive power. In the teachings of Antony (both in Athanasius's Life and in Antony's letters), demons are associated with "illusions" and with "unreality";[31] as he suggests, the more we live in unreality, the sicker and possibly more possessed or obsessed we become.

Though the desert Christians tended to personify their own inner drives, conflicts, or unresolved wounds from earlier life, and project them outwardly, demonizing them,[32] they did have a keen psychological awareness that many forces converge on a human being, many thoughts arise, many emotions can "possess" us, and many patterns, personal and social, can take on a vehement and destructive power that seems to exceed our own. The desert Christians' insight, and, in particular, Athanasius's, was the belief that a person couldn't handle all of these sometimes converging forces without the help of a higher power. As Christians, they identified that higher power as God, Jesus, the Holy Spirit, and prayed not only to God, but to Mary, Jesus' mother, and to the saints to protect them. Considering the theological conflicts following Nicea, in Athanasius's *Life of Antony* the power of Christ is especially frequently affirmed. To ward off evil Antony calls upon Jesus, uses His name in his battles with demons, sings psalms, and makes the sign of the cross. Any victories over evil are not due to Antony's personal power, Athanasius says, but to "the Savior's work."[33]

Solitude: Antony's Furnace of Transformation

After this first encounter with the woman and the black youth, Antony prepares to do future battles with the enemy by thoroughly adopting an ascetic lifestyle: *daily* disciplining his body through sleepless nights, constant prayer, and a strict diet—all practices that would help a person, both pagan philosophers and Christians believers,[34] contain "disordered" passions, especially those associated with sexual energies, personified, in

Antony's story, by the woman and the black youth. Spiritually invigorated, the desert father then goes to live by himself in the tombs outside the village, a time of solitude that becomes for him a "furnace of transformation."[35] Again, both pagan and Christian Egyptians occasionally engaged in this practice, believing that by dwelling in or near the tombs of the dead they could encounter the world of the spirits and of their ancestors, and experience there something of a "living death," a conversion as a person fasted and prayed.[36] Among the tombs, Antony, of course, encounters more demons, this time in the forms of lions, bears, leopards, bulls, serpents, wolves, and pigs—many later depicted so vividly in the horrific Renaissance paintings of Hieronymous Bosch (c. 1450–1516) and Mathias Grunewald (1475–1528).[37] Against all these animal figures, God is Antony's help, although Antony, it seems, is not always pleased with God's timing:

> ...the Lord did not forget the wrestling of Antony, but came to his aid. For when he looked up he saw the roof [of the tombs where he was staying] being opened, as it seemed, and a certain beam of light descending toward him. Suddenly the demons vanished from view, the pain of his body ceased instantly, and the building was once more intact. Aware of the assistance and both breathing more easily and relieved from the suffering, Antony entreated the vision that appeared, saying, "Where were you? Why didn't you appear in the beginning, so that you could stop my distresses?" And a voice came to him: "I was here, Antony, but I waited to watch your struggle. And now, since you persevered and were not defeated, I will be your helper forever, and I will make you famous everywhere."[38]

The dynamics of this scene recur frequently in stories of human transformation and in the history of Christian spirituality. Jesus, for example, hears a voice at his baptism that affirms him as God's Son (Matt 3:16 ff.); Paul sees a light and hears a voice on the way to Damascus that changes his life dramatically (Acts 9:3 ff.); Pachomius hears a voice, early in his career, advising him to "Struggle and settle down here";[39] Augustine in the garden in Milan hears the voice of a child that tells him, "Take it and read it [Holy Scripture]."[40] Pagan writers too refer to these types of experiences, sometimes in a way that is strikingly similar to the Athanasius's stories about Antony. In Porphyry's *Life of Plotinus,* for example, the author says that his teacher, the philosopher Plotinus (205–269 CE), experienced union with God at least four times, "pouring down before him a dense shaft of light" that "guided him."[41] Antony's experience, then, in the history of mysticism, great and ordinary, is not all that extraordinary—except, of course, for those who experience it for the first time. Nor is his anger at God all that unusual. If prayer is, as Teresa of Avila (1515–1582) says, "nothing else than an intimate sharing between friends,"[42] it will include at times—as any friendship does—uncomfortable feelings, including anger, that need to be expressed.

After this experience, Antony goes farther into the wilderness, eventually settling in the deserted fortress at Pispir, on the right bank of the Nile. There, Athanasius tells us, "he remained alone in the place, neither going out himself nor seeing any of those who visited." At the age of thirty-five, this was the time in which he continued to struggle with his demons, helped by ongoing visions from God and visits from friends, although the latter did not actually see him. This life of solitude and silence went on for twenty years—definitely a "desert" experience in which Antony learned not only about his shadow-side and his vulnerability to it, but about the grace of God, through his surrender to Jesus. This was a time of inner transformation, of both naming his demons and claiming his spiritual resources. It must also have been a time of naming and claiming his gifts, and the spiritual leadership to which he was called. However the transformation occurred, Athanasius shows him emerging from that difficult time a changed man.

As the story goes, when Antony's friends finally lose their patience and tear down the fortress door, they encounter

Antony, amazingly transformed, the epitome of the divinized figure who represents every Christian's potential. As Athanasius describes him:

> Antony came forth as though from some shrine, having been led into divine mysteries and inspired by God....When they beheld him, they were amazed to see his body had maintained its former condition, neither fat from lack of exercise, nor emaciated from fasting and combat with demons, but was just as they had known him prior to his withdrawal. The state of his soul was one of purity, for it was not constricted by grief, nor relaxed by pleasure, nor affected by either laughter or dejection. Moreover, when he saw the crowd, he was not annoyed any more than he was elated at being embraced by so many people. He maintained utter equilibrium, like one guided by reason and steadfast in that which accords with nature.[43]

What is striking about this description of Antony as he emerges transformed, an icon of divinization, is the similarity between him and that of certain philosophers as described by their pagan biographers. Again, Porphyry in his *Life of Plotinus* tells how his teacher who sought greatness of soul through physical deprivations was a "gentle friend" of the god Apollo, and how, when Plotinus spoke, his face was "visibly illuminated," radiating "benignity."[44] Like those pagan philosophers whom Athanasius hoped to convert to Christianity through his *Life of Antony,* Antony is shown to have learned in his solitude a way to live—and a way to die—well,[45] the sign of a truly wise person, according to Greek philosophers and Christian theologians alike. The major difference, of course, was that while pagan philosophers put so much of their reliance in reason, Christians like Athanasius and Antony put theirs ultimately in something radically new: faith in God and in Jesus Christ, fully human and fully divine.

What Antony Learned in Solitude

After this moving scene of a great teacher and hermit whose solitude and wrestling with demons have transformed him into a person of inner harmony, of "utter equilibrium," Antony begins his more "public" ministry—just as Jesus had done following his time in the desert facing his own demons (cf. Luke 4:14 ff.). At the age of fifty-five (an age many cultures associate with that of becoming an elder), Antony even appears as physically *unchanged,* an attribute that the classical culture of his time associated with being godlike, since divinity itself was considered all perfect, and thus neither subject to change nor aging. Although extreme by our standards, desert asceticism, including its diet, may also have contributed to Antony's appearance. As we recall, his followers commented on how he did not seem to have aged during his time in the fortress, and despite his strict asceticism, Antony did live to be one hundred and five years old! Another hagiography of a desert elder, Amma Syncletica, alludes to the same dynamics: "it was a wonder how, having spent so many years in such spiritual discipline and solitude, she remained at the peak of her youthful beauty."[46] More recently, Patrick Fermor suggests a similar view when he describes a visit to a Cistercian monastery, and how "the austerity of the diet, the arduous labour and the lack of sleep have on the monks the reverse of a debilitating effect and seem to furnish them with almost indestructible health."[47]

Following Antony's emergence from the fort, almost like Lazarus rising from the dead (cf. John 11), he begins his ministry of spiritual leadership that includes healing the sick, exorcizing demons, comforting the grieving, and, as other holy men of that time had done, reconciling "in friendship" those hostile to each other. He also persuades "many to take up the solitary life," Athanasius says, so that "from then on, there were monasteries in the mountains and the desert was made a city by monks..., and like a father he guided them all."[48] Here Athanasius is showing how the solitary life can produce great riches, resulting in benefits not only to oneself but to the larger community. He presumes what a more recent scholar of Christian spirituality, Louis Bouyer, says about the nature of *Christian* solitude: it is never just about oneself being alone with God, but "always bears fruits of love" in the lives of others.[49]

In this context, one of the first things that happens to Antony after coming forth from the fort is his being asked by certain monks to share his wisdom with them. He proceeds to do so happily, telling them that "I, as your elder, will share what I know and the fruits of my experience."[50] What he had learned in his silence and solitude evidently was quite extensive, so much so that his "lecture" constitutes a major part of the Life, extending from chapters 16–44. The major "fruit" of his wisdom, however, is on the meaning and importance of discernment: the ability to recognize differences between good spirits and evil ones, and thus distinguish between reality and unreality.

According to Antony, to become a discerning person, one must first cultivate certain inner qualities, many of which he had originally learned from his mentors: those of "prudence, justice, temperance, courage, understanding, love, concern for the poor, faith in Christ, freedom from anger, hospitality." A person begins to cultivate these virtues by "dying daily," he says, "for if we so live as people dying daily, we will not commit sin." His is thus a program of transformation that begins with oneself, and presumes *daily* attentiveness and surrender to God, with hearts, he says, always "watchful." Living this way of life, a spirituality based upon prayer, simplicity, and discipline, a person will be given, Antony tells his listeners, "the gift of discrimination of spirits," the ability to "recognize their traits."[51] To recognize these traits, a person must pay attention, he advises, to his or her *feelings*—certainly a somewhat radical stance considering how much *reason* and the *rational* side of humanity were affirmed at that time.

A good spirit, according to Antony, is identified by the lack of "disturbance" it causes. It is known by such feelings as tranquility, gentleness, joy, delight, and courage, all of which enter the soul, and make it thirst for the divine: "The soul is overcome by a desire for divine and future realities, and it desires to be entirely united with these beings, if only it could depart in their company." In other words, the sign of a good spirit is one that brings a sense of calm and inner harmony, along with the sense of being drawn to greater unity with God, others, and one's deeper self. The opposite is true of evil spirits: "The assault and appearance of the evil ones, on the other hand, is something troubling, with crashing and noise and shouting—the disturbance one might expect from tough youths and robbers. From this come immediately terror of soul, confusion and disorder of thoughts, dejection, enmity towards ascetics, listlessness, grief, memory of relatives, and fear of death; and finally there is craving for evil, contempt for virtue, and instability of character." Once a person has identified the spirit from its results, a person can then do something about it by seeking to affirm it, if it is good, or by finding help from God and one's community in expelling it, if it is evil. As Antony advises, "Certainly one must pray…to receive the gift of the discernment of spirits, so that we might not, as Scripture says, believe every spirit." To learn this, Antony says, one need not "go abroad on account of the Kingdom of heaven nor cross the sea for virtue. For the Lord has told us before, 'the kingdom of God is within you.'"[52]

Discernment: The Process of Attentive Listening

This, then, in all its simplicity, is what Antony learned from his own struggles: to begin to discern differences in one's life a person must be attentive to *what lies within,* to what brings and supports peace and tranquility or what produces and reinforces confusing, destructive behavior. This attentiveness means concretely taking time to *listen* to one's inner life. It presumes a discipline of being in or creating a quiet environment in which a person can begin to recognize what is happening internally. It presupposes that while any discernment process might necessarily include dialogue with others, it must include, above all, a dialogue with oneself—in relationship with God. Silence and solitude can provide this conversation. Such attentive listening can lead to less illusions and self-delusions (signs of the devil, according to Antony, as we've seen). It can also lead to greater knowledge of one's true self, a Self more grounded in truth, more capable of living *in reality*.

Antony himself in a personal letter uses this language when he tells a monastic group: "Prepare yourselves while you have intercessors to pray to God for your salvation, that He may pour into your hearts that fire which Jesus came to send upon the earth, that you may be able to exercise your hearts and senses, to know how to discern the good from the bad, the right from the left, reality from unreality."[53] This is what the solitary life provided Antony, and what led to his becoming such an effective spiritual mentor for others: a self-knowledge that includes *both* knowledge of one's demons *and* knowledge of one's resources for fighting them. All of this presumes the ability to discern differences, and make choices accordingly, by listening to the movements within, the movements of the heart. Such attentive listening and centering is what Buddhists call "mindfulness,"[54] a discipline that leads to new awareness. Without such listening, a person's self-knowledge will be extremely limited; without it, one might experience what Antony calls in another letter an "incurable wound." This is what happened, he says, to the heretic Arius, for "it is manifest that he did not know himself," and without that self-knowledge, he could not know the true nature of God.[55]

Later, in the *Life of Antony*, in another discourse before he dies, Antony, as spiritual guide, becomes more specific in how to cultivate this attentiveness to the inner life. Sounding again very much like the Greek philosopher Pythagoras,[56] Antony advises his followers to "examine yourselves and test yourselves:" "Now daily let each one recount to himself his actions of the day and night, and if he sinned, let him stop....Let each one of us note and record our actions and the stirrings of our souls as though we were going to give an account to each other." Above all, he says, "let us treat each other with compassion, and let us bear one another's burdens."[57]

The entire process of learning discernment, and of gaining self-knowledge, then, includes the following stages or steps, as outlined in the *Life of Antony*:

1. find a worthy spiritual guide or mentors from whom you can learn various inner qualities, and integrate them into your personality and spirituality;
2. through a simple life-style, learn to be disciplined, and through prayer, place yourself daily in the presence of God;
3. spend time daily in a personal inventory of how your life is unfolding or perhaps failing to progress; record this in some form, possibly through journaling;
4. when an unknown spirit, apparition, conflict, or experience needs clarification, ask "what is your name?";
5. listen attentively to the inner and outer responses that you receive or experience;
6. do not expect immediate clarification, but continue to listen, seeking help in prayer and from your fellows, colleagues, friends, and family;
7. persevere, even when no help nor clarification seems forthcoming, as Antony did in his desert life, remembering the words of the story, how "the Lord did not forget the wrestling of Antony, but came to his aid."

Thus, Athanasius, through Antony, provides his readers—and us—with something of a blueprint for learning to be discerning, for beginning to live with more self-knowledge and love, precisely because we have incorporated the monastic values of solitude and silence into our lives. Such discernment is an ancient Christian practice, one first referred to in the writings associated with Paul the Apostle (cf. I Cor 12:10; Heb 4:12; Gal 5:22) and John, the beloved of Christ (I John 4:1), and later incorporated into the *Spiritual Exercises* of St. Ignatius of Loyola (1491–1556), who encouraged a "daily examen" in which one pays attention to the inner life, and records what is happening.[58] Although Athanasius associates the process of discernment with Antony, it was something he also learned firsthand not only through his friendship with the desert elder who was like a father to him, but from his own sojourns as an exile in the desert regions, both those outside of Alexandria and those within his own heart.

Father Antony

Antony's feast day is celebrated January 17. Shortly before he died, he called his followers together and said to them, "I am going the way of the fathers....Be watchful and do not destroy your lengthy discipline....You know the treacherous demons—you know how savage they are, even though weakened in strength. Therefore, do not fear them, but rather draw inspiration from Christ always, and trust in him. And live as though dying daily...." Then, he added, "remember me as a father."[59]

This is how Antony is remembered by both Eastern and Western Christians throughout the world: as the "father of monks," a great spiritual leader whose effectiveness was not based upon an ecclesiastical position (he was never ordained), but upon the innate gifts that he received from God—and from his own hard struggles. According to Bernard McGinn, Antony's "greatest gift" was "the typical desert value of the discernment of spirits,"[60] a discernment learned in silence and solitude where a person eventually comes face to face with his or her true Self. Antony was the one who taught all Christians about the value of their struggles, and the spiritual resources that can help a person gain strength from them. In many ways, he embodies the best spirit of early monasticism, a man of serene courtesy and cheerfulness, whose life teaches that any Christian, *every* Christian, develops in holiness, as Antony did, *gradually,* over a lifetime. This is done by fighting one's demons, naming them, claiming them, and eventually taming them not by denial or avoidance, but by recognition and acceptance. He also shows that a person's struggles are not to be denigrated, but can be the source of both personal wisdom and ministry or service to others.

Within a few decades after the composition of the *Life of Antony* by Athanasius, it became a "best-seller," copied, read, and carried to Greek-speaking Christians in the eastern Mediterranean as well as to Latin Christians in Gaul and Italy, providing them and later generations with a new model of holiness, one replacing that of the martyr who dies for his or her faith. This new paradigm now became associated with a discipline and self-denial like a martyr's, but rather than dying in a dramatic way, it presumes a spirituality of *dying daily*, of letting go in surrender one day at a time. This desert spirituality takes very seriously the inner world, the discernment of inner realities, and the heart. With this spirituality, solitude and silence are valued, for they offer a person the opportunity to recognize the illusions and compulsions that feed the false self, and allow one to encounter, in the process, a loving God who offers himself as the substance of the new and true Self. With this spirituality too solitude is associated not only with times of being alone physically, but with a certain disposition, a quality of the heart: with having, as Antony says, a "watchful" heart. Another desert elder, a woman, Syncletica, explained it in a similar way: "It is possible," she said, "to be a solitary in one's mind while living in a crowd, and it is possible for one who is a solitary to live in the crowd of his [or her] own thoughts."[61]

Even though monastics would adopt more of the cenobitic life associated with Pachomius and Basil, because of Antony's story the eremetic life would not be forgotten. Later monastic communities throughout Europe would incorporate the values of solitude and silence into their spirituality. St. Benedict, for example, would devote a chapter in his Rule to silence, and Celtic monastics, along with Cistercians, would often build their monasteries in isolated regions, carrying on the spirit of the original desert hermits. Even those that emphasized communal life over the solitary would frequently allow an individual member to embrace life as a hermit for short periods of time, if not entirely after retiring from a long and active ministry. As we will see, many of the saints, including Martin of Tours, Benedict, as well as Celtic saints, like Kevin, Cuthbert, and Melangell, would be portrayed as heirs of Antony, and, as Douglas Burton-Christie notes, "during every monastic revival in the Middle Ages...the desert ideal of Egypt, and in particular the example of Antony, would be recalled."[62]

Henri Nouwen is right when he says that Antony is "the best guide in our attempt to understand the role of solitude in ministry,"[63] for Antony's life teaches us that solitude is the holy place where leadership emerges, and where spirituality and ministry embrace. His life also reveals a movement from solitude to greater communion with God, as well as a passage from being mentored to becoming a spiritual mentor—and all of our responsibility in doing so. The basis of that mentoring, as Antony has taught us, is simply sharing "the fruits" of what we have learned in solitude reflecting upon our own experiences.

Perhaps, most of all, Athanasius's *Life of Antony* shows how silence teaches us to know reality, and how silence and solitude will help us discover not just our demons, but that reality itself is ultimately blessed and graced. As Thomas Merton suggests in his writings, "In solitude we remain face to face with the naked being of things. And yet we find that the nakedness of reality which we have feared is neither a matter of terror nor for shame. It is clothed in the friendly communion of silence, and this silence is related to love."[64] Such an awareness helps us understand that silence itself is a quality of the heart, and that it often leads to hearts, like Antony's, set on fire for the love of God.

CHAPTER THREE

New Rays of Light—Martin of Tours and Hilary of Poitiers

In the nineteenth year of the reign of Constantine II the monk Antony died at the age of one hundred and five. Saint Hilary, Bishop of Poitiers, was sent into exile at the request of the heretics....At that period, too, our new luminary began to shine, and Gaul became bright with new rays coming from its lamps, for this is the moment when Saint Martin began to preach in this country. —Gregory of Tours, *The History of the Franks*

Upon leaving military service, Martin sought out St. Hilary, the bishop of the city of Poitiers, a man conspicuous at that time in the things of God and renowned for his steadfast faith.

—Sulpicius Severus, *Life of St. Martin*

The fourth century, as we have seen, witnessed the rise of a new hero of the Christian faith, the monk, and the spread of ascetic and monastic ideals. Athanasius's hagiography on Antony, and the holiness of Antony himself, of course, contributed significantly to this process in both the eastern and western parts of the Roman Empire. However, in the West itself, two other figures appeared who had a major impact on the spread of monasticism there and on the overall direction of Christian spirituality for centuries. The first was Martin (c. 316–397), bishop of Tours in Gaul. Unlike Athanasius, a bishop who loved monasticism and incorporated much of that spirituality into his life and ministry, Martin was the first monk who after becoming a bishop continued to live in a monastery. His hagiographer, Sulpicius Severus (c. 363–420), describes Martin in fact as the perfect combination of bishop and monk: "What he had been before (i.e., a monk), he firmly continued to be. There was the same humility in his heart, the same poverty in his dress. Lacking nothing in authority and grace, he fulfilled the dignity of a bishop, yet did not abandon the virtuous resolve of the monk."[1] In that capacity, Martin's hagiography provides us with the "earliest picture of the rise and spread of monasticism in Gaul," according to Nora Chadwick, "and an interesting contrast between the earliest monastic foundation in western Europe and the discipline which prevailed among the Desert Fathers in Lower Egypt."[2]

The second figure who had a major effect on the development of western monasticism was Hilary of Poitiers (c. 315–367), an early Christian leader who is often lost in the shadows cast by the light of Martin's fame. Although frequently referred to as "the Athanasius of the West" because of his early defense of orthodox theology, Hilary is perhaps the least studied of the great Western fathers, possibly due, as one scholar has stated, to his "heavy style and the profundity of his speculation."[3] Still, he was admired by numerous early theologians and church fathers, including Augustine who described him as "the illustrious doctor of the churches," and Jerome who said that he was a "most eloquent man, and the trumpet of the Latins against the Arians."[4] Rufinus, in his *Church History*, wrote that Hilary was "a man naturally gentle and peaceful and at the same time learned and most adept at persuasion" who "published some excellent books about the faith." He compared Hilary directly with Athanasius, "two men, like two great lights of the world, lit up Illyricum, Italy, and Gaul with their brightness, so that all the darkness of heresy was driven from even the most remote and hidden corners."[5] Cassiodorus, writing in the sixth century, considered Hilary "the sharpest and deepest of students in religious matters," and one of the "gleaming stars" in "the ecclesiastical sky."[6]

By his contemporaries and succeeding generations, Hilary was known primarily for his defense of orthodoxy and for his theological writings, especially on the Trinity. What is often overlooked, however, is how much, through his mentoring of Martin, he contributed to the development of monasticism in the West. Among the oldest of those teachers officially declared a doctor of the church, and the only one (thus far) who is known to have been a married bishop and the father of a child, Hilary was the one whom Martin first visited before becoming a monk, and from whom he learned a great deal about the faith. As Sulpicius says, Hilary was "a man conspicuous at that time in the things of God and renowned for his steadfast faith."[7] That faith of Hilary's and his explanation of it strongly affected Martin, for, as E. W. Watson writes, "the courage and tenacity with which Martin held and preached the Faith was certainly inspired to some considerable extent by admiration of Hilary and confidence in his teaching."[8]

This chapter examines the life and leadership of both men: Martin, a bishop-monk, and his mentor, Hilary, who as bishop first introduced Martin to monastic values, and, unlike other Gallic bishops who openly opposed the ascetic movement,[9] encouraged the foundation of monasticism in Gaul. If, as Robert Wilken suggests, "the way to God begins not with arguments or proofs but with discernment and faith,"[10] this chapter will focus specifically on faith, as chapter two focused on discernment. I agree with Marcus Borg that faith is "the heart of Christianity,"[11] and, I would add, the heart of monastic values too. Although Gregory of Tours (c. 540–94), a successor of Martin's, describes Martin as "our new luminary," and one of the lamps shedding "new rays" on Gaul,[12] by examining both men's lives we will begin to see how much his spiritual mentor Hilary contributed to that bright lighting, and how much faith itself is a lamp to the feet, a light on the road.

Sulpicius Severus, Martin's Hagiographer

To a large degree Sulpicius's hagiography on Martin was influenced by Athanasius's *Life of Antony*, and, like Athanasius,

Sulpicius knew personally the subject of his hagiography. A layman and a lawyer whose young wife had died soon after they were married, Sulpicius had read the book on Antony about 391, before traveling to meet Martin who had been bishop of Tours for some twenty years. Sulpicius was so impressed with Martin's holiness at that first meeting that he made a radical decision, like Antony, to sell most of his property, settle in his own house near Toulouse, and live a monk-like existence, possibly with his mother-in-law, Bassula, certainly with young male scribes, members of his household. He clearly had a warm and affectionate relationship with his mother-in-law who seems to have played something of the same part in his life and work that Paula did for Jerome, as we will see. His close friend, Paulinus, refers to her in a letter as "more generous than any parent," while praising Martin at the time for living as a *peregrinus,* a pilgrim, in the world. Instead of filling his home with furniture and wealth, Paulinus said, "you [Sulpicius] fill it with pilgrims and needy people, marking out one corner for yourself. You act as a fellow servant alongside the slaves of your household."[13]

In that one corner Sulpicius evidently did his work, surely rereading the *Life of Antony* after his first encounter with Martin, but also, most likely, the hagiographical works of Jerome as well as the writings of Hilary.[14] What was produced in his moments of solitude were a number of surviving works on Martin that represented, as Athanasius had done with Antony, his new hero as a saint of the people, having many of the same traits that made Antony so popular. Most of the Life was written while Martin was still alive, with Sulpicius completing it in 397 shortly after the holy man's death. He also wrote other works that give us further insights into the life and personality of Martin: three letters about the saint that have survived, the second and third (the latter addressed to Bassula) occasioned by the bishop's death; a *Sacred History,* or *Chronicle,* which, with brief references to Athanasius, Martin, Hilary, and the Arians, is a longer study of the history of the world from creation to 400 CE (the year it was published); and, finally, the *Dialogues,* written about 404, which seem to have been modeled on Plato's *Dialogues* with Socrates as well as Cicero's manuscript, *Laelius: On Friendship*. Sulpicius says in his *Dialogues* that he adopted that form "to allay boredom and lend variety to the narrative," although "it is historical truth [which] we have used as our foundation." Divided into three sections, the work provides further information on Martin, including "sayings" associated with him, accounts of his miracles, and, perhaps most interesting, stories of his conversations with such saints as Agnes, Thecla, and Mary Magdalene.[15]

The Life itself, Sulpicius says, was written because he thought Martin was someone worthy of imitation whose example would stimulate readers to "true wisdom,"[16] as the living Martin had done for him. Evidently, the book was a great literary success, judging from the remarks of Postumianus, Sulpicius's friend, who traveled extensively and appears in his *Dialogues.* "There is almost no place in the whole world," he tells Sulpicius, "where the happy story it tells is not commonly known....Copies [of it] were zealously snatched up all over the city [of Rome]. I saw the booksellers there carried away with joy. It was their most profitable item, they said; nothing sold more readily and nothing sold at a higher price." (One wonders if Sulpicius received *any* royalties!) From Rome to Carthage, to Alexandria, and then to Egypt and the desert regions—everyone, Postumianus said, was reading it.[17]

Martin's Early Life and His Meeting Hilary

According to Sulpicius, Martin was born in Sabaria (a town located in western Hungary), but was raised in Italy by pagan parents who were totally opposed to Christianity. Despite this, Martin had been attracted to the Christian faith since a young child, wanting to become a catechumen at the age of ten. Even more so, from the age of twelve, Sulpicius says, he had "longed... for the desert," "his spirit ever drawn toward monasteries or the Church." Alarmed by the prospect that his son might actually join a monastic community, his father, when Martin turned fifteen, forced him to join the army. For three years Martin lived an extraordinary life, considering his circumstances: "His kindness toward his fellow soldiers was great, his charity remarkable...." Patient, humble, and temperate, "even then he was considered not a soldier," Sulpicius says, "but a monk," as he assisted the sick, fed the hungry, and clothed the naked.[18] Then, while acting like a Christian without actually being baptized, Martin experienced something that became a turning point in his life.

As Sulpicius tells the story, "One day, at the gate of the city of Amiens, Martin met a poor man who was naked." It was the middle of winter, one "more severe than usual," and Martin was wearing only his armor and a simple military cloak. As in the gospel parable of the Good Samaritan (cf. Luke 10:29–37), other people had evidently passed by the begger without showing him any compassion. "Martin, however, filled with God's grace, saw that it was for him, when others had denied their mercy, that the suppliant was being reserved." Asking himself what he should do, he reached for the sword he was wearing and cut the cloak in two; "one part he gave to the pauper; in the other he again dressed himself." Later that night, while "he was deep in sleep, Martin beheld Christ, clothed in that part of his own cloak with which he had covered the pauper. He was told to look attentively upon the Lord and to recognize the garment he had given. And soon, to the throng of angels standing about, he heard Jesus saying in a clear voice, 'Martin, still a catechumen, has covered me with this cloak.'"[19]

Sulpicius provides his own theological interpretation of this powerful dream: "The Lord, in declaring that it was He who had been clothed in the person of the pauper, was truly mindful of His own words uttered long ago: 'As long as you did it to one of these my least, you did it to me' (cf. Matt 25). Further, to strengthen the evidence of such a good deed, He deigned to show Himself in the very garment the pauper had received." Moved profoundly by this dream, Martin, at the age of eighteen, was baptized "without delay." And then, "For about two years after his baptism," Sulpicius says, he "remained a soldier, though only in name."[20]

This would put Martin's age at twenty years, but scholars disagree with Sulpicius's chronology at this point: one posits that Martin left the army at the age of twenty-two; another, in 339 at the age of about twenty-four; still another, that he retired in 356 at the age of forty.[21] Whatever date or age, what happened next to him was highly significant—something that can positively affect every man, no matter how old: his finding a trustworthy mentor who can help him find his calling, and teach him wisdom. According to Sulpicius, Martin, "upon leaving military service…sought out St. Hilary, the bishop of the city of Poitiers, a man conspicuous at that time in the things of God and renowned for his steadfast faith."[22]

This Hilary with whom Martin lived for some time (Sulpicius is not clear for how long) was to have a major effect on the direction of the younger man's life, teaching him not only about orthodox Christian beliefs, but about Christian faith as a lived reality. It was this same Hilary who would introduce him to asceticism and communal living, for, evidently, as in the case of Sulpicius Severus and numerous others, Hilary, although a married bishop, had turned his house into a monastery, living with his wife, his young daughter, and other clergy—all committed to a life of fasting, scripture reading, and prayer.[23] This initial experience of a monastic lifestyle, along with Hilary's teachings and eventual encouragement for Martin to start his own monastery outside of Poitiers, would be the tremendous gift the older man offered his protégé. Although we might disagree with Nora Chadwick's evaluation of their relationship as one in which "Martin was not only Hilary's disciple; he was virtually his creation,"[24] it is clear that Hilary had a major effect on Martin's life.

The dynamics between them, as described by Sulpicius, are, to say the least, interesting. Hilary obviously has a great deal of affection and admiration for Martin, manifest in his attempts to ordain him a deacon; Martin, on the other hand, "insisted upon his unworthiness and repeatedly resisted." "A man of deep insight," Sulpicius admits, Hilary backs down, respecting the younger man's humility, and instead ordains him—with Martin's consent—an exorcist,[25] an important role, as it will turn out, considering Martin's later ministry, like Antony's, of exorcising demons. Shortly after this, Sulpicius says, the younger man received a dream inviting him to go back to his native land and visit his pagan parents. Martin sets out "with the consent of St. Hilary, but obligated by the bishop's repeated and tearful urging to return." While he is away, successfully converting his mother and numerous others (but not his father), Martin also "almost alone," Sulpicius says, confronts certain Arian bishops who, not appreciating his orthodox beliefs, beat and scourge him. Forced to finally leave his native land, Martin moves to Milan where he lives for a while as a monk, having learned that his mentor, Hilary, has been "forced into exile by the violence of the heretics."[26]

It is here in Sulpicius's story that we can leave Martin for a while, and turn to the life and thought of Hilary, since to understand the mentor better will provide insights into the future leadership of Martin, his protégé.

Hilary of Poitiers' Early Life and Conversion

Unfortunately, we do not have a lot of information on Hilary's early life, except what he refers to in his own writings, and those references are few. Church historians and writers, such as Rufinus, Sulpicius Severus, and Gregory of Tours, are not that helpful either since they mention Hilary only in regard to his later years, after he had become a bishop. The only extant hagiography on him was written some two hundred years after Hilary's death by Venantius Fortunatus (c. 530–609), a talented bishop of Poitiers who was a hymn writer, poet, and hagiographer of the saints.[27] Fortunatus wrote two works on Hilary: the first, "A Life," which is not all that helpful (Watson refers to it as "worthless");[28] and a second, "The Miracles of Hilary," which refers to the saint of Poitiers as "that unfailing light," and gives few biographical details other than a description of various miracles associated with him.[29]

By way of factual information, what scholars have been able to ascertain is that Hilary was born about 315 in Poitiers, a town located in the Poitou and Aquitaine region of southwestern Gaul. He was the son of wealthy pagans who evidently provided him with a good education, since his writings reveal an elegant Latin style, and reflect his knowledge of philosophy, especially Neo-Platonism, as well as such early Christian writers as Clement of Alexandria and especially Origen. Hilary, however, did not convert to Christianity until he was an adult, possibly about the year 350. In his major work, *De Trinitate (On the Trinity)*, he specifically refers to his own Christian conversion, evidently a long process of questioning the meaning of life, the existence of God, and his vocation. While R. P. C. Hanson suspects the veracity of the autobiographical references in that work,[30] I think that there is a personal ring of truth that pervades those passages.

In the opening pages of his *On the Trinity*, Hilary describes how as a young man he was searching for meaning, while growing increasingly restless under societal and cultural expectations of what constituted the happy life. He ties this search for meaning with vocational concerns as well: "When I was in search of an employment, proper to man and sacred which by its nature or through the researches of prudent men would result in something worthy of this divine gift which has been bestowed upon him for knowledge, many things came to my mind which according to the common opinion seemed to make life useful and desirable...." Traditional societal answers, however, such as the possession of leisure or wealth, did not satisfy his quest. He was dissatisfied with theories too that humankind is created only for pleasure or for death. Instead, "my soul," he says, hungered for God, "enkindled with the most ardent desire of comprehending and knowing Him."[31]

Asking himself which God to believe in, he turns to writers and teachers for guidance. Some, he says, spoke to him of "families of uncertain deities"; others "proclaimed that there were greater and lesser gods and gods differing in power." "Some asserted that there was no God at all and suggested only that nature came into existence through accidental movement or collisions. A great many declared in accordance with the popular belief that there was a God, but asserted that this same God had no concern or interest in human affairs. Some...worshipped those corporeal and visible forms of created things themselves in the elements of earth and heaven. Lastly, certain individuals placed their gods in the images of man, animals, beasts, and serpents, and confined the God of the universe and the Author of infinity within the narrow limits of metals, stones, and genealogies."[32]

Dissatisfied, again, with these responses, no matter how well intentioned, Hilary turns to scripture. One passage in particular from the Book of Exodus (3:14) seems to have touched his soul, where God the Creator, testifying about himself, says "I am who am." Hilary admits that "I was filled with admiration at such a clear definition of God, which spoke of the incomprehensible nature in language most suitable to our human understanding." For him, this brief utterance penetrated more deeply into the mystery of divine nature than anything else he had heard from the philosophers. "My soul," he says, "was filled with joy, therefore, at the contemplation of this excellent and ineffable knowledge...," especially affirmed by another passage from the Book of Wisdom (13:5): "For by the greatness of the work and the beauty of the creatures the creator of the generations is reasonably known."[33]

Still, what continued to cause him anxiety was the question of human mortality: yes, he seems to say, there may be an eternal God, one revealed in beauty itself, but what about death? Reason itself convinced him, he writes, "that it was unworthy of God to have brought man into this life as a sharer in His council and prudence in order that his life might one day end and his death last for all eternity." At this point in his search for answers to his theological questions, Hilary evidently turned to the New Testament, and the passage from the Gospel of John 1:1–14 (a favorite of Clement of Alexandria as we've seen), which describes God as Word, the Word proclaimed by John the Baptist who bore witness "concerning the light," "the true light that enlightens every man who comes into the world....And the Word was made flesh and dwelt among us." "By these words," Hilary says, "my fearful and anxious soul found greater hope than it had anticipated...[and] therefore gladly accepted this doctrine of divine revelation." Through Christ Jesus, "whom we are to confess as none other than God with the fullness of the Godhead," who died and rose from the dead, Hilary had found hope and consolation which made possible "the patient endurance of the present trials of life."[34] A short time later, about the year 350, he was baptized and received into the church.

What is important about this description of his conversion is his affirmation that questions on the meaning and understanding of God, tied in so closely to vocational issues, are significant. They need to be addressed openly, and guidance sought, for to ignore them is to deny a great deal of understanding not only about ultimate concerns, but about one's Self—or, as Hilary says, one's soul. To ignore such questions, to deny one's connection with God, is to severely limit one's human-divine potential, as well as the opportunity to develop a relationship of awe and gratitude with the wider universe rather than cynicism or abject despair. That Hilary turns to scripture, ultimately, for guidance is a characteristic of him, a quality (his love and knowledge of scripture) that he passed on to his protégé. As we read in Sulpicius's *Life of St. Martin,* "how penetrating, how forceful he [Martin] was, how quick and at ease in resolving questions from the Scriptures."[35] It is also significant, as we will see, that in order to explain his understanding of faith, Hilary turns to the Apostle John, in particular, for insight.

Bishop Hilary: A Prophetic Voice

Within three years of his baptism Poitiers' bishop died, and Hilary, in his mid-thirties, was elected as his successor. Such elections at the time included three groups of people: the laity, the clergy, and at least three neighboring bishops. Besides Hilary, other ecclesial leaders, such as Athanasius, Ambrose, Augustine, and Martin himself, were nominated and elected in that way, a fairly common procedure until the Roman emperors, due to their political agendas, began corrupting the process by nominating their own candidates and/or bribing those already in office.

Augustine, for one, according to his hagiographer, believed that anyone being ordained should have "the approval of the majority of Christians."[36] Hilary was married at the time of his consecration and the father of a young daughter, Apia, Apra, or Abra (the sources are not consistent), who is said to have later chosen a life of virginity, helping to promote the Christian faith around Poitiers until her early death at the age of eighteen. (Unfortunately, nothing has survived telling us about Hilary's wife.) Almost at once, however, Bishop Hilary was drawn into the great debate over the Trinity that was dividing the church. This was the time, following Constantine's death, when his son and successor, Constantius, emperor in the East, was increasingly favoring the Arian sympathizers rather than the bishops, such as Athanasius, who were defending the decisions of Nicea. Through his military achievements, Constantius had become emperor of both the East and the West by 353, and soon determined to make Arianism the dominant creed of the West too. Thus, early in his episcopal career Hilary found himself involved in the Arian controversy, even though he acknowledges in his writings some ignorance initially of the theological debates associated with Nicea. Still, the emperor was making his influence felt.

As the emperor promoted Arianism, Hilary, as bishop, was increasingly unhappy with episcopal and imperial leadership, and the direction the church was taking. This was about the time when Martin came to live with Hilary, and, of course, began to assimilate his mentor's views. Offering a prophetic voice to those in Gaul (and beyond), Hilary criticized Christian leaders who desired to construct fine buildings rather than to build up faithful communities: "What an evil it is, this love of building that possesses you: you think that roofs and walls make a church of God worthy of your reverence, and a setting fit enough in which to call down upon yourselves the blessings of peace....Safer by far, to my mind, are the mountains, the woods, the lakes—indeed, dungeons and pits: these are the places where, inspired by God's spirit, the prophets spoke...."[37]

Certainly influenced by ascetic ideals that were sweeping the empire, Hilary also became increasingly uncomfortable about those bishops and clergy who, it seemed to him, were too easily being seduced by the emperor and his wealth, compromising their own integrity. The temptation to give into such seductions, Hilary makes clear in one of his later writings, compiled during his exile, was not foreign to himself. Looking back at the period in which he had recently been made a bishop, he writes: "the possibility was offered me, as it was offered to others, of flourishing in the good things of this world, of enjoying domestic ease, of abounding in all sorts of advantages, of vaunting the emperor's familiarity, of living under the spurious title of bishop, of becoming, both publicly and in private, to all and sundry, formidable in lording over the church." Hilary implies here the need for bishops to be servant leaders, not lords, and recommends that they not give into temptations and intimidations.[38]

Hilary's views continued to develop along these prophetic lines. In a letter written to Constantius himself some years later,[39] Hilary does not mince words, developing further his critique of imperial power and its misuse. Here Hilary is extremely blunt in his criticism, stating that the emperor is not only another Judas, but indeed the Anti-Christ! While "pretending" to be a Christian, Hilary says, the emperor divided the flock; while professing loyalty to Christ, he tried to prevent Christ from being honored equally with God the Father; while "loading" the Church with gold and the spoils of pagan temples and granting tax favors to the clergy, he tempted them "to deny Christ." Hilary also accuses Constantius of imprisoning bishops, threatening them with force, and at one church council even starving them into submission. Professing peace, the emperor branded bishops on the forehead who disagreed with his Arian views, and sent them to labor in the mines. He even ordered soldiers to force their way through orthodox crowds of worshipers to tear their bishops from the altar. What right, Hilary asks, does Constantius have to give orders to bishops or to dictate the language of their sermons?[40]

These are strong words, revealing a great deal of courage on the part of Hilary. It is no wonder that he (and later, his protégé, Martin) are not appreciated by episcopal colleagues in Gaul, and certainly not by powerful emperors. Some of Hilary's critical attitudes toward those in authority can be seen in what Sulpicius says about Martin: how, for example, when Martin became bishop of Tours, he did not "sink to adulation of an emperor." As Sulpicius tells the story: "To the court of Emperor Maximus...there had come together numerous bishops from many parts of the world. Conspicuous in them all was their disgraceful flattery of the prince; yielding to a degenerate weakness, episcopal dignity was subordinated to patronage of the emperor." Not Martin, however! "In Martin alone," his biographer says, "apostolic authority remained firm. If it fell to him to intercede with an emperor on behalf of anyone, he commanded rather than pleaded."[41]

The views of both mentor and protégé resonate with Athanasius's own convictions when the bishop of Alexandria, for example, writes in his *History of the Arians:* "When did a judgment of the Church receive its validity from the Emperor? or rather when was his decree ever recognized by the Church? There have been many Councils held heretofore; and many judgments passed by the Church; but the Fathers never sought the consent of the Emperor thereto, nor did the Emperor busy himself with the affairs of the Church."[42] Although Hilary probably never met Athanasius face-to-face, it is certain that he was familiar with his writings, and agreed with them. His support of Athanasius, in fact, seems to have been what eventually caused Hilary trouble. Forced to attend the Arian-dominated Council of Beizers in 356, he openly sympathized with Athanasius's views, and, against the will of the emperor, refused to condemn the bishop of Alexandria. In reaction to this perceived disloyalty, Constantius forced Hilary to leave Poiters and his homeland, and go into exile. While personally very difficult for Hilary, we can see, in retrospect, what Lionel Wickham says about it: that "his career took a striking new turn, and his importance for his contemporaries and for us was dramatically enhanced" by this banishment.[43] As Hilary's writings show, he did not waver in his views, but courageously set forth on what he probably considered the next stage of his life's pilgrimage, determined to make the most of it.

Hilary's Exile

Hilary was gone from Poitiers for three or four years, probably from 357 to 361; scholars don't agree, but Sulpicius Severus, Martin's biographer, says in his *Sacred History* that Hilary spent four years in Phrygia (modern central Turkey), a land of rugged terrain and harsh climate.[44] This was to be the most important period of Hilary's life; certainly one of his most creative. At the same time, although facing great difficulties, being so far from home and family, it was an exile that had some advantages, especially when compared to Athanasius who had been, as we recall, hunted like an animal and even threatened with death. When Hilary was in exile, he still remained bishop of Poitiers, recognized as such by the government; he still was allowed to administer his own diocese, so far as administration by letter was possible. Most of all, in this case, like Athanasius, he was not forgotten by those back home. In effect, he became one of the great heroes of the day in his own country, especially because orthodox bishops in the West had not yet suffered for the faith, as Athanasius had.

Like many in history who have profited from exile or imprisonment, Hilary's time away was a period of tremendous intellectual and spiritual growth. His own faith certainly seems to have sustained him. In a book he wrote while in exile, entitled *Against Valens and Ursacius,* he quotes St. Paul and Jesus himself: "I had learned from the apostle, 'We have not received a spirit of fear' [cf. Rom 8:15]; and we have been taught by the Lord's saying: 'Everyone who shall acknowledge me before men I too will acknowledge before my Father who is in heaven' [Tim 1:7]; and by the same Lord's words: 'Blessed are they who suffer persecution for righteousness' sake, since theirs is the kingdom of heaven….'"[45] In another work, *On the Trinity,* which he largely wrote while in Phrygia, Hilary refers to his experience, identifying himself with numerous others, such as Athanasius, who had suffered for the sake of truth: "Although sound doctrine has been driven into exile by many who have brought together teachers according to their own desires, the true doctrine will not be banished by any of the saints. Although in exile, we shall speak through these books, and the word of God which cannot be bound will circulate in freedom....And we will not complain about the times, but will even rejoice....We glory in our exile and rejoice in the Lord...."[46] In another work, *De Synodis [On the Councils]*, he even says that he is willing to remain in Phrygia forever if it helps the orthodox cause: "May I always be an exile, if only the truth begins to be preached again!"[47]

While in Phrygia, Hilary learned a great deal about Eastern Christian spirituality and theology, knowledge which he later brought back to the West. He seems to have had some freedom in traveling about, and visiting with numerous monastic and ecclesial leaders. He also studied the Greek language and Greek literature, and made himself acquainted with the parties and doctrines of the Eastern church. Hilary's exile in the East confirmed for him what he already knew about the value of asceticism, and his own attempt at living it with family and friends in Poitiers. His visits with the monks, as Athanasius had done during his exile, reinforced his convictions about monastic values. When he returned, it would only have been natural for him to encourage his protégé Martin to become a monk and establish his own monastery, "the first western monastery," Judith Herrin says, "founded entirely on eastern lines."[48]

Relieved of administrative responsibilities for the most part, Hilary put his exile to good use, writing numerous works, some of which have been lost, a number of significant ones that have survived. One of the latter, which he completed in 359, *On the Councils,* mentioned above, is an historical survey of the confessions of the Eastern church, which became exceptionally helpful in explaining Eastern theology to Western bishops. Another, his major work, *On the Trinity,* incorporates theological ideas from the East with Hilary's own reflection and depth of insight. Of all his works, it was the most influential, especially as it included certain key themes of Eastern theology, which Hilary made available to those in the West. Ironically, as Archibald Robertson posits, the two bishops who contributed the most to the development of Christian theology and monasticism, both East and

West, were those who suffered for their beliefs in exile: Hilary, a Western spiritual leader, "who had learned to understand and sympathize with the East" during his exile, and Athanasius, an Eastern leader who became "the Oriental representative of the theological instincts of the West."[49]

Hilary's Understanding of Faith

Hilary writes with passion and his writings are based upon his strong conviction that our understanding of God has tremendous implications for daily living. His theology had been evolving since the time when he was questioning ultimate meaning and his own direction in life. After his conversion, his primary focus had been on exploring the meaning of Christian faith for his contemporaries and, most of all, for himself.

All of his works, from his first, *Commentary on Matthew,* written before or during the early days of his episcopate, to his last, *Homilies on the Psalms,* were composed with the strong conviction that God was not only *one* being, but *three* persons, reflected, as Hilary says, in the first book of the Bible, *Genesis.* "By declaring," Hilary writes, "'Let us make mankind in our image and likeness,' He [God] does away with any idea of isolation, since He reveals this mutual participation."[50] God, and those who are created in God's image, Hilary believes, are thus called to community, to participate and build in their own lives communities that reflect the God in whose image they have been made. This is a key element of Hilary's theology, which has implications for everyone who follows Christ.

A second conviction that colors all of Hilary's theology is his intense love of and loyalty to Jesus Christ. For Hilary, the Son of God was truly God not in name and metaphor only, but in the fullest sense and deepest reality. This personal relationship with Christ, in fact, is his primary motive for the writings on faith that he does. It is his reading and study of the sacred texts of scripture that inform his theology and the explanations he gives to justify belief in the power and equality of the Trinity. Ultimately his love of Christ relies not solely on intellect and intellectual arguments, but upon his intuitive senses, his heart. As Watson says, Hilary's "heart as well as his reason" was engaged in his doing theology, his theologizing.[51]

Hilary also learned from the Eastern fathers during his exile that to be a theologian was, above all, to be a person of prayer. They had taught him that all theology begins and ends in prayer. With this awareness, it was natural for him to conclude that "God cannot be known except by devotion." As he writes in his book on the Trinity, "What presumption to suppose that words can adequately describe God's nature, when thought is often too deep for words, and His nature transcends even the conceptions of thought....We must believe, must apprehend, must worship, and such acts of devotion must stand in lieu of definition."[52] For Hilary, what he learned from the Eastern fathers was the ancient Christian principle, *"lex orandi, lex credendi"* (the law of worship is the law of belief); in other words, how a person or community worships reveals what an individual or a community believes. Thus his understanding of faith is linked intrinsically with a life of prayer, one that includes the reading of scripture, yes, but also public worship and personal prayer. In this regard, no wonder Hilary not only recommends participation in the Eucharist, but, as a poet, was one of the first writers of hymns in the West.

A fourth element of his theology also reflects the teachings of the Eastern fathers, alluded to above, when Hilary says, "What presumption to suppose that words can adequately describe God's nature." Eastern theologians had taught him this apophatic theology: based upon the presupposition that words or dogmatic definitions cannot fully explain the profound mystery of God. Here Hilary anticipates the theology of later Eastern Orthodox Christians, the sixth-century writer Pseudo-Dionysius, and a number of medieval mystics, including the fourteenth-century anonymous English author of *Cloud of Unknowing* and the sixteenth-century Spanish poet, John of the Cross (1542–1591). Hilary states in his book on the Trinity that the very "purpose" of faith, what it proclaims, is that it cannot fully "comprehend that for which it is seeking."[53] Anything that is said is merely an attempt to wrap words around a mystery that is beyond verbal or intellectual explanation.

With that premise, one that presumes anything that is stated about God is necessarily said provisionally and, one would expect, with a great deal of humility, Hilary goes on to affirm that, for the Christian, *guidance* for understanding God can be found in scripture, as it had for him. In Book Six of *On the Trinity,* he even gets quite personal, naming those who helped him, he says, discover the true nature of God; who were, in effect, his spiritual mentors. Among those named from the Old Testament are David, Solomon, Isaias, Jeremias, and from the New Testament Matthew, Simon, Paul, and John. "These men taught me," Hilary says, "the doctrines which I maintain and which have been irrevocably impressed upon my mind."[54]

Listening to the Heartbeat of God

Of all of these mentors, Hilary seems drawn most to John the Evangelist, the one "who was deemed worthy," Hilary says, "of receiving the revelation of the heavenly mysteries because of his intimate association with the Lord...." Hilary affectionately refers to John as "the fisherman," a term that originated in the gospel story of Jesus calling two pairs of brothers, Peter and Andrew, and James and John, to leave "their nets," follow him, and become "fishers of men" (cf. Matt 4:18–22). Considering his frequent references to John in his writings, and his early reliance upon John's Gospel during his own conversion process, Hilary seems to identify more closely with him than with any of the others. In the section of *On the Trinity* in which he discusses his search for God, for example, Hilary says, "In solving these difficult questions that I have just mentioned, I am aided by the poor fisherman who stands at my side. He is unknown, unlearned, a fishing line in his hands; his clothes are drenched; he is oblivious to the mud beneath his feet...." He goes on to encourage his readers to do what John did with Jesus in their own search for meaning, truth, God: "Let us admire the doctrine of the fisherman and let us cling to and adore the confession of the Father and the Son, the unbegotten and the only-begotten, that cannot be expressed and that transcends the entire scope of our language and thought. According to the example of John, let us rest on the bosom of the Lord Jesus in order that we may be able to apprehend and to express these truths."[55]

In early Christianity no text was more beloved than the one found in the Gospel of John: "No one has ever seen God. It is God the only Son who is close to the Father's heart who has made him known" (1:18). As the Son was close to the Father's heart, so, in Eastern thought, John the "beloved disciple" was especially close to Jesus, resting his head on Jesus' chest, listening to the heartbeat of God. This image of listening to God's heartbeat became a metaphor for the listening to God that a person does in prayer, the listening that can inform what it is that we believe. Hilary, in his exposition on the Trinity, promotes this stance of listening to the heartbeat of God as a truly valid way of understanding God, and doing theology. He did not originate the idea. Origen, whose writings Hilary knew before going to the Phrygia, was in fact the first to use the image of the beloved disciple and his resting his head on Jesus' chest in his *Commentary on John's Gospel,*[56] and in his *Commentary on the Song of Songs* he interprets the phrase "Your breasts are better than wine" as referring to the *principale cordis,* the inner ground of the heart of Christ upon which John, the beloved disciple, reposed.[57]

Hilary understands that stance of listening to God's heartbeat as symbolic of a Christian's search for understanding God's profound mystery. It is based, as John's was with Jesus, upon a relationship of intimacy, of ongoing friendship, of deep love. Hilary presumes, as did the Eastern theologians, that this "listening," while it cannot in this lifetime provide absolute answers, can give intimations of God's presence, direction, and unconditional love—what, in fact, John received from Jesus in his lifetime.

Thus, in retrospect, Hilary recommends two primary ways to clarify, nourish, and enrich a life of faith. The first is for us to read the Holy Scriptures, reflect upon their stories, become familiar with them to a point where we see those stories as having relevance for our own lives. To read and to grow to love the scriptures, Hilary believes, is to experience some degree of light:

> For every step that our soul takes, let us use the word of God as a lantern—but as a lantern that is ever burning, always ready, through our foresight, to fulfill its function. The same word, moreover, which is a lantern for the feet is also a light on the road....For just as someone who goes out at night bears a lantern before him, looks carefully where he steps, and is cautious—with his lantern guiding his every step, so too every one of us, passing the night that is in him, holds before himself the word of God as a lantern for the course of all his deeds.[58]

A second way to clarify our questions and our faith, as we've seen, is through prayer, liturgical celebrations, and private devotions. In both forms, what is especially needed is what Hilary recommends: our taking time to listen, as John did, to the heartbeat of God.

These practices certainly were ones that Hilary passed on to his protégé Martin, possibly before their separation, but certainly after Hilary's return from exile. To incorporate these ways or practices in our daily living, we will be given, Hilary suggests, some degree of light in the darkness (the darkness *within* and the darkness without), as well as a suitable "foundation" for our faith: "This foundation stands firm and immovable against all the winds, rains, and torrents, and will not be overturned by the storms, or penetrated by the drops of rain, or washed away by the floods."[59]

Hilary's Reunion with Martin

Hilary's exile ended about 361 when he was allowed to return to Poitiers. Toward the end of it he had attended the Council of Seleucia, a meeting arranged once again by

Constantius's Arian bishops to neutralize the decrees of Nicea. Hilary courageously had defended the Nicene beliefs, and then had gone on to Constantinople to try to meet with the emperor himself. Constantius, hoping to limit his influence, sent him back to Gaul. As Sulpicius Severus says in his *Sacred History,* Hilary "was ordered to return to Gaul, as being a sower of discord, and a troubler of the East...."[60] Once back in Poitiers, among family and friends, Hilary assumed his pastoral responsibilities immediately, but, as a result of his exile and what he had learned in Phrygia, with a new determination to fight against the spread of Arianism. At the same time he continued his efforts at bringing the thought of the East and West together, especially educating the West about Eastern theological ideas. He thus came to be considered one of the first great ecumenical writers who was concerned, above all, about Christian unity.

Soon after his return, according to Sulpicius's *Life of St. Martin,* the two friends, Martin and Hilary, were finally reunited. While Hilary was away, Martin had lived for a while as a hermit in Milan, and, after being driven from the city by Arians, had moved to "an island named Gallinaria [on the Mediterranean Sea], accompanied by a priest," the two of them living on nothing but "the roots of herbs." Hearing that Hilary was returning to Poitiers, Martin sought to meet him in Rome, but "since Hilary had already gone ahead, Martin followed after." There in Poitiers, Sulpicius says simply, "he was welcomed by the bishop most graciously." While the two may have communicated by letters, both would have been overjoyed to see each other again, and both would have noticed significant changes in the other: While Hilary had matured spiritually and intellectually into a theologian of some repute, Martin's faith had deepened too as a result of his own experiences. Sulpicius doesn't elaborate on those dynamics, but, in his next sentence, following the brief reference to their reunion, he says, "Not far from the town he [Martin] set up a monastery for himself."[61]

This monastic venture was certainly due to Martin's intense lifelong desire for solitude, a longing for "the desert" that had come from his deepest Self. As we recall, it was something he had wanted since the age of twelve, "his spirit ever drawn toward monasteries." This move also was surely encouraged by Hilary, especially considering what he had learned firsthand during his exile about the various desert forms of the solitary and communal life. And so Liguge was born, possibly at the site of Hilary's country villa, located five miles outside of Poitiers. Its original name, *Locociacum,* meant "the place of the little cells," and was based upon a desert-style circle of huts. (Early Irish monastic communities would have a similar shape, as can be seen today in the ruins on Skellig Michael.) "The fact that Martin founded his hermitage within striking distance of Poitiers is significant," according to Clare Stancliffe, "for it shows that Martin, despite his earlier experiments, did not imitate Antony in settling in total isolation from society. It further implies that the bishop of Poitiers played an important role in Liguge's foundation, and in the spiritual formation of Martin. Disciples were attracted to Martin at Liguge, and traditionally this foundation marks the starting point of Gallic monasticism...."[62]

Martin spent ten years there, the happiest and most creative period of his life. Hilary would have continued to act as his spiritual mentor until his own death November 1, 367. (His feast day is celebrated January 14.) Martin would have grieved the loss of such a supportive friend, and probably quite frequently remembered Hilary in the following years when Martin himself was made a bishop. His own election had come, largely against his will, about 371, pushed upon him by the local people who were so impressed with his holiness. Needless to say, he was not everyone's candidate, especially as other bishops, Sulpicius tells us, thought "he was a contemptible person..., shabbily dressed, with unkempt hair, [and] unworthy of the episcopate."[63] He would have recalled what Hilary had taught him about the importance of Christian faith and of *servant* leadership, and, in his darker moments, been encouraged by the memory of Hilary's smiling face.

Still, unlike other bishops of the time, once Martin was bishop, Sulpicius says, he was "unable to bear up under the distraction caused by throngs of visitors," and quickly returned to living as a monk. He set up for himself a monastery some two miles outside the city of Tours at a location "so sheltered and remote that it could have been a desert solitude."[64] Disciples joined him there, constructing their own cells of wood or digging out caves from the rock in which to live. Sulpicius describes aspects of their way of life, the "earliest picture of a monastic community on a considerable scale in Europe, and probably the earliest in western Europe"[65]:

> The disciples numbered about eighty, all forming themselves after the model of their blessed master. No one there had anything as his own; all property was brought together for common holding....No art was practised there except that of the copyist, and to this work only the more youthful were assigned; the elders had their time free for prayer. Rarely was anyone found outside his own cell, except when they came together at the place of prayer. All had meals in common and after the hour of fasting. All abstained from wine, except when compelled by illness. The majority were dressed in camel's hair; the use of any softer clothing was held a serious offense.[66]

Thus arose the monastery of Marmoutier (the name derived from the Latin, *"magnum monasterium,"* meaning large or great monastery), one that became, after Martin's death, one of the most powerful Benedictine monasteries in western Gaul.[67]

Still, Martin did not avoid his episcopal responsibilities. While living in community outside the city of Tours, he also became a highly effective pastoral leader, healing the sick, and preaching throughout Gaul, including visits to Paris and Chartres, to evangelize. Evidently one of his main ministries to which he was most dedicated was that of exorcizing demons, something that Hilary had originally encouraged him to do. The stories of Martin's encounters with numerous demons who take various forms certainly reflect dimensions of Athanasius's accounts of Antony, and there is even one about Martin following Antony's advice when he encounters a "grim, unclean spirit" and "ordered him to speak out his name."[68] He is also portrayed as destroying various pagan temples and shrines in villages and countryside, replacing them, Sulpicius says, "with churches or monasteries."[69] In his dual role, bishop of Tours and head of a Marmoutier, Martin lived out the rest of his life as a highly effective spiritual leader who at the same time "guarded his solitude right up to the hour at which the regular public offices were to begin." He also evidently maintained his humility, refusing to sit on a "towering throne" that many bishops were increasingly using in their churches, preferring instead to be seated on a three-legged stool, Sulpicius says, "of the kind that slaves use."[70]

Fellow Workers in the Field of Faith

When Martin died in 397, Sulpicius wrote to his mother-in-law, Bassula, describing to her how "an unbelievably large crowd assembled for his funeral." "The whole city rushed out to meet the bier," he says, and "everyone from the fields and villages was present, as well as many persons from the nearby cities. All were deeply grieved, and especially sorrowful were the lamentations of the monks." More than two thousand monks, he says, "came together on that day" to honor Martin's accomplishments and his genuine holiness.[71] Writing to another friend, a deacon Aurelius, Sulpicius tells him of his own profound grief at the loss of his mentor, comforted only in knowing, he says, that he had "profited in a special ways from his goodness, for, in spite of my faults and unworthiness, he had a particular affection for me." Sulpicius was also comforted, it seems, by a dream he had had shortly before his mentor's death in which "I seemed to see the holy bishop Martin…[who] was smiling gently at me, and in his right hand was carrying the little book I had written about his life."[72]

As the years progressed, Martin's fame grew—largely due to Sulpicius's "little book" and the miracles associated with Martin's tomb. By the Middle Ages, the city of Tours was one of the most popular pilgrimage sites in Western Europe. Thousands of pilgrims traveled there for guidance, rejuvenation, and even physical healing, including Clovis, King of the Franks (c. 466–511); the church historian Gregory of Tours (c. 539–594); poet and hagiographer Venantius Fortunatus (c. 530–609); the great Irish missionary Columban (c. 543–615); as well as Charlemagne (c. 742–814) and Joan of Arc (1412–1431). They did so with the belief that to see the lighted candles, to breathe in the fragrance of incense, to touch the tomb of the saint who was considered, like them, a pilgrim, was to experience instant intimacy with him. A plaque on the tomb reinforced that perspective:

> Here lies Martin the bishop, of holy memory,
> Whose soul is in the hand of God's, but he is
> fully here,
> present and made plain in miracles of every kind.[73]

Pilgrims also made their way to Poitiers to the church of St. Hilary, which, along with Tours, became a major holy site on the way to Santiago de Compostela in northwestern Spain. Although Martin had become better known as time went on, Hilary had made his own mark, through his life and writings, upon the Church, especially its emerging understanding of the Trinity. As Stephen McKenna points out, while the subject of the Trinity had been treated "for so many years by the keenest minds in the Eastern Church, no Latin writer had written a scientific and systematic treatise before him....St. Hilary, therefore, was a pioneer."[74] Through his love of Martin, Hilary was also a pioneer in promoting the spread of monasticism in the West. In a real way, the two men stand together, "fellow-laborers equally successful in widely separate parts of the same field."[75]

Through the examples of their lives, both of them taught people about the importance of Christian faith and its various dimensions. Judging from the large number of stained-glass windows depicting him in churches throughout Europe, including Chartres Cathedral, the story of Martin that most affected the imagination of later churchmen, artisans, and pilgrims had to do with that of Martin's meeting a poor man on the road who had turned out to be Christ. His story, of course, reaffirms the importance of the social dimension of faith, compassion, and how Christ is to be found where he promised he would be: among the hungry, the thirsty, the poor, the imprisoned, the outcast (cf. Matt 25). To be a person of faith is to recognize these social dimensions of inclusivity toward the marginalized, and one's Christian responsibility in changing conditions that cause their exclusion and suffering. It presumes that we are all related somehow to one another, and that Christ's incarnation is physically manifest in all of humankind. Hilary knew this, of course, referring to Christ in his first work, *Commentary on St. Matthew,* as the One who "assumed the body of us all" and became "neighbor to each one of us by the condition of the assumed body...."[76]

In Hilary's writings on faith, we learn something more: the importance of *paying attention* to our questions of meaning and of vocation rather than losing ourselves in trivialities, distractions, and other forms of escape. In our search for truth, meaning, and authenticity, we are provided with resources, with guidance, Hilary teaches, from scripture, from one another, from listening to the heartbeat of God. The theology of Nicea, defended by Athanasius in the East and Hilary in the West, had at least this one profound result: that the divine being was understood now not as a power in splendid isolation (above/beyond this world as Plato, for one, suggests), but rather a profoundly interrelated communion of persons; a communion that presumed, by implication, that holiness is found in community and that authentic Christian spirituality has a communal dimension—even when one is physically alone. Athanasius and Hilary, by stressing Jesus' divinity in their writing, thereby encouraged humanity to embrace its own DIVINE possibilities: of living into, growing into, becoming more like, the image in which we are created, the image of God.

For anyone with monastic inclinations, to believe in the Trinity is to affirm that we as images of God are called to express our own creative, healing, and sanctifying powers, and to positively change the world in whatever way we can. Knowledge of God is necessarily participatory, and community begins with an inner attitude: the virtue, the value of faith. With it, nothing is impossible, as Jesus has said: "I tell you solemnly, if your faith were the size of a mustard seed you could say to this mountain, 'Move from here to there,' and it would move; nothing would be impossible for you" (Matt 17:20).

CHAPTER FOUR

Like a Kindling Fire—Augustine and Monica

These and other similar expressions of feeling, which proceed from the hearts of those who love and are loved in return, and are revealed in the face, the voice, the eyes..., were like a kindling fire to melt our souls together and out of many to make us one. It is this which we love in our friends....

And so, now that I had lost the great comfort of her, my soul was wounded and my life was, as it were, torn apart, since it had been a life made up of hers and mine together.

—Augustine, *Confessions*

Besides the type of monasticism that Hilary had encouraged his protégé Martin to create in Gaul, other forms of monastic life in the West continued to arise, influenced by the stories of the desert Christians, passed on by word of mouth and through the writings about them, especially as found in Athanasius's *Life of Antony.* Augustine (354–430), a teacher of rhetoric living in Milan with two close friends, Alypius and Nebridius, tells of his first hearing those stories from a man called Ponticianus who visited him and Alypius one day while Nebridius was away. "On his initiative," Augustine says, "a conversation began about the Egyptian monk Antony, whose name was very well known... although Alypius and I up to this time had never heard of him...." The two friends "were amazed as we heard of these wonderful works...which had been witnessed by so many people" and of the communities living in desert monasteries. Their visitor also told them another story of how two imperial officials on an afternoon walk in Trier had unexpectedly stumbled upon an ascetic household where they had found a book, most likely Athanasius's, on the life of Antony. Picking it up and reading from it, the two men had been so moved by the story of the desert elder that both, with hearts on fire, had decided to become "friends of God," staying in the house and embracing a monastic lifestyle.[1]

What is extraordinary about this account told by Augustine is his own response to the stories:

> This was what Ponticianus told us. But you, Lord, while he was speaking, were turning me around so that I could see myself; you took me from behind my own back, which was where I had put myself during the time when I didn't want to be observed by myself, and you set me in front of my own face so that I could see how foul a sight I was....I saw and I was horrified, and I had nowhere to go to escape from myself.

Ponticianus's stories, Augustine says, filled him "with a terrible kind of shame," and "now inside my house great indeed was the quarrel which I had started with my soul in that bedroom of my heart...." Turning to Alypius, he cried out, "What is wrong with us?" and then fled to the garden where he heard the voice of a child telling him to "take it and read." In tears, he snatched up the book of the Apostle Paul, opened it, and read the passage that named his own addictive inclinations: "Not in rioting and drunkenness, not in chambering and wantonness, not in strife and envying, but put on the Lord Jesus Christ, and make not provision for the flesh in concupiscence." "I had no wish to read further," he later wrote in his *Confessions.* "There was no need to. For immediately when I had reached the end of this sentence it was as though my heart was filled with a light of confidence and all the shadows of my doubt were swept away."[2] So moved by Antony's story, Augustine, at the age of thirty-three, after years of searching for truth and happiness, finally embraced Christianity wholeheartedly.

While Augustine's conversion story is quite well-known, the influence of Antony's story upon it is not; nor is Augustine's decision, following his conversion, to become a monk, a dramatic lifestyle-change, which he maintained throughout his later career as a priest, bishop, and the most prolific and significant of patristic writers. As George Lawless has stated, "Augustine's persevering response to a monastic calling, as he conceived of it in his own terms and in his daily life, is possibly the most underrated facet of his personality."[3] Instead of following Antony to the desert, however, or, like the officials in Ponticianus's story, joining an existing monastic community, Augustine stayed closer to home, setting up a number of Christian communities that expressed and nurtured his monastic ideals.

His first such venture took place in 386, shortly after his conversion. Accompanied by intimate friends and family members, Augustine moved to a villa called Cassiciacum, owned by his friend Verecundus, located forty miles northeast of Milan. There he intended to improve his poor health, and, most importantly, prepare for his baptism by his mentor, Ambrose, the bishop of Milan. The group of nine included his close friend Alypius; his son, Adeodatus; his older brother, Navigius; two teenage pupils, Licentius and Trygetius; and his cousins, Lastidianus and Rusticus. Augustine's mother, Monica, also joined them, most probably grateful and highly relieved that her worrisome son had at last seen the light. This group of friends was following the practice of ancient philosophers, discussing practical questions, and moral, philosophical, and political issues. Their discussions or "dialogues" resulted in Augustine writing four books at Cassiciacum, the first of many exploring and explaining Christianity.

His first book, entitled *The Happy Life,* examines humanity's inherent desire for happiness, and how to find it—a topic that was clearly important to Augustine himself at the time, considering the various paths he had taken through sensuality, philosophy, and Manichaeism before coming to Christianity. Some of the book's content and certainly its dialogical approach were derived from Plato's *Dialogues* and Cicero's *Hortensius.* While drawing upon these Greek and Roman writers for form and some content, Augustine in his book affirms that knowledge of the heart devoted to God is more valuable than the study of philosophical theories, and that a truly happy life consists of following Christ, "the Way, the Truth, and the Life" (John 14:6). As in the writings of Clement of Alexandria and Hilary of Poitiers, Augustine relies upon St. John's Gospel to explain his thought. As Ludwig Schopp says, "It is the light of St. John's Gospel, the Word of God, that enlightened Augustine."[4] Perhaps what is most intriguing about this first book is that Augustine adds a woman's voice, his mother's, to the discussion, showing how philosophy and theology (contrary to the culture of the time) were not the prerogative of men only. In fact, in his dialogues, Monica has a prominent role, and her views on faith, hope, and charity in the book are shown to be *the* prerequisites of recognizing God and truly attaining a happy life.

Augustine wrote three other books during his short stay at Cassiciacum from late 386 to early 387: *Answer to Skeptics, Divine Providence and the Problem of Evil,* and *Soliloquies,* all in the form of dialogues. (The last, *Soliloquies,* whose title and term he created, consists of a dialogue within Augustine himself.) The months spent at Cassiciacum, surrounded by intimates, may well have been the most tranquil in his life, as well as the happiest, for there is frequent mention of joy and laughter. Although scholars agree that this first communal experience was not, strictly speaking, a monastery, it did confirm Augustine's desire to eventually establish one. When asked the question in *Soliloquies,* "Why do you want the men you love to live or dwell in your company?" he replies, "so that we can all at the same time and in unity of heart seek our souls and God."[5] This "unity of heart" (his definition of friendship, as we will see) is precisely how he came to define monasticism in the Rule he later wrote for his monasteries, reflected in its opening lines: "Before all else, live together in harmony, being of one mind and one heart on the way to God."[6]

The experience of intimacy and happiness with friends at Cassiciacum must have affected Augustine profoundly, especially when we consider how in *Soliloquies* he says that one of his three greatest fears is "the fear of losing those whom I love,"[7] and that within a few short years not only did his colleague Verecundus and his dear friend Nebridius die, but also his son Adeodatus and his mother. Despite these personal losses or perhaps precisely because of the vital memories associated with them, Cassiciacum provided Augustine with the model for his future monastic endeavors: the first one, a community, established in 388, on his family estates at Thagaste, where, according to Possidius, his colleague and hagiographer, Augustine, with his friends, constantly meditated, serving God "by fastings, prayers, and good works";[8] the second, a community for lay brothers, established in the bishop's garden in Hippo in 391 after Augustine had gone to that city, as he says, "looking for a place to set up a monastery," and been "grabbed" by the populace and ordained a priest;[9] and a third monastery, this one for clerics, which he established in 395 or 396 after he had become bishop of Hippo upon the death of his predecessor. Based on the concept of the monastery as a community of friends, all of these monastic foundations would constitute "a new chapter in the history of early western monasticism."[10] While endeavoring to live according to the monastic values of Egyptian monasticism, this new form would place less emphasis on the strict asceticism of the East and more upon the value of friendship, what Jean Leclercq suggests "is most profound in the monastic soul."[11]

In this chapter we will focus upon the monastic value of friendship as it is expressed in Augustine's *Confessions,* the first spiritual and intellectual autobiography of the Western world. Henry Chadwick describes the *Confessions,* which contain Augustine's clearest statement on friendship, as "among the greater masterpieces of western literature,"[12] while Brian Patrick McGuire says that Augustine "took the lead in forging attitudes towards friendship"[13] that profoundly affected Western culture, theology, and monasticism itself. By examining the most significant of his friendships as discussed in that writing, we will be able to gain a better perspective on how to incorporate this value into our own lives—whether we live inside or outside monastic walls. What will become clear is that, of all his friendships, Augustine was especially close to his mother, the woman who gave him, he says so poignantly, "great comfort," and whose death deeply "wounded" his soul: "my life was, as it were, torn apart, since it had been a life made up of hers and mine together."[14] As we shall also see, Augustine closely identified all his close relationships and the interpretations of friendship that emerged from them with the imagery of fire.

Augustine's Youth and His Unnamed Lover

Augustine was born November 13, 354, in the town of Thagaste, located about sixty miles to the south of Hippo in the Roman province of Numidia in North Africa. His mother, Monica (332–387), was a devout Christian, and his father, Patricius, a pagan—although the latter became a catechumen during his son's adolescence and was baptized before he died. In Augustine's *Confessions*, probably completed about 397 at the age of forty-three (a little over ten years after his dramatic conversion, and within two years of his consecration as bishop), he tells his readers more about his early life and struggles than does any other figure from late antiquity.

As his *Confessions* reveal, from his youth, Augustine, like many charismatic leaders, was filled with a strong erotic drive, manifest in his great passion for union, love of beauty, and desire for wisdom. What also becomes apparent is how he describes his adolescence and the natural growth of puberty in the worst possible light. In Book II, for example, he tells his readers that "in that sixteenth year of my flesh...the madness of lust...held complete sway over me." He introduces that period of time with the imagery of fire: "For in that youth of mine I was on fire to take my fill of hell." He goes on to associate that fire with a quality, though disparaged, that stayed with him throughout his life. "And what was it that delighted me?" he asks, and immediately answers: "Only this—to love and be loved." He then links the fire imagery with the love of friendship. "But I could not keep that true measure of love, from one mind to another mind, which marks the bright and glad area of friendship."[15]

In Book III, Augustine uses the same imagery and makes the same connection. At the age of eighteen, he says, "I came to Carthage, and all around me in my ears were the sizzling and frying of unholy loves. I was not yet in love, but I loved the idea of love....It was a sweet thing to be loved, and more sweet still when I was able to enjoy the body of my lover." The very next sentence, after his reference to the body of his lover, is telling: "And so I muddied the clear spring of friendship with the dirt of physical desire and clouded over its brightness with the dark hell of lust."[16]

This sexual relationship with a woman who remains throughout his *Confessions* unnamed, lasted for thirteen years, from 372 to 385 CE. He identifies their union almost solely with lust, although he intimates something more when he acknowledges his fidelity to her: "In those years I lived with a woman who was not bound to me by lawful marriage; she was one who had come my way because of my wandering desires and my lack of considered judgment; nevertheless, I had only this one woman and I was faithful to her."[17] From their union came a beloved son, Adeodatus, born in 373, who emerges in Augustine's autobiography and earlier works, *The Happy Life* and *The Teacher,* as an exceptionally precocious child and close friend of whom he was extremely proud.[18] Although Augustine equates his relationship with the boy's mother with an inability to control his sexual desires, it is clear from the short description of its termination how much the two of them loved each other: "my heart, which clung to her, was broken and wounded and dropping blood. She had returned to Africa after having made a vow to you (God) that she would never go to bed with another man...."[19] What is also apparent from that short passage is that, although the Hellenistic culture that had shaped Augustine believed that only men could be friends (since friendship presupposed the full equality of those involved, and only men had that),[20] Augustine applied the term to his female lover and the mother of his child. Although some criticize him severely for not naming her in his account of her dismissal (largely due to Monica's desire that he move "up" socially by marrying someone from a wealthy family), perhaps he was respecting his lover's privacy, not wanting to publicize her name at a time when she surely was still alive.

Cicero as Friendly Mentor

The imagery of fire appears again shortly after Augustine's move to Carthage. His father had died when he was seventeen, and now at the age of nineteen and a student of rhetoric, he discovers a book called *Hortensius,* written by the famous Roman statesman M. Tullius Cicero (106–43 BCE). As a result of reading this book, Augustine tells us, "my spirit was filled with an extraordinary and burning desire for the immortality of wisdom....I was on fire then, my God, I was on fire to leave earthly things behind and fly back to you, nor did I know what you would do with me; for with you is wisdom. But that book inflamed me with the love of wisdom (which is called philosophy in Greek)." This discovery of Cicero's writings had a significant effect on the course of Augustine's life; it was in fact a turning point in which his heart was changed profoundly: "I was urged on and inflamed with a passionate zeal to love and seek and obtain and embrace and hold fast wisdom itself, whatever it might be."[21] Although another twelve years would pass before his Christian conversion, the mentoring that Augustine received from Cicero had a lasting effect on his life and thought, not only regarding his passionate quest for wisdom, but on his understanding of the meaning of friendship.

Of all the writers in the classical world, Cicero was the one who offered Augustine and his contemporaries the most comprehensive reflections on the topic of friendship. In his *Laelius: On Friendship,* written around 44 BCE, Cicero describes a friend as an *alter ego,* or another self. Relying upon Greek philosophers, such as Plato and Aristotle, who had preceded him, he considers friendship as the most important and attractive human bond between men, one based upon the common pursuit of virtue, not financial profit, flattery, or sensuality. "Friendship may be defined as a complete identity of feeling with all things in heaven and earth: an identity which is strengthened by mutual goodwill and affection. With the single exception of wisdom," he writes, "I am inclined to regard it as the greatest of all the gifts the gods have bestowed upon mankind." He associates friendship with *consensio,* harmony in both the human and the divine realms, and with trust and hope:

> It is the most satisfying experience in the world to have someone you can speak to as freely as your own self about any and every subject upon earth....And another of its very many and remarkable advantages is this. It is unique because of the bright rays of hope it projects into the future: it never allows the spirit to falter or fall. When a man thinks of a true friend, he is looking at himself in the mirror. Even when a friend is absent, he is present all the same.

The Latin word for friendship *(amicitia)* derives, Cicero says, from the word for love *(amor)*; it "comes from a feeling of affection," he says, "an inclination of the heart....The significance of friendship is that it unites human hearts." Because of this, "authentic friendship is permanent"; it cannot and will not die.[22]

Cicero's book on friendship takes the form of a dialogue whose main character is Gaius Laelius Sapiens. The occasion for this famous orator's reflections is the death of Scipio Africanus, his close friend. Cicero has Laelius saying at one point:

> Without affection and kindly feeling life can hold no joys. Scipio was suddenly snatched away....We shared the same house, we ate the same meals, and we ate them side by side. Together we were soldiers, together we travelled, and together we went for our country holidays. Every minute of our spare time, as you know, we

> devoted to study and research, withdrawn from the eyes of the world but enjoying the company of one another.[23]

As we shall see, Augustine uses similar language in his *Confessions,* describing his own friend who dies suddenly, as well as the sort of activities with other friends that helped assuage his extreme grief at that loss. The influence of Cicero, a man who lived over four hundred years before Augustine, reveals how friendship and mentoring are not limited to contemporaries. Along with Plato, Plotinus, and Porphyry,[24] Cicero was a significant teacher and spiritual mentor for Augustine. He obviously admired the great Roman statesman and orator, and wrote on the same subjects as Cicero, such as friendship and the happy life,[25] using the same dialogic approach. He also quotes Cicero's definition of friendship directly in an undated letter to Marcianus, whom he describes as "my oldest friend" whom he hopes will join him in baptism, so that their friendship finally will be as all true friendships are, united in Christ.[26] Writing at the age of 70, Augustine again echoes his mentor's words about the profound happiness and support associated with human friendship: "there is no greater consolation than the unfeigned loyalty and mutual love of...true friends."[27]

The Friend with Whom "My Soul Could Not Do Without"

Book IV of the *Confessions* contains Augustine's fullest explanation of what friendship is—and, by implication, *what it is not.* Again he uses a story from his life to explain his theology, and, once again, he begins this section of his autobiography with reference to those desires that he had earlier equated with fire: "So for the space of nine years (from my nineteenth to my twenty-eighth year) I lived a life in which I was seduced and seducing, deceived and deceiving, the prey of various desires."[28] We find him, at the beginning of manhood, living with his lover and their young son, teaching rhetoric, attracted to astrology and the "vanity of the stage." In 375, at the age of twenty-one, he moves back to Thagaste, his birthplace, to continue teaching. It is there that he introduces the reader to a close friend from childhood: "We were both of the same age...; he had grown up with me as a child and we had gone to school together and played together." This friendship, he says, "was sweeter to me than all the sweetness that in this life I had ever known."[29]

In some ways, their relationship today might be associated with youthful infatuation or homoerotic attraction. Margaret Miles, for one, suggests that when Augustine acknowledged that he "muddied the clear spring of friendship...with the dark hell of lust" (quoted above), he may be implying that he was sexually attracted to both women and men.[30] Many people, of course, in both the ancient and the modern world, have this attraction or orientation, and it would certainly not have been all that unusual for Augustine to have such feelings, considering the intimacy involved in male relationships in Hellenistic society.[31] He would also have been aware of the great myths and stories of male friendships that were popular at the time he wrote his *Confessions:* of Homer's *Iliad,* where the warrior Achilles, when he hears that his best friend Patroclus has been killed, speaks of him as "the man I loved beyond all other comrades, loved as my own life";[32] and of the beautiful story in the Hebrew Scriptures of David and Jonathan, where the latter loved David "as his own soul" (1 Sam 18:1–2), and David, after Jonathan's death, describes their love as "more wonderful than the love of a woman" (2 Sam 1:26). Whatever the literary associations or personal dynamics, Augustine himself acknowledges that "my soul could not be without" his friend, and "we depended too much on each other." He goes on to state (from the hindsight of his Christian conversion and his own developing theology) that the other was "not...a friend in the true meaning of friendship." Here in Book IV, chapter 4, Augustine most clearly defines what friendship from his perspective means: "there can be no true friendship unless those who cling to each other are welded together by you

(God) in that love which is spread throughout our hearts by the holy spirit which is given to us."[33]

Despite this later interpretation, at the time this friendship was highly valued by Augustine, one that "had ripened in the enthusiasm of the studies which we had pursued together." He identifies it with much happiness, and he was obviously devastated when his friend suddenly contacted a high fever, was baptized, enjoyed a brief remission from his illness, and then died. It was a tremendous blow, evidenced in the way Augustine describes this personal loss:

> My heart was darkened over with sorrow, and whatever I looked at was death. My own country was a torment to me, my own home was a strange unhappiness. All those things which we had done and said together became, now that he was gone, sheer torture to me. My eyes looked for him everywhere and could not find him. And as to the places where we used to meet I hated all of them for not containing him....[34]

Like the stories of the young Buddha on the road who encounters an elderly man, and Gilgamesh and the death of his friend, Enkidu,[35] the loss of Augustine's friend confronts him with his own mortality. Beside himself with grief, "I became to my self a riddle," he says: a person "tired of living and extremely frightened of dying." He found only tears, tears that "had taken the place of my friend in my heart's love....I was in misery and had lost my joy." And he adds, quoting the classical writer Horace:

> I agree with the poet who called his friend "the half of his own soul." For I felt that my soul and my friend's had been one soul in two bodies, and that was why I had a horror of living, because I did not want to live as a half being, and perhaps too that was why I feared to die, because I did not want him, whom I had loved so much, to die wholly and completely.[36]

Other Friends, Including Alypius and Nebridius

In an attempt to escape his extreme unhappiness, Augustine returned to Carthage in 376, knowing full well that the pain would go with him, "for my heart could not flee away from my heart, nor could I escape from myself." There we find him once more returning to the imagery of fire—associating it now not exclusively with sexual longings nor intellectual pursuits, but with the ties of friendship. The comfort he found in these other friendships in Carthage, Augustine says, "helped most to cure me" of his grief. Echoing the words of Cicero, he describes many of the joys of friendship:

> ...to talk and laugh and do kindnesses to each other; to read pleasant books together; to make jokes together and then talk seriously together;...to be sometimes teaching and sometimes learning....These and other similar expressions of feeling, which proceed from the hearts of those who love and are loved in return, and are revealed in the face, the voice, the eyes, and in a thousand charming ways, were like a kindling fire to melt our souls together and out of many to make us one.[37]

In this company of friends, Augustine continued his teaching, wrote two or three books on the topic of beauty, and, according to Book V of the *Confessions,* became a follower of Mani (also called Manes), a third-century prophet who started the heretical movement, Manichaeism, which stressed the evil of matter and the need for asceticism to free one's "true self." Manichees were divided into two classes, the "elect" (leaders) and the "hearers" (followers). Augustine was a "hearer" for nine years, until he met one of the elect, Faustus, who did not impress him at all. Moving eventually to Rome (in an attempt to flee unruly students), and then settling in Milan, Augustine met Ambrose, the bishop, someone who, Augustine says, "welcomed me as a father." To this important mentor, Augustine opened his heart: "I began to love him at first not as a teacher of the truth (for I had quite despaired of finding it in your church), but simply as a man who was kind and generous to me."[38]

In Book VI, with Ambrose's preaching, and, most of all, his acting as an exemplar of the Christian life, along with Monica's reentry into his own, Augustine's conversion process intensifies, helped on by those whom he refers to as his "intimate friends."[39] Two of them in particular, Alypius and Nebridius, were and remained lifelong friends. Alypius had been born in the same town as Augustine, was younger than he was, and a former student of his in Carthage. Despite the differences of age and education, mutuality was a key dynamic of their relationship: "He was very fond of me, because he thought me good and learned, and I was very fond of him because of his natural tendency toward virtue which was really remarkable in one so young."[40] They shared a love of learning, and, according to Augustine, "together with me he was in a state of mental confusion as to what way of life we should take."[41] As we recall, it was at this time that Alypius and Augustine met Ponticianus who told them about Antony and the other desert Christians—stories that moved both men to conversion. Living together at Cassiciacum and eventually baptized together, they lived a monastic lifestyle at Thagaste from 388 to 391. Some months before Augustine became a bishop at Hippo, Alypius was consecrated bishop of Thagaste where he remained until his death about 430. Years after his conversion, Augustine describes Alypius quite simply as "the brother of my heart," and in a letter to Jerome, written in 394 or 395, he states that "anyone who knows us both would say that he (Alypius) and I are distinct individuals in body only, not in mind; I mean in our harmoniousness and trusty friendship."[42]

The imagery of fire returns to Augustine's *Confessions* when he tells his readers about his other close friend, Nebridius, whom he had first introduced in Book IV, just before describing the death of his unnamed friend. He referred to Nebridius then as "a dear friend," and "a really good and a really pure young man, who used to laugh at the whole business of divination," which Augustine was then pursuing.[43] This wealthy young man had left his family estate near Carthage and journeyed to Milan in order, Augustine says, to "live with me in a most ardent search for truth and wisdom. Together with me he sighed and together with me he wavered. How he burned to discover the happy life! How keen and close was his scrutiny of the most difficult questions!" And so, he continues, "there were together the mouths of three hungry people, sighing out their wants one to another."[44] Others made plans to join them in a communal life in which all possessions would be shared, but the plans were abandoned as impractical, primarily due to the objections of the wives to whom some were married. The idea remained, as we know, and, along with Augustine's communal lifestyle with friends before and after his conversion, contributed to his writing in 397 CE the oldest monastic Rule in Western Christianity with its ideals of sharing all property, living together in harmony, and being "of one mind and one heart."[45]

Alypius and Nebridius continued as intimates of Augustine in that process to which he refers in Book VIII as God's "setting me in front of myself, forcing me to look into my own face." Again, as we recall, Alypius is with Augustine in the garden in Milan, hears his anguish and tears, and is present when "it was as though my heart was filled with a light of confidence and all the shadows of my doubt were swept away."[46] The two of them, together with Augustine's son, Adeodatus, are later baptized by Ambrose—with Monica looking on. As Augustine describes the scene, alluding to his own great appreciation of music and liturgy, and, perhaps more importantly, his tears of joy:

> And we were baptized....What tears I shed in your hymns and canticles! How deeply was I moved by the voices of your sweet singing Church. Those voices flowed into my ears and the truth was distilled into my heart, which overflowed with my passionate devotion. Tears ran from my eyes and happy I was in those tears.[47]

Augustine returns to Nebridius in Book IX of his *Confessions:* "Not long after our conversion and regeneration by your baptism, you (God) took him from this fleshly life; by then he too was a baptized Christian...." His great love and affection for this friend are clear, as is his belief that friendship in Christ survives even the yawning chasm of separation that death brings. In words that Dante will use in his *Divine Comedy* to refer to God, and C. S. Lewis will draw upon in his grief at the loss of his wife, Joy Davidman,[48] Augustine says this about his dear friend, especially remembered for his questioning mind:

> And now he lives in the bosom of Abraham. Whatever is meant by that bosom, there my Nebridius lives, my sweet friend....There he lives in a place about which he used often to ask questions of me, an ignorant weak man. Now he no longer turns his ear to my lips; he turns his own spiritual lips to your fountain and drinks his fill of all the wisdom that he can desire, happy without end. And I don't think that he is so inebriated with that wisdom as to forget me; since it is of you, Lord, that he drinks, and you are mindful of us.[49]

Augustine's Understanding of Friendship

With the conversion and baptism of Augustine and his eulogy to Nebridius, we have come full circle: from the sudden loss of his first friend with whom his soul was intertwined to that of the vision of his Christian friend drinking his fill of wisdom; from tears of anguish at his friend's death to tears of happiness at his own and his friends' baptismal regeneration; from fear of dying when he had first encountered his own mortality to the Christian faith that our friendships live on in a God who is always mindful of us; from the search for love and wisdom in many pursuits to centering his life in Christ. Augustine went on to live as a monk, a priest, and a bishop, and to write a monastic Rule, but it is only because of these early friendships, remembered in that "great harbor of memory" in the depth of his soul,[50] that he was able to write so insightfully about human friendships and the friendship of God.

What is true friendship, then, according to Augustine? Nothing else but the welding together of two souls who seek the same goal; nothing more than two hearts united by the Holy Spirit who is God. This is the understanding that emerges in Augustine's *Confessions* as well as other writings, including his letters. It is similar to that of Plato, Cicero, Plotinus, Horace, and classical writers who rated friendship and dialogue with friends as the highest calling of humankind. It is a pattern that Plato in his *Symposium* describes as that of being drawn, with the help of one's friends, from desire for beautiful bodies to love of wisdom to immortality.[51] That pattern in Augustine's youthful years is discernible in his *Confessions,* and one that he quite possibly consciously used to portray his own journey to Christian faith. But, for him, as a Christian theologian, there is one important difference between Platonic concepts and his own: While friendship by classical writers is described as a search together for beauty, truth, and wisdom, in Christian friendship the search ultimately leads friends to the Source who is Beauty, Wisdom, Truth, and Love. This personal God of the Christians, Augustine writes in one of his letters in which he quotes a line from scripture that Aelred of Rievaulx (1109–1167), the Cistercian writer on spiritual friendship, will take up and make his own, is a God of love, "and he who abides in love abides in God."[52] We see traces of this love—in all its wandering, pilgrim ways—in the life of Augustine and in those friendships, which, he says, "like a kindling fire melted our souls together and out of many made us one."

But what is the source of Augustine's own great passion to love and be loved, his yearning for truth and wisdom, his all-embracing desire for union with God? How does God work to lead him (as Augustine believed God does in all Christian conversions) to his true self? What accounts for Augustine's obvious ability to form such intimate friendships and find such joy in them? Here, I believe, we must turn to the one relationship only hinted at thus far, that of his mother.

Monica

Peter Brown says that Augustine's "inner life is dominated by one figure—his mother,"[53] and, according to Augustine's own story, she is with him at many crucial turning points. He first makes reference to her in Book I when he says that as a new-born he "was welcomed...with the comfort of woman's milk"; in Book II, he tells us that when he was entering adolescence Monica privately warned him "not to commit fornication and especially not to commit adultery with another man's wife"; in Book III, she has a dream in which "a very beautiful young man with a happy face" assures her that her son will later be converted, telling her that "Where you are, he is too"; in Book V, her bitter tears for Augustine "daily...watered the ground" when he plans to sail to Rome; in Book VI, she joins him in Milan, and plays, he says, "a large part" in getting rid of his lover so that he can be properly married; in Book VIII, she hears of his and Alypius's conversion; and in Book IX she dies at the age of fifty-six.[54] Augustine describes her death, however, only after he summarizes her life and one of their last meetings.

There at the coastal town of Ostia, located on the banks of the Tiber River, he returns to the imagery of fire and, significantly, the symbol of the eternal fountain that he had mentioned earlier in his eulogy to Nebridius:

> So we were alone and talking together and very sweet our talk was...discussing between ourselves and in the presence of Truth...what the eternal life of the saints could be like....Yet with the mouth of our heart we panted for the heavenly streams of your fountain, the fountain of life. Then with our affections burning still more strongly toward the Selfsame, we raised ourselves higher and step by step passed over all material things....[W]e came to our own souls, and we went beyond our souls....And, as we talked, yearning toward this Wisdom, we did, with the whole strength of our hearts' impulse, just lightly come into touch

> with her, and we sighed, and we left bound there the first fruits of the Spirit, and we returned to the sounds made by our mouths....[55]

Here, in this one scene, Augustine most clearly paints for us the meaning and direction of Christian friendship: two souls, two hearts united as one in the vision of eternal Wisdom. In this picture we also find a paradigm of the communion of saints: spiritual friends, transcending the ages, helping each other discover God's infinite love. It is no wonder that after this encounter and a lifetime of memories Augustine says at the death of his mother: "my soul was wounded and my life was, as it were, torn apart, since it had been a life made up of hers and mine together."[56] Monica surely was, as Henry Chadwick believes, Augustine's "supreme friend."[57]

In Augustine's friendship with Monica, we find not only the source of his adult religious convictions (what he himself refers to as "the religion woven into our very bones as children"),[58] but the origins of his own great capacity for intimate friendships with both women and men. Judging from references in his *Confessions* to Patricius, his father, Augustine had little regard or affection for the man (at least, not until after both his father's and mother's deaths).[59] As a result, Augustine searched throughout his life for father substitutes in his many male mentors. Besides Ambrose, there was Augustine's wealthy patron, Romanianus, who sponsored his early education, and remained a friend for life.[60] For nine years, the Manichaean bishop, Faustus, served as a kind of "long-distance" mentor until Augustine actually met the man and was disillusioned by his apparent ignorance.[61] Simplicianus, originally a mentor of Ambrose, became an important guide for Augustine, especially when he told Augustine in 386 CE the story of another man's conversion: "when [he] told me all this about Victorinus, I was on fire to be like him, and this, of course, was why he had told me the story."[62] Even the wisdom figures Augustine read, such as Plato and Cicero, or those whom he heard about through the stories of

Ponticianus, such as the desert solitaire, Antony of Egypt, acted in that mentoring capacity.

Despite the relationship with his father, or perhaps precisely because of it, Augustine is exceptionally close to his mother, and, as he says in his *Confessions,* she to him: "she loved having me with her, as all mothers do, only she much more than most."[63] The Swiss psychiatrist Carl Jung calls this a "mother-complex," and though it can be associated with psychological illness, in its wider connotations it can have very positive effects:

> Thus a man with a mother-complex may have a finely differentiated Eros....This gives him a great capacity for friendship, which often creates ties of astonishing tenderness between men and may even rescue friendship between the sexes from the limbo of the impossible. He may have good taste and an aesthetic sense which are fostered by the presence of a feminine streak. Then he may be supremely gifted as a teacher because of his almost feminine insight and tact. He is likely to have a feeling for history, and to be conservative in the best sense and cherish the values of the past. Often he is endowed with a wealth of religious feelings, which help to bring the *ecclesia spiritualis* into reality; and a spiritual receptivity which makes him responsive to revelation.[64]

All these attributes can be discerned in the writings and lifework of Augustine, and, with this interpretation of Jung, we may, finally, have been given a clue to the meaning of the imagery of fire that is so prevalent in Augustine's *Confessions.*

According to Jung, fire is a symbol of transformation and of eros, that powerful yearning within humankind for wholeness, unity, freedom, and wisdom. This "fire" is a *spiritual* force, a passion or enthusiasm for what and whom we love deeply that ultimately leads us *beyond* ourselves as well as *to* the deeper Self that lies within. While Augustine intellectually could and did acknowledge the spiritual side of that "flame," it is precisely the bodily aspect of eros that caused him so much anguish, personally and theologically. Personally, he struggled with a passionate nature that had difficulty in accepting limitations of any kind—whether sexual longings or limits on work.[65] Theologically, he was influenced by the Manichaeans, who condemned the body and procreation for the most part,[66] and by the Neo-Platonists, who, though acknowledging Eros's importance to the spiritual quest, ultimately distrusted it and one's affective side in favor of reason. Augustine shared this belief, immersed as he was in that philosophical tradition and classical culture. He describes in his book, *City of God,* how Socrates believed that "only...a mind purified from passion" could comprehend "the origin of all things," including "the will of the single and supreme Divinity." As a result, Augustine failed to fully appreciate the goodness of passion itself, denigrating and condemning not only his own sexuality, but almost every form of sexual expression, saying that passion paralyzes "all power of deliberate thought," and creates "a problem for every lover of wisdom...who is both committed to a married life and also conscious of the apostolic ideal....Any such person would prefer, if this were possible, to beget his children without suffering this passion....Wherever sexual passion is at work, it feels ashamed of itself."[67]

Modern writers would certainly disagree with him and all those who in order to affirm celibacy portrayed sexuality and eros as incompatible with the committed love of God. (Jerome, as we will see in the next chapter, would be one of them.) C. S. Lewis, for example, would point out, as he does in *The Four Loves,* how the so-called "highest" loves cannot stand without the "lowest."[68] Jungian psychologist Adolf Guggenbuhl-Craig would advise Augustine that all human relationships, including our friendships, have a bodily and sexual aspect to them, and that if there is no emotion, no affect or attraction between people, there will be no depth of intimacy either.[69] James Hillman, another analyst, post-Jungian, posits something more; that "the sexual is the way the soul speaks."[70] Rosemary Haughton, among contemporary theologians, would speak to him of how the incarnation makes holy all materiality and bodiliness, and how sexual passion can lead us to greater maturity and self-giving.[71] The mythologist Joseph Campbell would warn Augustine, as he would us all: "Be careful lest in casting out the devils you cast out the best thing that is in you."[72] Even Socrates' mentor, the priestess Diotima, believed that Eros is a great daemon that can act as a mediator between the human and divine.[73]

If Augustine had perhaps taken that message in Plato's *Symposium* more seriously, and listened more closely to his feminine side, he might have been a little more trusting of his own eros and appreciated it more genuinely as a vehicle leading him to wisdom, holiness, friendship, and God. Perhaps Christianity itself, so influenced by Augustine's theology, might have avoided being suspicious, if not at times outright condemnatory, of sexuality in whatever form, especially in the expression of genuine love, and thus more capable of healing the painful split between sexuality and spirituality from which so many suffer today.

From these perspectives, we can now see that references to fire in Augustine's writings are in fact references to Augustine's eros, and that, despite his own denigration of that passion as it is expressed sexually, eros in *all its manifestations* made him the person he was and the saint he was to become. Truly, his life (to use the poetic language of T. S. Eliot) was "tongued with fire,"[74] and the directions it took and the important relationships he made were touched by that fire: the fire of eros, the fire of friendship, the fire of God. Yes, eros, like fire, can have a destructive side, but it is also where the Holy Spirit works. This spiritual presence, as Augustine knew from his own experience, manifests itself in numerous ways, from the voice of a child in a garden to a kindling fire whose warmth and power unite human hearts. That spiritual power, in fact, most often seems to be manifest in the heart, and it is intriguing to note that whenever Augustine in his *Confessions* uses the imagery of fire, the image of the heart is in close proximity. That is where Augustine finally locates friendship, for, according to him, friendship is simply sharing the counsels of the heart.

This chapter, then, has been about Augustine's own erotic passage to ultimate Wisdom, and how, through his many friendships, he was led to the God who unites souls and hearts. As his life story clearly shows, it is true that a person can be known by the friendships that she or he makes, or, perhaps, more accurately, that he or she is given. Monica was a significant part of that process. She did what Augustine in his writings considered one of the chief duties of friends: that of drawing each other closer to God. Because of her love, prayers, and persistence, the dream of her son's conversion eventually came true.

A New City in the Heart

Augustine died August 28, 430, at a time when the Vandals from Spain were clamoring at the gates of Hippo and seeking to destroy it. He had spent some of his last days in his beloved library with his books, reevaluating and revising his extensive writings, "both those which he had written as a layman in the early days of his conversion," according to his monastic colleague, Possidius, "and those from his days as priest and bishop."[75] With the fall of Rome to the Goths earlier in 410, he, along with numerous other Christians, including Jerome, had become increasingly aware of the uncertainty of the times. In response to accusations that Christians were somehow responsible for Rome's destruction, Augustine had written his final great work, *City of God,* defending Christianity and articulating a theology that was to become a blueprint for the Middle Ages. In that book, he posits that we are all *peregrinati,* people on pilgrimage, on a journey; that our true home is "the great eternity," and the "new city" for which we are destined—one that lasts—is found "in the heart."[76] In one of his last sermons, he alludes to that theme, stating, "Whoever does not want to fear, let him probe his inmost self. Do not just touch the surface; go down into yourself; reach into the farthest corner of your heart."[77]

In retrospect, we can see that at the heart of all Augustine's writings is, quite simply, the heart—*his* heart. His *Confessions,* in fact, were truly an exploration of the heart, what he describes as a "restless heart" that could never be satisfied until he had surrendered it completely to God. Only then did he experience a heart "filled with a light of confidence" in which all the shadows of doubt had been swept away. Attentive to his heart, and the spirit of God moving within it, he could write later: "There is no doubt in my mind, Lord, that I love you. I feel it with certainty. You struck my heart with your word, and I loved you..., beauty so ancient and so new...."[78]

Augustine highly valued the wisdom of the heart. It is no wonder that the monastic Rule that he left behind to guide his communities has so many references to it (fourteen in its eight chapters). According to that Rule, monks who follow it are to "seek the nobler things" with their hearts; to pray with their hearts; to "see" with their hearts; to "prevent evil gaining a stronger hold in the heart"; and perhaps, most importantly, to forgive "from the heart."[79] If one considers Augustine's definition of friendship as "two hearts united as one," clearly Augustine perceived monks to be friends with one another, reflecting in their daily lives and work the friendship of God. To be a monk today or someone seeking to incorporate monastic values into his or her own life presumes being part of a community of friends, people with whom a person can share the counsels of the heart, and speak a language of the heart to one another—something we will take up further in chapter six on John Cassian and his friend, Germanus.

While other Rules had been formulated in the East under Pachomius in southern Egypt and Basil in Caesarea, Augustine's with its emphasis on the heart was to become the oldest monastic Rule in the West. What also made it unique was that it was intended to be used by both women and men in their separate communities. As George Lawless says, "Augustine's Rule stands alone...in the entire history of western monasticism as the single legislative text which does double duty since it met the needs of both men and women."[80] This compendium on monastic life affected countless individuals and communities, exerting "an unusually great influence on the Christian ideal of the religious life,"[81] and contributing in a significant way to the development of Western monasticism. Its influence can be seen by its use in

Gaul, Spain, and Italy during the two centuries following Augustine's death, and its effect upon numerous writers, including St. Benedict of Nursia, who, as we will see, wrote his own now famous Rule, beginning it with the words: "Listen carefully, my son, to the master's instructions, and attend to them with the ear of your heart."[82] The phrase "ear of the heart" was one first used by Augustine in his own writings.[83]

By the Middle Ages, both male and female religious were using the Rule of St. Augustine to define their monastic life, and Canon Regulars of St. Augustine, such as Norbertines and Crosiers, had adopted it for themselves. From it, and from Augustine's other writings, especially the *Confessions,* they learned of the importance of friendship, and of a God who is often revealed as a God of friendship, of fire, of love.

CHAPTER FIVE

Flashing Lightning—Jerome and His Female Friends

Every time I read him [St. Paul], I seem to be hearing not so much words as thunder. Read his Epistles, particularly those to the Romans, the Galatians and the Ephesians, where he hurls himself into the fray....Wherever you look, the lightning is flashing!

—Jerome, *Apology to Pammachius*

While Augustine was living as bishop in a monastery that he had founded in Hippo, another of the great spiritual and intellectual leaders of the early Christian Church, Eusebius Hieronymus, or, as we have come to know him, St. Jerome, was living in Bethlehem in a monastic community that he had founded there, surrounded by admirers and a constant stream of pilgrims and refugees to the Holy Land. Although the two men never met, they carried on an intermittent correspondence for twenty-five years.[1] Augustine's friend, Alypius, had initiated their exchange of letters through his visit to Jerome in Bethlehem in 393 when he recommended Augustine to Jerome, and, upon his return, Jerome to Augustine. Encouraged by Alypius's description of Jerome, Augustine had taken the initiative in writing the older man.[2] The two of them were probably less than ten years apart in age, but radically different in temperament and interests. As a result, throughout the long years of their correspondence, they were not always on the best of terms. Still, over time, as their surviving letters show, they developed a deep respect for one another, if not outright friendship.

The two of them did, after all, have some things in common. Both men loved Cicero, although, as we shall see, in Jerome's case it turned out to be a highly conflictual love; both shared a passion for friendship, desiring to live with or in close proximity to those whom they counted as spiritual friends; both as young men struggled with the sexual side of eros, but were finally able to channel that spiritual energy in positive directions; both, through their writings and ministries, influenced significantly the Church's understanding of itself and its emerging orthodox theology. Most of all, both men lived as monks who taught others in and outside of monasteries about monastic values. While Augustine's monastic Rule significantly affected the development of monasticism in the West, Jerome's monastic leadership in Bethlehem as well as his hagiographies on the desert elders, Paul of Thebes, Malchus, and Hilarion, contributed to the popularization of monasticism among educated Christians, both clergy and laity. Always controversial, Jerome wrote his *Life of Paul* (of Thebes) at least partly to challenge the view that Antony was the "first monk," while his *Life of Malchus,* most interestingly, spoke of the "inner monk" that needs to find expression in daily living.[3]

A man of fiery temperament (one biographer calls him the patron saint of "ill-tempered people"), Jerome once said of St. Paul the apostle, "Wherever you look, the lightning is flashing."[4] Considering his quarrelsome personality and numerous conflicts with colleagues as well as strangers, it is an image that Jerome could have applied to himself. At the same time, he was known for his friendships, and for the spiritual guidance that he provided friends. Much of this side of him is revealed in his letters, which, according to Jean Leclercq, were "models of the art of letter writing and a source for ideals on monastic asceticism."[5] Through those numerous letters, as well as his scripture commentaries, hagiographies, and especially his translation of the Bible into Latin (subsequently known as the "Vulgate"), Jerome had a tremendous influence upon the development of Western monasticism.[6]

In this chapter, those letters in particular will be examined for insight into Jerome's understanding of friendship, especially as it relates to three women who became his lifelong friends and who led monastic communities of their own: Marcella, Paula, and Eustochium. As will become apparent, Jerome's great capacity for friendship was precisely what formed the basis of his own significant ministry as a spiritual mentor. This ability to make friends and his work as a spiritual guide, among other ministries, make Jerome's considerable personality flaws more tolerable. His ministry as a spiritual mentor also suggests the importance of the monastic value and practice of mentoring in forming and nurturing our lives.

Early Life and Significant "Dream"

Scholars disagree on the year of Jerome's birth, but, judging from recent arguments,[7] he most likely was born to Christian parents, possibly of Greek ancestry, about 345 or 347 CE at Strido in Italy, not far from Aquileia, a village on the Adriatic coast. This would have been about the time Athanasius was returning to Alexandria after his first exile in Rome. When Jerome was twelve, his father sent him to Rome to be trained in the art of public speaking and debate, and to receive a classical education, which would have included study of such Latin authors as Virgil, Terence, and, of course, Cicero. Jerome was baptized in Rome—a baptism delayed until his late adolescence as was the custom at the time. He must have loved his Christian faith, for he wrote later how often he and his friends (although not without trepidation!) used to visit the catacombs, which had become the sites of pilgrimage. "They were so dark," he said, that "only here and there did a ray of light penetrate from above and relieve the horror of blackness....We would grope our way back..., remembering Virgil's line: 'Everywhere dread grips my heart; even the silence frightens me.'"[8]

In his early twenties, Jerome traveled with a friend, Bonosus, to Trier in Gaul, which was then the administrative capital of the western Roman Empire. Here is where he began to accumulate what would eventually become an extensive library of both classical and Christian authors, as well as to associate with a circle of devout ascetic clerics. His readings at that time included at least two writings of Hilary of Poitiers.[9] At some point, possibly as a result of such works and of his ascetic friendships, he resolved to devote himself to his first experiments in monastic living. What drew him to embrace this lifestyle is not clear, since he left no testimony about that decision, but, perhaps, as Stefan Rebenich suggests,[10] he, like the Trier officials in the story told to Augustine by Ponticianus, took steps to become a monk because of the heroic example of the desert Christians themselves. Whatever his original motivation, Jerome, in imitation of those desert elders, lived for some time with a group of friends in Aquileia, and, when that community broke up, embarked in 372 or 374, in his late twenties, on a pilgrimage to the East, taking his library with him. After a brief stay in Antioch where he was a guest of Evagrius, a Christian priest who had translated Athanasius's *Life of Antony,* he settled as a hermit in the Syrian desert of Chalcis.

While in Antioch or in the desert itself, Jerome became seriously ill and experienced an extremely vivid dream. As he described it years later in a letter: "in about Mid-Lent, a fever attacked my enfeebled body and spread to my very vitals…[and] without cessation it so wrought havoc upon my wretched limbs that my flesh could scarcely cling to my bones. Meanwhile preparations for my funeral were being made. My entire body was already cold." What happened then seems more like a near-death experience than a dream: "Suddenly I was caught up in the spirit and dragged before the tribunal of the Judge. Here there was so much light and such a glare from the brightness of those standing around that I cast myself on the ground and dared not look up. Upon being asked my status, I replied that I was a Christian. And He who sat up the judgment seat said: 'You lie. You are a Ciceronian, not a Christian. Where your treasure is, there is your heart also.' I was struck dumb on the spot. Amid the blows—for He had ordered me to be beaten—I was tormented the more by the flame of conscience....I began to cry aloud and to say with lamentation: 'Have mercy on me, Lord, have mercy upon me.'"

As the "dream" continued, Jerome says, the bystanders fell to their knees, asking the Judge to forgive his enthusiasm for the pagan classics, and allow him to do penance. Jerome himself swore an oath, "O Lord, if ever I possess or read secular writings, I have denied you." After uttering these words, "I was discharged and returned to the world above." Jerome mysteriously suggests that this dramatic experience was *not* a dream, when he adds: "That had not been mere sleep or meaningless dreams....My shoulders were black and blue, and I felt the blows after I awoke from sleep." Whatever happened, besides the black and blue marks on his body, the experience made a significant impression on his soul: "After that I read God's word with greater zeal than I had previously read the writings of mortals."[11]

Whenever this experience occurred, it evidently became a turning point in Jerome's life, "akin both to an ecstatic vision and to a conversion more profound than the earlier ones...."[12] If it occurred while he was residing in Antioch, it led him to go into the desert of Chalcis, or, if in the desert, to become even more committed to his ascetic life. Wherever it happened, he would always remember his oath to remain loyal to Christ—although, as we will see, his love for the classics and Cicero in particular would never be totally extinguished.

Jerome stayed in the desert wilderness for two, three, possibly even five years (scholars are not sure), fasting and, like Antony, fighting his demons. He also evidently fought with numerous other hermits in the area over theological issues and the authority of the bishop of Rome. Unhappy and unsatisfied for a variety of reasons, he eventually moved back to Antioch where he was ordained a priest, traveled to Constantinople, and from 382 to 385 was in Rome where he served as a secretary to Pope Damasus. It was in Rome that he made so many enemies by satirizing the Roman clergy for their hypocritical piety and lives of luxury (they looked more like bridegrooms than clerics, he said), as well as campaigning passionately in favor of Eastern ascetic ideas and monastic values. Rome was also where he functioned as a spiritual mentor to numerous laypeople, including women. Three of those women, Marcella, a wealthy Roman widow; Paula, another widow; and her daughter, Eustochium, were especially important to him. Of the three, the latter two eventually joined him in Bethlehem where in 386 he established a monastic community of his own, one which expressed his ascetic ideals and provided him, at last, some degree of happiness—perhaps, most of all, because of their friendship.

Jerome's Passion for and Images of Friendship

If anything can be discerned in Jerome's writings, it is that his passion for friendship, both women's and men's, was matched only by his passion for books.[13] His letters betray an exceptionally needy man in this regard, one who is deeply hurt and quickly angry when his friends fail to live up to *his* expectations of them: to write back to him, to visit him, to stay with him, to return his affection. In one of his early letters that have survived, he writes to "the virgins of Haemona" from his retreat in the desert of Chalcis: "But now, I beg you, pardon me for having a grievance. I am saying it because I am hurt. I say it in tears and in anger: you have not addressed a single syllable to one who so often bestows his affection on you."[14] In another letter, he addresses Antonius, a monk living in the same area: "Ten times already, if I am not mistaken, have I sent you letters full of kindness and entreaties. But you do not deign to utter even a grunt, and though the Lord spoke with His slaves, you, a brother, do not speak with your brother....But as it is human to become angry and Christian to abstain from harm, I return to my old way: I entreat you once more to love me as I love you and, as a fellow servant [of Christ], speak to your fellow servant."[15] In effect, Jerome wanted his friends to love him *as he needed loving*. His correspondence shows that, along with a keen intellect, he had strong emotions, and was definitely not afraid of expressing them. For whatever reason, his writings reflect great passion *and* his great need for love.

No one work on friendship can be found in Jerome's writings, no unified statement explaining his theory of friendship or its practice. His opinions on the topic, however, emerge in the one hundred and fifty letters of his that have survived. What becomes clear is how much he thinks and speaks of friendship in classical terms, especially as reflected in the writings of Cicero. In particular, Cicero's *Laelius: On Friendship* is quoted frequently by Jerome in his own writings, suggesting how much his theology of friendship (as was true of Augustine's) was influenced by the Roman writer.[16] Despite his dramatic dream or visionary experience about Cicero, when Jerome speaks of friendship, he often uses Ciceronian images and phrases. A friend, according to Jerome, is half of one's soul,[17] and another self. As he says in a letter to Augustine, the correspondent who shared with him a profound appreciation of friendships: "Friendship ought to be free from all suspicion and one should be able to talk to a friend as to a second self."[18] These references to friendship as consisting of two bodies sharing one soul or to a friend as a second self are found in numerous classical writings[19] with which Jerome would have been familiar. Like Cicero, Jerome also believed in the permanence of friendship, echoing the Roman writer's words when he states in an early letter to Rufinus (in retrospect, quite ironically, since his close friend later became his bitter enemy): "a friend is long sought, is rarely come upon, and is hard to keep....Friendship that can cease was never real."[20]

Differences, however, can be found between Cicero's classical philosophy and Jerome's Christian theology of friendship. While Cicero suggests that *sapientia,* wisdom, is the virtue that creates and maintains friendships, Jerome believes friendship to be tied not only closely with wisdom, but with the activity, the work of Christ. In a letter to a Florentinus, he says: "Though absent in person, I do come to you in love and in spirit, earnestly beseeching you that no extent of time or space may tear asunder our growing friendship, cemented as it is in Christ."[21] Christ is the cement, the glue that binds friends together, and, thus, every

Christian friendship consists not of just two persons, but of three. As Jerome explains in a letter to his longtime friend Heliodorus, such relationships transcend geographical distance and the passage of time: "We write letters and send replies, our messages cross the seas, and as the ship cleaves a furrow through the waves the moments we have to live grow less. We have but one profit: we are joined together by the love of Christ."[22] While Cicero uses a mirror as a metaphor of friendship, Jerome compares friendship to an open door. In a letter to Exuperantius, a Roman soldier whom he invited to live with him in Bethlehem, he writes, "I have now knocked at the door of friendship: if you open it to me, you will find me a frequent visitor."[23]

Jerome's Women Friends

From his extant letters as well as numerous prefaces to his scriptural commentaries, we know that besides the male friends whom he loved (and with whom he frequently fought), Jerome loved women, beginning with his grandmother from whose arms, he says, he was torn and dragged off to school as a child.[24] If, as Elizabeth Clark says, "his relations with women remain to this day somewhat of a puzzle…[when he] confesses his love for them yet warns clerics against associating with them,"[25] Jerome's own feelings were probably just as mysterious to him, if not more so. Perhaps he loved women too much; perhaps this is why he seems to distance himself from them by adopting a highly critical, if not outright hostile, attitude toward many of them, or a paternalistic stance. Possibly he did this in order to protect himself from his own passionate nature, as well as the rumors from his detractors that he paid too much attention to women. J. N. D. Kelly sheds light on this: "Strongly sexed but also, because of his convictions, strongly repressed as well, his nature craved for female society and found deep satisfaction in it when it could be had without doing violence to his principles."[26]

Jerome alludes to some of his struggles with eros in his letters: the fact that he was not a virgin,[27] and that, while in the desert of Chalcis, visions (or was it memories?) of dancing girls filled his cell. Despite his extreme ascetical practices there, "the fires of the passions kept boiling within me."[28] Even when he was much older, he spoke of "that uniquely burdensome tyrant, sexual desire," which he compared, as did Augustine, to fire.[29] No wonder he would disagree with men like Evagrius of Pontus who believed that *apatheia*, a state of inner harmony, was a worthy *and attainable* goal. Based upon his own experience, Jerome thought such a state impossible except, he says, if one were a stone—or God.[30] That he identifies himself with Mary Magdalene, whom he saw as the sinful but contrite woman who washes Jesus' feet with her tears (Luke 7:39),[31] is quite revealing of his own inner state—and ongoing struggles with eros. That he identifies himself with a female at all, considering some of his statements on women, is also quite surprising! Jerome gives us a clue to how he handled his erotic energies when he tells the young virgin, Eustochium: "It is hard for the human soul not to love, and it is necessary that our mind be drawn into some sort of affection. Love of the flesh is overcome by love of the spirit. Desire is quenched by desire."[32]

Jerome's affection and his desires seem to have been sublimated into works of ministry and into spiritual mentoring, precisely what he did when he left the desert and moved to Rome. There his life revolved around the aristocratic women of the Aventine whom he counseled and taught, and with whom he corresponded: Furia, Fabiola, Asella, and, above all, the two wealthy widows, Marcella and Paula, and Paula's daughters, Blesilla, Paulina, and Eustochium. These women and others, including men, frequently met with Jerome in prayer, study, and care of the poor. What brought them together was what Cicero links with friendship: "an inclination of the heart," a "mutual belief in each other's goodness,"[33] and certainly a great deal of mutual affection. As Cicero says, "Friendships...are formed when an exemplar of shining goodness makes itself manifest, and when some congenial spirit feels the desire to fasten on to this model. Then the result will be affection."[34] That is how Jerome must have been perceived by them: as an exemplar, someone known for his scholarship and writings who elicited affection—and gratitude—when he acted as their teacher and spiritual guide. In one of his letters, Jerome tries to explain how these women had become intimates and friends: "Frequently I was surrounded by a throng of virgins: to some of them I often discoursed on the Scriptures to the best of my ability; study brought familiarity, familiarity friendship, friendship confidence."[35]

James Hillman, in his book, *The Soul's Code*, associates mentoring with having a "perceptive eye," that is, having the ability to see something "essential" in the other. This "eye," he says, is "the eye of the heart. Something moves in the heart, opening it to perceiving the image in the heart of the other": the image of potential greatness, of calling, of vocation which the mentor, with his or her perceptive eye, can then help foster in the life of the protégé. These relationships, characterized by great affection and love, begin, Hillman says, "when your imagination can fall in love with the fantasy of another." "An erotic component is necessary," he adds, "as it has been essential to education since Socrates...." Hillman makes clear that this erotic component is not necessarily genitally expressed, but associated much more with, as the poet John Keats said, "the holiness of the Heart's affections and the Truth of the Imagination."[36] Eros, as the Greeks and Keats himself believed, was a holy power, the spiritual power of connection, of affection for someone or something that meets our very human needs for affirmation, wisdom, and love.

This dynamic can be discerned in Jerome's friendships with the three Roman women to whom he was most attracted, and for whom he felt the most affection: Marcella, Paula, and Eustochium. All were deeply in love with God; all were bound together, over time, with the cement, the glue of Christ; all were in love, already, with the "fantasy" of the ascetic and monastic life. As in the case of many people of late antiquity, including both Augustine and Jerome, each of their imaginations had caught fire from the stories of the desert Christians. Despite his obvious misgivings about women of wealth, Jerome was attracted to these particular women, widows and a virgin, because of the ascetic ideals that he so admired. They, in turn, looked to him for wisdom and encouragement—which he happily gave. Unfortunately, we do not have *their* words to tell us what sort of relationship they had with him, but what we find reflected in Jerome's letters are his deep love and admiration for them, as well as intimations of the "give-and-take," the mutuality that characterizes all true friendships and mentoring relationships.

Marcella, Jerome's Questioner

The clearest description of Marcella can be found in a letter that Jerome wrote to Principia, a "virgin of Christ" who had taken Jerome's place as Marcella's "close companion" after he had left Rome. The letter is, in reality, a memoir of Marcella's life whose death had occurred about two years before, at the time Rome was pillaged by Alaric and the Goths in 410. Jerome speaks of his "incredible grief," which had so overwhelmed him that he could not write until now. In telling her story, he describes how the stories of the two desert fathers, Antony and Pachomius, were brought to Rome by Bishop Athanasius and other priests of Alexandria, as was mentioned earlier, and how Marcella was the first to adopt a simple lifestyle, practicing fasting "in moderation," and visiting the churches of the apostles and martyrs for "quiet prayer." Soon, Jerome says, a community of virgins and widows formed about her. When he came to Rome, "I in my modesty was inclined to avoid the gaze of ladies of rank," but she insisted, he says, upon his helping her understand the scriptures: "She never met me without asking me some questions about them, nor would she rest content..., but would bring forward points on the other side...." When Marcella bought a farm outside of Rome that she chose for its solitude, she turned it into a monastery where she lived until her death. Because of her leadership, Jerome implies, "I had the joy of seeing Rome become another Jerusalem" with the building of numerous monasteries for virgins and monks.

Jerome also discusses Marcella's spiritual mentoring: "Her friendship was enjoyed by the revered Paula, and in her cell that paragon of virgins Eustochium was trained. Such pupils as these make it easy for us to judge the character of their teacher." He believed, according to his own familiarity with the classical writers, that character (and the wisdom associated with it) was shaped by how well one prepared to die. Marcella was truly wise, Jerome suggests, for she "in all the days of her life remembered that she must die" and prepared for that day of reckoning. When the barbarians entered her house after they had invaded Rome, they "beat her with sticks and whipped her" because she, in her poverty, had so little to give them. Some months later she died as a result of that physical abuse, but smiling, he says, "conscious of having lived a good life." Jerome, at this point in the letter, cannot refrain from quoting the Roman poet Virgil, another favorite classical writer of his, when describing the plunder of Rome at an earlier time:

> Who can tell that night of havoc, who can shed
> enough of tears
> For those deaths? The ancient city that for many a
> hundred years
> Ruled the world comes down in ruin: corpses lie in
> every street
> And men's eyes in every household death in countless phases meet.[37]

That one of the dead was the wise woman Marcella seems to have made, for Jerome, the fall of Rome in his own time all the more difficult to bear, and accept.

Besides this moving testimonial to Marcella, we find intimations of another side of her leadership in an earlier letter that Jerome wrote directly to her. In it, he acknowledges that if he found (or placed) himself in the role of a teacher and spiritual mentor to Marcella, Marcella, he says, was not afraid of challenging his authority, of pushing him to further clarify his scholarship, of even acting as a *moderating* influence, a voice of reason when his inclination was to overreact:

> I know that as you read these words you will knit your brows, and fear that my freedom of speech is sowing the seeds of fresh quarrels; and that, if you could, you would gladly put your finger in my mouth to prevent me from even speaking of things which others do not blush to do.[38]

Paula, Fellow Pilgrim

The second woman with whom Jerome was particularly close was Paula whom he seems to have loved the most, and whose friendship caused him the most difficulty. As he candidly admits, "Of all the women in Rome, but one had power to subdue me, and that one was Paula." Unfortunately, it was precisely his friendship with her and the other women that became the source of rumors in Rome that contributed to the demise of his reputation, and his eventual departure. As he states in a letter written onboard a ship at Ostia in August, 385, after leaving Rome for the East, "Before I became acquainted with the family of the saintly Paula, all Rome resounded with my praises. Almost everyone concurred in judging me worthy of the episcopate. [Pope] Damasus, of blessed memory, spoke no words but mine. Men called me holy, humble, eloquent."[39] Some of his attraction to Paula, on an unconscious level, may have been due to her family connections. Jerome frequently quoted the Roman poet Virgil and identified himself with Virgil's hero Aeneas. He may have been attracted to Paula precisely because she had been married to Toxotius "in whose veins," he says "ran the noble blood of Aeneas."[40] Consciously, however, Jerome says that he was drawn to her solely because of her holiness and asceticism: "She mourned and fasted, she was squalid with dirt, her eyes were dim from weeping. For whole nights she would pray to the Lord for mercy, and often the rising sun found her still at her prayers. The psalms were her only songs, the Gospel her whole speech, continence her one indulgence, fasting the staple of her life."[41]

Paula eventually joined Jerome in Palestine, a move that did not lesson rumors of impropriety back in Rome. Before settling with him in Bethlehem, she, along with Eustochium, visited Egypt and the monasteries of Nitria where the desert monks lived. She also went as a pilgrim to sacred sites in the Holy Land. Jerome describes her enthusiasm: "Moreover, in visiting the holy places so great was the passion and the enthusiasm she exhibited for each, that she could never have torn herself away from one had she not been eager to visit the rest. Before the Cross she threw herself down in adoration as though she beheld the Lord hanging upon it; and when she entered the tomb which was the scene of the Resurrection she kissed the stone which the angel had rolled away from the door of the sepulchre." When Paula finally saw the cave in Bethlehem where Jesus was born, she reveals a rich and vivid imagination that anyone trained in the Ignatian method of prayer and discernment would appreciate: "she protested in my hearing that she could behold with the eyes of faith the infant Lord wrapped in swaddling clothes and crying in the manger, the wise men worshipping Him, the star shining overhead, the virgin mother, the attentive foster-father, the shepherds coming by night...." With such a response, it is no wonder that she and Eustochium decided to settle in Bethlehem with Jerome, in a cave not far from Jesus' birthplace.

There, while Jerome supervised a monastery for monks, Paula was in charge of a community for women. Increasingly, she became known for her compassion. "No poor person went away from her empty-handed," Jerome says. In terms of the mutuality that seems to have characterized their relationship, it is obvious how much Paula meant to him, and how much Jerome appreciated her fervor, her love for the poor, her overall holiness. At the same time, as a friend, he seems to have had to challenge her constantly to be more moderate in her spending on the poor—an unusual role for him who was not particularly known for moderation in anything. As he says, "Her liberality knew no bounds. Indeed, so anxious was she to turn no needy person away that she borrowed money at interest and often contracted new loans to pay off old ones....[She left] her daughter overwhelmed with a mass of debt. This Eustochium still owes and indeed cannot hope to pay off by her own exertions; only the mercy of Christ can free her from it."[42]

When Paula died in 404, Jerome was shattered. "I have suddenly lost," he wrote, "the comforter...."[43] For almost twenty years, their lives had been closely intertwined. Only the presence of her daughter, Eustochium, who succeeded as head of her convent, seemed to offer him the strength to go on.

Eustochium, Protégé and Spiritual Daughter

Jerome describes Eustochium in a famous letter to her as "daughter, lady, fellow-servant, sister—for one name suits your age, another your rank, another our religion, another my affection...."[44] Whether that affection was only paternal or fraternal as he implies, it is obvious from his letters and commentaries how much affection he had for her. In one letter he compares her to "a precious necklace."[45] From the first time they met until her death in 418 or 419, a year or so before his own, there seems to have been a tender, loving relationship between the two of them despite their significant age-difference. As her spiritual mentor in Rome and in Bethlehem, Jerome provided her with guidelines on how to live, and encouraged her to pray and learn. "Read much and learn as much as possible," he told her early in their friendship, and "let sleep creep upon you with a book in your hand...." Wisely, he offers Eustochium the example of Jesus by which to live her life:

> Hear Jesus, speaking to the apostles: "Be not solicitous for your life, what you shall eat, nor for your body, and what you shall put on. Is not the life more than the meat, and the body more than the raiment? Behold the birds of the air, for they neither sow nor do they reap, nor gather into barns; and your heavenly Father feeds them." If clothing is lacking, consider the lilies. If you are hungry, hear the blessedness of the poor and the hungry.

Defending her virginity, however, Jerome disparages marriage and even opposes her "consorting" with married women. (It's a good thing her mother was a widow by this time!) And, in one of the most egregious statements which he was to make, he tells her, "I praise marriage, I praise wedlock, but I do so because they produce virgins for me. I gather roses from thorns, gold from the earth, the pearl from the shell."

Aside from some of these lessons magnifying virginity and denigrating marriage, perhaps the most valuable gift Jerome gave Eustochium was what Hillman suggests a good mentor will do: a vision that touched her imagination. In this case, he offers her in his letter a promise that if she lives a holy life, she will experience union with God, Jesus, Mary, and all of the saints, including Paula, her mother, and Marcella, her "spiritual mother":

> ...picture before your eyes the reward for your present labor....What shall that day be like when Mary, the mother of the Lord, shall come to meet you, accompanied by bands of virgins?...Then, too, shall your Spouse Himself come to meet you and shall say: "Arise, come, my love, my beautiful one, my dove, for winter is now past, the rain is over and gone...." Then also another chaste company shall come to meet you....Your mother in the flesh and your spiritual mother shall be there in different companies. The former will rejoice that she bore you, the latter will exult that she taught you.

He concludes this vision of heaven, of the communion of saints, with the words, "Begin to be what you shall be. And you shall hear from your Bridegroom: 'Put me as a seal upon your heart....'"[46]

Years later, when Eustochium died suddenly at the age of fifty, after having been his spiritual daughter since her youth and serving him in all sorts of ways in Bethlehem (especially the fifteen years following the death of her mother), Jerome was once again in grief. "I have been saddened beyond measure by Eustochium's unexpected passing," he writes; "it has virtually altered the whole tenor of my existence."[47] Surely, considering the vision of heaven he offered Eustochium when she was young, he too hoped to be one of those in the heavenly company, along with Marcella, Paula, and Eustochium—all united in the friendship of Christ.

Last Days

Jerome died September 30, 420, resting at last from a full, highly productive, and at the same time contentious life. Some of that contentiousness was due to his personality, some perhaps to his training. Along with a keen intellect, Jerome had strong emotions, as we know from his correspondence, and was definitely not afraid of expressing them. Some of the vindictive tone of his writings certainly is related to this quality in him, as well as to his extreme sensitivity toward *any* criticism—which he took, as we know, quite personally! Besides his emotional side and a highly competitive streak, some of his sarcasm and malicious comments toward his perceived enemies could be attributed to his early training in rhetoric that had a tendency to exaggeration,[48] or to his own identification with certain classical writers of satire, such as Horace and Juvenal.[49] Jerome's at times extreme approach may also have been due to the poor example of lawyers. As he says about his own formation: "When I was a young man declaiming controversies at Rome, preparing for real contests by imaginary pleadings, I went much to the law courts. I saw the most eloquent of the orators arguing among themselves with extraordinary animosity. Often, leaving aside the matter under discussion, they took to personal insults, mocking and sneering at one another furiously."[50] Despite all this (whether we blame lawyers or not), Jerome, before his death, was surely able to look back with some sense of happiness and of accomplishment. His spiritual mentoring, his writings on and in defense of monasticism, his own pioneer leadership in Bethlehem, all had contributed a great deal to the spread of monasticism and monastic values.

Still, Jerome's last days were difficult for him, judging from writings that have survived. He was shocked by the fall of Rome, and by the numbers of refugees who streamed into Bethlehem, "men and women who once were noble and abounding in every kind of wealth, but are now reduced to poverty." "We cannot," he says, "relieve these sufferers; all we can do is to sympathize with them, and unite our tears with theirs." Deprived of his closest companions, he also was frustrated by the physical limitations of old age: "my eyes are growing dim…[and] I am quite unable to go through the Hebrew books with such light as I have at night, for even in the full light of day they are hidden from my eyes owing to the smallness of the letters."[51] Like Augustine, he worried too about the spread of Pelagianism, and wrote vehemently against the followers of the Christian Celt, Pelagius, whom he describes (in his usual immoderate way) as a "stupid fool, laboring under his load of Irish porridge."[52]

Postumianus, a friend of Sulpicius Severus, visited Jerome in Bethlehem before he died, and reported back to the biographer of Martin of Tours how much Jerome's vehemence elicited a backlash: "he [Jerome] is hated by the heretics because he never stops assailing them. He is hated by the clerics because he censures their vicious mode of life." "On the other hand," he added, "Jerome has the admiration and affection of all good men." In his discussions with Sulpicius, Postumianus also made another significant observation about the sage of Bethlehem: "He is always fully absorbed in reading and in books. Day and night he takes no rest. He is continually reading or writing something."[53] Considering his vast outpouring of letters and manuscripts, it is no wonder that Jerome has been called the patron saint not only of ill-tempered people, as mentioned earlier, but also of book lovers.[54] The female Christian humanist, Isotta Nogarola (1418–1466), later wrote this about him: "He read so much we can hardly imagine how he found time to write; he wrote so much that it is difficult to believe he could have found time to read."[55] Thus, it is understandable how Jerome came to be so frequently depicted by artists as seated alone in some monastic cell, hunched over a manuscript, scribbling with a quill pen. In particular, the 1514 engraving of Albrecht Durer (1471–1528), one of the greatest artists of the Northern Renaissance, is especially moving, showing Jerome at work in his study with his only companions, a small dog and a lion asleep next to each other. This picture, "St. Jerome in His Study," symbolizes much about the man: his study as "a place of monkish peace, psychologically distant from the town and the marketplace," the dog, a frequent comrade of Christian scholars, as a symbol of fidelity, and the lion symbolizing Jerome's monastic vocation, his attempts at taming his passions, the wild beast within—over a lifetime, one day at a time.[56]

When Jerome died, he had produced such a great body of works that, as Rebenich says, "next to Augustine he was the most prolific of all Christian Latin authors in the ancient world,...a literary exponent of the ascetic movement and of Nicene orthodoxy, a biblical scholar, and [like Athanasius and Hilary] a mediator between eastern and western theology."[57] Finally, his quill pen put down, he was buried close to the graves of the two women (Paula and Eustochium) whose lives had been so intertwined with his, not far from the Church of the Nativity, the site to which all three had been drawn, and which had touched so powerfully Paula's imagination.

In the years following his death, Jerome's fame increased steadily, taking on legendary proportions. Augustine and John Cassian (c. 360–435) compared him to a divine lamp lighting the world, while Alcuin (c. 735–804), the lead scholar at the court of Charlemagne in Aachen, Germany, called him *maximus doctor,* the greatest of teachers.[58] By the eighth century, along with Ambrose, Augustine, and Gregory the Great, he was declared a "Doctor of the Church," the first of many to be honored for their spiritual leadership and significant contributions. Unlike these other doctors, however, who were bishops and even a pope, Jerome, the monk, never advanced beyond the priesthood. Still, later generations "promoted" him, identifying him as a "cardinal priest" (since he had worked for a pope), which is why he is frequently portrayed by artists as dressed in the red vestments of a cardinal or with a cardinal's hat nearby. Besides the Vulgate, his scripture commentaries, and his extensive correspondence, medieval Christians came to love especially his *Life of St. Paul* (of Thebes), the story of the two desert monastic pioneers, Antony and Paul, who shared bread together before the older man died, revealing the eucharistic dimension of all spiritual friendships and mentoring.[59] Though Martin Luther, who favored Augustine in his Reformation theology, said that he knew of "no writer whom I hate so much as I do Jerome; all he writes about is fasting and virginity,"[60] among Celtic Christians Jerome was held in high regard, described in one ninth-century Irish martyrology as "the sound, well-tongued sage, fair Jerome of Bethlehem, whom our sisters [Paula and Eustochium] used to visit."[61]

A life filled with controversy as well as genuine accomplishments, surely one of Jerome's most significant was the spiritual mentoring he did for numerous people, especially women. At a time in late antiquity when women in the Roman Empire had few rights and roles outside the home and were not considered capable of genuine friendships with men, Jerome advocated their education, scholarship, and spiritual formation. Despite his misogynous statements, he was the one who remarked that what God values is not gender but the heart, supporting his view by listing examples from secular and sacred history women distinguished for their virtue and learning, and reminding his readers that after his resurrection, Jesus had appeared to women first, women, like Mary Magdalene who had become "apostle to the apostles."[62]

Ironically, from the time he left the desert of Chalcis and moved to Rome and eventually to Bethlehem, his closest friends were women. The irony is evident when one considers his diatribes against certain types of women in his letters, his caricatures of them, and his warnings about keeping their company. Granted, his polemic was most often directed at corrupt nuns or against wealthy, worldly women who were not committed to asceticism as Marcella, Paula, and Eustochium were. Some of his comments, however, from a contemporary perspective are indefensible: when he, for example, told a young priest, Nepotian, "Remember always that a woman drove the tiller of Paradise from the garden...," or when he warned a young mother not to let her daughter see pregnant women because they are "a revolting sight."[63]

Still, in practice, Jerome was capable of having intimate friendships with women, relationships that changed his life. Paula and Eustochium, in particular, with their knowledge of Hebrew and Greek, provided him with help in translating, and encouragement in composing the commentaries that he wanted to write.[64] They also gave him the support that he needed in fighting all those foes whom he perceived as challenging his theology. In their own way, his female friends changed Jerome's theology, as can be discerned in the letter he wrote after the death of Marcella: "The unbelieving reader may perhaps laugh at me for dwelling so long on the praises of mere women; yet if he will but remember how holy women followed our Lord and Saviour... and how the three Marys stood before the cross and especially how Mary Magdalene...was privileged to see the rising Christ first of all before the very apostles, he will convict himself of pride sooner than me of folly. For we judge of people's virtue not by their sex but by their character...."[65]

Above all, these women provided him with a community that helped assuage his great needs for affection, for love—what he kept crying out for in the loneliness of the desert of Chalcis. Whether he could admit it or not, he, in his spiritual mentoring, and they, in their intellectual stimulation and, yes, patience with his fiery personality, did find in each other an open door and "another self." Against cultural taboos and Jerome's personal hesitancy, theirs was a friendship truly brought about by "an inclination of the heart," as Cicero had so wisely said. Together, they reveal the importance of spiritual mentoring as a practice and as a resource for those who are attempting to follow a spirituality today based upon monastic values. The stories of Jerome, Marcella, Paula, and Eustochium also reveal how much mentoring itself is a *mutual* relationship; that as one gives, one also receives. Jerome obviously recognized this to some degree when he dedicated a number of his later works to his close friends, Paula and Eustochium.[66]

CHAPTER SIX

A Kind of Fire—John Cassian and the Desert Elders

My sons, it is your zeal which led me to speak for so long. Because of your eagerness, some kind of fire has given a more urgent sense to what I have been saying.

—John Cassian, *Conference One*

As Jerome was preparing for his own death in Bethlehem, another monk was founding two monastic houses in Marseilles, on the coast of southern Gaul. This monk had once traveled to the Holy Land with a close friend of his about the year 380. The two of them had spent time in Bethlehem where they had joined a monastery near the cave of the Nativity, and remained there for several years sharing a common cell. Although the younger of the two later read and recommended Jerome's writings to his own readers, the two friends evidently did not stay with him, since Jerome had probably not yet founded his monastery in Bethlehem. Whatever the situation, the two friends moved on to Egypt, after what the younger man called "too short a training," where they lived with various desert solitaires for the next fifteen years or so.

What drew them to the desert regions around such places as Cellia, Scetis, and Nitria was their longing, the younger man tells us, to learn "the rules" and to receive "spiritual instruction" from those mature and wise teachers whom he called "the Elders."[1] The intense desire of the two friends was clearly evident to at least one of the desert fathers with whom they lived, for, in the description of their meeting with Abba Moses, we find the old man pausing for a moment, astonished by their enthusiasm, and then telling them: "My sons, it is your zeal which led me to speak for so long. Because of your eagerness, some kind of fire has given a more urgent sense to what I have been saying."[2] This fire, this eager yearning for wisdom on their part, can be discerned a few paragraphs later when the writer describes how, after listening to the old man, they found it difficult to sleep, "at once burning with joy as a result of the conference that had been given and excited by the prospect of the discussion that had been promised."[3]

Years later in recalling that conversation with the elder and what may well have been one of many sleepless nights, the writer implies that, though he and his older friend had started their spiritual adventure in the desert as intimates, the time they spent together fighting the first of their spiritual battles strengthened even more the bonds of friendship between them. Echoing the words of Augustine, their contemporary, he wrote that as a result of the communal life and desert experiences which they shared, "we were one mind and soul inhabiting two bodies."[4]

The two friends who spent so much valued time together were John Cassian and Germanus. Although biographical information on both men is limited,[5] it is the younger of the two, John Cassian, who is better known because of his gift of storytelling, his work as a pioneer in the monastic movement in southern Gaul, and his extraordinary writings explaining various dimensions of monastic living. Unlike Augustine who explores almost every aspect of his life in his *Confessions*, Cassian seems to have been an intensely private man, someone who, while emphasizing in his works what he called "the inner man," gives only the briefest glimpse of his own interior and exterior life. Probably born about 360 CE in what today is identified as Romania in eastern Europe, he was a member of what seems to have been a well-to-do family, which provided him with a fine education in classical literature. We know nothing of his early life, until he and Germanus as young men (i.e., Cassian was about twenty years old) decided to journey to Palestine and live as monks. The two remained companions for at least the next twenty-five years. It was in Bethlehem that Cassian specifically reported on a life-changing event: their meeting an old monk named Pinufius who told them about the hermits in Egypt, lighting the fire in them to go and live there themselves. As a result of that adventure, Cassian wrote two major works, *Institutes* and *Conferences,* explaining to a much larger audience basic monastic dynamics and principles.

Like the others in this book, Cassian is considered a leading Father of the early Church, and one of the most influential writers on the development of Christian monasticism in both East and West.[6] Owen Chadwick, his biographer, has stated that "all the guides to spirituality in which western Europe later abounded were his descendents."[7] However, as Cassian himself implicitly acknowledged, the insights about monasticism and desert spirituality expounded in his writings were a product of both his and Germanus's experiences and the friendship they shared.

This chapter offers a brief analysis of what the two friends learned about formation and spiritual direction from the "daily exhortations and examples"[8] of the desert elders. By critically examining Cassian's *Institutes,* written to explain desert monasticism to a Western audience, and, *Conferences,* a compilation of instructions on the spiritual life as expressed by specific anchorites, we may be able to discern the importance of spiritual formation for any Christian leader today, as well as of the monastic value of confession, of disclosing the secrets of the heart if one is to discern and maintain any degree of spiritual health.

It should be noted at the outset, however, that although Cassian refers only to male elders throughout his writings, women in his own time, such as Sarah, Theodora, Matrona, and Syncletica, were also recognized for their competence and holiness as spiritual guides in the desert. Various collections of the so-called "Sayings of the Desert Fathers" also include statements by women, and, of these women, Blessed Syncletica's teachings were the most extensively quoted.[9] Palladius (c. 365–425 CE), a frequent visitor to the desert Christians, states in his "Foreword" to *The Lausiac History* that one of the reasons he wrote his book was "to commemorate women far advanced in years and illustrious God-inspired mothers who have performed feats of virtuous asceticism in strong and perfect intention...."[10] Early hagiographies of desert women, such as St. Mary of Egypt, Pelagia, and Thais, also offered others examples of repentance and great holiness.[11] Recognizing their historical importance, we will, however, concentrate here on the contribution of male elders as described in Cassian's works, while presuming that much of what he says about them would apply to the women in the desert regions as well as to their own significant ministry of spiritual guidance.

The Importance of an Elder and of an Apprenticeship

According to Cassian, he and Germanus went to Egypt specifically to learn about the "rules of the Elders." Throughout his writings he refers constantly to the "old sayings and opinions of the fathers" and to what the desert elders thought or said.[12] He saw it as his task, because of the gift of wisdom that he had received from them, to hand down for posterity their teaching. One of the key lessons he learned from them was the importance of an elder: a wise, holy, and experienced person who can act as a teacher and guide for an individual or community. Among the many sources of guidance recognized by the desert Christians as helpful to their spirituality, such as reading the scriptures, participation in Eucharist, and sitting quietly in a cell, they considered an experienced guide to be, Cassian says, "the greatest gift and grace of the Holy Spirit."[13] In fact, such a person is linked directly with the spirit within and the transforming power of God. Besides the terms of *abba* for a male or *amma* for a female wisdom figure, the spiritual guide was identified as a *pneumatikos pater* or *pneumatike mater*: a spirit-bearer who acts as a kind of foster parent or midwife of souls. Desert Christians believed that a relationship of friendship with these guides could have a major effect on the direction of one's spiritual journey, for, as they learned from the gospels, one person's spirit is very much affected (for good or for ill) by another's.[14] They also knew from the personal example and the stories of such desert elders as Antony, Paul of Thebes, Pachomius, and others of the value of such a spiritual mentor in their lives. Thus, because of his own formation by the desert elders, Cassian firmly espouses the belief in his writings that God's guidance and wisdom come most often through human mediation, especially, as he says, through the "experience," "sure example," and "spirit" of the desert elders.[15]

Cassian makes clear that a desert elder's competence as a spiritual guide is not guaranteed by his white hair or length of years. Rather, as he states in his *Conferences,* "we should follow those who we recognize have shaped their lives in a praiseworthy and upright manner as young men, and who have been instructed not in their own presumptions but in the traditions of their forebears."[16] Whether one lived within a monastic community or as an anchorite alone in the wilderness, to be recognized as a trustworthy guide one must have gone through some form of apprenticeship with a more experienced person—as Antony had done before he began his solitary living. Any kind of effective leadership within a community depended upon an apprenticeship, Cassian says in his other work, *Institutes,* for "to rule or to be ruled well needs a wise man," and, "no one is chosen to be set over a congregation of brethren before he who is to be placed in authority has learnt by obedience what he ought to enjoin on those who are to submit to him, and has discovered from the rules of the Elders what he ought to teach to his juniors."[17]

An apprenticeship with a wise person or elder could take different forms in the desert. One that was highly popular during the fourth and fifth centuries CE was informal and sometimes quite spontaneous: that of simply going out into the wilderness and asking to live near or with a specific elder—as Germanus and Cassian did while they were in Egypt. A story told about one of the desert elders refers to this practice. When someone asked Abba Paesius, "What should I do about my soul?" he replied, "Go, and join a man who fears God, and live near him; he will teach you, too, to fear God."[18] The other more structured form of apprenticeship was that of joining a formation program provided by the desert monasteries. Both informal and structured apprenticeships included experienced teachers and guides, as well as educational and confessional elements that might be equated with "spiritual direction." While it is obvious that Cassian greatly appreciated the training he received from various charismatic teachers who lived in solitude, he seems more concerned in his writings (because of the rise of monasticism in the West) with describing the formation process specifically found within a monastic community. Let us turn first to his description of that formation program, and then examine those elements of spiritual direction within it.

Monastic Formation: Becoming a Mature Monk

Beginning in Book IV of his first book, *Institutes,* Cassian explains the dimensions and different stages of formation that desert monks passed through. Anyone who wished to join the desert community, he says, had to first stand outside the monastery's walls for at least ten days. While this waiting period was much longer than that advocated by the Rules of Basil or Pachomius or the later Benedictine Rule, considering the desert heat, it certainly must have proved a young man's sincerity, if not his persistence! Once this initial test had been withstood and he was welcomed in, the neophyte or novice laid aside his own clothes, was clad in a monastic habit, and "given into the charge of an Elder." For a year, he lived only with this older, more experienced monk, since no mixing with other members of the religious community was allowed. This elder usually lived near the entrance to the monastery and evidently functioned as a guest master, for, according to Cassian, he was "entrusted with the care of strangers and guests, and bestows all his diligence in receiving them kindly." During that first year, the novice was to do the same type of work as his master, without complaint, giving "evidence of service towards strangers." In this way, the young person is "initiated," Cassian states, into "the first rudiments of humility and patience."[19] As is apparent in the reference to serving "strangers," the novice is also introduced to the practice of hospitality, a virtue recognized throughout the history of Judeo-Christian spirituality as one of the most important qualities a person can have.

This initial part of his formation process truly was an initiation for the young man, one in which he not only learned his first lessons about the prayer, work, diet, and qualities that might be expected of any monk, but a time in which the elder came to know his charge intimately. Theirs was a daily routine of sharing responsibilities and unpleasant tasks, eating simply, praying quietly, sleeping in close proximity, and rising early to face another day. Like a Zen Master who must get to know his students before setting them on the Zen way,[20] this first desert elder, after a year of intimacy with his student, was capable of making an informed judgment on whether to recommend the young man or not for more training in the spiritual life. If the novice's personality and character were deemed worthy, he proceeded to a second phase.

At this second stage in the formation program, the young man, whom Cassian now terms a "junior monk," joined a community of at least nine other peers, all of whom were under the direction of another elder. This second elder, according to Cassian, was primarily responsible for teaching each student self-control; that is, the ability to conquer "his own wishes." The desert Christians believed that this was essential, for "a man who has not first learnt to overcome his desires cannot possibly stamp out anger or sulkiness, or the spirit of fornication; nor can he preserve true humility of heart, or lasting unity with the brethren, or a stable and continuous concord." Junior monks learned self-control through a strict regimen of fasting and abstinence, of daily prayer and work. They were taught to call nothing their own—neither book, tablets, pen, coat, nor sandals. They were to sit in their cells and devote "their energies equally to work and to meditation."[21] Work was highly valued by the desert fathers, for, as Cassian states, "they never allowed the younger ones to be idle." This work included projects related not only to maintenance of the monastery, but also to visiting prisoners in nearby cities and even to collecting food and provisions for the starving people of Libya during times of famine.[22] Above all, they were expected to do as they were told. They were not to exercise any judgment of their own, nor do anything on their own authority. Their primary responsibility was that of obedience: attentiveness to the words and advice of the elder, and readiness to follow his commands, even if they might appear impossible or ridiculous. "Make yourself," Cassian says, "a fool in this world that you may become wise."[23]

Cassian's theology of formation is constantly clothed in human flesh and expressed in vivid stories. Throughout his writings he provides examples from what he calls "the deeds of the elders," telling his readers that these holy men provide "a model" for what he is proposing in regard to monastic life. One of the elders he describes in the *Institutes* is Abba John of Lycopolis who from youth to manhood was "subject to his senior" until the older man died. This John was so humble and obedient, Cassian says, that his senior monk was suspicious of his intentions, wondering if he was merely being compliant or acting sincerely in his religious quest. So he ordered John to do many superfluous and at times impossible tasks, including watering a stick until it might strike roots and bloom, and moving a giant boulder. Eventually, he and the other elders became convinced of John's sincerity, since the latter "shone forth more and more with the grace of humility" and "the sweet odor of obedience."[24] For Cassian, John is a paradigm of the truly obedient junior monk.

The exact opposite of John is the monk named "Heron" whose story is related in Cassian's second book, *Conferences*. This monk destroyed himself by following only his illusions, especially the "illusion of the devil" to which everyone is prone: that of failing to recognize evil masquerading as good. According to Abba Moses, a wisdom figure whom Cassian dearly loves and whom he calls "the chief of all the saints,"[25] Heron lived fifty years in the desert, maintaining "a rigorous abstinence with extraordinary strictness, and with a marvelous zeal he went more deeply into the desert than anyone else living here." Heron, however, "preferred to be governed by his own understanding of things rather than to obey the counsels and conferences of the brothers." When Satan appeared to him disguised as an angel of light and told him that he would suffer no harm, Heron foolishly believed him and threw himself headlong into a well, only to die two days later from his injuries. True discernment is obtained, Abba Moses concludes, only when one humbly submits every deed and thought to the discretion of the elders.[26]

This is precisely what the elder in charge of the junior monks attempts to discern during his time with them: whether they "are grounded in a false and imaginary or in a true humility."[27] Humility for the desert Christians was the opposite of pride, the sin they considered to be the most dangerous of all. Thus, to be grounded in humility was the greatest sign of maturing holiness. Humility also had much to do with clear-sightedness: a holistic sense of reality and an awareness of the awesomeness of the universe—and one's place within it. To discern the growth or decline in humility, the elder, as his predecessor had done, closely observed and noted the junior monks' actions and various responses to assigned work, prayer, and study routines. Desert Christians believed that the inner life is manifest outwardly, or, as Cassian expresses it, "you can tell a man's inward condition from his outward gait." Revealing his own astute psychological insights and obvious observation skills, Cassian outlines some "signs" of pride to watch for in a monk: "To begin with, in conversation the man's voice is loud; in his silence there is bitterness; in his mirth his laughter is noisy and excessive; when he is serious he is unreasonably gloomy; in his answers there is rancor; he is too free with his tongue....He is utterly lacking in patience, and without charity...."[28] In another part of the *Institutes,* Cassian lists ten positive signs of genuine humility that the elder might look for in his charges. They include whether the young man mortifies his desires, puts no trust in his own opinions, and does not conceal any of his actions or even of his thoughts from his superiors; in effect, that he does "nothing to which he is not urged by the Common Rule or by the examples of the elders."[29]

Besides close observation of their behavior, the second way the elder discerns the junior monks' obedience and humility is in their willingness to fully disclose what Cassian describes as "any itching thoughts in their hearts."[30] This honest sharing of what lies within one's heart (precisely what the monk Heron avoided doing) is an essential aspect of formation. It is also one of the main dynamics of the spiritual direction that is found within the entire formation process outlined by Cassian. This spiritual direction, Cassian's writings make clear, consists of both educative and confessional elements that lead to the type of self-knowledge that not only heals, but also frees one to love more fully and genuinely.

Learning Discernment and True Self-Knowledge

As we first saw with the *Life of Antony,* the literature of the desert Christians is closely identified with the practice of spiritual direction in which a person helps others discern the movement of God in their lives and hearts. They believed that discernment was "the begetter, guardian, and moderator of all virtues,"[31] the virtue that teaches one to recognize differences and to avoid extremes. As apprenticeship in the desert tradition could be either informal or highly structured, so also the practice of spiritual direction could consist of simply living near or with a solitary elder, and asking him or her questions arising in one's spiritual life, or it could be part of a monastic formation program in which the same dynamics coexist. In either case, education in human nature and self-knowledge was taught, and an elder and a student spoke as friends do, openly and honestly acknowledging to each other human struggles and sinful deeds. As was true of the relationship between Jerome, Marcella, Paula, and Eustochium, mutuality in the relationship between elder and protégé was presupposed, apparent in the words of Antony to his own followers: "...it is good for us to encourage each other in the faith. Now you, saying what you know, bring this to the father like children, and I, as your elder, will share what I know and the fruits of my experience."[32]

"Conferences," or meetings between elders and their students, were a standard method of doing this spiritual direction.[33] Many of these sessions evidently began quite spontaneously with a request on the part of the student: "Abba, teach me a word so that I may be saved" or "so that I may live." The "word" given was not necessarily a direct answer, nor was it an extensive list of recommendations for improving one's spiritual life; more often than not it took the form of a simple suggestion for further reflection by the neophyte, a prayerful process that might more readily lead the younger person to discover wisdom in his or her own heart, the place where conversion happens (cf. Matt 6:33). Desert Christians presupposed that their primary task was not to give advice, but to evoke a response; not to get others to rely upon them for discernment, but to encourage others to rely upon God. Favorite topics of many of these conferences seem to have been the "passions," which they associated with overindulgent sensuality or sicknesses of the soul.[34] Contrary to some modern views, desert Christians were not just morbid or depressed individuals with an overly pessimistic attitude toward life. Rather, they presupposed that before one can get well physically and/or spiritually, a person needs to first name that which keeps him or her sick or in bondage. Such soul-sickness and self-destructive patterns of behavior the desert elders called "sin," and spent many conferences describing and analyzing the kinds, origins, and causes of it. But, as Cassian shows in his writings, these desert guides taught their students remedies for overcoming sin as well. Through words, and most importantly, through their example, they taught their protégés about the need for each of them to develop patterns in their own lives and spirituality that would contribute significantly to spiritual health and holiness, what Augustine and other Early Church writers refer to as "greatness of soul."[35]

From Books V–XII of his *Institutes* and throughout his *Conferences,* Cassian names and describes what he calls the "eight principal faults": gluttony, fornication, covetousness or avarice, anger, dejection, accidie ("heaviness or weariness of heart"), vainglory, and pride. He also discusses, with a great deal of psychological astuteness, how they are interconnected with each other, and how they might be remedied. All of them, he says, keep a person from true self-knowledge, and are personally harmful to that person's soul and to the community to which one belongs. All must be "laid open by the teachings of the elders."[36] Remedies can be found, according to Cassian, not by concentrating on the vices to be eradicated, but on their opposites or "contraries."

Thus, if a person hopes to be freed of certain faults or sins, rather than focusing attention and energy upon the vice, one instead seeks to develop its opposite virtue. Cassian states, for example, that in order to overcome the vice of gluttony, a person needs to develop the virtue of discretion: not commanding oneself to "stop eating" since that frequently makes "the forbidden" even more attractive, but rather beginning the practice of discerning what food is appropriate to eat, in what moderate proportion, and when. He thoroughly discusses this "recovery program," explaining as he does what each fault is and what its remedy might be. The "opposite" virtue he lists is not always what one might initially expect, but, upon reflection, Cassian's insights make a great deal of sense. The opposite of fornication, he says, is selflessness; the opposite of avarice (jealousy about someone else's good fortune or possessions) is patience with one's own life; anger's opposite is detachment; dejection's is hope or equanimity; accidie's is persistence; vainglory's is practicing genuine care; pride's opposite, of course, is humility. What this training in self-knowledge, sicknesses of soul, and their remedies is meant to do ultimately is to produce genuine liberation: freedom of soul and body from those things that keep us, Cassian says, "deaf and dumb and blind."[37]

Disclosing the Secrets of the Heart

The effectiveness of these conferences and, by implication, of the entire formation program that Cassian describes seems to be related not only to the theological insights an elder shares with his charges about sins and their remedies, but especially to the elder's willingness to disclose personal struggles and what he has learned from them. Such disclosures can be truly educative, not only benefiting the younger, more inexperienced monks intellectually, but actually bringing about healing to those who are present as listeners:

> For unless the different kinds of sins are first explained, and the origin and causes of diseases traced out, the proper healing remedies cannot be applied to the sick, nor can the preservation of perfect health be secured for the strong. For both of these matters and many others besides these are generally put forward for the instruction of the younger brethren by the elders in their conferences, as they have had experience of numberless falls and the ruin of all sorts of people. And often recognizing in ourselves many of these things, when the elders explained and showed them, as men who were themselves disquieted by the same passions, we were cured without any shame or confusion on our part, since without saying anything we learnt both the remedies and the causes of sins which beset us....[38]

Although Cassian doesn't mention it, the healing brought about by the self-disclosure of the elders may have taken place precisely because the younger monk discovers that he is not alone. Such was the case, at least, of the desert writer Palladius, who tells in his *Lausiac History* that he almost left the desert because of "concupiscence" until Abba Pachon admitted his own lifelong difficulties with eros.[39] It seems that when an elder openly acknowledges his very human struggles to grow in holiness, hope is often born. *Both* speaker *and* listener are given one of the greatest of spiritual strengths in overcoming faults and entrenched life-patterns: the assurance that, despite the difficulties, spiritual progress can be made—with God's help. Whatever happened with the self-disclosure of the older monks, it was meant to be, according to Cassian, a reciprocal process.

As the elders modeled self-disclosure to their charges, so the younger monks were expected to acknowledge their own "secrets," inclinations, and woundedness. An essential aspect of formation in general and spiritual direction in particular was what Cassian calls revealing the "counsels of the heart."[40] Throughout his writings there are numerous references to the importance and healing effects of speaking directly from the heart to another person—as many early Church fathers, including Augustine and Jerome knew. This self-disclosure was a form of lay confession, since most of the elders and desert guides were not ordained. It was a practice that later spread to Ireland and contributed to the rise of the *anamchara,* or soul-friend, tradition, which in its creative origins also included, as did the practice of the desert Christians, both female and male confessors, laity and ordained.[41] Before disclosing any sickness or sin to another person, however, Cassian advises in his *Conferences* that the monk engage in a personal inventory or general examination of his life. "All the secret places of our heart," he writes in Conference Two, quoting Abba Moses, "therefore, must be constantly scrutinized and the prints of whatever enters them must be investigated in the most careful way, lest perchance some spiritual beast, a lion or a dragon, pass through and secretly leave its dangerous traces." Only then will we manage "to root out from ourselves the nests of harmful animals and the hiding places of venomous serpents."[42]

After this inventory, Cassian recommends that its results and everything arising in the heart be shared with the elders, for "after it [an evil thought] has been disclosed, this most wicked spirit will no longer be able to disturb you, nor shall the filthy serpent ever again seize a place to make his lair in you, now that by a salutary confession he has been drawn out from the darkness of your heart into the light." Such open and honest confession can help set a person free of all kinds of forms of captivity. Through the power of such self-disclosure "the wicked foe has been revealed, [and] he will never again have a place in you."

Cassian relates the story of Abba Sarapion, who, when he confessed his dishonest actions to his elder, says: "To such an extent has the domination of that diabolical tyranny in me been destroyed by the power of this confession and been rendered forever ineffective that the enemy has never again tried to stir up the thought of this desire in me [to steal], nor after this have I ever again felt myself shaken by the temptation to pursue that furtive desire." When one confesses to some spiritual person who is immersed in the all-powerful words of scripture, a cure can be found immediately for these "snake bites," as well as the ability to "draw the snake's venom out of a person's heart."[43] This healing and the knowledge of self that comes through self-revelation to another can help a person avoid the repetition of self-destructive patterns of behavior that previously characterized one's personality and life. As Alcoholics Anonymous discovered in the past century,[44] Cassian is simply saying that a personal inventory and confession to a reliable guide on a regular basis are good for the body and for the soul.

The elder's responsibility in receiving another's confession of the heart is to listen without judgment, for, as one of the holy men wisely tells Cassian, "not only are someone's openly confessed sins not to be reproached, but also...the pain of a suffering person is not to be despised in belittling fashion."[45] With such compassion and deep respect for another's suffering, the elders act, Cassian tells us in his *Institutes*, as a kind of "glass" or mirror by which the younger monks "learn both the causes of the sins by which they are troubled, and the remedies for them." Thus, he says, the elders minister to their protégés as "true physicians of the soul," listening to their self-disclosures attentively, and, "by means of spiritual conferences," explaining to the junior monks "the causes of the passions which threaten them, and the remedies which heal them."[46]

Cassian is not clear in his writings when the formation process came to an end for the junior monks, but he implies that termination depended more upon individual spiritual progress than on a definite length of time shared by all. He compares the entire formation program to the preparation athletes go through to participate in the Olympic and Pythian games of ancient Greece. Only after proving their competence, strength, and valor are the youths allowed, he says, "to mix with full-grown men and those of approved experience."[47] It seems to have been the same for a junior monk. When the elders discerned that he was making progress in self-knowledge, compassion toward others, and intimacy with God, that person was welcomed into the community as a full member. What came with this change of status, of course, was the very likely prospect of becoming an elder and spiritual guide oneself to those who traveled to the desert, as Cassian and Germanus once had, seeking wisdom and the holy life.

Leadership Formation Today

The formation process that Cassian outlines in his writings is by contemporary standards a rigorous one, but all ancient societies believed that adulthood, maturity, and leadership itself can be achieved only through some form of initiation and apprenticeship. They recognized the need in everyone for a second birth in which one begins to take seriously the spiritual realm. They also believed that tribes and communities depended upon regeneration and spiritual leadership if they themselves were to survive.[48] This initiation process required the active intervention of elders: men and women of vision, experience, and wisdom whose knowledge of the spiritual journey and of the human heart was a resource not only for younger people but the entire tribe.

Those of us living today in an increasingly complex world are aware of the need for good and creative leadership on all levels of our social, political, and ecclesial life. In the midst of changing roles and cultural perspectives, as well as conflicts over who is a qualified leader and questions on how best to prepare someone for that role, Cassian can become a contemporary guide. Without seeking in any way to merely "duplicate" the past, his wisdom can teach us what could be considered key elements for the spiritual development of Christian leaders today, especially those who are seeking to incorporate monastic values into their own lives. Whether such formation programs are found in parishes for volunteers, at retreat houses for workshop participants, or in academic or pastoral settings where ministers (lay, vowed religious, and ordained) are being prepared, the following components would benefit everyone:

First, those who are preparing for leadership need immersion in some form of community: a group of people who both support and challenge us, and invite the expression of our creativity, energy, and love; a place where we are stimulated intellectually and where we are personally affirmed. In such a group and environment, questions are welcomed, stories are shared, and knowledge of our spiritual traditions is freely given. If one is a layperson, this "immersion" does not necessarily have to mean leaving one's family and work for extended periods of time. It would consist, however, of participation in the life of a group on a regular basis (perhaps weekly or monthly) so that a person can imbibe its spirituality, be enriched by its liturgical life, while contributing to both. As Cassian and Germanus learned from the desert elders, one can either live in a community for some time or one can stop and visit for a while, asking questions and seeking guidance. The important thing is connecting in depth with a supportive group, a vibrant community, or at least one other spiritually mature person, and thus opening up to a larger reality, a "higher power" greater than oneself.

The search for a genuine community in which one can be nourished spiritually and to which a person can contribute one's gifts is a pervasive aspiration of many people in today's world. Diarmuid O'Murchu, theologian and counselor, describes how this is what the Christian churches "hail as their primary goal," but do not always accomplish. Many spiritual seekers frequently seem to find this experience of community, he says, only "on the margins and liminal places"[49] of their lives: sometimes, in fact, only when their lives have fallen apart due to sickness or addiction, injury or loss, rejection, dejection, depression, despair. This, of course, is when many are most open to change and spiritual growth, and when they hunger most for spiritual nourishment. This is also when and where leadership is often born: in experiences of powerlessness, emptiness, and spiritual hunger; in the determination not only to survive sicknesses and losses, but also to give back and share what has been learned from those wounds. Everyone is called to such generative leadership, especially as a person grows older: helping others, as a result of one's own learning, name their talents, clarify their dreams, and fulfill their potential in church and society. Such leadership is what individual monks in Cassian's day received from their elders as they moved from being neophytes to becoming themselves elders and spiritual guides for others. Such leadership also emerged, as the history of desert Christianity and monasticism itself vividly reveals, on the margins of institutional church life.[50]

A **second component** that Cassian taught in his writings, and that fosters the emergence of competent leaders today, is personal commitment to *inner* work. This inner work is mainly discussed in Cassian's *magnum opus, Conferences,* which, as he says, focuses on "the discipline of the inner man and the perfection of the heart."[51] While the *Institutes* is concerned with what he calls "the external and visible life of the monks," *Conferences* turns toward "deeper waters," "the invisible character of the inner man."[52] As the desert elders taught him, spiritual formation is ultimately about inner transformation: a change of heart in which one identifies with Christ and seeks to become like him. It means taking on aspects of servant leadership in one's own life, transforming the outer world as one's inner world is changed; no longer being victimized by personal obsessions or institutional dysfunctions that keep a person (to use Cassian's terminology) "deaf and dumb and blind."

Desert Christians realized this gradual and extremely difficult process of liberation begins with oneself. They believed that as much as "outer" work is important for the health of a person's mind and body and for the well-being of his or her community, inner work is even more so. They equated this inner work with the acquisition of a "single eye": a stripping away of illusions so that one can finally "see God" and oneself realistically.[53] They also associated it with becoming "single-hearted," attentive to God and one's relationship to God above everything else.[54] This "reality therapy" presupposes that less time and energy are spent in analyzing or critiquing others and more on knowing oneself and reforming one's own life. Cassian learned this lesson directly from Abba Machetes: "Each one therefore ought only to judge himself, and to be on the watch, with care and circumspection in all things not to judge the life and conduct of others in accordance with the Apostle's charge,…'Judge not, that ye be not judged.'"[55]

For perspective leaders, then, inner work is based upon a "recovery program" similar to the one the desert Christians not only taught verbally, but lived. Such a program would begin with prioritizing present responsibilities and commitments, and clarifying future hopes and dreams. It would include some form of personal "rule": a daily routine of prayer, work, learning, and leisure in which quality time is set aside for family, friends, and "strangers"—the poor, abused, and homeless who are too often overlooked. A discipline of simplicity would be developed and maintained in which diet, exercise, communion with nature, and a daily inventory had their place. This inventory might take the form of journaling, guided imagery, meditation, prayer. However it is done, reasons for gratitude and personal needs are acknowledged, areas of "sickness" named, and new directions for their "contraries" explored.

Essential to all of this inner work is attentive listening to the heart, that deepest part of a person that is frequently expressed in our feelings, intuitions, imagination, yearnings, dreams, and tears. Cassian makes clear in his writings that this discernment process can be helped tremendously by an elder or a spiritual mentor who on a regular basis helps us to identify the movement of God in our hearts and lives; who helps us coax out the wild beasts and venomous serpents that dwell within, waiting to be tamed and befriended. Considering the importance of that human need and the long history of that ancient Christian practice, it is no wonder that Poemen, one of the desert elders, advised his protégés: "Teach your lips to speak what lies within your heart."[56]

Taking all of the above into account, the **third component** of any program that hopes to encourage Christian leadership is making sure participants have access to those with experience who can speak a language of the heart. In retrospect, we can see that at the center of the formation process and the practice of spiritual direction that Cassian describes is the meeting between an experienced guide and a person seeking holiness and wisdom. In fact, underlying all of Cassian's theology is the conviction that those who commit themselves to Christian living require the guidance another person in whom they can confide. Thus, Cassian's formation program in theory and practice is intimately related to mentoring: a relationship of friendship with a person a little more advanced or mature in some area of life with whom one can share the counsels of the heart. Any formation program today that hopes to elicit competent participants and future leaders needs a mentoring component at its core.

Mentors: The Ministry of Inspiration

As the story of Cassian and Germanus reveals, as well as those of Athanasius and Antony, Hilary and Martin, Augustine, Jerome, and their friends, all true leadership is intrinsically related to mentoring: leading people to new perspectives, facilitating personal and institutional growth, encouraging the discernment of vocational possibilities. This means, concretely, that persons who are themselves leaders in any Christian community or church are invited to help plan spiritual formation programs as well as to become mentors to participants when they are in place. Depending on their own years of experience and innate gifts, such people might act in a variety of mentoring roles—from host to teacher to spiritual mentor or guide.[57] Each mentor should be chosen because of the wisdom they have acquired, the overall quality of their lives, and their willingness to share their struggles without pretension. Like the desert elders, both women and men, they are to model not perfectionism, but a healthy acceptance of themselves, a commitment to truthfulness, and a certain transparency that makes others feel at-home. *Unlike* some of the male desert elders whose condemnation of women seems to have been related to an extreme fear of their own eros and sexuality, mentors today of either gender are inclusive of women in all decision-making and leadership roles. They do not at all espouse blind obedience to themselves as a way of teaching humility, but rather encourage in participants something that is even harder to maintain (and what the word "obedience" really means): attentiveness to one's own experiences, the questions they raise, and the responses that they invite. After reflecting upon their own lives, they believe that such attentive listening to one's experiences is in fact listening to God, and they realize how much suffering and courage such obedience can entail. This type of mentoring, then, leads others not to greater dependency upon the mentors themselves, but to greater intimacy and reliance upon the Holy Spirit, the true guide of souls.

Judging from what Cassian has written and perhaps what our experiences have taught us, one of the most important roles of any elder, mentor, or leader is that of being someone who inspires in others the confidence to pursue their own goals and dreams. This role cannot easily be defined, nor is it something that anyone through personal effort can induce or make happen, since it has so much to do with the mentor's personality and a protégé's unconscious needs and expectations. Quite simply, it is the role of being an exemplar who teaches more by example than by words. Cassian acknowledges that this role can take all sorts of approaches and include all kinds of personalities, but the crucial element is related to the mentor's spirituality and relationship with God.[58] Rather than intimidating us by their experience and expertise, such a person has the gift to truly "inspire": to infuse, animate, breathe into us enthusiasm for our gifts and for our own sacred journey. If, as one of the greatest of desert mothers, Amma Syncletica, said, "Our God is a consuming fire; hence we ought to light the divine fire in ourselves,"[59] then an important dynamic of mentoring is providing this fire, this inspiration, this passing on of wisdom from one spirit to another through the union of minds and hearts.

Such a ministry of inspiration is not one-sided, but reciprocal, as the story of Cassian and Germanus with Abba Moses, told at the beginning of this chapter, demonstrates and as Jerome's spiritual mentoring in the previous chapter affirmed. If we recall from Cassian, it was the old man, Abba Moses, whose inner fire was constellated by the enthusiasm of the two young men. He is the one who said, "My sons, it is *your* zeal which led me to speak for so long. Because of your eagerness, some kind of fire has given a more urgent sense to what I have been saying." Through this experience of mutuality, trust is born, allowing a person to eventually confess the inner workings of the heart, a key monastic value that nurtures spiritual health and personal integrity; that fosters a single eye and a single heart.

One Kind of Love

Cassian died about 435, and his feast day is celebrated in the West on July 23. Years before his death, he and Germanus had left Egypt and spent some time with the Church Father John Chrysostom (c. 347–407) in Constantinople where Cassian was ordained a deacon and Germanus, a priest. About 415, we know Cassian had moved to Marseilles to found his monasteries, but his friend Germanus had evidently died about 405, since there are no further references to him after that time. Cassian's writing of his *Conferences,* which take the form of dialogues between him, Germanus, and the desert monks, most likely served as his tribute to his older companion and friend, since Germanus plays such a prominent role within them. According to Nora Chadwick, that work may have been influenced by the *Dialogues* of Sulpicius Severus, Martin of Tours' hagiographer, but unlike Sulpicius's, "Cassian takes us into the actual presence of the Desert Fathers, and we are, as it were, present at their dialogues"; whereas the dialogue in Sulpicius's writing takes place when the pilgrim, Postumianus, returns to Gaul and relates his stories about the desert elders.[60]

Both his *Conferences,* as well as the work that preceded it, his *Institutes,* clearly show that Egypt was the center of Cassian's life, the source of many cherished memories that continued to teach him about Christian spirituality and the God whom he called "the Creator and Healer of All."[61] He preached loyalty to those traditions because his own heart had been set on fire by the desert elders in their mutual quest for God. His goal in writing was to pass on to others, as Athanasius said about Antony, the fruits of his experience. One of the primary things that Cassian's storytelling reveals is that to be formed by an elder is to learn from his or her spirit, and through that ministry of mentoring to be brought to the threshold of God's. Cassian refers to this "union of spirit, not of place" in Conference Sixteen "On Friendship" where he seems to allude not only to his friendship with Germanus, but also to those desert elders who in memory guided him years after his return from desert lands:

> Among all of these there is one kind of love that is indestructible and that is founded not on a good reputation or on the greatness of one's title or one's gifts or on some business obligation or on natural need but on likeness of virtue alone. This, I say, can never be cut off for any reason: Not only are distance and time unable to undo and destroy it, but even death itself does not sunder it. This is the true and indissoluable love that grows by the combined perfection and virtue of friends....With God it is common behavior rather than a common location that joins brothers in a single dwelling....[62]

While Owen Chadwick says that the core of Cassian's spirituality is found in Conferences Nine and Ten on prayer and Conference Eleven on perfection,[63] a major part of it, surely, is found in this Conference Sixteen on friendship. After all, it was Cassian's friendship with Germanus that perhaps first gave him the courage to embark on his pilgrimage into the desert regions. It was the friendship provided by the desert elders that taught them both so much about the God of fire who transforms minds and hearts. It is the stories Cassian tells that remind us of how much our own elders and wisdom figures have changed our lives by their acceptance, love, and inspiration.

Cassian's teachings profoundly affected monasticism's development in both the Eastern and the Western churches. St. Benedict whose Rule was to become a standard for many monasteries in the West gives pride of place to Cassian, recommending to his followers that they read his *Institutes* and *Conferences.* Cuthbert Butler writes that "St. Benedict was familiar with Cassian's writings and was saturated with their thought and language, in a greater measure than with any other, save only the Holy Scriptures." For him, Cassian's work searches "most deeply into the human, or at any rate, the monastic heart."[64] Thus, through the Rule of St. Benedict, the writings of Cassian entered into the tradition of monasticism in the West, and the teaching of Cassian was woven into the very structure of the monastic life, forming the basis of monastic spirituality. As William Harmless concludes, "If Benedict created the institutional frame of Latin monasticism, then Cassian helped define its inner life, its mystical aspirations. At the same time, Cassian's quite distinctive interpretation of Egypt became normative—*the* definition of desert spirituality. Cassian, more than anyone else, brought Egypt to the West."[65]

This was especially true of the monasticism that arose in those lands associated with the culture and spirituality of the ancient Celts. In Ireland, England, Scotland, Wales, the Isle of Man, Brittany in Gaul, and Galicia in Spain, the monks and those people with families attached to the monasteries loved Cassian.[66] They deeply appreciated his description of monasticism as found in his writings, and, most especially, his recommending the practice of disclosing one's heart to a trusted confessor, someone the Christian Celts came to identify as an *anamchara,* a soul friend.

CHAPTER SEVEN

Golden Sparkling Flame—Brigit of Kildare and Irish Monasticism

Brigit, excellent woman, a flame, golden, delightful,
May she, the sun dazzling, splendid, guide us to the eternal Kingdom.

—"Life of Brigit," *Book of Lismore*

In the last chapters, we have seen the spread of early monasticism from the desert sands of Egypt, Palestine, and Syria to the lands of Gaul, Italy, and Africa. Spiritual leaders, in love with monastic spirituality, contributed to its establishment and growth. However, in a different part of Europe, on the margins of the Continent itself, another form of monasticism arose. Although highly appreciative of the early fathers and their spiritual wisdom, this one was less patriarchal in structure and emphasis,[1] saw itself linked intrinsically with nature, and was openly respectful of women's gifts. This *Celtic* monasticism, a blend of orthodox Christian beliefs and practices as well as of customs and outlooks of the ancient Celts, offered a different expression of Christianity than that of the more "Roman" model developing on the Continent. What emerged in those lands where the Celtic culture flourished and where Roman culture and institutions were not dominant was a Christian church more monastic than diocesan in its structures, one that at the same sought to incorporate the ascetic values of the desert Christians into daily life. As

John Ryan says, this monasticism, especially in Ireland, "achieved a popularity without parallel in any age or country."[2]

Celtic Christians were familiar with and highly appreciative of such literary works as Athanasius's *Life of Antony*, John Cassian's *Institutes* and *Conferences*, as well as the *Life of Paul* by Jerome. Their love of the desert heroes is reflected artistically on the high crosses that are scattered throughout the landscape of the Celtic churches, especially those found in Ireland, Scotland, Brittany, and the Isle of Man. While most of these crosses bear scenes from the Old and New Testaments, some of their panels show a solitary Antony being tempted in the wilderness or the two desert elders, Antony and Paul, together as spiritual friends. In Ireland alone, there are at least ten crosses depicting the two saints sharing Eucharist, constituting the largest number of such depictions anywhere in western Europe.[3] While Anglo-Saxon monks in England would identify with St. Benedict (c. 480–550 CE) and his monastic Rule, as we will see, in Celtic lands the two desert friends whose story was first told by Jerome were the ones especially revered. In Brittany, the monks considered those two men as the first teachers of the monastic and solitary living that they followed.[4]

No one knows precisely when or how Christianity arrived in Ireland, England, Scotland, Wales, Brittany, Galicia, and the Isle of Man. The conversion of Ireland, however, is associated with the spiritual leadership of one man, the great missionary bishop, St. Patrick (c. 390–461). Though he was possibly educated at Lerins, a famous monastic site located off the coast of southern Gaul, and thus shaped by the monastic traditions of Gaul and of St. Martin, Patrick brought with him to Ireland an ecclesiology that was diocesan in organization, based upon the urban settings and secular divisions of the late Roman empire found on the European mainland. Whether this diocesan system took root in Ireland at all is questionable, considering its largely rural environment and tribal system. According to Richard Sharpe, "there is no evidence pointing to a clearly defined hierarchical structure, no evidence for a canonically recognized metropolitan authority; in short, no sign that growth of the church or its organization were the subject of any form of control."

Instead, Sharpe posits a great deal of diversity and independence: "An essential characteristic of the Irish church, at all times between the earliest evidence and the twelfth century or later, seems to be the very great degree of independence enjoyed by individual churches....Its shape reflects growth *in situ,* local solutions to local needs, and is not an imposed structure."[5]

While there is still controversy today among scholars over the issue of ecclesial authority in the early Irish Church and the shape that churches took,[6] it seems that monasticism had become a dominant form of church life within a century or two of Patrick. Certainly, as Bernard McGinn suggests, "almost all the notable figures of early Christian Ireland were monastics."[7] By 600 CE, there were in Ireland more than eight hundred monasteries, including the most prestigious: Finnian's Clonard, Ciaran's Clonmacnoise, Comgall's Bangor, Brigit's Kildare, Ita's Killeedy, Kevin's Glendalough, Brendan's Clonfert, and Columcille's Durrow and Derry. (The latter saint also established one of the greatest Celtic monasteries of all time in 563 at Iona, off the coast of Scotland.) During this "Age of the Saints," monastic leaders, both female and male, were frequently more powerful administratively than any bishop, though bishops frequently may have been members of their communities or abbots themselves.[8]

Male monastic leaders who followed the first generation of monastic founders were either ordained or lay. Many were married, and in some monastic communities the abbacy descended from father to son.[9] Among female Celtic leaders, a great number held powerful ecclesial positions in communities consisting of *both* women *and* men. These "double monasteries" were evidently a normal feature of the earliest monastic life in Ireland and Britain. Whether monastic leaders were married or celibate, the monasteries that they headed had many laypeople (known as *manaigh*) attached to them, and were thus definitely family-oriented and dependent on the contribution of the laity. Irish scholar Colman Etchingham posits how there seems to have been "a blurring of distinctions" and "a fluidity of definitions" regarding membership within these monastic communities between "true monks" and what he calls "paramonastics": laypeople attached to the monasteries, some of whom were undergoing penitential rehabilitation, while others were "monastic clients" who often participated in the work and liturgical life of the monastery. "The Irish material [i.e., written sources] seems unusual," Etchingham concludes, "in often applying without distinction monastic terminology and ideas to such a range of types: true monk, rent-payers, servile retainers and aristocratic adherents."[10]

The earliest surviving Irish hagiography, one on the life of St. Brigit of Kildare, seems to confirm this composition of diverse monastic members of both genders, ordained, celibate, lay, and married, all of whom came together to celebrate the Eucharist at Brigit's double monastery. As Cogitosus (c. 620–680), a monk of Kildare, describes the monastic church within a hundred and fifty years or so of St. Brigit's death:

> Due to the increased numbers of the faithful of both sexes, the original church has been enlarged. Its ground-plan is large, and its roof rises to a dizzy height. Its interior contains three large oratories, divided from one another by walls of timber, but all under the same roof of the larger church. One wall, covered with linen curtains and decorated with paintings, traverses the eastern part of the church from one side to the other. Two doors stand in either side of this wall: through the door on the right the bishop, with his clerics and those assigned to celebrate the holy rites, proceeds to the sanctuary and to the altar to offer the divine sacrifice to the Lord; through the door on the left the abbess enters with her virgins and with pious widows in order to participate in the Supper of Jesus Christ, which is His flesh and blood. The remainder of the building is divided lengthwise into two equal parts by another wall, which runs from the western side to the transverse wall. The church has many windows. Priests and lay people of the male gender enter by an ornamented door on the righthand side; matrons and virgins enter by another door on the left. In this way the one basilica is sufficient for a huge

> crowd, separated by walls according to order, station, and gender, but united in the Spirit, all praying to Almighty God.[11]

In addition to the inclusivity of Irish monasticism reflected here and which was quite extraordinary,[12] there was, as already mentioned, its valuing of women's gifts. While other Christian churches during late antiquity and the early medieval period increasingly isolated women from positions of authority and relationships of friendship with males, the early Celtic Church, and the Irish Church, in particular, influenced by the pagan Celts' belief that women were equal to men and had similar legal rights, encouraged their leadership. Contrary to the prevailing dualistic tendencies found in the Roman culture and churches, and even more so among the desert Christians, the early founders of the Irish Church "did not reject," according to a ninth-century manuscript, *Catalogue of the Saints in Ireland,* "the service and society of women."[13] The oldest monasteries of women recorded in Ireland are those of Brigit at Kildare, Moninna at Killeevy, and Ita at Killeedy. Passing references to quite numerous female foundations in the early period suggest that the great Irish monastic movement was, in fact, pioneered by communities of women from as early, perhaps, as the fifth century.

Among the founders of the early Irish monasteries, St. Brigit is the best-known, a woman whose pioneer work and pastoral leadership touched many lives. Although historical knowledge of her is extremely elusive, since her life is so interwoven with pagan myth and Irish folklore, the *Annals of Ulster* tell us that she lived from about 452–524. As founder of Kildare and spiritual guide of both women and men at her monastery, she was considered such an important female wisdom figure to the Irish that she was named "the Mary of the Gael." She is described in an ancient Christian Celtic hymn as "ever excellent woman, golden sparkling flame."[14]

As we examine in this chapter the stories of Brigit, we will discover important aspects of her spiritual leadership, especially the monastic value specifically linked with it: the value of compassion.

The Fire at Kildare

Sometime in the 1180s, the medieval churchman, pilgrim, and storyteller, Gerald of Wales, visited Kildare, Ireland, made famous, he says, by the "glorious Brigit." There, as he tells us in the controversial book he wrote after his tours of Ireland, he found Brigit's fire, said to be inextinguishable: "It is not that it is strictly speaking inextinguishable, but that the nuns and holy women have so carefully and diligently kept and fed it with enough material, that through all the years from the time of the virgin saint it has never been extinguished."[15] Gerald of Wales, of course, was not the first pilgrim to visit Kildare, but he has provided one of the most vivid accounts of that monastic site and the legends associated with it centuries after the death of its foundress. Judging from his books on Ireland and Wales, he evidently discovered there (as many do when they travel to foreign shores) that the holy places and the tombs of the saints often provide a location for the healing, forgiving, and guiding powers of God.

That is evidently how numerous pilgrims experienced Kildare from the earliest days of the monastery. A place originally associated with ancient druidesses, Kildare was "a centre of pilgrimage,"[16] one of the four major pilgrim sites of the early Irish Church, largely because of the notoriety of Brigit herself. By the Middle Ages, she was considered the patron saint of travelers and pilgrims everywhere. As a soul friend with whom that ancient tradition of spiritual guidance is very much identified, Brigit, the powerful Christian saint, is linked with a Celtic goddess that preceded her. Described by the Irish poet, Padraic Colum, as "she who had the flaming heart,"[17] Brigit will show us through her stories not only that her monastery is associated with flames of fire, but her life and ministry as well—a flame of holiness that continues to blaze and give light even though the fires at Kildare of which Gerald of Wales wrote were extinguished during the days of the Protestant Reformation, only to be relit recently.[18]

Brigit, the saint, was an intimate part of the early Irish Church, and her life, ministry, and spirituality were heavily influenced by the spiritual heritage of the Celts. To understand the saint better, we first need to turn briefly to the world of pagan Celtic mythology, and then to early and medieval Christian hagiographies associated with her. Though historians differ in their assessment of how much about Brigit as a saint is historically accurate, we must not limit ourselves to only considering absolutely verifiable evidence (i.e., "the facts"). While historicity is an important criterion when we examine the lives of the early saints,[19] for a spiritual theologian it is not the only one to be considered. Our task is that of discerning and naming the larger truths the stories from mythology and Christian hagiography reveal, and what sort of meaning and guidance they might provide.

As we shall see, we do know that there is a very long and ancient tradition linking a woman named Brigit with the monastery at Kildare, and that she was extremely popular—judging from the spread of her cult and the numerous stories about her. These early Christian legends were based upon the collective memory of a people (not only those in her original monastery) who obviously admired and loved her, and recognized in her tremendous spiritual power. With the help of the stories, and the images and symbolic language they contain, we can begin tentatively to identify important dynamics and qualities of the saint's personality, life, and leadership that endured the ravages of time and formed the basis of her spiritual power.

Let us turn first to her pagan origins, for to understand Brigit, the Christian saint, we need to know something about Brigit, the Celtic goddess. As the Irish scholar Donncha O'Haodha states: "There is no doubt that the enormous cult of Brigit, as well as many of its features, must have benefited from the coincidence of the saint's name with that of the Celtic goddess…."[20]

Brigit, the Goddess of Fire

The Celts were a branch of the Indo-European family from which most of present-day European, Middle Eastern, and Indian races are descended. Called *Keltoi* by the Greeks and *Galli* by the Romans, they were Europe's dominant power by the third century BCE, some of whom invaded Ireland between 900 and 300 BCE. Their mythology was as diverse as their lives and as vivid as their imaginations. As animists, they believed that the supernatural pervaded every aspect of life, and that spirits were everywhere: in ancient trees and sacred groves, mountaintops and rock formations, rivers, streams, and holy wells. Theirs was a faith that worshipped the great forces of nature (i.e., moon, ocean, sun, and wind), and, like the Greek, Roman, and Norse pantheons, their Celtic gods and goddesses governed all aspects of human life.[21] One of their great fertility gods was named Dagda, or "Good Father," while possibly the most ancient deity was a goddess named Danu, who was also called Ana. Some scholars believe that the legends associating Danu as universal mother and oldest of the gods show that in its origins Celtic society was matriarchal. This could well account for the Celts' great respect for women and the equality women seemed to have.

Some of Dagda's most famous children were Angus, called "the Young God," a Gaelic Eros representing eternal youth; Ogma, the god of literature and eloquence; and Brigit or Brighid ("the exalted one"), a diety worshipped by the *filid,* the pagan poets, who considered poetry itself as "an immaterial, supersensual form of flame."[22] The goddess of wisdom, poetry, and song, Brigit was especially known as the goddess of fire and of hearth. Like other Celtic goddesses who were more primitive and, according to Katherine Scherman, more "veiled in shadows" than "the clear, bright singleness of the male deities,"[23] Brigit was something of an amorphous figure with what might be called multiple personalities. We know, for example, that, as the most important child of Dagda, she is associated with two sisters by the same name—one who is patron of healing, and the other of the smith's craft. All three with their different attributes were identified with the goddess Brigit whose feast was celebrated every February 1st on Imbolc, one of the Celts' four most important feasts. This was the festival of spring when the sun emerges from its winter sleep and the goats and sheep begin to produce milk for their young. Brigit, the Celtic saint, would eventually have her feast on the same day, and be considered the guardian of farm animals, of healers, and of childbirth, including midwifery. (One of her legends says that she was present as midwife at Christ's birth.)

What is interesting to note here is that triple aspect of the goddess's identity. For the Celts, the number three had special significance and was equated with "added strength or potency."[24] Many allusions to this triple feature occur in Celtic mythology and Irish literature, and Brigit was not the only Celtic goddess associated with that number. Three mother goddesses of war, for example, Morrigan, Macha, and Bodb, were known collectively as Morrigna. As we shall see, the mystical number three will appear again when we consider the legends of Brigit, the Christian saint—as will the powerful imagery of fire.

Both the number three and the symbol of fire have been associated in human history with the mysterious presence and power of God, not only in pagan cults, but in our Judeo-Christian spiritual traditions. Three symbolizes spiritual synthesis; the solution of the conflict posed by dualism, and, as Trinity in Christianity has been expressed symbolically in a number of ways—from a triangle to an Irish shamrock. The symbol of fire appears in both Old and New Testament stories—from the burning bush of Moses to the tongues of fire at Pentecost—and is also equated with the powerful presence of God. As is evident in this book, images of fire, along with those of light, appear often in the writings of Christian wisdom figures from both the West and the East. Abba Syncletica in the Egyptian desert speaks of God as "consuming fire";[25] John Cassian uses fire to describe the highest form of contemplative prayer (Conferences 9 and 10); the twelfth-century Rhineland mystic Hildegard of Bingen associates her spiritual awakening at midlife with tongues of fiery flame; the fourteenth-century English mystic Richard Rolle describes Jesus as a "honeyed flame," and tells how God "sets our hearts aflame so that they glow and burn."[26] In the twentieth century, T. S. Eliot sees the paradox of suffering and love resolved in the heavenly contemplation of God when "the fire and rose are one,"[27] while the Swiss psychiatrist Carl Jung describes individuation, the painful process of moving from an ego-centered existence to a Self-directed one, as that of "being near the fire."[28]

A powerful symbol of creativity, spiritual awakening, and rebirth, as well as of healing, cleansing, and being purged, the image of fire will appear (as we saw with Augustine's autobiography) at certain turning points in Brigit's life and ministry. It was also, as we've seen, associated with Kildare (which means the "Church of the Oak") even before St. Brigit's time. According to some historians, female druids or vestal virgins resided there, and, like those in Rome, kept a perpetual fire burning. Their leader supposedly was a high priestess who bore the name of the goddess Brigit, since she was regarded as the Goddess's incarnation.[29] While this has not been definitively proven, the great Irish scholar James Kenney believes that these legends have some plausibility.[30] What we lack in historically verifiable facts about Brigit, the goddess and the saint, however, we can tentatively deduce from the early and medieval lives of the Christian saint.

St. Brigit and Her Stories

St. Brigit's stories and legends are part of the history of Christian hagiography, that genre of literature that first became popular among Christians, as we saw, with Athanasius's *Life of Antony*. That first hagiography and all of the succeeding Lives that it influenced were written to present a certain saint as a spiritual mentor or soul-friend,[31] someone capable of teaching readers and listeners about the importance of holiness, as modeled in the lives of the saints. Later, as Christianity developed and pilgrimage became a dominant practice, hagiographies were also often used to support the political prominence and economic well-being of the monastery or shrine with which a saint was identified. The Lives of the saints, especially the earlier ones, are not biographies in the way we understand that term today, but stories with a theological message. They contain the larger truths of the saints' lives that moved them (and can move us) toward greater self-awareness and self-acceptance, wholeness and holiness, meaning and God.

Like the world of mythology, hagiography is full of symbols, mythic components, and the language of dreams, of fairy tales, and of the soul. It is a language describing, not only historical facts in the "outer world," but realities in which inner experiences, feelings, intuitions, and thoughts are often expressed *as if* they were sensory experiences or events in the outer world. These inner experiences, of course, are no less "real" than the outer ones, for often they determine and profoundly influence the shape and course of outer events. To understand the Christian Brigit better, we need to consider specific legends and the symbolic language and imagery they contain. We also must be attentive in the stories about her to what is emphasized and what is not. When compared to other Lives of the early saints, these clues may provide us with traces of the original personality and historical figure.

Brigit's hagiographies were influenced greatly, as were so many of the early Celtic lives and others, by those Christian classics that had preceded hers, especially Athanasius' *Life of Antony* and Sulpicius Severus' *Life of St. Martin.* In the emerging tradition of Christian hagiography, Brigit too is portrayed as a heroic Christian, worthy of emulation—yet, like other lives, not at all removed from human suffering. Like many of us, she experiences headaches, is sometimes overcome with poor eyesight, and can be at times a difficult person with whom to live. Yes, she feeds the poor and shelters the homeless, cures lepers and heals the blind, but she also isn't afraid of cursing those who get in her way (an old druid custom), seems a bit overly fond of beer and ale (we find her making quite a lot of it on various occasions), and even gives so much of her community's goods to the needy that her companions complain, "Little good have we from your compassion to everyone, and we ourselves in need of food and clothing."[32] Like us (again), there seems to be a thin line between her strengths and very human limitations.

Unlike other early lives, however, that present asceticism and an eremitic lifestyle as the ideal of holiness,[33] Brigit's life from the beginning is associated with ministry: deeds of hospitality and generosity, of kindness and compassion. Even her apparent love of beer can be seen in this way. As a poem attributed to St. Brigit from an eighth-century manuscript reveals, she does not make it for herself alone, but to give away to others, including the entire communion of angels and saints, so that they might enjoy the celebration of God's love:

> I should like a great lake of ale
> For the King of Kings.
> I should like the angels of Heaven
> To be drinking it through time eternal.
> I should like excellent meats of belief and pure piety.
> I should like flails of penance at my house.
> I should like the men of Heaven at my house;
> I should like barrels of peace at their disposal;
> I should like vessels of charity for distribution;
> I should like for them cellars of mercy.
> I should like cheerfulness to be in their drinking.
> I should like Jesus to be there among them.
> I should like the three Marys of illustrious renown
> to be with us.
> I should like the people of Heaven, the poor, to be
> gathered around us from all parts.
> I should like to be a rent-payer to the Lord
> So that should I suffer distress
> He would bestow a good blessing upon me.[34]

Also, unlike the stories and legends of the male founders of the other great Irish monasteries, Brigit is not at all portrayed as a "reluctant" spiritual mentor, but as a woman who constantly draws people together because she wants to—out of love for them, not because it is her "duty." In fact, in the earliest surviving *Life of Brigit,* there is a clear allusion to her pastoral care and desire for collaboration:

> Wishing to provide wisely and properly for the souls of her people, and anxious about the churches of the

> many provinces that had attached themselves to her, Brigit realized that she could not possibly do without a bishop to consecrate churches and supply them with various levels of ordained clergy. So she sent for a distinguished man, known for his virtues, who was then leading a solitary life in the desert. Going herself to meet him, she brought him back into her company....From then on the anointed head and leader of all bishops and the most blessed leader of virgins, in pleasant mutual agreement and with the helping aid of all the virtues, built her principal church at Kildare.

Though Cogitosus' *Life of Brigit* provides us with more of a fascinating glimpse into the life of a double monastery *during his time* than extensive biographical information on Brigit, we can see other images of collaboration, mutuality, and inclusiveness that surface in his account that surely reflect the original values of the foundress. For example, in the church at Kildare, "the glorious bodies" of Brigit and the bishop repose in sarcophagi, placed, we are told, "the one to the right and the other to the left of a beautifully adorned altar." Her community, consisting of both women and men, also continues to welcome, as was mentioned above, ordinary laypeople to its prayer and Eucharist.[35]

This early *Life of Brigit* by Cogitosus, according to Kenney, "forms the basis of Brigitine hagiography,"[36] and, as her cult spread, its contents were incorporated into later Lives. By the Middle Ages Brigit's Lives had been translated into Old French, Middle English, and German, and had become quite popular among monks and educated laypeople who loved monastic heroes. From the earliest to the later medieval Lives, a pattern can be discerned in Brigit's legends consisting of various stages that is similar to other hagiographies, especially those of the Celtic saints. To help trace that pattern, we will concentrate upon "The Life of Brigit" as found in the *Book of Lismore,* compiled from various manuscripts in the latter half of the fifteenth century. This life, of course, like others about her, is based upon stories going back to the sixth century, and includes some of the same material as found in the *Life of Brigit* by Cogitosus and other early Lives written in Latin and Irish.

A Pattern in Brigit's Lives

The first stage of this pattern usually begins with mention of the saint's royal lineage and distinguished ancestry, and how his or her birth is often preceded by extraordinary events and prophetic dreams. In the case of Brigit, we are told that her father is a Leinster nobleman by the name of Dubthach, who, although living with his wife, has intercourse with Broicsech, one of his slaves, who becomes pregnant. From the outset we see traces of Brigit's liminality, that state of being "betwixt and between" many marginalized people experiences, which, though often painful, can lead to transformation and the first stirrings of leadership.[37] Brigit is definitely portrayed in this light, for she will not only be a link between pagan and Christian spiritual traditions, but she will be born illegitimate, perhaps always feeling deeply a sense of not-belonging. (This may account for the many stories of her compassion toward those who are poor and rejected, and her own desire to found a community in which, as it turns out, both genders are welcome.)

Liminality is further expressed quite clearly when her birth is prophesied by *both* pagan *and* Christian holy men. As Dubthach and Broicsech ride by in a chariot before Brigit's birth, a druid prophesies that their child who will be born to them will be "marvelous": "her like will not be on earth...a daughter conspicuous, radiant, who will shine like a sun among the stars of heaven."[38] Not to be outdone, two bishops, Mel and Melchu, come from Scotland to prophesy about her and to bless her. Because of the jealousy of Dubthach's wife, however, Dubthach sells the pregnant slave to a druid, and it is in the latter's house that Brigit is born—but not before at least one more portent. A holy man and friend of a poet sees "a flame and a fiery pillar" rising from where Brigit's mother resides in anticipation of Brigit's birth—a fiery manifestation that appears at other critical junctures in Brigit's life. Perhaps most dramatic of all, she is born when her mother "went at sunrise with a vessel full of milk in her hand, and when she put one of her two footsteps over the threshold of the house, the other foot being inside, then she brought forth the daughter, Saint Brigit."[39] The symbol of liminality couldn't be clearer.

A second stage of an unfolding pattern in a saint's life occurs when the saint finds a worthy mentor or mentors from whom wisdom is learned. These sometimes take the form of both human and angelic guides. (St. Patrick, for example, had an angel, Victor, as his guardian and soul friend.) In Brigit's story, she not only later finds worthy bishops, Mel and MacCaille, who receive her vows and help her build Kildare, but is *first* mentored by the druid, already mentioned, with whom her mother now lives. This anonymous druid evidently raises Brigit as his own daughter, acting as her foster father, teacher, and friend. He is certainly one of the most significant persons, besides her mother, in Brigit's important formational years. One day, when the druid is sleeping, he awakes to find three angels, disguised as clerics, baptizing her. The third angel, in fact, tells the druid what to name her. The number three is important here, for, as we've already seen, it emphasizes this young child's holiness and great potential as a Christian saint. It is noteworthy too that it is an angel, a messenger symbolizing the love and care of God, who names her.

As the child grows older, stories alluding to her generativity are told, and the *Book of Lismore* clearly states that "everything to which her hand was set used to increase," while she goes about tending sheep, caring for birds, and feeding the poor.[40] By the time she is a young woman, her druid-mentor takes the initiative and reunites Brigit with her natural father. This druid's love and compassion, especially manifest in his seeking out her natural father, must have taught her the importance not only of those qualities, but also of her value as a woman. Such affirmation surely contributed to the emergence of her as a leader mentoring others in return.

A third stage that consistently appears in saints' lives is one in which the saint performs numerous miracles, demonstrating his or her spiritual power. These miraculous deeds often take the form of Jesus' own, such as healing the sick, casting out demons, multiplying food, and even raising the dead. In the stories of Brigit, manifestations of her power seem divided between two periods in her life: the first, when she rejoins her natural father, and a second and much longer phase when she has committed her life to virginity and church work. This latter phase, especially associated with a ministry of healing, seems to coincide with her progress in holiness and years.

What becomes clear in the first phase is how spiritually precocious she is for a young woman, *and* how much her father comes to resent her care and generosity. This generosity is manifest in numerous stories. Brigit, for example, makes beer out of well water for a sick nurse, and churns endless hampers of butter for her original mentor, the druid, who is so grateful to her that he is eventually baptized and, we are told, "remained till his death in Brigit's company." Expressing the Celtic trait of kinship with animals, she even gives bacon from her father's table to a hungry hound. This is evidently not the only instance of Brigit taking such initiative, for the *Book of Lismore* says: "of her father's wealth and food and property, whatsoever her hands would find or would get, she used to give to the poor and needy of the Lord." The conflict between Brigit and her father finally reaches a climax when she gives away his prized sword:

> He asked Brigit what she had done with his sword. "I gave it," Brigit said, "to a poor man who came to beg of me." Dubthach was extremely angry with her for having given the sword away. When Brigit came before the king, he said: "Why did you steal your father's property and wealth, and, what is worse, why have you given the sword away?" Then said Brigit: "The Virgin Mary's Son knows, if I had your power, with all your wealth, and with all your Leinster, I would give them all to the Lord of the Elements." Said the king to Dubthach: "It is not right for us to deal with this

> maiden, for her merit before God is higher than ours."
> Thus was Brigit saved then from bondage.

Shortly after the episode with the king, Brigit's father tries to get rid of her in another way—by marrying her off to a suitor. Brigit refuses in a dramatic way by plucking her eye out of her head, "so that it lay on her cheek." When Dubthach and her brothers behold this, they promise that "she should never be told to go to a husband unless she liked the man." After obtaining this promise (and healing her eye!), Brigit goes with some of her female friends to Bishop Mel in Telcha Mide to take the veil. It is here when the story in the *Book of Lismore*, as well as earlier Lives, takes a particularly interesting turn, to which we will return shortly. Two things, however, are worth mentioning, again because they give us insights into her character: first, "a fiery pillar rose from her head to the roof-ridge of the church" at the time of her vows, and, second, while the other virgins with her each choose during the ceremony a particular beatitude to live by, "it was the beatitude of mercy that Brigit chose."[41]

Stories in abundance connected with her mercy and compassion, her healing and generative powers, follow this turning point in her life. Too numerous to mention here, a great number are associated with her healing powers. Her ministry to the poor and to lepers in particular seems to be characteristic of her entire adult life. Surely the lepers symbolize those people who are most feared and despised by others, and, perhaps most tragically, filled with self-loathing as well. Other stories reveal intriguing aspects of her life and ministry. Her girdle, for example, has special miraculous features; she gives a man an aphrodisiac so that his wife "could not stay away from him";[42] she meets Patrick and is evidently not all that impressed with his preaching, since she falls asleep during one of his homilies; she defends a bishop falsely accused of fathering a child; and she prays with a scholar who complains that "I have no leisure."[43] What we see is the gradual emergence of Brigit as a powerful spiritual leader who often ministers to those whom others will not. *The Book of Lismore* tells the story of Brigit's visit to a certain church at Easter:

> The prioress of the church said to her maidens that on Maundy Thursday one of them should minister to the old men and to the weak and feeble persons who were living in the church. Not one of them was found for the ministering. Said Brigit: "I today will minister to them." There were four sick persons in the church: a consumptive man, a lunatic, a blind man, and a leper. Brigit ministered to these four, and they were healed from every disease which they had.[44]

This capacity for healing seems to have been hers precisely because of her compassion, and her acceptance of being in need of healing herself. This important dimension of her ministry—that of being a wounded healer—is illustrated symbolically in another story:

> At the same time a disease of the eyes came to Brigit, and her head seemed exceedingly weary. When Bishop Mel heard of that he said: "Let us go together to seek a physician, so that you may have your head cured...." As they were going forth, Brigit fell out of her chariot and her head smashed against a stone. She was greatly wounded and the blood gushed out. Then with that blood were healed two mute women who were lying on the road.[45]

Brigit's ministry flourishes and she eventually turns to Bishop Mel, and asks him to give her land for a monastery. Despite the initial opposition of a wealthy man, Ailill, son of Dunlang, "Saint Brigit's great house in Kildare," we are told, "is built."[46] Her community of both women and men grows, her care for the poor and lepers continues, and other stories reveal certain psychic abilities that could be equated with "second sight." By this time too, she is evidently becoming an important wisdom figure and *anamchara*, for there are numerous stories not only of ordinary people seeking her out, but even of bishops, sometimes seven at a time. Brendan the Navigator, one of Ireland's most famous saints, comes to visit her at Kildare. He asks her why on his travels a certain monster in the sea had given honor to her and not to him:

> Brigit said to Brendan: "Make your confession, O cleric, first, and I will afterwards." "I declare," said Brendan, "that since I entered devotion, I never crossed seven furrows without turning my mind to God." "Good is your confession," said Brigit. "So now make your confession to me," replied Brendan. "I confess," said Brigit, "that since I first fixed my mind on God, I have never taken it from Him. "It seems to us, O nun," said Brendan, "that the monsters are right to give honor to you."[47]

In addition to welcoming these worthy guests, as well as presumably responding to ever-increasing responsibilities, we still find her milking cows (so that the bishops will have something to drink), saving a wild fox from certain death, and evidently always drawing upon the transforming power of prayer, "for," as the *Book of Lismore* says, "everything that Brigit would ask of the Lord was granted her at once."[48]

The last stage of the pattern that often appears in saints' Lives includes the saint traveling to other parts of the country or to foreign shores, and, finally, being forewarned by a divine visitor or angel of his or her impending death. This death may be preceded by a deathbed scene like those found in many saints' Lives, including those of Antony, Macrina, and the Celtic saints, David, Columcille, and Cuthbert, when final words of wisdom or warning are imparted as a sacred legacy. With Brigit's story, however, there is no deathbed scene; hers is a legacy not of words, but of a lifetime of ministry. And rather than traveling to Rome before she dies, someone from Rome travels to be by her side:

> Now when it came to the last days for Brigit, after founding and helping cells and churches and altars in abundance, after miracles and marvels whose number is as the sand of sea, or stars of heaven, after charity and mercy, then came Nindid Pure-hand from Rome

> of Latium....And he gave communion and sacrifice to Brigit, who sent her spirit to heaven.

Her story concludes where it began—with the powerful imagery of flames:

> Her relics are on earth with honour and dignity and primacy, with miracles and marvels. Her soul is like a sun in the heavenly Kingdom among the choir of angels and archangels. And though great be her honour here at present, greater by far will it be, when she shall arise like a shining lamp in completeness of body and soul at the great assembly of Doomsday...in the union that is nobler than every union, in the union of the Holy Trinity, Father, Son, and Holy Ghost.[49]

Brigit's Spiritual Power

What has emerged in the stories about St. Brigit is the portrait of a woman who was a powerful leader, healer, and spiritual guide. She has the power associated with those beloved of God, the saints, who are able, as the scholar Peter Brown says, to see two worlds, the visible and the invisible.[50] Brigit transcends both realities, bringing about a new interior synthesis and holiness that are put at the service of others. Hers is a spiritual power that comes to her from God out of the struggles of her life. While other saints, such as Antony, are known for their fights with the demonic, in Brigit's stories we find few encounters with the devil. Instead, she fights for self-worth and vocational discernment against the taboos of illegitimacy, and the opposition of men: father, brothers, and even, as we saw, a wealthy man's attempts to keep her from building her monastery at Kildare. She is a woman too who builds a lifetime—and an eternal reputation—on her generosity, her healing ministry, and her outreach to the poor, the most neglected, and to lepers, the most rejected of society. Hers was the sort of personality, quite clearly sexually integrated and spiritually mature, that could attract celibate women and men, as well as those with families. No wonder, then, that she was remembered for qualities described in a hymn attributed to the great Columcille:

> For this was her desire: to satisfy the poor, to expel every hardship, to spare every miserable person....Her heart and her mind were a throne of rest for the Holy Spirit. She was simple towards God; she was compassionate towards the wretched; she was splendid in miracles and marvels; thus her name among created things is Dove among birds, Vine among trees, Sun among stars.[51]

Perhaps of all her qualities compassion was her greatest, and the one on which her spiritual power was based. This is the quality—so closely intertwined with that of generosity—that many remembered about her, and with which her own community had such great difficulty. Here, I believe, because of the consistency of the stories told about her, we can discern traces of the original historical personage of Brigit the saint. When we consider her life, it is clear why she chose the beatitude she did at the time of her vows: "Happy the merciful; they shall have mercy shown them" (Matt 5:7), and how much she came to personify compassion itself.

Certain symbols have also emerged as important indicators of her leadership and spiritual power: she is born on a threshold; she is baptized by three angels; she has healing powers; and perhaps, most significantly, her life, to use T. S. Eliot's poetic language once more, "is tongued with fire."[52] This fire, like that at Pentecost, announces the holy, creative, transforming power of God. We find these same symbols of liminality, the number three, and fire in one last story about her. Found in other Lives, including that of the *Book of Lismore,* this one is from a manuscript called by scholars the *Old Irish Life,* the earliest surviving life of Brigit written largely in Irish, composed in the eighth or ninth century. It is the legend that Brigit was ordained, and, although scholars such as John Ryan call the story absurd,[53] its meaning is clear to those who understand the language of symbols.

In this story we find Brigit first entering a state of liminality, but then helped unexpectedly by a youth—*and* her own determination and assertiveness. Watch closely for the symbolic imagery:

> On a certain day she goes with seven virgins to take the veil to a foundation on the side of Crochan of Bri Eile, where she thought that Mel the bishop lived. There she greets two virgins, Tol and Etol, who lived there. They said: "The bishop is not here, but in the churches of Mag Taulach. While saying this they behold a youth called MacCaille, a pupil of Mel the bishop. They asked him to lead them to the bishop. He said: "The way is trackless, with marshes, desert, bogs and pools." The saint said: "Extricate us from our difficulty." As they proceeded on their way, he could see afterwards a straight bridge there.

As the story continues, angels unexpectedly appear and then the powerful presence of the Spirit, imaged as fire:

> The hour of consecration having arrived, the veil was raised by angels from the hand of MacCaille, the minister, and is placed on the head of saint Brigit....The bishop being intoxicated with the grace of God there did not recognize what he was reciting from his book, for he consecrated Brigit with the orders of a bishop. "This virgin alone in Ireland," said Mel, "will hold the episcopal ordination." While she was being consecrated a fiery column ascended from her head.

And, finally, the mystic number three, a sign of Brigit's generativity and transforming power, appears in the story:

> Afterwards, the people granted her a place called Ache hI in Saltus Avis. Remaining there a little while, she

> persuaded three pilgrims to remain there and granted them the place. She performed three miracles in that place, namely: The spring flowed in dry land, the meat turned into bread, the hand of one of the three men was cured.[54]

It is, of course, typical of Brigit that she gives the place away!

This legend vividly confirms the spiritual power and leadership of Brigit—whether she was ordained or not, as we understand that term today. The point of the story is that, as head of a major monastery, spiritual guide to many, and healer of many broken lives, she quite clearly was a powerful spiritual leader who had all the gifts of creativity, inspiration, and holiness associated with ordained ministry. This, the legend says, was recognized by the angels, and, most importantly, by God. That was enough for even Bishop Mel, surprised as he was by his own actions, to recognize that what he had done was of the Holy Spirit, the Person of the Trinity, whose life is "tongued with fire."

Brigit's Fire Today

We have passed over on pilgrimage to the life of Brigit, and discovered an amazing woman whose spiritual leadership was not based first upon ordination, but upon a previous and continuous pattern of assertive, healing, and compassionate ministry. People of her time recognized this about her, and in the years following her death, her cult became so popular that hundreds of churches and holy wells were named after her, not only in Ireland, but also in such countries as France, Portugal, Italy, Switzerland, Belgium, Germany, and Austria. In England alone, there are nineteen churches dedicated to her, including the oldest place of Christian worship, St. Bride's, on Fleet Street. In Salzburg, Austria, an ancient litany invokes her name, along with two other well-known female soul friends, Sts. Ita and Samthann. By the Middle Ages her relics were highly valued. Though we do not know for certain where her body lies (a number of stories link it with Downpatrick in Northern Ireland), her purported head is venerated at the Church of Lumier, near Lisbon, Portugal, and her cloak in the cathedral at Bruges, Belgium. In a Swiss church at Liestal, near Basel, a lamp has been kept burning in her honor since the thirteenth century.

Today, especially, with her fire at Kildare lit by the Brigidine nuns once more, Brigit has something to teach Christians about women's leadership and the full recognition of their gifts. She reminds us how many women's ministries and vocational calls go unrecognized or are treated as illegitimate in our own times, and how their lives often seem to be in some sort of liminal state or twilight zone. Despite this, her story offers hope to those of us yearning for the full equality of women in all aspects of social, political, and religious life. For it shows what qualities are truly important when it comes to our ministries, whether we're female or male, ordained or not, and how in fact our churches will finally come to accept and even welcome the full equality of women. That will happen when all of us, particularly those in leadership positions in the Church, finally recognize what harm the deprivation of those gifts is causing the entire People of God—AND, when they discover, as Bishop Mel did, that God's spirit, power, and love are greater than any cultural and theological stereotypes that presuppose that God's inspiration and creativity somehow ended with the last apostle.

Perhaps, most of all, Brigit's story, as well as the numerous stories of women like her involved in all sorts of ministries today, teach us that spiritual power in our churches must take a different form—not that of spiritual aggression, as symbolized in the story of Brigit's father and his sword, but of greater compassion, justice, and love. It was, after all, Brigit who gave the sword away, and who told the king that if she had his power and wealth, she would give it all to "the Lord of the Elements." Her life and ministry remind us of the principle enunciated by Carl Jung: "Where love reigns, there is no will to power; and where the will to power is paramount, love is lacking."[55]

For those seeking to incorporate monastic values into their lives today, the history of the early Irish Church encourages us to remember, as is true today of many monastic communities, that there was a certain fluidity of definitions regarding membership between "true monks" and "paramonastics," laypeople attached to the monasteries in various ways. In particular, Brigit's life reminds us especially of the overall importance of compassion—whether one is a full-time monk in community or one who seeks to bring monastic values into the wider world. This value, of course, is reflected not only in the stories of so many monastic leaders, from Antony to Martin to Cassian and the desert elders, but in the life and ministry of Jesus himself. He is the one who identified intimately with marginalized people, reminding us of how important it is that our own lives be characterized by compassion, inclusivity, mutuality, concern for the poor and the outcasts, and a profound respect for the diversity of women's gifts.

In the following chapter, we turn to the life of another great monastic leader who was born about the time Brigit died, a man who has been called "the greatest statesman of the early medieval church":[56] Gregory the Great. As we will see, it was Gregory's support and protection of nascent Benedictine monasteries and, in particular, his writing of the only Life of St. Benedict that had a major effect on the continued growth of monasticism in the West from late antiquity on into the Middle Ages. Although chronologically Benedict preceded Gregory by a few years (the latter was about seven years old when Benedict died), we will consider the life and writings of Gregory first in order to better understand his depiction of Benedict and the theology associated with the holy man and his sister, Scholastica.

CHAPTER EIGHT

A Candle in the Darkness—Gregory the Great

He [a spiritual leader] should...be polished long by religious meditation, that he may be well-pleasing and so shine as a candle placed on a candlestick....

—Gregory the Great, "Letter to Bishops Syagrius, Aetherius, Virgilius, and Desiderius"

Gregory, called "the Great," was much loved by the people of the early Irish Church, including the missionary Columban (c. 543–615), who in his correspondence to Gregory addressed him as "holy Lord," "father in Christ," and "fairest ornament of the Roman Church."[1] Alcuin, a monk educated at Clonmacnoise in Ireland and later, in 796 CE, made abbot of the monastery of St. Martin in Tours, spoke of him with affection at the court of Charlemagne.[2] Bede the Venerable (c. 672–735), in addition to the Celtic saints, counted Gregory one of his heroes, and described him as "a man eminent in learning and in affairs."[3] Highly influenced by the writings of Augustine, Jerome, and John Cassian, whom he greatly admired, he was the first pope with that name, a name that derives from *egregora,* perfect tense from the Greek verb, *egeiro,* to wake up. This state of transformation, of personal spiritual awakening and of awakening others, typified his life and leadership.

Along with Ambrose, Augustine, and Jerome, Gregory is counted as one of the four great Latin doctors of the Church, and considered one of the most significant figures in Western

Christianity and the history of Christian mysticism. He was bishop of Rome from 590 to 604, at a time described by historians as "the Dark Ages" when the structures and cultures of the West were being laid waste by the so-called "barbarians": Goths in Germany, Franks in Gaul, Visigoths in Spain, Anglo-Saxons in Britain, and, in Italy, the Lombards. The latter tribes had been threatening the gates of Rome itself before Gregory's pontificate, and continued to confront him when he became bishop of Rome.[4] This was the time too when the prophet Mohammed was uniting vast regions in the East under his religious leadership, while the Roman emperors had moved their capital to Constantinople, thus leaving the West largely undefended, especially the city of Rome.

As a result of this military and political vacuum, the office of the bishop of Rome began to grow in prominence, with the pope increasingly taking responsibility for civil and religious stability. Gregory himself was highly instrumental in laying the groundwork for the papacy's emerging influence and power in the Middle Ages. Under his leadership, "the city of the Caesars was in process of becoming the city of the Popes,"[5] the Rome of the apostles and martyrs increasingly the center of churches, monasteries, and pilgrim shrines. Pope and pastor, contemplative and mystic, Gregory epitomizes the transition between the world of late antiquity and the rise of the Middle Ages, a man who guided the Church through a most difficult period of history when one world was dying as another was being born.

Gregory's writings on pastoral leadership and the lives of the saints, in particular on the life of St. Benedict, along with his extensive volumes of letters, commentaries, and homilies, had a great impact on medieval church life. Jean Leclercq describes him as "the spiritual father of the Middle Ages in the West," and says that Gregory's teaching became the chief source of medieval spirituality. His life, Leclercq says, "varied during long periods between one of involvement in the world, contemplation in a monastery, and the labors of a pastor of souls."[6] It was precisely this "mixed" life of prayer, writing, and of ecclesial, social, and politic engagement that produced, as we will see, such creative and effective leadership, but also, for Gregory, so much personal distress.

Gregory's anguish was largely due to the fact that he was by temperament and proclivity a monk, a man who before he was elected pope had lived in a monastery and had grown to deeply love what that monastic life provided: solitude, peace, serenity, and the opportunity to commune, uninterrupted, with God. Considered to be the first monastic pope, Gregory had not sought out the papal office, and, in fact, resisted assenting to the election. Throughout much of his pontificate, he grieved the loss of his former life to which he longed to return. No wonder Bernard McGinn states that "what was central to his own experience and his spiritual message" was "the painful but necessary tension between action and contemplation."[7]

In this chapter, through our exploration of the life and thought of Gregory as expressed in his writings, we will begin to discover the significance of the monastic value of contemplation, which he personally loved and missed so much. Despite his numerous complaints, we will also learn how action and contemplation are not necessarily antagonistic, but complementary in significant ways. As Gregory advised certain bishops to "be polished by religious meditation" in order to "shine as a candle placed on a candlestick,"[8] we will be able to discern how he himself illuminated the darkness of his own time, providing a light then and even now in an uncertain and violent world.

Gregory the Monk

Gregory was born about 540 into a wealthy Roman family, and grew up in a palace on the Caelian Hill. From his home, he could see the Appian Way, the Circus Maximus, the Palatine, even the Arch of Constantine and the Coliseum, as well as the area in Rome where St. Jerome in the 380s had acted as a spiritual director to noble women before he left for the Holy Land. Gregory grew up with three sisters, Tarsilla, Aemiliana, and Gordiana, and a brother (whose name is unknown). Their parents' names were Gordianus and Silvia. In his comprehensive biography on Gregory, F. Homes Dudden acknowledges the parental inheritance Gregory received: "From his mother he doubtless derived his almost feminine tenderness and power of sympathy, his innate bent towards asceticism, his religious mysticism, his self-sacrificing, self-effacing disposition. From his father, no less certainly, he inherited his administrative capacity, his legal acumen, his unswerving love of justice…."[9] Both parents were Christian, and Gregory's lineage included ordained clergy, even a pope.[10]

As was the case for the nobility still living in Rome, Gregory received a classical education, and, as he grew to adulthood, was soon recognized for his leadership qualities. In 573, he was made Prefect of Rome, a prestigious position that carried with it notable responsibilities: the management of all important affairs in the city, care of grain supplies, distribution of free doles, repair of the aqueducts, baths, sewers, as well as helping defend the city against the invading Lombards. All that he did as Prefect, of course, would contribute later to his competent administration as the bishop of Rome. At this stage of his life, Gregory was a devout layman, seemingly intent upon pursuing a pious *and* highly political life. Yet, something about his life in general and his work in particular seemed unsatisfactory. As he expressed it, years later, to his close friend Leander: "While my mind obliged me to serve this present world in outward action, its cares began to threaten me so that I was in danger of being engulfed in it not only in outward action, but, what is more serious, in my mind."[11] This state of dissatisfaction went on for some time—until a painful event seems to have forced him, as Augustine says about his own conversion, to "look into his face."[12] His father died, a man whom he loved dearly. Perhaps influenced by the story of the desert father, Antony, who became a monk after the death of his parents, Gregory disposed of his family's extensive landholdings in 575, and established a monastery, dedicated to St. Andrew, on his parents' estate in Rome. He then entered this community—not as abbot, as one might expect, but as an ordinary monk. There he remained approximately four years, establishing six other monastic communities on family properties in Sicily.

The relatively few years in St. Andrew's monastery seem to have changed Gregory profoundly as he attempted to live a life of solitude and quiet, prayer and contemplation. In imitation of the desert Christians, he adopted an extremely ascetic lifestyle. Peter Brown believes that, as a result of this asceticism, Gregory "ruined his health," and that "from then onwards his energies were sapped by constant illness."[13] This is probably an accurate analysis, since there are numerous references to illnesses in Gregory's later correspondence that kept him low throughout his papacy. Although he knew of the Rule of St. Benedict, and obviously admired the great abbot of Monte Cassino (as his later hagiography on St. Benedict attests), Gregory did not adopt that Rule for himself and his fellow monks. In fact, he may have not done so precisely because of his desire to live an extremely ascetic lifestyle rather than the more moderate one described in Benedict's Rule.

A story in his *Dialogues*, a book written while he was pope, relates how sick Gregory was as a monk, and possibly what caused it: "Once while I was still living in the monastery, I was seriously ill with sharp, throbbing pains in my intestines. I felt that death was approaching in a matter of hours because of the frequent spasms of intense pain." Grieving, he says, not because he was sick, but that the illness was not allowing him to fast during Holy Week, he asked Eleutherius, a visiting monk known for his holiness, to pray for him. As a result of his "sincere and tearful prayer," Gregory's "weakened body" was healed—enough so that he could continue his fast![14] As was true of Augustine and Jerome, Gregory seems to have been ill a lot, probably due to this initial monastic asceticism, and then his hectic pastoral life as pope, as well as his prolific output of writings and correspondence. It also may well have contributed to his later belief that sickness may be a "gift," teaching humility, gratitude, and compassion.[15]

Like the desert Christians whom he sought to emulate, Gregory as a monk also became known for his hospitality to strangers, and his generosity to the poor—qualities that would characterize his papacy and the servant leadership associated with it. These characteristics are alluded to in another story, told by a Gregorian hagiographer, John the Deacon. One day when Gregory was writing in his cell, a man disguised as a shipwrecked mariner appeared and begged alms. Twice Gregory gave him something, but when the man returned a third time, there was no more money in the community to be given away. Then Gregory remembered a silver dish that his mother had sent him, a cherished legacy from his father, and without hesitation presented that to the beggar so that "a poor man who asks to be comforted may not depart in sorrow."[16] As in the popular story of St. Martin of Tours' dividing his cloak and finding later that the poor man to whom he gave it was Jesus, Gregory discovers that the supposed mariner was not who he seemed to be, but an angel sent from God.

Overall, his years as a monk at St. Andrew's were when he "breathed in the wisdom of the past."[17] Life in the monastery afforded him the opportunity to read and study without bothersome interruptions. Besides becoming familiar with the works of Augustine, Jerome, John Cassian, and other Church fathers, Gregory was especially drawn to sacred scripture. He seems to have had, as Charles Kannengiesser says, "an uncommon capacity to memorize it," and his comprehensive reading of it was later "to infuse all his later writings."[18] To read Gregory is to become aware of how much his life and thought were thoroughly immersed in scripture. No wonder that at another time he would act as a teacher of scripture to his fellow monks.

What Gregory seemed to love most as a monk was the opportunity to pray. As he wrote later, "When I was in the monastery, I could refrain my tongue from idle words and keep my mind almost continually in an attitude of prayer."[19] This may well have been when he first began to experience contemplation, what he associates in his later writings with mystical experiences of union with God, which, although transitory, linger on in memory, producing intense longings for more. Gregory expressed this holy desire in his book *Dialogues*, after becoming pope, when he says: "I recall those earlier days in the monastery where all the fleeting things of time were in a world below me, and I could rise far above the vanities of life. Heavenly thoughts would fill my mind, and while still held within the body I passed beyond its narrow confines in contemplation."[20] Such experiences, Gregory equated with sweetness, joy, and ecstasy as well as fire and light—especially light. As Cuthbert Butler rightly posits, "Gregory's favorite symbol, to which he returns again and again in describing contemplation is Light."[21] One dramatic expression of this can be found in a scene from the hagiography he later wrote on St. Benedict, perhaps the most famous nonbiblical vision in the early Middle Ages:

> Long before the night office began, the man of God was standing at his window, where he watched and prayed while the rest were still asleep. In the dead of night he suddenly beheld a flood of light shining down from above more brilliant than the sun, and with it every trace of darkness cleared away. Another remarkable sight followed. According to his own description, the whole world was gathered up before his eyes in what appeared to be a single ray of light.[22]

Although most people do not have such powerful experiences of transcendence, all, Gregory came to believe, are capable of at least temporary encounters with God, which result in sometimes dramatic life-changes. As he said in one of his homilies as pope, "the minds of those that contemplate, although they have but a slight glimpse of the true light, yet are they enlarged within themselves with a great amplitude." And he adds, "Therefore, there is no Christian state from which the grace of contemplation can be excluded. Whoever has an interior heart can be illuminated by the light of contemplation...."[23] Drawing upon concepts from Augustine, Gregory speaks of contemplation as "the search for Truth," and "the contemplation of Truth"; as "a sight of the true Light" or of "the eternal Light."[24]

Contemplation, for Gregory, was *both* an *experience* of God *and* the *discipline* of prayer; the first comes as gift, and cannot be controlled by human efforts; the second, however, is something everyone can do. Gregory equated contemplation with "fire" and the rekindling, reenergizing of holy people and spiritual leaders:

> Holy men are sent and go forth as lightnings, when they come forth from the retirement of contemplation to the public life of employment....But after the outward works which they perform, they always return to the bosom of contemplation, there to revive the flame of their zeal, and to glow as it were from the touch of heavenly brightness. For they would freeze too speedily amid their outward works, good though they be, did they not constantly return with anxious earnestness to the fire of contemplation....[25]

Contemplation is the attempt to "fix the eye of the heart on the very ray of the unencompassed Light." It is associated with communion with God, and being "on fire with love."[26]

These were some of the insights Gregory was beginning to learn in his days as a monk; that is, until his life of prayer and contemplation, reading, and pastoral outreach were interrupted by a summons from the pope in 578. Remembering his abilities in the public sphere, Pope Benedict I (575–578) or his successor, Pelagius II (578–590), asked Gregory to leave the monastery and travel as a papal representative to Constantinople at a time when the popes were in special need of obtaining help against the Lombards. Surely with major misgivings and regrets, Gregory agreed to go.

Papal Envoy to Constantinople

In Constantinople, after being ordained a deacon by the pope, Gregory lived in a house for papal visitors near the seashore, not far from the Imperial Palace and the magnificent church dedicated to the Mother of God, the Hagia Sophia (the title that means "Holy Wisdom"). This religious and physical landscape contributed significantly to his developing theology. Certainly, his life and leadership reflect a deep desire for wisdom, manifest in his numerous writings, commentaries, and sermons. The church, Hagia Sophia, surely reminded him of his heart's desire for wisdom, and engendered his enthusiasm for obtaining it.

The seascape around Constantinople also deeply affected him. As an image, the ocean appears often in his writings, and not always in the best possible light. Gregory seems to have been starkly aware, not only of its beauty as he watched the sun's reflection at dawn over the incoming waves or the moon glow at night on placid waters, but also of its potentially destructive power. The inherent dangers of the sea he could recognize by observation when storms off the coast suddenly arose, sending swelling surf and breakers into land. He also would have experienced this firsthand on his own sea voyages that he made to and from Constantinople. Stories probably contributed too. Maximianus, an abbot of St. Andrew's monastery, for one, evidently told him of his near-fatal difficulties on the open sea, while Agatho, bishop of Palermo, described to him his own dangerous passage.[27] There were also the stories of Homer's Odysseus and his perilous wanderings over the ocean to find home with which Gregory would have been familiar, as well as references to storms and leaking ships found in the writings of his hero, St. Augustine.[28] Along with his own experiences, all of these stories and references must have made a vivid impression on Gregory's thought and psyche, for, as we will see, he frequently returns to images of the sea and compares a life without contemplation to being "sunk by storms."[29]

Gregory spent approximately six years in Constantinople, conducting official papal business, multiplying contacts with high-level officials, meeting foreign visitors, even talking with those identified as heretics. As Jerome had done when he lived in Rome, Gregory also acted as a spiritual guide to numerous women, including Rusticiana, an exile from Rome, her daughter Eusebia, and at least two noble women at court, Dominica and Gregoria. Formal contacts and personal friendships acquainted him with invaluable knowledge of the Byzantine administration, which would serve him well when he became pope.

Despite his hectic schedule in Constantinople, Gregory continued his monastic lifestyle as best he could, living with several monks from his St. Andrew's community who had accompanied him. "By their example," he later wrote, "I was bound, as it were by the cable of an anchor, when tossing in the incessant buffeting of secular affairs, to the placid shore of prayer. For to their society, as to the bosom of a most safe harbor, I fled for escape from the rollings and the billows of earthly action; and, though that ministry had torn me from the monastery, and cut me off by the sword of its occupation from my former life of quiet, yet among them, through the converse of studious reading, the aspiration of daily compunction gave me life."[30]

In this monastic environment he began his life as a writer, influenced especially by the words of scripture, the works of Augustine, and the writings of Cassian. From Augustine, Gregory learned of that fierce longing for God that characterized his own life, while Cassian taught him the value of holy conversations of the heart. Gregory's first major writing, *Morals on Job,* dedicated to his friend Leander, a Spanish bishop from Seville whom he had met in Constantinople, addressed the problem of suffering, and was written as a guide for the moral life. It derived from Gregory's meditation on the stories from the Book of Job, a man with whom, as is clear in his references in other writings, he identified. Gregory's approach is that of a spiritual guide, someone who, in the long tradition of the Greek philosophers, Roman sages, and desert Christians, attempts to help his readers come to a clearer understanding of themselves, their motivations, and their continuous search for self-integrity.

This work also contains an exposition on the relationship between action and contemplation, an issue with which Gregory was then struggling. The controversy had its origins in the writings of Origen, expressed as the contrast between the two sisters in the Gospel of Luke: Martha, scurrying about to make Jesus feel welcome in their home, who would come to represent the active life, and Mary, symbolizing the contemplative, who sat at Jesus' feet and listened to him speak. According to Jesus, "It is Mary who has chosen the better part" (cf. Luke 10:38–42). Origen, and others influenced by him, interpreted this story as meaning that contemplation was superior to action. Gregory, however (although he much preferred the contemplative life), takes a different stance. In *Morals on Job* he clearly states that the *union* of the two lives should be the goal of the followers of Christ, inspired by his example:

> Christ set forth in Himself patterns of both lives, that is the active and the contemplative, united together.... For when he wrought miracles in the city, and yet continued all night in prayer on the mountain, He gave His faithful ones an example not to neglect, through love of contemplation, the care of their neighbors; nor again to abandon contemplative pursuits through being too immoderately engaged in the care of their neighbors....[31]

This insight would later be expressed in a homily preached in Rome after he had become pope, revealing what Gregory had learned from his struggle about the *complementarity* of contemplation and action. Quite clearly, he says, the one can enrich the other:

> We must note that just as the right order of life is to tend from the active to the contemplative; so the soul often reverts profitably from the contemplative to the active, so that the contemplative life having kindled the mind, the active life might be the more perfectly led. For the active life should convey us to the contemplative; but sometimes the contemplative life should send us back to the active life from what the mind turned in on itself beholds.[32]

Choosing to be contemplative in a world of action, however, presumes a certain discipline: "If we wish to contemplate things within, let us rest from outward engagements. The voice of God is heard when, with minds at ease, we rest from the bustle of this world, and the divine precepts are pondered by us in the deep silence of the mind."[33]

Sometime in 585 or 586, Gregory was allowed to return to Rome and to reenter his beloved monastery where he was elected abbot. According to his own evaluation, he considered the following years before becoming bishop of Rome as his happiest, allowing him the freedom to pursue his passions of reading, writing, teaching, and prayer. As in the Benedictine monasteries that were beginning to multiply, Gregory's days were filled with an "order," a daily routine of prayer, study, and work. He was able to write, and, as a teacher, to lecture his fellow monks on the meaning of Holy Scripture. These lectures were transcribed, and later published as a series of commentaries. He also completed the final edition of *Morals on Job,* a major accomplishment.

Gregory's joy, however, ended abruptly in 590 when he was—against his own desires—made pope. Although others before him, such as Martin of Tours, Ambrose of Milan, and Augustine of Hippo, had initially been reluctant to accept ecclesial advancement, Gregory seems to have resisted the most, sending a letter to the emperor begging him not to endorse the election. The emperor, however, "who loved the deacon dearly," according to Gregory of Tours, a church historian in Gaul, "gave thanks to God that he could now promote Gregory to such a place of honor," and "issued a diploma ordering Gregory to be enthroned."[34] Until his death in 604, Gregory would perceive his life as bishop of Rome (with all the accompanying pastoral, political, and administrative responsibilities) in terms of a single phrase from the Book of Job: "Behold, the giants groan beneath the waters" (26:5).

Pope Gregory: Guardian, Teacher, and Servant Leader

By inclination and temperament, Gregory was a man who loved solitude and an ordered life, and, even after becoming pope, always remained a monk at heart. At the same time, as earlier accounts of him reveal, he was extremely pastoral, often manifesting a solicitous concern for the poor, the destitute, the outcast. In fact, in his *first* letter as pope he asks the bishops of Sicily to attend to "the relief of the necessities of the poor and oppressed."[35] This concern of his became a priority under his leadership, especially reflected in a principle, based upon his reading of the gospels, he later enunciated that was radical for his day—and for our own: "When we administer necessities to the needy, we give them what is their own, not what is ours; we pay a debt of justice, rather than do a work of mercy."[36]

Combining in himself both a love of contemplation and a desire to serve, Gregory knew from the earliest days of his papacy that integrating those two passions would be a difficult, if not at times a seemingly impossible, task. Although he would come to understand *intellectually* the need to integrate contemplation and action (and then go on to clearly articulate for other spiritual leaders the need to do so in their lives), *emotionally* he never seems to have accomplished this, frequently stating in his correspondence—up to his last days—his unhappiness with "occupations" that "irk" him, and complaining of his "bitterness of heart."[37] As is clear from his numerous accomplishments, however, this tension within, this struggle in his very soul, was not debilitating, but highly creative.[38] Still, Gregory felt the need to make his misery known, often returning to the imagery of the sea. One of his first letters as pope is to Theoctista, sister of the emperor who had forced him to agree to become bishop of Rome, which clearly reveals the anguish he associated with his new job: "...under the color of episcopacy, I have been brought back to the world; in which I am involved in such great earthly cares as I do not at all remember having been subjected to even in a lay state of life. For I have lost the deep joys of my quiet, [and]...on every side I am tossed by the waves of business, and sunk by storms, so that I may truly say, 'I am come into the depth of the sea, and the storm has overwhelmed me' (Ps. 69). After business, I long to return to my heart...like Mary, in Luke's gospel, 'I have longed to sit at the feet of the Lord with Mary, to take in the words of His mouth; and lo, I am compelled to serve with Martha in external affairs, to be careful and troubled about many things.'"[39]

Gregory became pope at the age of fifty, an age that he himself associated with becoming "a guardian of sacred vessels" and a "teacher of souls."[40] As a "guardian," he was intensely involved in the religious and political conflicts of his time, attempting to settle doctrinal disputes, encourage orthodoxy, and get other ecclesial leaders, especially the Patriarch of Constantinople, to honor the primacy of the Roman see. As bishop of Rome, Gregory guarded the city itself, and dealt firsthand with the daily concerns of the Roman people. As a former monk, he also actively defended the rights of monasteries over those of bishops seeking to control them.[41] By granting the monks special privileges of independent rule that restricted episcopal jurisdiction, he laid the foundations for the later exemption of religious orders that brought them under direct papal protection and control. This was not appreciated by the bishops or by his fellow clerics in Rome, who were largely drawn from the local nobility. The latter had not been his initial supporters when he became pope, and, while they tended to admire monks from a safe distance, they had not wanted to be ruled by one. Nor did they appreciate his promoting the building of Benedictine monasteries in the territories under his jurisdiction.[42]

Other decisions of his in which he acted as a "guardian of the sacred" would have direct effects upon the contours of the medieval Church. He encouraged the veneration of relics, frequently passing on to rulers and others whom he hoped to influence various holy items especially associated with Sts. Peter and Paul and the wood of the cross on which Christ had died. According to Dudden, Gregory "used the whole weight of his unrivalled authority to encourage popular veneration for the relics of the saints,"[43] an endorsement that would encourage the rise of the practice of pilgrimage, which would be so popular in the Middle Ages. Gregory also made important changes in the liturgy, writing prayers for the Sacramentary that eventually was named after him, and promoting the development of liturgical music. Due to his influence, the simple beauty of plainsong became known as "Gregorian Chant." Gregory also developed the doctrine of Purgatory, teaching that the suffering of the souls detained there could be relieved by the celebration of the Eucharist. He thus encouraged praying *to* the dead, the holy saints, for help, but also *for* the dead, those still in purgatory. This latter practice, so much a part of medieval life, would eventually be linked with the gaining of indulgences to relieve the "poor souls" in purgatory.

Another significant area of his influence was his opinion regarding religious art. Writing to Serenus, bishop of Marseilles in Gaul, Gregory reproved him for his "inconsiderate zeal" in having religious art destroyed. While he commends Serenus for forbidding holy paintings and pictures of the saints to be adored, he blames him for their outright destruction. In his reprimand, Gregory enunciates a principle that would be honored throughout the Middle Ages when the great churches and cathedrals were built with their stained-glass windows and fine religious paintings: "Say, brother, what priest has ever been heard of as doing what you did?...To adore a picture is one thing, but to learn through the story of a picture what is to be adored is another. For what writing presents to readers, this a picture presents to the unlearned who behold, since in it even the ignorant see what they ought to follow; in it the illiterate read...." Gregory asks the bishop to do all in his power to explain to his people "that it was not the sight itself of the story which the picture was designed to show that displeased you, but the adoration which had been improperly paid to the pictures."[44] Gregory's views would be used by later popes in the eighth century to counter those of the Greek iconoclasts.[45]

As a "teacher of souls," Gregory was concerned about the spread of Christianity in Western Europe. While happy with the results of the evangelization made in Spain, Gaul, and among the Germanic tribes, he especially took delight in sending in 596 Augustine, a prior of his former community of St. Andrew's, to Canterbury, resulting in one of Gregory's major accomplishments: the conversion of England to Christianity. Inspired by the works of John Cassian who taught him that the highest form of leadership was to act as a spiritual guide or mentor to those one served, Gregory also acted as a teacher-guide to his contemporaries through his preaching, writing, and, most especially, his personal example of servant leadership. This servant leadership is identified in the first letter he wrote as pope, mentioned above, in which he describes himself as "servant of the servants of God," a designation which he was not the first pope to use, but probably the first to use so consistently.[46] Following the example that Jesus set, loving service and commitment are major concerns of Gregory's throughout his pontificate, something he linked intimately with spiritual leadership. As in St. Benedict's Rule in which the abbot serves the needs of the community,[47] Gregory saw the need for every Christian to serve, not dominate, those one is called to lead. As Jesus had said, "anyone who wants to be great among you must be your servant, and anyone who wants to be first among you must be your slave, just as the Son of Man came not to be served but to serve....(cf. Matt 20:24–28).

Gregory as Pastoral Theologian and Writer

If the vocation of teaching, according to Thomas Aquinas, is *tradere contemplativa,* "to share the fruit of contemplation,"[48] Gregory, through his writings, was truly a great teacher. What is amazing, considering his intense involvement in the issues of his time, is that he had time to write at all. And yet, in the midst of multiple responsibilities, he is known as one of the most prolific of popes, producing in addition to numerous homilies that were later published as books, *Gospel Homilies* and *Homilies on Ezechiel,* two other major works, *Pastoral Care* and *Dialogues,* which became primary sources of guidance for succeeding generations, and among those most widely read in the Middle Ages. In all of them, Gregory writes as more of a pastoral than an academic theologian: someone more prone to telling stories and administering pastoral counsel than to abstract, theoretical thought. He recognized the power of stories to teach, and that many people of his time were more apt to be stirred by a story than by a precept, especially if the stories were about the saints. "The lives of the saints," he writes, "are often more effective than mere instruction for inspiring us to love heaven as our home."[49]

He also made use of extensive storytelling when he preached. Dudden acknowledges this: "Gregory was the first great preacher who attempted in anything like a systematic fashion, to introduce non-scriptural illustrations into his instructions, to drive home a religious truth with the help of an apposite story. He was the first to experiment in a method which at a later period was almost universally adopted. He opened the way for the popular orators of the Middle Ages."[50] Besides stories from his own life, Gregory incorporated stories of holy men, as we will see, especially St. Benedict's, and holy women, including St. Scholastica's, into his own storytelling, most of all, because he loved listening to them. As he says about his soliciting narratives for his book, *Dialogues:* "...if I could, I would never do anything else than listen to such excellent stories."[51]

Gregory also acted as an effective writer in his correspondence with a wide variety of people, including archbishops, bishops, priests, deacons, abbots, and abbesses (as might be expected of the pope), but also emperors, senators, queens, noble women as well as ordinary lay women and men. Much of this correspondence (over 850 letters have survived) contains dramatic intimations of his loving care for others, his offering them guidance, encouragement, and sometimes outright challenge. In one letter to Clementina, a noble woman, he strongly advises her to let go of her resentments: "For indeed it has been reported to me that, when anyone has offended you, you retain soreness unremittingly. Now if this is true, since the more I love you the more grieved I am, I beg that you would nobly rid yourself of this fault...."[52]

Always in his extensive correspondence, Gregory applies a pastoral principle that he associates with effective ministry. In a letter to Conon, abbot of Lerins, an island off the southern coast of France, he commends him for the kind of leadership he provides his own monks. In his words to Conon, we find the pope's pastoral approach: "Wherefore let the good feel you sweet, the bad a corrector. And even in correction know that this approach should be observed, that you love persons and confront faults; lest, if you should be disposed to act otherwise, correction might pass into cruelty, and you should destroy those whom you desire to amend....Let your very sweetness be wary, not remiss; and let your correction be loving, not severe."[53] In all of his writings, Gregory seems guided by this stated principle, but most especially in his two major literary accomplishments as pope: his *Pastoral Care,* written in the first year of his pontificate, and his *Dialogues,* probably completed in 593–594.

Gregory's Pastoral Care

Pastoral Care, the book R. A. Markus sees as "the key" to all Gregory's work,[54] focuses specifically on the topic of spiritual leadership. Though written primarily for bishops, it presumes a wider audience, and has implications for anyone called to spiritual leadership, whether a bishop, abbot, clergyperson, or lay. In words that surely reflect his own struggles as both a layman and now a bishop of Rome, Gregory explains how difficult it is to maintain any semblance of a contemplative life when one is a leader: "Often it happens that when a man undertakes the cares of government, his heart is distracted with a diversity of things, and as his mind is divided among many interests and becomes confused, he finds he is unfitted for any of them...; the mind cannot possibly concentrate on the pursuit of any one matter when it is divided among many. When it permits itself to be drawn abroad by concerns intruding upon it, it empties itself of its steadying regard for its inmost self." Contemplation is the way, Gregory says, for one to gain knowledge of the inner self. Disciplines, such as prayer and contemplation, also help one focus and not dissipate one's energies. Here is where "the heart is forced to discipline itself."[55]

A primary understanding of contemplation is Gregory's associating it with light, as we've already seen. Here, in *Pastoral Care,* he says: "Now that man is blind who is ignorant of the light of heavenly contemplation." The leader who does not take time to contemplate becomes "oppressed by the darkness of the present life," and "does not behold the light to come as he does not love it, and, therefore, does not know where to direct the steps of his conduct." Taking time to contemplate and pray provides light, guidance in one's daily affairs and decision-making. An effective leader "must not be remiss in his care for the inner life by preoccupation with the external; nor must he in his solicitude for what is internal, fail to give attention to the external." Good leadership presumes the setting of limits in order to maintain any semblance of an interior life: "For it commonly happens, as I have said, that when the hearts of rulers are incautiously occupied with temporal cares, their interior love grows cold, and immersed in external affairs, they do not fear forgetting that they have undertaken the guidance of souls. Consequently, the care that is expended externally on their subjects is to be kept within defined limits."[56]

Gregory also states his belief that so much of effective leadership depends upon self-care. "In restoring others to health by healing their wounds," he says, a leader "must not disregard his own health...." "Let him not, while helping his neighbors, neglect himself; let him not, while lifting up others, fall himself." This self-care presupposes knowledge of oneself, one's own sinful potential as well as one's own limitations and "infirmities." Such self-knowledge presumes a life of interiority where time is set aside for reflection and self-examination. Gregory also strongly intimates that a life without contemplation can often lead to violence when, for example, a person, "forgetful of his own estate," "violently rushes into reproof of the frailty of his neighbor." Patience and compassion are required.[57]

A truly effective leader, Gregory suggests, is one who "walks the talk," who in his or her daily life and ministry mirrors what he or she teaches and preaches. All true and effective leadership depends, Gregory says, upon maintaining a discipline, a lifestyle of contemplation, while responding as best one can to the needs of one's fellows, one's community. As Gregory suggested in his earlier writing on Job, the model for any Christian leader is

Christ himself who in his very active life set aside times and places for prayer. The call to leadership presumes an attempt to integrate contemplation with action, and action with contemplation, resulting in a more effective servant leadership characterized by humility. Returning to the sea imagery, Gregory says that any "unskilled seaman can guide a ship on an even keel in a tranquil sea," in a sea "tossed with tempestuous waves, even a skilled seaman is greatly troubled"; so "the ship of heart" can be "shaken by hurricanes of thought," and founder "on confronting rocks."[58]

The Dialogues of Gregory

In Gregory's second major work as pope, *Dialogues*,[59] the author does precisely what he implicitly advocates in *Pastoral Care* all spiritual leaders should do: meditate on Christ and the lives of the saints, incorporating their qualities and values. Gregory models his writing on the earlier works of Sulpicius Severus, the *Life of St. Martin of Tours* and *Dialogues*.[60] As Severus had done, the pope presents his material in the form of a dialogue, a literary device, as we've seen, quite common among pagan classical authors, such as Plato, Aristotle, and Cicero, as well as patristic writers, including Origen and Augustine. Later Cistercian writers, Bernard of Clairvaux and Aelred of Rievaulx, will do the same. Gregory's dialogue partner is Peter, a deacon, whom Gregory describes in Dialogue One as "my dear son," "a very dear friend to me from his early youth," and "my companion in the study of sacred Scripture."[61] Both Gregory and Peter are portrayed as contemplatives in a world of action: while Gregory primarily teaches, responding to Peter's questions, both men show in their discussion a reflective, contemplative side, despite their obviously being busy men. Peter brings to the text concerns and questions that the reader might reasonably ask, and, as James O'Donnell says, "between his figure and that of the character portrayed as Gregory, we are led to see models of contemplation rather than action, or rather of active figures still rooted in contemplation."[62]

Peter was a real person—not a fictitious character; someone who often acted as Gregory's representative in social, political, and ecclesial conflicts. Judging from the numerous letters sent to Peter, Gregory seems to have trusted him implicitly to carry out his decisions regarding church governance and care for the poor. In one letter, Gregory asks Peter to "see whether there be any worthy of the office of priesthood among the clergy of the churches [in Sicily]," and, "after enquiring into the gravity of their behavior, send them to us, that the flock of each place may not be found destitute for any length of time through the lapse of its pastor....For it is not right that from the deviation of one the Lord's flock should be in danger of wandering abroad among precipices without a shepherd."[63]

In another letter, Gregory tells Peter of his pastoral concern regarding a recent decision that affected married subdeacons in Sicily: "Three years ago the subdeacons of all the churches in Sicily, in accordance with the custom of the Roman Church, were forbidden all conjugal intercourse with their wives. But it appears to me hard and improper that one who has not been accustomed to such continency, and has not previously promised chastity, should be compelled to separate himself from his wife, and thereby (which God forbid) fall into what is worse."[64] Peter was to attend to this matter. On another occasion, he asks Peter to distribute gold, wine, lambs, oil, and hens to the poor when an oratory was to be dedicated to Blessed Mary at a certain monastery.[65] Obviously fond of Peter, Gregory at the same time does not hesitate to challenge him, in one letter, for example, telling Peter to "read all these things over carefully, and put aside all that familiar negligence of yours."[66] In the *Dialogues,* Peter's extensive questions and comments give Gregory the opportunity to explore his own theological views and to provide guidance to his readers.

Book One of the *Dialogues* opens significantly with the scene of Gregory, contemplating his recurrent state of feeling overwhelmed by his responsibilities: "In my grief I retired to a quiet spot congenial to my mood, where I could consider every unpleasant detail of my daily work and review all the causes of my sorrow as they crowded unhindered before my eyes." Peter finds him there, and, as any close friend would do, quickly recognizes Gregory's mood. He asks, "Have you met with some new misfortune? You seem unusually sad." Gregory replies, grateful to have the opportunity to identify the source of his unhappiness, "Peter, this daily sadness of mine is always old and always new; old by its constant presence, new by its continual increase." He speaks of the monastic life, which is no longer his where he had the opportunity for contemplation: "But now all the beauty of that spiritual repose is gone, and the contact with worldly men and their affairs, which is a necessary part of my duties as bishop, has left my soul....I am so distracted with external occupations in my concern for the people that even when my spirit resumes its striving after the interior life it always does so with less vigor." As Gregory continues, he turns, once again, to the metaphor of the sea: "I am tossed about on the waves of a heavy sea, and my soul is like a helpless ship buffeted by raging winds."[67]

Gregory is not a happy camper, and, in recognizing his friend's anguish, Peter invites him to transcend it by telling stories, perhaps intuitively realizing that stories can often nourish the spirit—and the body—more than food. He asks Gregory if he knows of "any person in Italy whose life gives evidence of extraordinary spiritual powers": "This land of ours has undoubtedly produced its virtuous men, but to my knowledge no signs or miracles have been performed by any of them; or, if they have been, they were till now kept in such secrecy that we cannot even tell if they occurred." Peter's ignorance seems to be enough for Gregory to launch into his narratives: "On the contrary, Peter, the day would not be long enough for me to tell you about those saints whose holiness has been well established and whose lives are known to me either from my own observations or from the reports of good, reliable witnesses."[68]

Much of the rest of the *Dialogues* contains the stories of the saints whom Gregory obviously wanted to use to educate his people, and to inspire their own search for holiness. While, from a modern perspective, the stories themselves of visions, prophecies, and miracles seem for the most part quite incredible and somewhat repetitious (Gregory needed a good editor), they do reveal interesting references to Gregory's life and his associates. They also provide a perspective on the beliefs and practices of Christianity prevalent at the time. There are, for example, stories about visions of heaven and hell, near-death experiences, ghosts, even a discussion on the origins of dreams. Despite the disturbing stories associated with a vengeful God and a sense of living in apocalyptic times, there are stories of hope of the presence of angels and loved ones when a holy person is about to die: "It often happens that the saints of heaven appear to the just at the hour of death in order to reassure them, sometimes even accompanied by heavenly music....And, with the vision of the heavenly company before their minds, they die without experiencing any fear or agony." There is even a poignant story about two soul-friends who die together and "live together in one dwelling in heaven."[69]

What is especially interesting, however, is that, for the most part, Gregory's stories are about *living* holy men rather than dead ones, about very ordinary Christians, not all of whom are ordained. Many of these saints too are from rural areas rather than major cities. Considering the cultural and religious views of his time, Gregory is teaching, through his stories, a significant lesson about where God's presence is found and how it is expressed: on the margins, in "ordinary" lives. Also, these "saints" are portrayed as accessible soul friends. As in the writings of Augustine, Jerome, and Cassian, friendship is an important theme in the writings of Gregory, and friendship with the saints a presumed reality. Gregory says how, after our deaths "there is something even more wonderful in store for God's chosen ones. They will recognize not only those whom they knew on earth, but many saintly men and women whom they had never seen before will appear to them as old friends."[70]

One of Gregory's "old friends," surely, was St. Benedict, and in Dialogue Two we find Gregory's finest and most complete life of a saint. Although Benedict's life will be examined more closely in the next chapter, it is enough to say here that the narratives of Benedict (and those too of his sister, Scholastica) clearly describe Gregory's understanding of contemplation itself. Although he often gives the impression of favoring contemplation over the life of action, his depiction of Benedict affirms that it is possible to combine effectively and creatively both action and prayer. Benedict is seen as doing so: seeking solitude and quiet, but also serving and guiding others. In Gregory's stories of Benedict, he shows how another man, like himself, was pulled between a desire for quiet, a life of contemplation, and a very active ministry. Contemplation, Gregory once again affirms, can lead a person to "inner light,"[71] a greater ability to integrate action and contemplation in one's life, ministry, and work.

Gregory's Death and Legacy

Gregory's final days were filled with the physical suffering of gout and the emotional pain of melancholy and depression. In one of his last letters to his friend, Leander, "whom," he says, "I greatly love," he returns to the theme found throughout his writings and letters: his unrequited longing for God, and his supposed failure to incorporate adequately contemplation into his daily life: "For indeed, good man, I am not today the man you knew....My heart has no rest. It lies prostrate in the lowest place, depressed by the weight of its cogitation. Either very rarely or not at all does the wing of contemplation raise it aloft." "Pray for me," he tells Leander, "for I sailed as it were with a prosperous breeze when I led a tranquil life in a monastery, but a storm, rising suddenly with gusty surges, caught me in its commotion, and I lost the prosperity of my voyage; for in loss of rest I suffered shipwreck. Lo, now I am tossed in the waves...."[72]

Gregory died on March 12, 604, at a time when the Lombards were poised to attack Rome once more, and when the city was suffering from a terrible famine. The Romans whom he had served so well, looking for a scapegoat, had turned on him, and converged on the Lateran, wanting to burn his books. Only Gregory's friend, Peter, was able to intervene and stop the madness. Although Christians in the East celebrated him as a saint while those in Spain revered him as a great writer and, in

England, as their "apostle,"[73] in Rome there was almost complete silence until the ninth century concerning him. Only when Pope John VIII commissioned the Roman deacon John to write a life of Gregory from Roman sources was his reputation rescued. As Jeffrey Richards suggests, this lack of enthusiasm for Gregory's leadership locally "can be attributed almost certainly to his elevation of the monks as a rival centre of power to the clerical establishment."[74]

This tragic ecclesiastical rivalry would not have agreed with Gregory. He would have been the first to acknowledge that, no matter what one's station in life, everyone should have a bit of the "monk" within, manifest in developing an interior life, a life of contemplation. Gregory knew this wisdom firsthand, reminding his contemporaries and people today of the importance of acquiring the monastic value of contemplation. As his life shows, contemplation can have a significant effect on any individual's personal transformation or any leader's creativity. Contemplation leads to unity with God and with one's deepest Self. It is quite simply, as Gregory reminds us, about developing the awareness of God's presence in our lives. As such, it can make the difference between merely living life, half-awake, or living joyfully. Or as Gregory says, "To live in God is one form of life; to live simply as created beings is another. The former consists in living a life of happiness; the latter, in merely being alive."[75]

Gregory reminds us also of how much contemplation is intrinsically linked with community. In community is where we can contribute our talents and energy through our service and leadership, and it is there that we can find, through communal liturgies and prayers, rich sources for spiritual nourishment. Contemplation, communing with God, Gregory believed, leads not to isolation, but to community, and to some form of service. Christian leadership is based upon the interconnection of action and contemplation, as service and contemplation complement each other in the pastoral life. While there are more writings available today on leadership, not all recognize what Gregory knew from his own experience: how crucial prayer, reflection, and contemplation are as the foundation of any effective leadership that we do. Contemplation and action are not apart from each other, but are parts of each other. Gregory's feastday is celebrated on September 3 in the West, and March 12 in the East. Contrary to his own evaluation, his life, leadership, and ministry bore much fruit—his success closely tied to his ongoing attempts to unite his longing for contemplation with his desire to serve. Though his life seemed to be frequently tossed by waves and winds as if upon the open sea, Gregory taught by example that if we cannot direct the wind, we can at least adjust the sails, and, by doing so, shine like a candle in the darkness.

CHAPTER NINE

The Glittering Road to Paradise—Benedict and Scholastica

That day two monks, one of them at the monastery, the other some distance away, received the very same revelation. They both saw a magnificent road covered with rich carpeting and glittering with thousands of lights. From his monastery it stretched eastward in a straight line until it reached up into heaven. And there in the brightness stood a man of majestic appearance, who asked them, "Do you know who passed this way?" "No," they replied. "This," he told them, "is the road taken by blessed Benedict, the Lord's beloved, when he went to heaven."

—Gregory the Great, *Dialogue Two*

Monasticism in the early medieval period continued to spread in the West, largely due to the stories of the Italian holy man, Benedict (c. 480–547), as told by Gregory the Great, and to the influence of Benedict's Rule. Augustine, the missionary-monk from Gregory's monastery in Rome, took with him to Canterbury in 596 the Rule of St. Benedict, an important first step to the establishment of Benedictine communities in England. In seventh-century Gaul, at Luxeuil, followers of the Irish missionary, Columban, promoted its extension, often combining their leader's Rule with that of Benedict's. Benedictine monks eventually took over the holy sites of the Celtic saints at Glastonbury and Lindisfarne in England, Iona on Scotland's western edge, and Mont St. Michel in Normandy. Benedict's Rule was known at Jarrow in northern England where Bede did his writings and at Rievaulx Abbey where Aelred wrote his book on spiritual friendship. Today, Benedictine communities sing their daily office in St. Peter's Abbey in Solesmes, France, Glenstal Abbey in Ireland, Melk Abbey in Austria, Montserrat in Spain, St. Gallen and Einsiedeln in Switzerland, and St. John's Abbey in Minnesota—to mention only a few of the hundreds of abbeys worldwide. The Rule of St. Benedict has affected and continues to influence the spirituality of countless Christians. According to William Harmless, it "came to define Western monasticism, its institutional contours and its spiritual temper; and it remains, to this day, a vital constitution for monastic communities around the world."[1]

Much of this influence and popularity has to do with the "adjustment" Benedict himself made to the monastic Rules of his own day which tended to follow the strict asceticism of the desert monks. As F. Homes Dudden, the biographer of Gregory, states: "the monasticism which had been imported into Gaul from the East had not yet become adapted to the conditions of Western life." Asking Western monks to imitate the Eastern ascetics had its dire consequences, Dudden suggests: "Though a few monks and anchorets lived up to the Eastern standard of asceticism, the majority of religious found the ideal too high for them, and, in despair of attaining to it, became careless and lax."[2] The genius of Benedict was his adapting the East's highly ascetic lifestyle to a more moderate one in the West to which many would feel drawn—as well as more capable of sustaining. Rather than seeing monasticism as a form of living martyrdom, Benedictine monks would seek on a daily basis to live out in community gospel values. As one Benedictine scholar says, "Benedictine life is not, and is not intended to be, what is called 'a penitential life.'"[3]

At the same time, intimately acquainted with monastic literature, including the writings of the early Fathers, such as Augustine, Cassian, and Basil, Benedict summarized and transmitted monastic values to a much wider audience in the West. As a result, it is no wonder that while Antony is considered "the first monk," Benedict is called "the patriarch" of *Western* monks. He had, quite simply, as

Justin McCann says, "assimilated the best elements in the teaching of his monastic predecessors and reproduced them all transfused with his own fatherly wisdom and his eminent moderation."[4] This moderation was reflected in Benedict's prescribing for his own monks, unlike many of the desert Christians, sufficient food, ample sleep, and proper clothing.

Unfortunately, other than the Rule of St. Benedict, the only source of information about the life of its author is found in Gregory's *Dialogues*. Thus, while some scholars suggest that Gregory should be considered Benedictine monasticism's "cofounder," others would go so far as to conclude that there might not have been a Benedictine religious order at all except for Gregory and his writings on Benedict.[5] Whatever one's conclusion, the monastic tradition as it evolved during the Middle Ages in the West "is founded principally on two texts," according to Jean Leclercq, "which make of it a 'Benedictine' tradition: the Life of Saint Benedict in Book II of the *Dialogues* of Saint Gregory, and the *Rule for Monks*, traditionally attributed to St. Benedict."[6]

In this chapter, both Life and Rule will be examined to gain a better understanding of the key ideas and character of Benedict, as well as the spirituality that he espoused. Special focus, however, will be on the monastic value of stability. One of three vows that every Benedictine promises, it is considered "fundamental to St. Benedict's concept of the religious life."[7] This vow and the value it represents were affirmed by Benedict precisely at a time when there was so much social chaos and unrest in Europe and in the East; so much social *instability*. This was also about the time that wandering monks, missionaries, and pilgrims, especially those of Irish descent, began to traverse continental Europe. While the latter, in particular, would in the following centuries emphasize wandering as a legitimate form of penitence (what Irish Christians called "white martyrdom," an expression of their religious commitment to spread the gospel), Benedict saw some monks of his own day whom he called "gyrovagues" quite differently, condemning in his Rule those who "spend their entire lives drifting from region to region," never settling down.[8]

In contrast to this type of monk, and to the later dedicated Christian Celts who seemed to be constantly on the move, followers of Benedict chose to remain in one place. According to Cuthbert Butler, "St. Benedict's most special and tangible contribution to the development of monasticism was the introduction of the vow of stability," one of the "most characteristic features of Benedictine monachism."[9] So underrated in contemporary Western society, which values mobility, geographical escape, and change (sometimes it seems "for change's sake" alone), stability provides a foundation that can lead to greater depth and intimacy in relationships with families and friends, and greater personal freedom in the midst of chaos and uncertainty. It is the value of staying where one is planted—or where one plants oneself. Ironically, it seems, it is precisely this monastic value of *staying put* that can help us *travel* along the heavenly road to paradise, as Gregory's story of Benedict reveals, a road "glittering with thousands of lights."[10]

Gregory's Life of St. Benedict

Gregory's Life of Benedict is found in his second Dialogue. It consists of thirty-eight chapters, and describes the main incidents and miracles of the saint's life. Gregory wrote that dialogue less than fifty years after Benedict's death, and states early in it that he is relying upon key "witnesses," four of Benedict's own disciples, to verify some of the stories: Constantine, "the holy man who succeeded Benedict as abbot"; Valentinian, "for many years superior at the monastery of the Lateran" in Rome where Benedict's followers moved after the destruction by the Lombards of their monastery at Monte Cassino between 581–589; Simplicius, Benedict's second successor; and, finally, Honoratus, who was still abbot of the monastery at Subiaco where Benedict first lived at the time Gregory was writing. Born a few years before Benedict's death, Gregory would have been twenty when Constantine, Benedict's successor, died, and in his forties when the Benedictines settled in Rome. Gregory may have known some of the latter monks; he certainly was acquainted with the Rule, and admired it, as well as Benedict himself whom he describes in Dialogue Two's opening lines as "a man of saintly life;...blessed also with God's grace."[11]

Clearly, as R. A. Markus posits, "of all the holy men in sixth-century Italy, Benedict was the one Gregory most admired."[12] To express his love and admiration, Gregory employed the use of the genre of literature that Athanasius used to write of Antony, Sulpicius Severus of Martin of Tours, and Cogitosus of Brigit, the Irish saint. As we learned already, while hagiography does not intend to impart historical truth per se, its symbolic language tells of truths more profound than historical data. Some of this symbolism is revealed in the use of numbers to explain the sacred dimensions or mysterious happenings in a saint's life. Like the hagiographers of St. Brigit, Gregory employs this approach in his account of Benedict. For example, as Terrence Kardong rightly points out, "it can hardly be coincidence, that the number of chapters in the four books of *The Dialogues* is 150, to match the number of psalms in the Psalter," or that "the number of saints described in the first three books is 50, the Jubilee number," or that "there are 38 chapters in Dialogue II, to match the number of saints in Dialogue III." Gregory's obvious message is that Benedict alone is equal to a whole crowd of other saints. This latter symbolic depiction of Benedict's "superior" holiness may also be reflected in the very structure of the entire Gregorian Dialogues. Again, according to Kardong, "Gregory also seems to be using a Byzantine structural pattern as seen in those icons where a great saint is pictured as surrounded by many little saints. Thus Benedict, the towering hero of Dialogue II, is framed in Dialogues I and III by a multitude of lesser Italian saints,"[13] possibly revealing what Gregory had learned about icons and their symbolic meaning while ambassador to Constantinople before he was made pope.

Whatever way meaning was intended to be conveyed, the Benedict that emerges in Gregory's account is a highly mythological figure, similar to Antony, Martin, and others, as well as those heroes found in scripture itself. Peter, Gregory's dialogue partner in his writing on Benedict, relates to these scriptural allusions directly following a story about a raven that takes a poisoned loaf of bread from the holy man and flies away with it in its beak:

> This whole account is really amazing. The water streaming from the rock reminds me of Moses, and the iron blade that rose from the bottom of the lake, of Eliseus. The walking on water recalls St. Peter, the obedience of the raven, Elias, and the grief at the death of an enemy, David.

Peter's conclusion: "This man must have been filled with the spirit of all the just."[14]

Although, as Bernard McGinn acknowledges, "we know so little about the historical Benedict,"[15] at the same time we can find within the stories some clear insights into the type of person he was and the spiritual leadership he provided. By analyzing Gregory's stories, we will discover, in the process, how much Gregory himself relied to a great degree upon earlier hagiographies to introduce his readers to the man. Like all hagiographers, however, Gregory's primary intent was to show how Benedict himself "possessed the spirit of one man only, the Saviour, who fills the hearts of the faithful."[16]

Birth and Early Life

Benedict was born of "distinguished" parents, according to Gregory, in the district of Nursia, some seventy-five miles north of Rome, probably about 480. Although Gregory says nothing about Benedict's mother and father, we discover later in his narrative that he had a sister, Scholastica, who "had been consecrated to God in early childhood."[17] While Gregory tells us little, tradition has it that they were twins, which may be true, since they seem to have been exceptionally close, as we will see.[18] However, the main focus of Gregory's *Dialogues* is on Benedict who "even in boyhood... showed mature understanding" and "strength of character far beyond his years."[19] Like Jerome, Benedict moved to Rome probably in early adolescence to gain a classical education. This move on his part is the first of only four major moves that Benedict makes in his entire life: from parental home to Rome; from Rome to Subiaco (after a short stay in a village called Affile); from Subiaco to a monastery which he abruptly leaves for good reason, returning to Subiaco once more; and, finally, to Monte Cassino, the monastery outside of Rome where he ministered and eventually died. Through all this, whether intentionally or not, Gregory seems to provide us with the suggestion that some degree of stability characterized Benedict's life and that *constant* movement is not a prerequisite for the development of holiness and wisdom. In fact, it may even be detrimental.

As a student in Rome, however, Benedict seems to quickly recognize the dangers inherent in acquiring a classical education, especially "when he saw," Gregory says, "many of his fellow students falling headlong into vice." This awareness of spiritual danger and, perhaps most of all, of his own strong "desire to please God alone" contributed to Benedict's giving up home and inheritance, and resolving to embrace the ascetic life. Accompanied only by an older woman, described by Gregory as his "nurse" who loved him dearly, Benedict "abandoned his studies to go into solitude."[20]

This is where we can begin to see similarities between Benedict's story and those of the desert father Antony of which Gregory was obviously acquainted. Like Antony, we will see Benedict increasingly seeking places of solitude; like Antony and Jerome, he too will be tempted by women or the memory of them; again, as in the case of Antony, Benedict will be approached by crowds of people seeking his guidance and help as a spiritual mentor. There will, however, be significant differences in Benedict's stories. Unlike Antony, Benedict eventually will decide on a communal life rather than a solitary one, and, again, unlike Antony, will reject the strict ascetic lifestyle for a more moderate one. But, first, the similarities.

As Benedict and his nurse-companion travel through Affile, a little hill town about thirty-five miles outside of Rome, a number of holy men invited them to stay, giving them lodging near the village church. The first of Benedict's miracles occurs here when the nurse accidentally breaks a tray for cleaning wheat. Benedict prays over it, and its two pieces are joined together again. This simple, certainly minor "miracle" by any standards, causes quite a stir. News of the miracle spreads, and people rush to see Benedict, so much so, that, in reaction to this unsought publicity, "he stole away secretly from his nurse and fled to a lonely wilderness…called Subiaco."[21] Here, Benedict resides for three years in a narrow cave, a highly symbolic place where saints from Jerome in Bethlehem to Kevin in Glendalough to Ignatius of Loyola in Manresa were surely reminded by their surroundings of both womb and tomb, the mystery of their birth and origins, and of their ever-approaching death. Subiaco is an important place for Benedict where he comes to know more about his true Self. He does so, Gregory implies, precisely by staying put, and confronting his demons one at a time.

Subiaco: Confronting Demons

According to Gregory, Benedict's stay at Subiaco was not without interruptions. Romanus, a monk from a nearby monastery, would visit him occasionally, while a priest came to share with him an Easter meal. Even some nearby shepherds wanted to speak to him, recognizing this man, wearing the rough skins of wild animals, as a true "servant of God." As was true of Antony, "his name became known to all the people in that locality and great numbers visited his cave, supplying him with the food he needed and receiving from his lips in return spiritual food for their souls." At the same time, when alone in his cave at Subiaco, Benedict was besieged by the demonic—as was true of Jesus in the desert before him and Antony in the tombs as well. After some minor encounters, the first major temptation comes to Antony in the form of a blackbird that one day began to flutter in his face. So close was the bird, it is said, that Benedict could have captured it with his hands, but instead he simply made the sign of the cross, and the bird flew away. As soon as it left, however, Benedict was seized by "an unusually violent temptation" in which the memory of a woman he had once seen seized him, his emotions nearly carrying him away. "Almost overcome by the struggle," Gregory writes, "he was on the point of abandoning the lonely wilderness, when suddenly with the help of God's grace he came to himself."[22]

This coming "to himself," of course, presumes that there is a Self to which to come. *To be himself,* to follow his true calling, Benedict decided *not* to follow the temptation to abandon his chosen place. He chooses to remain there instead, following the virtue, the value that he will eventually affirm as of such significance to his monks in his Rule: that of *stabilitas,* of stability. To maintain that stance, however, Benedict employs an ascetic practice followed by other early monks, especially those in the desert regions: the practice of disciplining one's body or, as Gregory puts it, of conquering pleasure with pain. Here, Gregory tells us, Benedict, in response to the temptation, throws off his clothes, and rolls naked in a thick patch of briers and nettles until his whole body is in pain and covered with blood: "Before long, the pain that was burning his whole body had put out the fires of evil in his heart. It was by exchanging these two fires that he gained the victory over sin. So complete was his triumph that from then on, as he later told his disciples, he never experienced another temptation of this kind."[23] This scene reminds the reader of the one when, after years of confronting demons in solitude, Antony comes forth, transformed, from the tombs: a man who is at-one with himself and with God, experiencing *apatheia,* peace, and joy.

According to Gregory, Benedict has conquered his erotic desires: temptations associated with lust or "concupiscence." Normally, Gregory tells his dialogue companion, Peter, the lessening of one's erotic desires does not occur until one reaches the age of fifty, the time of becoming an elder. While Jerome, for one, would probably disagree with the pope's assessment that any male, no matter what his age, could achieve total *apatheia,* clearly at this point in his life Benedict himself is still only a young man. Nonetheless, Gregory says, "with the passing of this temptation, Benedict's soul, like a field cleared of briers, soon yielded a rich harvest of virtues." Because of this transformation (what Cassian would associate with purity of heart and people recovering from any form of addiction with surrender), Benedict was now prepared to be a more effective spiritual guide. As Gregory says, "for now that he was free from these temptations he was ready to instruct others in the practice of virtue."[24] Word of his holiness, of course, spreads, and one day an entire monastic community approaches Benedict, pleading that he become their abbot after their own abbot had died. Benedict's positive response to them, following some time of careful discernment, leads him to another stage of his life-journey to self-knowledge on the road to paradise.

Vicovaro and Benedict's Search for His True Self

Benedict's journey to the monastic community at Vicovaro,[25] a village about twenty miles down the Anio from Subiaco, is his third major move—a "major" move not necessarily in terms of the length of time spent there, but in the significant insights about his true self that he would gain by living with these recalcitrant monks. When he accepted their invitation, he did not do so immediately; "for some time," Gregory says, Benedict tried to discourage them, refusing their request. Perhaps his intuition was warning him to avoid this situation; perhaps he realized on some level that he and they would not be compatible. Still, they persisted, and he finally agreed. This is where Benedict's life diverges from Antony's; this is when his true Self leads him away from the solitary life to his first experiences with the communal. It is not a good experience, but it is one that teaches him, by its sheer negativity, what a *positive* experience of monastery might be, including what sort of Rule would be needed to guarantee that monastic life be more positive.

As Gregory tells the story, "At the monastery Benedict watched carefully over the religious spirit of his monks and would not tolerate any of their previous disobedience." Obedience, as we will see, is extremely important to Benedict, one of the three vows he later requires for every *Benedictine* monk. The monks at Vicovaro, however, "clashed with the standards he upheld, and in their resentment they started to reproach themselves for choosing him as abbot." They turned sullen, and then, even worse, murderous, plotting to poison Benedict's wine! Here Gregory demonstrates Benedict's miraculous powers once more, having him make a sign of the cross over the poisoned wine that was offered to him. As a result of his blessing, the pitcher shatters immediately. Benedict's response is characteristic of him; he tells the monks, "May almighty God have mercy on you," and then, after some reflection, decides to return "to the wilderness he loved, to live alone with himself in the presence of his heavenly Father."[26]

This story provides Peter in Gregory's Dialogue the opportunity to ask what the pope meant by saying "to live with himself." Gregory elaborates, and, in so doing, explains to his protégé (and the reader) the importance of discerning whether a person should stay in one place or leave it in order to preserve one's physical, psychological, emotional, and even *spiritual* health. While the Benedictine value of stability may be very much worth affirming, as Benedict's Rule would later advocate, Gregory's stories show that it does not eliminate the need for ongoing discernment. As he says:

> These monks had an outlook on religious life entirely unlike Benedict's own....Now, if he had tried to force them to remain under his rule, he might have forfeited his own fervor and peace of soul and even turned his eyes from the light of contemplation. Their persistent daily faults would have left him almost too weary to look to his own needs, and he would perhaps have forsaken himself without finding them.

And Gregory adds:

> For, whenever anxieties carry us out of ourselves unduly, we are no longer with ourselves even though we still remain what we are. We are too distracted with other matters to give an attention whatever to ourselves.

Here Gregory is alluding to decisions every person must make regarding his or her associates, and perhaps the environment in which one works. Sometimes, as Benedict did, a person may have to choose between staying put (a decision that may well contribute to one's self-destruction) or to moving on in order to defend and protect one's Self. According to Gregory, Benedict "can be said to have lived 'with himself' because at all times he kept such close watch over his life and actions. By searching continually into his own soul he always beheld himself in the presence of his Creator"[27]—and made decisions accordingly, in that light.

Thus, implicit in his story, is the lesson that while stability is a value worth affirming, a person must always also take into account her or his personal health and integrity. Having a Self presumes *self*-care, as well as having the courage to change when one must. Contemplation, of course, in all of this discernment process is essential. As Gregory advises Peter:

> There are two ways in which we can be carried out of ourselves, Peter. Either we fall below ourselves through sins of thought or we are lifted above ourselves by the grace of contemplation.

Contemplation allows a person to ask pertinent questions, and seek direction in one's search for suitable answers. Here Gregory has Peter asking him in Dialogue Two whether it was right for Benedict "to forsake this community [at Vicovaro], once he had taken it under his care?" Gregory responds:

> In my opinion, Peter, a superior ought to bear patiently with a community of evil men as long as it has some devout members who can benefit from his presence. When none of the members is devout enough to give any promise of good results, his efforts to help such a community will prove to be a serious mistake, especially if there are opportunities nearby to work more fruitfully for God. Was there anyone the holy man could have hoped to protect by saying where he was, after he saw that they were all united against him?

Gregory concludes with a telling principle that has implications for many in their personal and professional lives:

> In this matter we cannot afford to overlook the attitude of the saints. When they find their work producing no results in one place, they move on to another where it can do some good.[28]

Finding and protecting one's true Self involves the sometimes extremely painful process of asking whether it is right to stay put or to move on.

Return to Subiaco, and Eventual Move to Monte Cassino

As we know, Benedict made the decision to move on; that is, to return to his former place of serenity and quiet at Subiaco. But, as is common for spiritual leaders, we learn that his "influence spread over the surrounding countryside…[and] a great number of men gathered round him to devote themselves to God's service." In response to these numbers, Benedict established twelve monasteries, while remaining within his own hermitage, surrounded by a few monks. Scholars believe that Benedict stayed at Subiaco for about thirty years, teaching sons of noblemen who left them with him "to be schooled in the service of God."[29] (This latter phrase written by Gregory is intriguing, for in Benedict's Rule, the monastery itself is portrayed as a "school of service," and the Rule's prologue begins with the evocative words, associated with teaching, "Listen carefully, my son, to the master's instruction, and attend to them with the ear of your heart.")[30] Benedict also continued to act as a spiritual mentor to the monks in the other monasteries he had established, including helping one who was bothered, as Antony had been in the desert, by a black youth who kept "pulling at the edge of his habit."[31]

Around 529 CE, at about the age of fifty, Benedict left Subiaco for Monte Cassino, located about eighty miles south of

Rome. This would be his fourth and final major move. It was a significant time for him in his becoming an elder, as we know it was for Gregory when he turned fifty and became pope. At their age, both men must have realized the added responsibility of sharing the wisdom with others that they had gained over a lifetime. At the same time, Benedict's decision to move, according to Gregory, was precipitated by the antagonism of a jealous priest named Florentius who did everything he could to destroy Benedict, even sending a raven with a poisoned loaf of bread to kill the holy man. This story of the raven that flew away with the loaf and deposited it in a distant place, far from the holy man, is the origin of the countless statues and pictures showing Benedict with a black bird, traditionally a harbinger of death, yet in this instance more symbolic of what Carl Jung would equate with wisdom and angelic protection.[32] When Florentius persisted by sending seven "depraved women" into Benedict's monastic garden, Benedict finally relents, and, out of concern for his younger monks, decides to find, Gregory says, "a new home."[33]

The new home that Benedict and his monks built was located on the "towering mountain" near the fortified town of Cassino; hence the name, Monte [Mount] Cassino. On its summit stood an ancient pagan temple dedicated to Apollo, to whom worshippers offered sacrifices in "groves dedicated to various demons." This is where Benedict's stories become similar to those of St. Martin of Tours who had gone about destroying pagan temples in his own locale.[34] In this case, it is Benedict and his monks who destroy the idol, overturn the altar, and cut down the trees in the surrounding sacred groves. As if to establish clearly Benedict's connection with St. Martin, Gregory states that "Then he [Benedict] turned the temple of Apollo into a chapel dedicated to St. Martin," and "gradually the people of the countryside were won over to the true faith by his zealous preaching."[35]

The monastery that was built on Monte Cassino was "destined," Cuthbert Butler writes, "to be the one monastery before all others associated with St. Benedict's name, ever after looked on as the center of Benedictine life and spirit, the Holy Mount of the Benedictines, whence flowed over Europe streams of religion and civilization and culture."[36] At this point in Benedict's life Gregory shows him to have miraculous powers, as Martin had (and, of course, Jesus before him), for healing the sick and lepers, exorcising numerous demons, prophesying, reconciling, raising the dead. Gregory adds more intriguing stories of Benedict confronting a dragon, putting to rest the ghosts of two dead nuns, even helping a layman in debt who was "tormented by a creditor"! Benedict was able to do all these things, Gregory explains to Peter, precisely because "the man who unites himself to the Lord becomes one spirit with him..., for all who follow the Lord wholeheartedly are living in spiritual union with Him." Not only his miracles revealed this union of Benedict's spirit with God's, but "there was a trace of the marvelous in nearly everything he said, Peter, and his words never failed to take effect because his heart was fixed in God."[37] Even so, Gregory implies, Benedict was far from perfect. At times he seems to have been a bit overly concerned, if not obsessive, about order in his life, and about his need to have or maintain control—a character trait that perhaps only a sister could remedy.

Scholastica, Beloved Sister

Columba Stewart says that Gregory's story of Benedict and Scholastica "is perhaps the most famous in the *Dialogues*."[38] It is told toward the end of Dialogue Two, and provides the only reference to Scholastica that we have. Gregory introduces her by telling his readers that Benedict's sister "used to visit with him once a year." On each of these occasions, Benedict would go down to meet her in a house that belonged to the monastery, located near the monastery's entrance at Monte Cassino. On this particular visit, Gregory says, Benedict "joined her with a few of his disciples and they spent the whole day singing God's praises and conversing about the spiritual life." The scene of brother and sister, together, discussing spiritual matters is reminiscent of Augustine's and Monica's conversation at Ostia, shortly before the latter's death. Gregory's story, however, has a different twist, for he tells how the siblings kept talking after darkness had set in and after sharing a meal together. By this time, it was "quite late," when Scholastica said to Benedict, "Please, do not leave me tonight, brother. Let us keep talking about the joys of heaven till morning."[39]

Benedict's response reveals a great deal about his character, and Scholastica's, about hers. "What are you saying, sister?" he replies. "You know I cannot stay away from the monastery." Here, as Gregory portrays him, Benedict is shown to be more concerned about following rules than responding to the deep, heart-felt wishes of his sister. To heighten the tension of the moment, Gregory describes Scholastica's response while alluding to the natural elements:

> The sky was so clear at the time that there was not a cloud in sight. At her brother's refusal, Scholastica folded her hands on the table and rested her head upon them in earnest prayer. When she looked up again, there was a sudden burst of lightning and thunder, accompanied by such a downpour that Benedict and his companions were unable to set a foot outside the door. By shedding a flood of tears while she prayed, this holy nun had darkened the cloudless sky with a heavy rain. The storm began as soon as her prayer was over. In fact, the two coincided so closely that the thunder was already resounding as she raised her head from the table. The very instant she ended her prayer the rain poured down.[40]

At this point in the story, Gregory, a good storyteller, is revealing the effectiveness of Scholastica's prayers, and how not only God, but nature as well, listens to her. Without realizing it, perhaps, Gregory's depiction of Benedict's sister links her with the powers of a shaman, the spiritual leader and healer of ancient tribes who often has the ability to make rain.[41] Rain itself is a powerful symbol of renewal, and rain, thunder, and lightning are associated with the divine, "spiritual influences of heaven descending upon earth."[42]

Gregory's story shows that God definitely takes the side of Scholastica. Realizing this, Benedict still can't resist complaining, "God forgive you, sister! What have you done?" Scholastic simply responds, "When I appealed to you, you would not listen to me. So I turned to my God and He heard my prayer." Overwhelmed with the evidence that such was the case, Benedict finally accepts the truth of her statement. According to Gregory, "he had no choice now but to stay, in spite of his unwillingness." As a result, brother and sister "spent the entire night together and both of them derived great profit from the holy thoughts they exchanged about the interior life."[43]

The entire story of the two siblings' conflict and its resolution, of course, contains one of the most significant lessons Gregory wants to impart: the importance of love in our relationships with one another, of love above everything else. So it was that Benedict's desire to return to his monastery, Gregory says, "was thwarted by a miracle almighty God performed in answer to a woman's prayer." And he adds, "We need not be surprised that in this instance she proved mightier than her brother; she had been looking forward so long to this visit. Do we not read in St. John that God is love? Surely it is no more than right that her influence was greater than his, since hers was the greater love."[44]

Through her persistence, Scholastica reminded Benedict and all of Gregory's readers of this rule of love that overrides every other rule, of "the superiority of *agape* over law."[45] She taught Benedict at a time when he may have just finished writing his own Rule that while order is important when dealing with groups of people or communities, love is even more so. That conviction, as we shall see, is clearly reflected in the Benedictine Rule, which was eventually promulgated.

Scholastica's and Benedict's Deaths

The next morning, following their meeting, Scholastica returned to her convent, located at Plumbariola, about three miles from the foot of Monte Cassino.[46] Three days later, according to Gregory, she died, revealing perhaps why she had been so insistent that her brother stay with her for what would be their last time together (in this life, at least). On the day of her death, Benedict, while standing in his room, actually sees her soul leave her body and enter "the court of heaven in the form of a dove." Filled with joy "at her eternal glory," he gives thanks to God, and sends some of his monastic brothers to bring her body back to the monastery and bury it in the tomb he had prepared for himself. "The bodies of these two were now to share a common resting place," Gregory says, "just as in life their souls had always been one in God."[47] This burial of "twins" or "doubles" in a common tomb seems to have been a popular practice in ancient and medieval times; in Greek mythology, for example, Patroclus and Achilles are said to have shared a common grave, as did Sts. Bernard of Clairvaux and Malachy of Ireland centuries later. This was also the case of two brothers, Vincent and Theo van Gogh, whose remains today lie next to each other in a cemetery in Auvers, France, outside of Paris. Obviously, Benedict's desire to share his grave with his sister shows how much he thought of her as his double or twin.

Benedict himself was soon to join Scholastica. Shortly after her death and his own mystical experience in which "the whole world was gathered up before his eyes in what appeared to be a single ray of light" (related in the preceding chapter on Gregory), Benedict "breathed his last," surrounded by his monastic colleagues. On the same day, according to Gregory, two monks saw a "magnificent road covered with rich carpeting and glittering with thousands of lights," stretching from his monastery, reaching up to heaven. In the brightness, they noticed a mysterious man of "majestic appearance" who told them that "this is the road taken by blessed Benedict, the Lord's beloved, when he went to heaven." With such a vision affirming Benedict's holiness, as well as the miracles that followed his burial, Gregory ends his account of the Italian saint, but not without stating his own conviction about Benedict's greatness:

> There is one more point, however, I want to call to your attention. With all the renown he [Benedict] gained by his numerous miracles, the holy man was no less outstanding for the wisdom of his teaching. He wrote a Rule for Monks that is remarkable for its discretion and its clarity of language. Anyone who wishes to know more about his life and character can discover in his Rule exactly what he was like as abbot, for his life could not have differed from his teaching.[48]

With this reference to Benedict's Rule, Gregory invites us to turn directly to it for further understanding not only of Benedict's character, but especially of the monastic value of stability.

Benedict's Rule

Between 400–700 CE, some thirty "Rules of Life" appeared in Western Christianity, primarily composed in Italy and Gaul, but also Spain and Ireland. The Rule of St. Benedict, however, was "decisive," Bernard McGinn says, "for the future of monasticism and indirectly for western mysticism as well." Benedict's Rule, he posits, "is the single most important document in the history of western monasticism, and arguably the most significant text from the whole late antique period."[49] Considering its significance, it is all the more important to remember that Benedict's Rule was not written by a priest or bishop, but by a layman dedicated to the search for God—a layman who, as his Rule shows, was somewhat suspicious of the ordained, associating them with pride and presumption[50]—as many desert Christians had before him. Benedict's own extensive knowledge of the monastic tradition as well as the writings of the Fathers certainly confirms that theological competence and organizational skills—in any age—are not limited to the ordained.

Benedict's Rule was probably begun at Subiaco, but finished at Monte Cassino, around 530–540, when Benedict would have been in his fifties. Certainly it was a Rule that was lived before it was codified. Still, Benedict seems to have made extensive use of an earlier *Rule of the Master*,[51] probably written in Italy a few decades before. Benedict shortened it dramatically, however (i.e., the *Rule of the Master* is three times longer than Benedict's), and added his own interpretation and particular emphases. As is clear from his references, Benedict also made use of a wide variety of sources, primarily Judeo-Christian Scriptures,[52] of course, but also the writings of the early Fathers of the Church, especially Augustine, Jerome, Cassian, and Basil from whom he borrowed freely, while recommending their works be read by all of his monks. As is clear from the text, Benedict knew the early monastic literature well.

The Rule itself is a short document of some nine thousand words in length, at least a thousand of which are merely the numbers of psalms to be said or other purely liturgical instructions concerning the singing of the Divine Office, what Benedict refers to as the *Opus Dei*, the "Work of God." In addition to these instructions, the Rule is, above all, a *spiritual guide*, offering short, concrete, practical principles and precepts for his followers to live together as a genuine community, showing mutual respect. As stated in chapter 72, the second to the last of the Rule:

> This, then, is the good zeal which monks must foster with fervent love: "They should each try to be the first to show respect to the other" [Rom 12:10], supporting with the greatest patience one another's weaknesses of body or behavior, and earnestly competing in obedience to one another. No one is to pursue what he judges better for himself, but instead, what he judges better for someone else. To their fellow monks they show the pure love of brothers; to God, loving fear; to their abbot, unfeigned and humble love. Let them prefer nothing whatever to Christ, and may he bring us all together to everlasting life.[53]

Considering the ideal of love that the Rule emphasizes, one might readily agree with the interpretation David Knowles first suggested in the twentieth century, followed by numerous other more recent writers, that the Rule can apply to any family or community: "Indeed, we should not be far wrong in considering the Rule simply as a guide to the human relationships of a Christian family, where all are to be patient of the weaknesses of the body and character of others, where mercy is to take precedence of justice, where every kind of inconsiderate word and action is to be avoided, and where all are to be more concerned with another's interests than with their own."[54]

Benedict's Rule reflects the wisdom of a man well acquainted with human foibles when he, for example, presumes that there will be late arrivals for prayer and for meals, that complaints will be made about the quality of clothing, that when arising from sleep, everyone should "quietly encourage each other, for the sleepy like to make excuses."[55] At the same time he is not afraid of holding up, even to the most recalcitrant, certain ideals, all of them personified in Christ. As Owen Chadwick says, Benedict "knows human nature, its weaknesses as well as its potentialities."[56] Monastic leaders, in particular, are to follow Christ, imitating "the loving example of the Good Shepherd," and showing "every care and concern for the sick, children, guests and the poor." Not only monastic leaders have this responsibility, but every monk "should serve one another...in love," by seeing Christ in everyone, most especially, as St. Martin's famous story of the beggar revealed, in the stranger; for Benedictines, the stranger who comes as guest to the monastery: "All guests who present themselves are to be welcomed as Christ, for he himself will say: 'I was a stranger and you welcomed me' [Matt 25:35]. Proper honor must be shown 'to all, especially to those who share our faith' [Gal 6:10] and to pilgrims."[57]

Major Sections of the Rule

With love and hospitality as significant foundation stones, Benedict's Rule consists of four major parts. The first includes a Prologue, inviting the individual Christian to follow the monastic life, as well as seven initial chapters, outlining primary aspects of Benedictine spirituality, including an overall plan for living, entitled "Tools for Good Works" (chapter 4), on obedience (chapter 5), on "restraint of speech" (chapter 6), and on humility (chapter 7). As if having the Beloved Disciple, John, in mind, or the understanding Cassian had of the desert elders, Benedict opens his Rule with the moving words, "Listen carefully, my son, to the master's instructions, and attend to them with the ear of the heart. This is advice from a father who loves you; welcome it, and faithfully put it into practice."[58] Throughout the rest of the Rule, *listening* is one of the primary disciplines that every monk is called to learn to practice, and constitutes Benedict's primary understanding of "obedience" itself.

In the second major section, chapters 8–20, specific instructions are given regarding the structure and content of the communal prayer, the Divine Office, which consists of eight canonical hours sung throughout the day and night: matins, lauds, prime, terce, sext, none, vespers, and compline. Benedict believed that this "Work of God" was essential to Benedictine life. According to Cuthbert Butler, this emphasis in his Rule upon the Divine Office "must be counted among the innovations he made in the monastic life, for it was not part of the inheritance he received from the earlier monasticism."[59] This second section ends with the profound faith statement that "the divine presence is everywhere," and the suggestion that private prayer itself should be "short and pure, unless perhaps it is prolonged under the inspiration of divine grace."[60]

The third major section of the Rule, chapters 21–67, outlines the structures and practices of the common life. This section covers a wide variety of elements in monastic living, including responsibilities of abbot, deans, cellarer, and kitchen servers, as well as directions for sleeping arrangements, reproving and educating the young, private ownership (none was tolerated), silence, proper diet, and manual labor. Perhaps the most enduring aspect of this section has to do with the Rule's affirmation of work. Contrary to Late Antiquity's Greek and Roman cultures, manual labor is seen by Benedict as extremely worthwhile, contributing to one's colleagues' well-being and one's own salvation. "The brothers should serve one another," Benedict says in chapter 35. "Consequently, no one will be excused from kitchen service unless he is sick or engaged in some important business of the monastery, for such service increases reward and fosters love." In chapter 48, he states, "Idleness is the enemy of the soul. Therefore, the brothers should have specified periods for manual labor as well as for prayerful reading....When they live by the labor of their hands, as our fathers and the apostles did, then they are really monks."[61]

Section four of the Rule is made up of the last six chapters (68–73), none of which appears in the *Rule of the Master*. With its emphasis on moderation, common sense, mutual obedience, and humility (i.e., the Rule itself is referred to as "this little rule that we have written for beginners"),[62] many Benedictines see this last section as providing the most direct access to Benedict's own experience of monastic living and to his own theology and spirituality. At the same time, with its emphasis on love (chapter 72, quoted above, is called Benedict's "hymn of love"),[63] this is where the influence of Scholastica upon Benedict may well be the most evident.

Overall, Benedict's Rule describes a monasticism whose daily schedule is fairly circumscribed, divided between three primary actions: prayer (the Divine Office), work, and *lectio divina* (some form of sacred reading). It is a communal life, under the leadership of an abbot, with the monastery itself significantly described as a "school for the Lord's service."[64] The leader of each community, the abbot, then, is meant to be primarily a teacher, an exemplar, a spiritual guide; above all, a pastoral leader who cares for each monk with the same attribute of adaptability that Gregory the Great associates with leadership in his book, *Pastoral Care*. As Benedict's Rule explicitly states, "In his teaching, the abbot should always...vary with circumstances, threatening and coaxing by turns, stern as a task master, devoted and tender as only a father can be. With the undisciplined and restless, he will use firm argument; with the obedient and docile and patient, he will appeal for greater virtue; but as for the negligent and disdainful, we charge him to use reproof and rebuke....He must so accommodate and adapt himself to each one's character and intelligence that he will not only keep the flock entrusted to his care from dwindling, but will rejoice in the increase of a good flock....He should keep in mind that he has undertaken the care of souls for whom he must give an account."[65]

Under the abbot's leadership, a spirituality of simple, ordinary living emerges. As Cuthbert Butler suggests, looking back to the first Benedictines, "St. Benedict's own monks": "A simple life it was, made up of a round of simple duties....And so they lived together their common life, serving God by the daily round of duties in choir, in farm and garden, in kitchen and bakehouse and workshop—chanting, praying, working, reading, meditating—their life-work and their life-interests being concentrated as far as possible within the precincts of the monastery or its immediate vicinity." It was a life that offered stability, precisely because it was based upon stability, a monastic value reflecting, some would say, Benedict's own personality. One of the three vows every Benedictine makes, the introduction of stability, according to Butler, "was St. Benedict's most important and characteristic contribution to the course of Western monachism," helping "every Benedictine monastery...to be a home."[66]

Stability in Benedict's Rule

As is clear from the first chapter of Benedict's Rule, he affirmed the two forms of monasticism that he had lived at Subiaco and Monte Cassino, the anchorite and cenobite, while condemning two others evidently popular in his time: those whom he called "sarabaites" (monks who "with no experience to guide them, no rule to try them" do "whatever strikes their fancy"), and "gyrovagues" (those who "never settle down, and are slaves to their own wills and gross appetites").[67] Numerous scholars, including David Knowles, believe that Benedict's endorsement of stability as a vow was not only a reaction to those monks whose behavior he found abhorrent, but also a reflection of his own formation years and his Roman character. Benedict was, above all, Knowles says, a Roman, "one of the last of the Romans, more truly Roman in spirit than even Gregory the Great." The "noblest Romans," according to Knowles, were known for such qualities as strength, moderation, and stability, and "it is noteworthy that in such a short document as the Rule the word *gravitas* (dignity) occurs five times, *rationabilis* (reasonable) and its adverb five times, *imperium* (authority) six times, *stabilis* and *stabilitas* (steadfast, stability) six times, and *mensura* and *mensurate* (measure, moderation) ten times." No wonder, then, that "this sense of strong government, of stability and yet of moderation, was precisely the quality most needed in one who was to hand down the wisdom of the desert to a new, adolescent, uncultivated age of shifting landmarks and people."[68] Naturally, Benedict would incorporate stability itself as a primary value and vow into his understanding of monastic life.

The origin of the English term "stability" is the Latin word *stabilitas,* derived from the Latin infinitive *"stare"*: to stand, to be still, to be in and know one's place. As such, specific use of the term is found scattered throughout the Rule. In chapter 4, on "The Tools for Good Works," we have its first mention, with the statement that "the workshop where we are to toil faithfully at all these tasks is the enclosure of the monastery and stability in the community." In chapter 58, under the title, "The Procedure for Receiving Brothers," it is referred to twice: the first time, in reference to how a new member can be received into the community for a longer period than an initial two months if he is found acceptable by an elder monk and "if he promises perseverance in his stability." The second time it is mentioned is in the context of listing all three Benedictine vows when, following a year's observation, the novice, if proven worthy, "comes before the whole community in the oratory and promises stability, fidelity to monastic life, and obedience." In chapter 60, on "The Admission of Priests to the Monastery," the Rule states that "any clerics who...wish to join the community" can do so, "but only if they, too, promise to keep the rule and observe stability." And, finally, in chapter 61, on "The Reception of Visiting Monks," the Rule states: "If after a while he wishes to remain and bind himself to stability, he should not be refused this wish, especially as there was time enough, while he was a guest, to judge his character."[69]

Although these few references to stability do not adequately describe Benedict's understanding of it, by making it a requirement for acceptance into his communities by the novice, the cleric, and visiting monk, he quite obviously sees it as central to Benedictine life, not only essential for communities, but for each individual member. Despite Benedict's lack of explanation, numerous scholars throughout the centuries have attempted to explain what stability means to Benedictines as they have lived according to the Rule. Not everyone agrees with every interpretation, but most scholars today maintain that there are three primary understandings of stability implied in the Rule: (1) *stabilitas loci:* a commitment to stay in a specific geographic place where a monastery is located; (2) *stabilitas communitate:* a commitment to stay with a particular community, with all of its human gifts and foibles, where a monk has made profession; and (3) *stabilitas cordis:* an attitude and disposition of the heart.[70]

Stability of Place

The first understanding of stability that related to geographical location or sense of place recognizes the monastic value of staying put, affirmed by the desert Christians in one of their wisdom sayings: "Sit in your cell, and it will teach you everything."[71] While the desert Christians often spoke of the necessity of remaining in one place to counteract the dreaded demon of accidie who, according to the desert writer, Evagrius Ponticus, "instills in the heart of the monk a hatred for the place, a hatred for his very life itself...,"[72] Benedict was "the first to bind a monk to his monastery by an express vow of stability,"[73] affirming the essential need of staying put as a way to self-knowledge and Christian holiness. Stability is perceived as an antidote to the restlessness of mind and heart in which a person constantly searches for new experiences, new relationships, and new geographical locations to escape difficulties or to solve problems by avoiding them. This unceasing search for the new and extravagant, of course, can too often make life and relationships superficial, and any intimacy between people extremely fragile. Stability, however, can help a person stand still and listen, *truly listen,* as the Rule encourages one to do. It is similar to what Quakers call "centering down" and Buddhists, "mindfulness": the discipline of paying attention to "what is going on in the present moment," which can give rise "to insight, awakening, and love." As the Buddhist monk Thich Nhat Hanh says, "When we practice this exercise, it takes us directly to a place of peace and stability, to the most calm and stable place we can go."[74]

In contrast to society today in which many voices tell us to keep moving, to change houses or partners or jobs, to keep searching for the new, the amazing, and at times the bizarre, Benedict cautions us against the trend of making rootlessness a virtue. Rather, he counsels us to be mindful of the moment, to stay rooted in the present, perhaps above all to learn to wait patiently. Stability of place, he advises, is crucial to anyone's spirituality, a belief affirmed by the contemporary writer Scott Sanders when he says: "I cannot have a spiritual center without having a geographical one; I cannot live a grounded life without being grounded in a *place.*"[75]

Granted, being rooted in a place does not mean that one *always* stays there. After all, Benedict, as portrayed by Gregory, did move, however infrequently, when he judged it necessary, and Benedictines today are frequently given permission to spend time away from their primary monastery for study, pastoral work, or teaching. Some even are sent to start new houses, new monasteries, when it seems appropriate. But always, with those decisions to be away for a while or to move, there is a discernment process that includes, as it did for Benedict, prayers to God and consultation with others.

Stability of Community

For Benedictines, commitment to place is related directly to committing oneself to a specific community, a particular family of monks. Stability in this sense involves embracing one family, one community; opening oneself to the conflicts and growing pains, joys and celebrations of particular relationships of friendship and love. Benedict's Rule helps us see that geography of place and geography of family are one terrain. Columba Stewart believes that one of the primary elements that shapes every Benedictine monastery is that of "life together in community." Stability, for him, means commitment to the community where the monk has professed his vows, the daily decision of each member to be faithful to that community or not. "A monastery is not an accidental agglomeration of passers-by," he writes, "but an intentional community of those who have, in their various ways, responded to an inner urging traditionally termed a 'call' or 'vocation.'" For Stewart, the spiritual value of stability lies in the commitment to a particular community, a specific group of people, with whom one has the opportunity to grow in holiness, wisdom, and depth. It implies a certain groundedness that helps a person avoid the "allure of fantasy and self-deception." "Having committed both spiritual and material fate to a particular community," Stewart adds, "a Benedictine has a stake in keeping the community focused on what they are meant to be about."[76]

This commitment to a specific community or family or community can lead to greater freedom and joy as one at the same time learns firsthand the meaning of loyalty, persistence, patience, and forgiveness; the ability to accept and work with others' limitations as one learns to accept one's own.

Stability of Heart

Many commentators on the Rule also believe that both stability of place and stability of community are ultimately related to and fostered by stability of heart. Esther deWaal, an Anglican laywoman, writes that while all three Benedictine vows, stability, fidelity to monastic life, and obedience "constantly illuminate, deepen, and depend on each other," the vow of stability is "altogether fundamental, for it raises the whole issue of commitment and fidelity," which is so alien to contemporary Western life. She reminds us that we cannot confront the basic questions of life without stability, and that without it we cannot come to know our true selves. As others do, she links stability with patience and perseverance, virtues that can be acquired only by stability of heart; that is, by surrendering oneself to God. She quotes Psalm 57, "My heart is fixed, O God, my heart is fixed," relating that stance to the discovery, as Benedict's Rule affirms, that God is everywhere; that we have no need to seek God elsewhere, but in our daily lives and relationships, our daily routine. Quoting another spiritual writer, Catherine de Hueck Doherty, deWaal says, "You must understand that the *poustinia* [the Russian word for a place of solitude where one can communicate with God] begins in your heart. It is not a place, a geographical spot. It is not first and foremost a house or a room. It is within your heart."[77]

In retrospect, this examination of various meanings of stability helps us begin to see that centering our hearts on God can counteract our inner restlessness of heart, which Augustine describes in his autobiography. It can help us to listen, as John the beloved disciple did, to the heartbeat of God. It can also give us the courage to open the secrets of our hearts to one another, as John Cassian recommended. Benedict's gift and intuition were that stability of place and of community is ultimately about stability of heart. This is why, most likely, he begins his "Tools for Good Works" in chapter 4 with the admonition of Jesus: "First of all, 'love the Lord God with your whole heart, your whole soul and all your strength, and love your neighbor as yourself.'"[78] In staying grounded, sitting in one's cell, paying attention to the moment, we too might experience not only the presence of God, but also revelations that come, as they did for Benedict, in a flash of light. Stability of heart, centering our hearts in God, allows us to truly listen to the heart and the wisdom it waits to convey.

Stability is the opposite of geographical escape or even more subtly, escape into fantasies, the source of addictive thinking and addictive behaviors. With a commitment to stability, whether we live in a monastery or not, we can begin to experience the wonders of springtime, as portrayed by the American artist Grant Wood in his beautiful—and hopeful—painting, "Spring in Town," where a man, half naked, digs in a garden from which bulbs that have survived winter are just beginning to bloom. Stability can provide those who value it with a path to spiritual growth, a road to Paradise, as the vision of Benedict's followers after his death reveals.

The Benedictine Legacy

Benedict died March 21, 547, and was buried, as Gregory tells us, in the same tomb as his sister, Scholastica. Within a generation, about the year 581, Lombard tribes attacked Monte Cassino and the monks fled to Rome where they established a house by the Lateran Church. (This may have been the community that Gregory got to know before he became pope, and the one that perhaps most influenced his ideas about Benedict.) What is interesting to note, in light of later history, is that, after the destruction of Monte Cassino, Gregory's and Scholastica's bodies were evidently left behind. In the year 673, the two saints' bodies were taken to the abbey of Fleury in France. The theft of relics was becoming more common at this time, and, according to Paul the Deacon, in his *History of the Lombards*, written about 790, "where there had been for many years a deserted solitude, some Franks, coming from the regions of Le Mans and Orleans and pretending to keep vigil at the venerable body, took away the bones of the same venerable Father and likewise of his reverend sister Scholastica and carried them to their country."[79] While Scholastica's relics were eventually moved to Le Mans, Benedict's remained at Fleury, which became a major center of pilgrimage during medieval times. Evidently some relics or ashes of Benedict were later returned to Monte Cassino after its restoration, but the church of Fleury-St.-Benoit continues to be the honored site of Benedict's remains.

Benedict's spirit, of course, along with that of his sister's, never died, continuing to affect significant aspects of Christian spirituality up to our present age. While Benedict became, after Jesus, a primary exemplar for his followers, Scholastica herself was recognized as the patroness of Benedictine women. During the Middle Ages, in addition to the Irish monasteries where many people received a free education, Benedictine monasteries were the chief cultural, educational, and spiritual centers of Europe. Gregory's *Life of Benedict,* of course, had a major effect on these developments, becoming one of the most influential of Christian hagiographies of all time. Countless medieval saints' Lives were modeled on those of Antony, Martin, and his. Benedict's Rule too had a major effect on medieval life. One of the two best-known medieval documents (the other being Boethius's *Consolation of Philosophy*), it was one of the three most commonly followed in the Middle Ages (the Rules of St. Augustine and of St. Francis being the other two). "The promotion" of his Rule as "the Western standard" with which all others were compared, became, according to Peter Levi, "the keystone of monastic reform for centuries, and the most important single factor in creating the monasteries of the West as they have been ever since."[80]

One such monastic reform, under the leadership of Bernard of Clairvaux (1090–1153), resulted in the creation of a new religious order, the Cistercians. Bernard is linked directly by Jean Leclercq with Benedict in the spread of monasticism and monastic values in the West.[81] In the following chapter, our last, we turn to Bernard who emphasized, as had Scholastica in her teaching of Benedict, the Christian monastic value of love above everything else.

CHAPTER TEN

Valley of Light—Bernard of Clairvaux

I remained with Bernard for a few days, and as I looked about me I thought that I was gazing on a new heaven and a new earth, for it seemed as though there were tracks freshly made by men of our own day in the path that had been trodden by our fathers, the Egyptian monks of long ago. —William of St. Thierry

The place was to become famous as Clairvaux, the "Valley of Light;" famous because of Bernard its abbot, because of the saints who lived there, because of the life they lived, because of the God whom they had found. —Thomas Merton

In the twelfth century, over five hundred years after Benedict, Scholastica, and Gregory the Great, the age that Bernard McGinn calls "the richest development of the monastic mystical tradition in the West"[1] began. This was the century that laid the foundations for the universities, those new cathedrals of knowledge, such as Oxford, Cambridge, Salamanca, the Sorbonne, the Louvain, Bologna, whose influence still shapes our modern world. It was a time of extensive travel when increasingly more people set forth on pilgrimage to visit holy sites associated with Jesus and the saints or on crusades to defend those places against the "infidel." The twelfth century also witnessed the appearance of the first Gothic cathedral, Saint-Denis, outside of Paris, an old abbey church renovated by Abbot Suger (c. 1081–1151) with numerous stained-glass windows and marvelous displays of light.[2] According to art historian Kenneth Clark, this was the age "which gave European civilization its impetus: our intellectual energy, our belief that God may be approached through beauty, our feeling of compassion, our sense of the unity of Christendom."[3] In many ways, the twelfth century was marked by an explosion of creative energy similar in its intensity to that found in the fourth century when Christianity was just emerging from the catacombs.

Christianity itself was undergoing major changes. On all levels, reform was happening, initiated by the highly talented Benedictine monk Hildebrand (c. 1020–1085), who, as Pope Gregory VII, started what became known as the Gregorian Reform, which attacked ecclesial abuses as well as strengthened dramatically papal power in the West. Reform at the grassroots, in monastic communities, was also taking hold. It had begun in the early tenth century with the founding of the French monastery of Cluny in Burgundy. This Benedictine monastery, placed under the direct control of the papacy, was free to elect its own abbot unhindered by outside secular or episcopal authorities. In less than a century, according to Cuthbert Butler, "it became not merely the most important Benedictine monastery in the world, but the chief ecclesiastical center outside of Rome, the abbot of Cluny being, next to the pope, the most prominent churchman in western Europe."[4] While successful as a reform movement (it gave birth to fifteen hundred daughter-houses by the end of the twelfth century), certain critics came to associate it with liturgical grandiosity, a church architecture of overly elaborate sculpture and rich decorations, and an ever-lengthening Divine Office that replaced the manual labor of the monks.[5]

In reaction to these Cluniac "extremes," a small group of Benedictine monks in 1098 moved to the French abbey of Citeaux, hoping to recover the original charisms of St. Benedict as well as "the ideals of an older and purer monasticism," that of the desert Christians.[6] These reform-minded monks became known as Cistercians (Citeaux in Latin is *Cistercium*). Wearing white habits made of coarse, undyed sheep's wool in contrast to the black of the original Benedictines, this monastic group "dominated the life of the whole Western Church," according to

David Knowles, "and built the abbeys whose remains or ruins are a familiar sight in every land."[7] In imitation of the desert Christians, they built their monasteries in remote regions of the countryside, while adopting a stricter, leaner diet and a daily schedule of silence, study, prayer, and work. Their impact was profound as their reform-minded monasteries repopulated monastic Europe at an astounding rate, to such a degree that the twelfth century itself became known as "the Cistercian century."

In the works of the early Cistercians, we find a vigorous flowering of the patristic tradition. Along with their deep love of scripture and daily immersion in it, these monks knew and loved the patristic writers, from Origen to Gregory the Great. They not only read the works of the Fathers and copied them in their scriptoria, they *lived* what those books contained. Theirs was a monastic spirituality that united head and heart, daily work and prayer, contemplation and action, theology and spirituality. Because of them, medieval monastic culture was, Jean Leclercq posits, "a patristic culture, the prolongation of patristic culture in another age and another civilization....By prolonging patristic culture in a period different from that of the Fathers, they produced a new and original, yet traditional culture deeply rooted in the culture of the first centuries of Christianity."[8]

The twelfth century, then, was an exceptional time, culminating in a monastic culture that looked back to the patristic period for guidance and inspiration as well as ahead, with faith and hope, to the unfolding of what later historians would identify as the late Middle Ages, the Renaissance, and the Reformation.

If leaders are those who often best represent the views of an age and most effectively contribute to its social and religious development, then one person in particular emerges as the representative figure of the twelfth century: Bernard of Clairvaux, a monk, mystic, and reformer who from 1115 until his death in 1153 attempted to remain simply abbot of his monastery, and yet who was constantly called upon to settle ecclesial disputes outside its gates, far from home. A man of frail health, he was intensely involved in the political and religious issues of his time, yet able to help establish, during his tenure as abbot, at least sixty-eight Cistercian houses scattered across Europe, as well as to author at least nine major treatises, 332 authenticated sermons, and at least a thousand letters, some 550 that have survived. His writings affected not only the rise of courtly love and poetry in the West, but also of mysticism and the language medieval mystics, both female and male, used to describe their experiences of God. If the first thousand years of Christianity had emphasized Christ's divinity, it was Bernard who helped swing the pendulum in the direction of Christ's humanity, a key aspect of medieval spirituality that would be reflected in the works of such mystics as Francis of Assisi, Julian of Norwich, and Ignatius of Loyola. A monk who longed to return to his community as had Gregory the Great, Bernard refused numerous offers to become bishop or archbishop, and yet was such a powerful figure that, as he complained to the new pope, Eugenius III, "they are saying that it is not you but I who am the Pope, and from all sides they flock to me with their suits."[9]

Bernard left his mark on many areas of medieval life, including, Thomas Merton says, "on schools of spirituality, on Gregorian chant, on the clerical life, and on the whole development of Gothic architecture and art."[10] He also made a notable contribution to the Middle Ages through his affirmation of friendship, his devotion to Mary, and, most especially, his consistent assertion of the importance in everyone's life of discovering and responding to God's love. The central core of his teaching from his first to his last works, as we will see, is contained in the words from St. John, "God is love" (I John 4:8). As Bernard wrote in one of his letters, "Let no one who loves God have any doubt that God loves him [or her]. The love of God for us precedes our love for God and it also follows it."[11] As a result of his convictions, he became, according to Leclercq, a reformer not only of monasticism, but also of "all sectors of the Church's life, both for love of the Church and in order to see it daily become more worthy of love and to see it lovingly served."[12]

This chapter examines the life of Bernard of Clairvaux, concentrating on the monastic value of love as Bernard expressed it in his writings, especially in his letters and his most famous and most important work, his *Sermons on the Song of Songs.* Monasticism has always been oriented toward love; it is the foundation for monastic communities everywhere, and for any individual seeking to follow Christ. With that understanding, it is no coincidence that while the Rule of St. Benedict referred to the monastery as a "school for the Lord's service," Bernard and other Cistercians, such as William of St. Thierry, referred to it as a "school of charity," a school of love.[13]

As we will see, Bernard (with all his faults and human limitations) was, above all, a lover: a person in love with God, with others, and with his own spiritual heritage. In that regard, he read daily from the scriptures and the writings of the Fathers, loving especially the works of Origen, Augustine, Jerome, Cassian, Bede, Benedict, and Gregory. Immersing himself in their wisdom, he did not see them as dead and gone, but spiritual mentors very much alive, offering their insights to him in prayer and contemplation. With that appreciation, he did all that he could to get others to have a relationship with them as he did. In that capacity, it seems appropriate that this book on "the monk within" concludes with Bernard of Clairvaux, a monk considered to be "the last of the fathers" as well as "the symbol of a whole spiritual world, a whole literature which is a prolongation of the patristic age."[14] If, as Benedicta Ward suggests, he is "the wisest of all spiritual guides,"[15] we will see how much of a competent and wise guide Bernard was for his contemporaries, and can be for us today.

Bernard's Early Life

A basic source of information on Bernard's life is found in a series of hagiographical accounts written by those who knew him. The most significant is the one entitled *Vita Prima,* "the First Life," started by his close friend, William of St. Thierry, probably in 1147, the year before William died. Like Sulpicius Severus's Life of St. Martin of Tours, William's account was begun while the subject of the hagiography was still alive. After the deaths of both William and Bernard, it was completed by a Benedictine abbot,

Arnold of Bonnevaux, and a third biographer, Geoffrey, Bernard's secretary at Clairvaux. Each added his own perspective and interpretation of the saint's life. At times, hagiography and history seem to clash, and the reader of this first hagiography of Bernard finds it following too closely the mythical pattern of earlier Lives, so much so that the authentic Bernard seems lost in the sometimes flamboyant, uncritical praise of the man. The *real* Bernard, the much more appealing historical figure, comes through more profoundly in his letters and his sermons, as we will see.

Bernard was born at Fontaines les Dijon in Burgundy sometime during the year 1090. His father, Tescelin, was a nobleman who had the reputation of being a brave and honorable knight. His mother, Aleth, also came from an upper-class family. The two of them had seven children: six sons and one daughter, of whom Bernard was the third. Their names according to birth were Guy, Gerard, Bernard, Hombeline, Andrew, Bartholomew, and Nivard. (The second child, Gerard, was Bernard's favorite brother to whom he was passionately devoted.) Bernard himself seems to have been exceptionally close to his mother who encouraged him to pursue a literary career as well as a religious one. While his brothers were learning to ride and hunt, Bernard was sent to a school with the Canons Regular of St. Vorles at Chatillon-sur-Seine, a town about fifty miles north of Dijon. There he would have received a thorough education in Christian scripture, as well as gained familiarity with the Latin Classical poets and writers, especially Cicero. The latter's work, in particular, *On Friendship,* probably had a major influence on Bernard—as it had on Augustine and Jerome, as well as other spiritual writers in the twelfth century, such as Aelred of Rievaulx (c. 1110–1167).[16]

Although we know little about his youth and adolescence, Bernard's first biographer, William of St. Thierry, says he was precocious, learning "much more quickly than the other boys his own age," and a lover of solitude (i.e., "he loved to be alone"). A tall, blonde, and exceptionally handsome young man, he was also known to have had numerous friendships. Because of his good looks and charm, women were naturally attracted to him. In imitation of St. Antony's temptations, William shows that

Bernard too faces his own: In one case, a young woman climbed naked into his bed while he was asleep, and in another story, a married woman attempts to seduce him. Neither made any headway, perhaps because, like the Celtic saints, Bernard "would leap into a pool of cold water," William says, "and stay up to his neck in it until the blood had almost frozen in his veins and his lust had been cooled by means of grace."[17]

Whether these early stories of his youth are historically accurate or not, what is certain about the young Bernard is that he was profoundly affected by the death of his mother.[18] Bernard, an adolescent at the time, deeply grieved for her. Like Augustine's mother, Monica, Aleth had a major influence on her son's life and spirituality. According to William, in her own lifetime she had evidently adopted monastic values for herself: "at home in her household, in her married life, and in her dealings with the world around her, she seemed to imitate the life of a hermit or a monk."[19] As Bernard's biographer Bruno James suggests, it was she who "had inspired him with the desire to serve God either as a monk or as a priest and...who had insisted on his being educated for the Church."[20] This loss of his mother may have contributed to Bernard's lifelong devotion to Mary, the mother of Jesus, and, through him, to his followers,' the Cistercians,' and the Western Church's. "Marian devotion of the Middle Ages," according to Henri Daniel-Rops, "is inseparable from Saint Bernard," a devotion that included depictions of a kneeling Bernard receiving milk directly from Mary's breasts.[21]

Not much is known about Bernard between the year his mother died and 1111 when he definitely made up his mind to become a monk. At least one story describes how, in a state of indecisiveness, he had gone into a roadside church and, praying for guidance from God, had left convinced that he should enter a monastic community and become a monk. Considering his earlier proclivities, such a vocational decision was probably not all that surprising to his family and friends. What was surprising was the monastery he intended to join: not the prosperous abbey of Cluny, but that of Citeaux, a poor and seemingly insignificant community of reform-minded monks who had originally come from Molesme. Bernard had a reason for choosing the lesser one: "I chose Citeaux in preference to Cluny not because I was not aware that the life was excellent and lawful but because 'I am a thing of flesh and blood, sold unto the slavery of sin.' I was conscious that my weak character needed a strong medicine."[22]

Considering Bernard's love of friends and family, however, he did not plan to go into the monastery alone, but to take them with him! This is precisely what he did, eventually persuading all of his brothers except Gerard (who was a prisoner of war at the time) and Nivard (who was still a child) to give up whatever plans they had, and come with him to Citeaux. He also convinced friends and acquaintances to join him, so much so, that, as the First Life says, "mothers hid their sons when Bernard came near, and wives clung to their husbands to prevent them from going to hear him."[23] The number of those desiring to join the monastic life grew to about thirty men, all of whom gathered together at Chatillon in October 1111 where, for the next six months, they discussed their plans, reflected on their vocations, and prayed. This time together is compared by some scholars to Augustine's gathering of friends at Cassiciacum before his baptism, and to John Henry Newman (1801–1890) and his followers in retirement from 1842 to 1846 at Littlemore, outside of Oxford.[24]

At the end of March or early April 1112, all thirty men traveled to Citeaux where they are welcomed with open arms by Stephen Harding, a monk originally from England who was at that time its abbot.[25] No novices had entered the community for several years, and the monks were few in number. The addition of so many new members at once, of course, changed communal dynamics dramatically. All seem to have adjusted to each other well, and to the new monastic routine. Bernard was then almost twenty-three years old, a young, highly idealistic adult with a great deal of energy. He spent his early days at Citeaux learning to integrate work, prayer, and study into a daily rhythm that fostered peacefulness, silence, and solitude. This was the time he began to study the Bible in earnest and the writings of the Latin fathers. He also followed an extreme asceticism, William of St. Thierry tells us: "short hours of sleep coupled with a very scanty diet," which led to "his physique" becoming "quite broken by his fasts and vigils." The result of Bernard's self-imposed hardships was "that he could not keep down anything that he ate, so that whatever food he did manage to take, he vomited up before it could be digested."[26]

This rigorous regimen would contribute to Bernard's lifelong struggle with poor health—something, as we've seen, that also characterized the lives of Augustine, Jerome, and Gregory. Whether his superiors counseled him against this lack of self-care is not known. They may not have said anything, considering their own depreciation of the body, an inheritance from the desert Christians and their attempts at *"apatheia."* Whatever response they may have given Bernard, Abbot Harding decided after three years to send him and twelve other monks to found a new house in Champagne. Despite his youth, Bernard was to be the abbot of the new community.

Clairvaux: The Valley of Light

In 1115, Bernard and his monks settled in a dark valley that was surrounded by a forest, described by William of St. Thierry as a place that "had for many years been used as robbers' lair." "Of old it was called the Vale of Absinth," he writes, "either because wormwood grew there in great abundance, or because of the bitter sorrow felt by those who fell into the hands of the robbers who lived there. Such was the place in which the men of God from Citeaux settled. Formerly it had been a place in which fear and loneliness held sway, but they made this den of thieves into a temple of God and a house of prayer." The abbey they built there they named "Clairvaux," which means the "Valley of Light." As Abbot Suger's cathedral of light, Saint-Denis, would inspire Gothic art and architecture in the twelfth century, Bernard's Clairvaux, in the valley of light, would provide the stimulus for a new interpretation of the monastic life. In imitation of the first Benedictines, "they began to serve God here in poverty of spirit, in hunger and thirst, in cold and nakedness, and in long vigils...."[27]

There at Clairvaux, Bernard's "greatest desire," William writes, "was for the salvation of all mankind, and this has been the great passion of his heart from the first day of his life as monk even on the day on which I am writing this." "Like a mother's devoted care for her children," Bernard's longing was "to draw all people to God." This would be the great conflict that Bernard faced that would color all his days as a monk: "his great desire for souls and the desire to remain hidden from the attention of the world."[28] They constituted two loves that others before him had faced seemingly at odds with each other: the love of souls, of people, manifest in his desire to serve, and the love of God, reflected in his desire for quiet, solitude, and prayer.

Quiet was definitely a characteristic of the early community at Clairvaux, as it is today in Cistercian monasteries worldwide. William tells how "men who come down from the hills around into the valley of Clairvaux for the first time, are struck by an awareness that God dwells there....They find that the silence of the deep of night reigns even in the middle of the day, although in this valley full of men there are no idle souls [here William subtly refers to the perceived differences between Cistercian and Cluniac lifestyles], and everyone busies himself with the tasks entrusted to him. The only sound that can be heard is the sound of the brethren at work or singing their office in praise of God. Even worldly men are filled with much awe by this atmosphere of silence, with the result that not only are they slow to indulge in any idle or improper chatter, but keep their talking to a minimum." And, to reinforce the ties between the first Benedictines and the Cistercians, he adds: "The loneliness of this place, hidden among the woods and closed in by the surrounding hills, was comparable to the cave where the shepherds found our holy father Saint Benedict, so closely did the monks of Clairvaux follow his form of life and style of dwelling....[This] way of life helps to establish an inner solitude in the depths of the heart."[29]

Although enjoying the landscape and the silence, the first monks at Clairvaux experienced extreme hardships. The land was poor and their bread was of coarse barley; boiled beech leaves were sometimes served in place of decent vegetables. Like Benedict in his early years, Bernard seems to have been as hard on the monks as he was on himself, coming down on them for the smallest transgressions. This approach led many of them to become discouraged, probably in turn discouraging Bernard. It is known too that he was not the best of administrators, "inclined to overlook," William says, "necessary matters." He seemed to enjoy "his conversation...in heaven" to such an extent that "occasionally, they had to force him to come down to earth for awhile to discuss business."[30]

Within a year or two of Clairvaux's foundation, Bernard's health had grown worse, and he was in danger of physical collapse, if not of dying. During this crisis, a nearby bishop, William of Champeaux, who had originally ordained Bernard a priest and installed him as abbot at Clairvaux, came for a visit. He had once been mentor to Peter Abelard (1079–1142), a monk, who was later to become known for his controversial theological views and his life with Héloïse, a former student. Bishop William had had a falling-out with Abelard earlier due to what he perceived to be the younger man's arrogance. Now William became one of Bernard's most significant sponsors and, according to Bruno James, one of his "firmest friends." It was Bishop William who "first spread the fame of Bernard throughout France, while his influence on Bernard's intellectual outlook may well have been responsible for the strong line he [Bernard] later took in combating Abelard."[31]

At this point in Bernard's life, however, it was William of Champeaux who proceeded to take matters into his own hands, telling the young abbot that there was hope for his recovery, but only if Bernard would follow his advice, allowing "his body just the small degree of care and attention required by the nature of the illness." When Bernard stubbornly refused, the bishop performed what today would be called an "intervention" to save the young monk's life. Going directly to a general chapter of abbots at Citeaux, William received their permission to keep Bernard under his obedience for a year. Only then did Bernard finally agree to follow his advice. The bishop ordered a hermitage to be built for his protégé outside the boundaries of the monastery where the sick man could begin his recuperation. "By his express command the abbot was not to be held to any of the restrictions of food and drink imposed by the rule of his Order. Nor were any problems concerning the care and upkeep of the monastery to be brought to him for decisions; instead he was to be left quite unhampered to follow the way of life which the Bishop laid down for him."[32]

During this time of recuperation and prayer Bernard's future hagiographer, William of St. Thierry, had his first meeting with him, an encounter that changed both men profoundly. As was the case when Sulpicius Severus first met Martin of Tours, he, William, at the time a Benedictine abbot of the monastery of St. Thierry, was strongly impressed with and inspired by the Cistercian monk, stating that "the sweetness of Bernard's character so attracted me to him and filled me with desire to share his life amid such poverty and simplicity, that if the chance had then been given to me I should have asked nothing more than to be allowed to remain with him always, looking after him and ministering to his needs."[33] Bernard was also affected by William, since it was at the latter's instigation that he, Bernard, later wrote a number of important works, including his *Apologia* (which was dedicated to William), *Concerning Grace and Free Will, Concerning the Errors of Abelard,* and probably his *Sermons on the Song of Songs.*[34]

Besides being impressed with Bernard, William was also affected dramatically by the monastery of Clairvaux, stating that "as I looked about me I thought that I was gazing on a new heaven and a new earth, for it seemed as though there were tracks freshly made by men of our own day in the path that had first been trodden by our fathers, the Egyptian monks of long ago."[35] The friendship between the two men continued to grow—even when Bernard initially rejected William's request to join his community. Obviously influenced by St. Benedict's affirmation of the vow of stability and an abbot's responsibilities, Bernard tells William in a letter: "Hold on to what you have got, remain where you are, and try to benefit those over whom you rule. Do not try to escape the responsibility of your office while you are still able to discharge it for the benefit of your subjects. Woe to you if you rule them and do not benefit them, but far greater woe to you if you refuse to benefit them because you shirk the burden of ruling them." This was Bernard's thought, although he makes clear his advice had nothing to do with a lack of love for William. As he says in two other letters, affirming their friendship: "…your charity is greater than mine," and, "I am yours and shall be yours as long as I live."[36]

William evidently listened to Bernard at the time, but eleven years later gave up his Benedictine abbacy and retired to the Cistercian monastery of Signy in the diocese of Rheims. There he continued writing a number of spiritual works widely read in monastic circles, including the first part of Bernard's *Vita Prima*.[37]

Besides this initial meeting with William when Bernard was recovering his health, this well might have been the time that the abbot of Clairvaux began to learn a greater compassion not only toward others in his community, but also toward himself. In an essay that he wrote much later, he seems to be drawing upon this earlier experience and what it taught him about self-care. He addresses a five-volume work, "On Consideration," to the newly elected Pope Eugenius III, who had once been a monk at Clairvaux and was in need of the wisdom that one spiritual leader could provide another. Bernard chose the title of the writing because it was the term Gregory the Great had used to describe a bishop's task in his book, *Pastoral Care*. "Action itself certainly gains nothing from a lack of prior consideration," Bernard tells the pope. "Again, if you want to live wholly for others, like Paul who became all things to all men, I salute your humanity, but only on condition it be all-inclusive, and how can it be that if it excludes yourself? You too are a man. If your humanity, therefore, is to be entire and whole, you too must be clasped in your all-embracing arms. Else what does it profit you, as the Lord said, if you win every human life and lose your own? In view of the fact that all have you, make sure you are one of the haves. Why should you alone be cheated of your reward?"[38]

As Bernard painfully learned these truths, and began perhaps to follow his own advice, word spread about his holiness and that of his community's. Like the desert father Antony and so many others after him, large numbers of people traveled to Clairvaux, while more men began to apply for entrance. Even Bernard's aged father, Tescelin, and his younger brother, Nivard, in 1119, finally joined the community, as his other male family members had done earlier. (At this time, even his sister, Hombeline, left her husband and joined a Benedictine convent.) Increasing numbers of monks at Clairvaux as well as those in other countries, inspired by Clairvaux's example, led to the establishment of monasteries in France and other parts of Europe. Some of the most well-known were Tintern Abbey in Wales in 1131, and in England, in 1132, Rievaulx Abbey, where the spiritual writer Aelred eventually became abbot, and Fountains, which, by the time of Henry VIII, was the largest and wealthiest abbey in all of England.[39] In 1142, Mellifont Abbey in Ireland also became a daughter-house of Clairvaux. Eventually, under Bernard's leadership, sixty-eight houses linked with Clairvaux were founded in Flanders, England, Wales, Ireland, Germany, Spain, Italy, Portugal, Sicily, Sweden, and, of course, France. From what we know, Bernard was personally involved in the establishment of most of these.[40]

As more members were joining Clairvaux (there were two hundred monks under him by 1130), his letters are full of references to incessant worries and tasks. In one letter, he writes in response to the complaint from his friend, Oger, a Canon Regular of Mont-Saint-Eloith, that he, Bernard, does not answer his letters promptly: "So I will not make any more of what you regard as dubious excuses. I will merely point out to you as a friend what you must believe to be a fact, namely that because of the short summer nights and the full days I have not had one moment of leisure in which I could attend to your business....To tell the truth, dear Oger, although my conscience bears witness that I am only trying to serve charity yet, for your sake, I cannot but be exasperated with all my cares. I bear them only for the sake of charity, because I am debtor to the wise and unwise...."[41]

Bernard's monastic life was filled with people and responsibilities that tried his charity and patience. At the same time, events outside his monastery increasingly called forth a response. In retrospect, William of St. Thierry saw this period in Bernard's life, "although he could not foresee where it would lead him," preparing Bernard "for work not only on behalf of his own Order but also on behalf of the whole Church....And so it was that his reputation spread among men so widely that the Church could not afford not to use so valuable a member of Christ's body for its designs."[42] What helped spread his reputation were not only the rumors of his competence and holiness, but his early writings on topics that appealed to his contemporaries.

Bernard's Early Writings

While Bernard's first ten to fifteen years as abbot of Clairvaux were occupied with the establishment of his community and with monastic business, his work as a writer began about 1124. That was the year when his treatise, *On the Steps of Humility and Pride,* was published. Described as his "first masterpiece,"[43] it reveals Bernard's keen psychological insights into human behavior, and also shows the influence of the Rule of St. Benedict, especially chapter seven, on his thoughts. Unlike Benedict's twelve steps of humility, however, Bernard spends more time discussing twelve steps to pride. He does so, he says humorously, because he knows more about pride than humility, and so he writes about what he knows best. Still, in using the metaphor of a ladder, Jacob's ladder (Gen 28:12), Bernard presumes that in describing the steps "down" (away from God) that pride entails, a person can learn the steps "up" to true humility.

In other words, Bernard is advocating what Cassian did in his own writings on "contraries": *do the opposite*. "I have nothing to set before you," Bernard writes, "except the order of my descent. But if you look carefully," he tells his reader, "you will find there the way up....Similarly, in these steps of our descent you will perhaps find steps up. As you climb, you will read them better in your heart than in this book." Humility, Bernard defines as, "the virtue by which a man recognizes his own unworthiness because he really knows himself." This self-knowledge is related to truth and love: "What is this refreshment that Truth promises to those who are climbing and which he gives to those who reach the top? Perhaps it is love itself?...Truly, love is a sweet and pleasant food, which refreshes the weary [and] strengthens the weak (Isa 35:3)....The way of humility is good (Ps 118:71), for by it we seek truth, attain love, and share the fruits of wisdom."[44]

In this first work, Bernard offers Mary, Jesus' mother, as the model of true humility, and also refers directly to the Hebrew poem, the "Song of Songs," associated with King Solomon. This was to become the basis of his theological reflection on the union between Christ and the Church, and (Bernard's more original contribution) between Christ and the individual soul: "Love is a good food, which is placed in the middle of Solomon's plate (Song 3:9), fragrant with the many scents (Song 1:2) of the virtues as if with a multitude of spices (Song 3:6)."[45]

About the same time he wrote his first treatise, he composed what came to be called the "Letter of Love," addressed to Prior Guy and his monks of the Grande Chartreuse. This was Bernard's initial attempt to describe the love of God that would eventually lead to his greatest work, his *Sermons on the Song of Songs.* According to Jean Leclercq, this composition, "Letter of Love," was "the first and most detailed explanation of monastic love in the twelfth century."[46] Shortly after its publication, due to the positive response it received, Bernard incorporated it into his next treatise, "On Loving God," a work that incorporated insights he had gained by reading or rereading Cicero's essay, "On Friendship."[47] In both of his own writings on love, Bernard posits that the spiritual life is ultimately about growth in the love of God, beginning with the realization that our chief reason for loving God is (and he quotes St. John) that God loved us *first* (cf. 1 John 4:9–10). Incorporating that realization more deeply into our lives and consciousness may eventually lead, through a series of stages, to the experience of spiritual union, communion with God.[48]

Other works followed. One was a series of four homilies, *In Praise of the Virgin Mary,* which contributed significantly to the development of Marian spirituality in the later Middle Ages.

These latter homilies, Bernard says, he felt compelled to write: "my devotion has been urging me to write something...in praise of the Virgin Mother."[49] Next came his *Apologia,* written at the request of William of St. Thierry who wanted Bernard to respond to certain accusations against the Cistercians by the monks of Cluny. Bernard was at first hesitant to join the debate, but eventually acceded to William's desire. His treatise, "An Apologia for Abbot William," written in 1125, is a hard-hitting satire against the abuses of certain clergy, all done out of Bernard's concern for ongoing monastic and ecclesial reform. In language that St. Jerome would have appreciated, Bernard condemns clerical excess—whether in the consumption of fine meals, too much wine-drinking, or ostentatious clothing. Regarding the latter, he writes, "today's religious is less concerned with keeping out the cold than with cutting a good figure," and describes how some monks to buy a cowl "traipse from town to town and trail round the markets, visiting every booth..., unrolling the huge bolts of cloth, fingering, peering, holding the lengths up to the light and rejecting anything coarse or faded."[50] He is especially critical of superiors who fail to put a stop to such behavior.

All of Bernard's criticism is done in the name of improving monastic behavior so that it might be more in line with the original Rule of St. Benedict as well as earlier monastic leaders. He asks, for example, "Is that what Basil taught or Anthony began? Is that the life the Fathers lived in Egypt?" When Bernard describes monks who traveled on horseback with huge retinues of followers, he asks: "what evidence is there of humility when one solitary abbot travels with a parade of horseflesh and a retinue of lay-servants that would do honor to two bishops? I swear I have seen an abbot with sixty horses and more in his train. If you saw them passing, you would take them for lords with dominion over castles and counties, not for fathers of monks and shepherds of souls."[51]

Bernard is also especially critical of the extravagance spent on churches and relics to supposedly impress the faithful while actually soliciting their money: "You spend to gain, and what you pour out returns as a flood-tide. A costly and dazzling show of vanities dispose to giving rather than to praying....When eyes open wide at gold-cased relics, purses do the same." He goes on to take exception to certain types of church art: "Instead of crowns one sees in churches nowadays great jewelled wheels bearing a circle of lamps, themselves as good as outshone by the inset gems. Massive tree-like structures, exquisitely wrought, replace the simple candlestick....What is this show of splendor intended to produce? Tears of contrition or gasps of admiration? O vanity of vanities, but above all insanity!" The Church, according to Bernard, has other obligations: "The walls of the church are ablaze with light and color, while the poor of the Church go hungry. The Church revets its stones in gold and leaves its children naked. The money for feeding the destitute goes to feast the eyes of the rich. The curious find plenty to relish and the starving nothing to eat." All of this, of course, was especially directed at monks. "What possible bearing can this have on the life of monks," he asks, "who are poor men and spiritual?"[52]

This was a scathing attack on monastic excess, and, though it may never have been intended to give an accurate picture of life in a typical Benedictine monastery of the time, it no doubt contained enough truth that it both hurt as well as amused. It certainly hurt at least one monk in particular: Suger, who had been appointed abbot of the abbey of Saint-Denis in 1122. He was one who had been seen traveling with sixty horses or more in his retinue, and it was his church, decorated so lavishly with gold and jewels, that contained, we know, large golden candlesticks of unusual height and beauty, looking like trees.[53] We know that, in fact, between the publication of Bernard's *Apologia* in 1125 and a long letter written to Suger by Bernard in 1127, Suger had experienced some form of dramatic conversion. In the letter, Bernard states that "the good news of what God has done in your soul has gone forth in our land encouraging all the good people who hear it....Even those who have not known you, but have only heard how great has been the change from what you were to what you are, marvel and praise God in you." He describes how "now the vaults of the great abbey that once resounded to the hubbub of secular business echo only to spiritual canticles," and seems to include himself with those "who used to abhor your folly," but "now praise your wisdom."[54]

The two abbots remained, after this, lifelong friends who frequently corresponded with each other and collaborated on French political and religious affairs. Years later, in a moving letter sent to Suger on the abbot's deathbed, Bernard addresses him as his "dear and intimate friend," and assures the dying man of his continued love and prayers, telling him, "Fear not, man of God, to put off the earthy man which is holding you down to the earth...when you are about to put on the garb of immortality in heaven." Bernard wants to visit the abbot, but is not sure if he can, "but whatever happens, I who have loved you from the first shall love you without end...." And he continues, in words that anyone who has lost a loved one understands: "I say with all confidence that I can never lose one whom I have loved unto the end: one to whom my soul cleaves so firmly that it can never be separated, does not go away but only goes before. Be mindful of me when you come to where I shall follow you, so that I may be permitted soon to come after you and come to you. In the meantime be sure that I shall never lose the dear memory of you, although to my sorrow I lose your dear presence."[55]

Suger died January 13, 1151, a monk who not only significantly contributed to the emergence of Gothic architecture and art, but was even Regent of France, the most powerful government official acting in the name of King Louis VII while the king was off fighting the Second Crusade. However important, Suger was only one person touched by Bernard's *Apologia,* a treatise that clearly reveals Bernard's love of the Church and his commitment to reform—as well as the *two sides* of love he would speak of in other contexts.

Bernard's Increasing Involvement outside Clairvaux

Bernard's *Apologia* met with a wide readership for, Jean Leclercq says, "From that point on, Bernard of Clairvaux was no longer simply a monastic teacher, but was asked to extend his teaching office to those engaged in pastoral care and to other areas of Church life."[56] As a result, the year 1130 became a turning point in Bernard's life. Before that year, his life and energy had been primarily centered on Clairvaux and its relationship to other religious houses. After that time he entered onto the broader European stage, becoming deeply immersed in ecclesial arguments (a papal schism), doctrinal disagreements (a confrontation with Peter Abelard), even preaching a crusade against Moslems. It seemed that each time he attempted to help resolve these complex issues and then to return to Clairvaux to live the simple life of a monk he was expected to help solve yet another crisis.

One of the first major controversies in which Bernard played a primary role involved the papal election of 1130. Pope Honorius had died, and the cardinals were divided in their opinion as to who should be his successor. Some, evidently a majority, elected Gregory, cardinal deacon of Sant'Angelo, as Pope Innocent II; a smaller faction elected Peter Leonis (Pierleone), Cardinal Priest of St. Calixtus, and a former monk of Cluny, who took the name Anacletus. The latter was a member of an influential Roman family liked by the populace in Rome. Innocent was forced to leave the city and move to Pisa, but not before petitioning the bishops of France to help him. They, in turn, summoned a council to be held at Etampes. Bernard was sent by the king to resolve the matter. He went there reluctantly, "realizing the weight of responsibility involved."[57] When he arrived at Etampes, he discovered that the bishops and the king wanted him not only to facilitate the discussions, but to make a recommendation to them about who should be recognized as the true pope. After a time, Bernard decided *for* Innocent II, and the whole council acclaimed Innocent as rightful heir to St. Peter. "It was at the Council of Etampes," biographer Watkin Williams says, "that St. Bernard's influence first began to be widely felt."[58]

At this point, rather than returning to Clairvaux, Bernard set out across France, often in the company of the pope, to elicit support for Innocent's legitimacy. In this capacity, Bernard, a highly skillful and persuasive person, met with delegations from

Germany and even Henry, the king of England. Pope Innocent seems to have relied a great deal on Bernard, since, according to Arnold of Bonnevaux (the hagiographer who followed William of St. Thierry), "in all matters, particularly those of a more secret nature, Bernard's advice was always sought" by the pope. Over the next eight years, numerous meetings and councils followed. In France, Germany, and Italy, Bernard continued to be "constantly at the Pope's side, taking part in all the discussions...."[59] Finally, in 1139, Peter Leonis was excommunicated at the Second Lateran Council, and his followers dispersed. Historians agree that the resolution of the schism over rival popes by the abbot of Clairvaux was "a masterpiece of statecraft on Bernard's part."[60]

This was only the beginning of Bernard's religious and political involvements. For Bernard, it was not only "who you know" that accounts for his rise to power and influence; it was also "what you know." His intelligence, his skills as a speaker and writer, his personal charisma,[61] and, not least, his reputation for honesty and holiness engendered respect, which in turn led to increased demand for him to settle other monastic, ecclesial, and even civil disputes. Merely to peruse his correspondence on so many different issues with every class in medieval society is to realize how truly involved he was!

His Letters: The Two Sides of Love

Bernard's letters are addressed to all classes of men and women in medieval Europe—from monks, nuns, abbots, and abbesses to bishops, archbishops, cardinals, and popes; from ordinary laypeople to dukes, duchesses, kings, queens, and emperors. These letters, which begin about 1119, paint "as it were unconsciously," Watkin Williams says, "the portrait of himself."[62] Unlike the early hagiographies about Bernard, which emphasize his greatness to the exclusion of his failures and disappointments, Bernard's letters provide a vivid and animated self-portrait of the man who emerges as no plaster saint but someone who, like ourselves, had to contend at times with poor health, depression, and ill temper. While they sometimes seem to ramble on (Bernard himself often apologizes for his "wordiness" and being "too long-winded"),[63] they reveal a spiritual leader highly involved in the issues of his time—despite the fact that he was a monk. In these letters, he frequently asks for prayers, sounding very much like Gregory the Great. In one, he writes: "I am obliged to spend most of my time out of my nest exposed to the tempests and troubles of the world. I am shaken and upset like a drunken man, and cares devour my conscience." His friends, especially, he accuses of "always trying to drag me...from the cloister to the cities," telling him "that the matter is important and the necessity grave." Why, he asks, has "God called me to be a monk...if (as his friends imply) I am necessary to the world, a man without whose aid the bishops cannot settle their own affairs?"[64]

Surely, despite his complaints, Bernard always had the ability to say "no" to such pressures and invitations, but it seems in many instances that his reticence in saying no had much to do with his sense of pastoral responsibility *and* his genuine love for people. Although he was not afraid of showing passion and great affection, this love of his was far from sentimental, but often challenging and confrontative, as was clearly demonstrated in his relationship with William of St. Thierry and Abbot Suger of Saint-Denis. Overall, what Bernard's numerous letters reveal are his consistent attempts to be a loving and compassionate person, while increasingly aware that love itself can be expressed in different ways, can have two sides. These are the two sides of love that Bernard constantly seems to have struggled with, and that every parent and teacher, leader and friend, frequently ask: In my loving others, when should I be compassionate and when challenging? In his writings, Bernard associates compassionate acceptance with a mother's love, and challenge and judgment with that of a father's. He believed that every spiritual leader must incorporate both approaches into his or her life, what we today might call "unconditional love" and "tough love." All of Bernard's letters reflect to one degree or another these two expressions of love.

In some of Bernard's correspondence "father-love" is more pronounced, although always in the context of caring and compassion. He tells Master Walter of Chaumont, for example, not to allow his mother to make decisions for him: "the love you have for your mother prevents you from following your convictions….Choose which you prefer: you can either serve her wishes or both her salvation and yours. If you truly love her, it is for her good that you should leave her."[65] To Romanus, a subdeacon of the Roman curia, he advises: "Have done with delay and do at once what you say in your letter you intend to do! Prove by what you do the sincerity of what you write….Fly, I implore you, and linger no more where sinners walk."[66] To Henry Murdac, abbot of Vauclair, then abbot of Fountains, and finally archbishop of York: "Believe me who have experience, you will find much more laboring among the woods than you every will among books. Woods and stones will teach you what you can never hear from any master."[67] To Thomas of Saint Omer, after he had broken his promise to become a monk, Bernard explicitly refers to his paternal role and feelings: "I confess that I feel your turning away just as if my heart were being torn from my body, for you are very dear to me and I regard you with all the affection of a father. For this reason every time I think of you I feel a sword of anxiety pierce my soul….I see many fearful things threatening you while you delay to come to your senses…."[68]

With another monk, Aelred, a fellow Cistercian and abbot of Rievaulx in northern England, Bernard demonstrates his "tough love" side, demanding that the younger man compose a treatise on love that Aelred was refusing to write, citing all sorts of excuses that Bernard lists: "You have said that you are ignorant of grammar, that you are almost illiterate; that you have come to the desert, not from the schools, but from the kitchen [a reference to Aelred acting as a steward at the Scottish royal court]; that you have since lived a rustic and rough life amidst rocks and mountains, earning in the sweat of your brow your daily bread with axe and maul; and that flights of oratory ill become your poor fisherman's clothes." Bernard is not buying any of these: "I do not blame your excuses, but I do reproach your obstinacy." In fact, the more Aelred protests, the more impressed Bernard is, telling him that his excuses "serve rather to inflame than extinguish the spark of my desire, because knowledge that comes from the school of the Holy Spirit rather than the schools of rhetoric will taste all the sweeter to me." Dropping any pretense of politeness, Bernard concludes his letter to Aelred, not with another invitation, but a command: "I therefore order you in the name of Jesus Christ, and in the Spirit of our God, that you do not delay to write down those thoughts that have occurred to you, in your long meditations, concerning the excellence of charity, its fruit, and its proper order, so that we may see in what you write, as if in a mirror, what charity is, how great sweetness there is in the possession of it...."[69] Bernard even tells Aelred what to call his work: *Mirror of Charity,* a book that was to become a classic, and lead to other significant writings, including Aelred's most famous, *Spiritual Friendship.* For those who are familiar with Aelred's work, especially the latter, we can only say, thank God for Bernard's challenging the Yorkshire monk!

In other letters, Bernard's more "motherly," feminine side comes through. To Thomas, provost of Beverley, he reveals his ability to confront, yet not from a position of superiority, but of compassion: "A sinner myself, I feel no repugnance towards a sinner. I do not spurn the diseased, since I am aware that I too am diseased....No matter how great your sins may be, how foul may be your conscience,...yet you shall be cleansed and become whiter than snow....A good conscience is a mine of wealth....What is there on earth to give such peace and such serenity?"[70] With Ermengarde, formerly a countess of Brittany, he acts as a spiritual mentor, telling her: "Search your heart and you will find mine there too....It is for you to see that you have me always by you; for my part, I confess, I am never without you and never leave you....I have received what has given delight to my heart, the news of your peace. I am glad because you are glad...for now you are living humbly instead of in state, as one of no consequence instead of as a great lady, as poor instead of rich....Without doubt your joyfulness can only be of the Holy Spirit."[71]

In another letter to perhaps his most famous female correspondent, Hildegard of Bingen (1098–1179), a mystic from the Rhineland in Germany, whom he addresses as his "beloved daughter in Christ," he writes: "I congratulate you on the grace of God that is in you and admonish you to regard it as a gift and respond to it with all humility and devotion." Affirming her ministry, he says: "...you who are favored with hidden knowledge..., it is rather for me to beg that you may not forget me before God, or those who are united to me in spiritual fellowship....We pray without ceasing for you that you may be strengthened in all good, instructed in interior things, and guided to what endures, so that those who put their trust in God may not fall by losing faith in you, but may rather derive strength, so as to make ever greater progress in good...."[72]

In other letters, both father-love and mother-love are expressed. To an anonymous nun, he writes a letter of encouragement and challenge, telling her that "after a wretched slavery" of broken vows, she is "leaving the shadows and entering the light": "From now on the integrity of your life will not be undermined by the corruption of your heart, nor will you any longer sully the title of virginity by your evil life." Not afraid of mincing words, he writes: "From now on there will be no deception in the name you bear, and the veil you wear will not any longer be meaningless."[73] To another nun, this one from the convent of St. Mary of Troyes, he writes: "Either you are one of the foolish virgins (if indeed you are a virgin) or you are one of the wise. If you are one of the foolish, the convent is necessary for you; if you are one of the wise, you are necessary for the convent....If you are a saint, try to edify your sisters by your example. If you are a sinner, do not pile one sin on the top of another but do penance where you are...."[74]

One letter in particular explicitly acknowledges the two sides of Bernard's love when he tries to console the parents of Geoffrey, one of the youths of the nobility whom Bernard converted when he was traveling in Flanders, and who was then joining his monastery: "It is true that he is going to God, but you are not losing him; on the contrary, through him you are gaining many sons. All of us at Clairvaux or of Clairvaux will receive him as a brother and you as our parents....Have comfort, do not worry, I shall look after him like a father and he will be to me a son until the Father of mercies, the God of all consolation, shall receive him from my hands....I will be for him both a mother and a father, both a brother and a sister. I will make the crooked path straight for him and the rough places smooth."[75] As we will see when we consider his great work, *Sermons on the Song of Songs*, Bernard's theology, his understanding of God and of life itself, reflects this two-sided dimension.

The "Absent Abbot" and "Difficult Saint"

As reflected in his vast correspondence, Bernard was intensely involved in the controversial issues of his time. From the early 1130s to the late 1140s, in fact, Bernard was gone from Clairvaux much of the time—to such an extent that Brian Patrick McGuire calls him an "absent abbot."[76] This engagement outside the monastery was a source of seemingly tremendous inner conflict as he was torn between his love of solitude and his sense of pastoral responsibility; between his longing to remain a simple monk and his burning desire to reform the current abuses in the Church. In one letter to a Carthusian prior, he alludes to his extreme regret in this regard: "I am a sort of modern chimaera, neither cleric nor layman. I have kept the habit of a monk, but I have long ago abandoned the life."[77] His letters to his community back in Clairvaux reveal a defensiveness as he attempts to justify his absence. He complains that he is only gone because of the commands of his superiors, civil and ecclesial, especially the pope. He even suggests that he really isn't always absent, telling his monks that he returns to the monastery "in spirit" at least once a year to inspect it, and make sure that everything is being done properly.[78] (This form of "spirit travel" may sound a bit bizarre, but to be fair to Bernard it is important to acknowledge that there are records of others, such as the Spanish mystic Maria de Agreda and the Native American shaman Black Elk, who engaged in this practice.)[79]

At other times his correspondence appears a bit manipulative as he attempts to gain sympathy from his colleagues. In one letter to them, he says: "Your own experience can tell you how much I am suffering. If my absence is irksome to you, you can be sure it is much more to me." In another, he writes: "Sorrowfully and reluctantly, weak and sickly, and (I must admit) ever haunted by the wan spectre of pale death, I have bowed before the urgent request of the Emperor, the command of the Apostolic See, the prayers of the Church and of secular princes....Pray for the peace of the Church, pray for my health, pray that I may see you again, live with you, and die with you."[80]

Certainly, these were heartfelt sentiments, but nonetheless some in his community must have wondered why, if he was missing them so much and even perhaps betraying his vocation as a monk, he didn't simply say, "No!" Today, we might interpret this inability to set limits as "codependency." Certainly, on numerous occasions Bernard seems to have taken on more than he could handle—to the detriment of his physical, emotional, and spiritual health. He complains, for example, in a letter written in 1137 that his life was "over-run in all quarters with anxieties, suspicions, cares, and there is scarcely an hour that is left free from the crowd of discordant applicants, from the trouble and care of business. I have no power to stop their coming and cannot refuse to see them, and they do not leave me even the time to pray."[81]

When the papal schism had finally ended, Bernard returned to Clairvaux, hoping at last to settle into the simple routine of being a monk and abbot. He also wanted to work more on the sermons he had begun writing in 1135 on the "Song of Songs." Unfortunately for him and for his community, he did not stay long. The 1140s saw him in even greater demand, as he was, according to Michael Casey, "at the height of his power and prestige."[82] Following the death of Pope Innocent in 1143, Bernard again was called upon to resolve another papal struggle, this one between the Roman Senate and the new pope. When the latter prelate died, a Cistercian monk from Clairvaux was elected in 1145, becoming Eugenius III (1145–1153). A close friend of Bernard's, Eugenius, as noted earlier, had to suffer the rumors that even though he was pope, Bernard really held that position. This caused further pressure on Bernard when "Clairvaux became like a branch of Rome, and more in high places saw it as a rival."[83]

As the decade progressed, however, Bernard experienced two major frustrations that would severely tarnish his reputation: his verbal fight with the controversial monk, Peter Abelard, and his preaching a crusade, the Second, which ended in disaster. Bernard had initially wanted to take on neither conflict, but once persuaded to do so he seems to have put his whole self into it. Numerous scholars believe that he was exceptionally unfair to Abelard, although Bernard, in a way that was characteristic of him, sought forgiveness from the controversial thinker before the latter died in 1142.[84] Regarding his preaching a second crusade, many also believe that he went too far in his desire to serve the pope and the youthful king of France, Louis VII, who wanted it. Again, despite his initial reluctance, Bernard seems to have embraced his mission wholeheartedly, first preaching it on March 31, 1146, to a huge throng of people at Vezelay, a famous French pilgrimage site dedicated to Mary Magdalen,[85] and then in the following year and a half (from the autumn of 1146 to spring 1148) traveling great distances in France, Germany, and Switzerland to promote it. By the time Bernard had ended his mission, Christian leaders in the West had decided to fight not only Moslems in the Holy Land, but also pagan Slavs on their eastern borders as well as Moors in Spain!

Although sympathetic biographers defend Bernard's call to arms, it is difficult today to appreciate what many would associate with religious fanaticism. While this second crusade failed miserably for a number of reasons, it, along with other crusades in Christian history, contributed greatly to Moslem distrust, if not outright hatred, of Christians everywhere. This is when Bernard can be seen most clearly as not only a "difficult saint,"[86] but as perhaps most human, overcome by his passion for protecting the Christian holy places and for spreading the Christian message to everyone. Some of the stridency too in his preaching may have been due to extreme fatigue. Nevertheless, one might ask how a monk, a mystic, a writer on the love of God, could call for the extermination of Slavs, Moors, and Moslems? We can only agree with Dennis Tamburello's assessment of Bernard: "Like many great people in history, he was a complex individual who had both strengths and weaknesses. One thing that can certainly be said about Bernard is that he was not lukewarm."[87]

Love in Bernard's Sermons on the Song of Songs

By the time the Second Crusade had failed miserably in late summer, 1148, Bernard was back at Clairvaux. Despite intermittent absences to settle more ecclesial conflicts, he remained there, perhaps seeking to hide from the numerous accusations against him about the debacle, but perhaps, most of all, because he wanted the solitude to write. During these years, he completed his work, "On Consideration," which in addition to offering counsel to the new pope included an attack on the Roman curia, which, he said with great foresight, had a tendency toward centralization. He also began composing a Life of St. Malachy (1094–1148),[88] about the great Irish reform bishop who had initially wanted to join the Cistercians, but whose request, like that of William of St. Thierry, Bernard denied. (Instead Malachy was responsible for bringing the first Cistercians to Ireland when Mellifont Abbey was established there.) As is clear from that hagiography, Bernard loved Malachy as a soul friend to such a degree that when the Irish bishop died unexpectedly on a visit to Clairvaux, Bernard had him buried in Bernard's own habit, and even prepared a tomb that he would share with Malachy,[89] as Benedict and Scholastica shared theirs.

Bernard also continued to write his sermons on the *Song of Songs,* which he had begun years before.[90] In these eighty-six sermons (which were probably never preached as such, but written to inspire and educate monks and laity alike), he attempts to explain the spiritual meaning of the great love poem found in the Hebrew scriptures, interpreting its two main figures as "The Bridegroom is our Lord, and we, I say in all humility, are the Bride."[91] Throughout the sermons, he focuses upon the significance of this love, stating repeatedly that "Love is a great reality," and "How great is the power of love."[92] Inspired especially by the writings of Origen on that Old Testament book,[93] he also drew upon those of John the beloved disciple, Augustine, Cassian, Benedict, and Gregory. In his own sermons on the *Song of Songs,* he starts with the presupposition that humankind, created in God's image, necessarily longs for, desires, God's love. As he writes in sermon eighteen, "God himself is love, and nothing created can satisfy the person who is made to the image of God, except the God who is love, who alone is above all created natures."[94] This innate desire for God is "that spark of unfulfilled love which exists in the human heart."[95]

According to Bernard, each of us is created with a deep inner void that can be filled only through an intimate relationship with God. As Buddhists posit the concept of "the hungry ghost" and those with addictions know firsthand of a seemingly great emptiness which no drugs, possessions, or sexual experiences can fill, so Bernard suggests, as had Augustine, that only with our hearts united with God can we begin to experience true liberation, joy, healing, satisfaction. The soul, the eternal in us all, inherently thirsts for union with God, what Bernard associates with the experience of "spiritual marriage" to which the *Song of Songs* alludes. Though our experiences of union may be rare and brief (as he states in sermon twenty-three: "Alas! how rare the time; how short the stay!"),[96] we must still prepare ourselves for those visitations.

For Bernard, love is a passion, a burning desire, a taste, a touch, a kiss. The latter, the kiss, is the primary image in the *Song of Songs* around which Bernard develops his theology of union and communion with God—much as Teresa of Avila centuries later would develop hers around the castle image. According to him, before a person experiences union with God, what he calls "the kiss of the mouth," one must have already exchanged two other kisses. The first is that of the "kiss of the feet" of Jesus: this is the stage of repentance when a person recognizes sin and the need for confession and forgiveness; a "kiss" Bernard links with conversion and the traditional mystical stage of *purgation.* The second stage, according to Bernard, is "the kiss to the hand" when spiritual progress is made by Jesus lifting a person up, drawing him or her to himself, the traditional stage of *illumination*. These two stages lead to the third, that of *union* with God or "spiritual marriage," what Bernard calls "the kiss to the mouth." He believes that "every soul, if it is vigilant and careful in the practice of all virtues, can arrive at this holy repose and enjoy the embraces of the Bridegroom," and that for "a person so disposed, God will not refuse that most intimate kiss of all, a mystery of supreme generosity and ineffable sweetness."[97]

In this teaching on love and spiritual marriage between God and the individual, Bernard frequently alludes to his own experiences, while inviting his listeners or readers to reflect on theirs. He presumes, as he says in sermon twenty-three, that while "instruction" can make us "learned," "experience makes us wise."[98] Jean Leclercq believes that, for Bernard, "the first and most important of his sources" as a writer and theologian "was his own experience," and, in that way, "he did not delight in abstractions; rather, he loved the concrete and experiential. From experience he took his starting point, and it was to experience that he wanted to lead."[99] Michael Casey agrees with Leclercq, seeing Bernard not as an academic, but fundamentally "a monk."[100] I would agree with both scholars, while adding the perspective that Bernard was, in the context of experience, a pastoral theologian, above all: someone who as pastor or spiritual guide helps others to understand their experiences in light of scripture and tradition. Bernard, as other patristic writers had done, thus emphasizes in his writings experience over instruction, love over knowledge, and wisdom over the mere accumulation of "facts." His theology was the result of a lifetime of commitment, contemplation, and prayer, and written primarily for the instruction and guidance of others.

In more than one place in the sermons, Bernard gives descriptions of those experiences that he likely associated with "spiritual marriage." In sermon seventy-four, for example, he writes:

> I want to tell you of my own experience, as I promised. But I make this disclosure only to help you, and if you

> derive any profit from it I shall be consoled....I admit that the Word has also come to me—I speak as a fool—and has come many times. But although he has come to me, I have never been conscious of the moment of his coming. I perceived his presence, I remembered afterwards that he had been with me; sometimes I had a presentiment that he would come, but I was never conscious of his coming or his going. And where he comes from when he visits my soul, and where he goes, and by what means he enters and goes out, I admit that I do not know even now; as John says, "You do not know where he comes from or where he goes" (John 3:8)....

Bernard then gets more specific, rhetorically asking a key question related to discernment, and to movements of the heart:

> You ask then how I knew he was present, when his ways can in no way be traced? He is full of life and energy, and as soon as he enters in, he awakens my slumbering soul; he stirs and soothes and pierces my heart, for before it was hard as stone, and diseased....Only by the movement of my heart, as I have told you, did I perceive his presence; and I knew the power of his might because my faults were put to flight and my human yearnings brought into subjection.

A different experience other than that of being energized, however, evidently happens when God leaves him:

> But when the Word has left me, all these spiritual powers become weak and faint and begin to grow cold, as though you had removed the fire from under a boiling pot, and this is the sign of his going. Then my soul must needs be sorrowful until he returns, and my heart again kindles within me—the sign of his returning. When I have had such experience of the Word, is it any wonder that I take to myself the words of the Bride,

> calling him back when he has withdrawn? For although my fervor is not as strong as hers, yet I am transported by a desire like hers....As often as he slips away from me, so often shall I call him back. From the burning desire of my heart I will not cease to call him, begging him to return, as if after someone who is departing, and I will implore him to give back to me the joy of his salvation, and restore himself to me.[101]

As is clear, much of Bernard's teaching on spiritual communion has to do with the movements of the heart, and being attentive to them. This is perhaps why he relates, as Origen and Hilary of Poitiers had done, to the figure of John the beloved disciple. For Bernard, John the evangelist is the primary symbol, after the Bride in the *Song of Songs,* of the individual soul, while St. John's writings, in particular, his gospel and first epistle, are Bernard's primary source for interpreting the *Song of Songs.*[102] As he says in sermon fifty-one, alluding to both Bride and beloved disciple: "Happy the soul who reclines on the breast of Christ, and rests between the arms of the Word!"[103] In another sermon, Bernard, quoting John, describes how any revelation of God, for a Christian, finds its primary source in "the only Son, who is in the Father's bosom," and who "has made it known" (John 1:18). He elaborates:

> But he has made it known, I will say...to John, the Bridegroom's friend, whose words these are....For his soul was pleasing to the Lord, entirely worthy both of the name and the dowry of a bride, worthy of the Bridegroom's embraces, worthy, that is, of leaning back on Jesus' breast. John imbibed from the heart of the only-begotten Son what he in turn had imbibed from the Father.[104]

Here Bernard is teaching a basic belief in Christianity: that, as Jesus, the Son of God, learned knowledge of God by listening to God the Father, so also, like John, the Church and the individual Christian can gain wisdom and holiness by listening to the heartbeat of God; that is, by paying attention to what God is teaching us in our daily lives and sometimes most confusing experiences. With this stance of listening, of paying attention, of being mindful (as Buddhists would say), we can begin to experience union with God, a union that is expressed—and needs to be expressed—in our loving actions, in our love.

In light of this theology as well as the imagery of John's "imbibing" from the heart of Jesus, it is interesting to note that Hildegard of Bingen, a contemporary of Bernard's and a mystic, as we recall, whose writings he had sent to the pope, uses a similar motif when she describes her mystical experiences: "from God's inspiration as it were drops of gentle rain splashed into the knowledge of my mind, just as the Holy Spirit permeated John the Evangelist when he sucked supremely deep revelation from the breast of Jesus."[105] Other medieval mystics evidently appreciated the intimacy between Jesus and John as symbolic of their own potential relationship with God. According to art historian Rolf Toman, "from an early date the motif of the close personal relationship between Christ and St. John was taken up both theologically and iconographically, and was linked with the bridal symbolism of the Song of Songs." In the early fourteenth century in southwest Germany a sculptured carving of the two men with the younger man resting his head on Jesus' heart became highly popular. The emergence of this Gothic sculpture, Toman says, "corresponded particularly closely to visionary images conceived by some German women mystics of the thirteenth century and given vivid expression in their writings. In the convents, the friendship between Christ and St. John, intensified by the bridal symbolism, was a subject for profound mystical contemplation, which could lead to the *unio mystica* in which the nuns experienced the union of their souls with God....A feeling of deep peace and intimate tenderness emanates from this statue in its portraying of the mystical union of the disciple with God."[106]

A person, then, who has this intimate relationship with God or at least is attempting to develop it, will necessarily reflect, Bernard believes, the God in whose image he or she has been created. Like the spiritual life itself, such a God, according to

Bernard, has two sides, one that he associates—as he did in his letters—with a father's love (that of "judgment" and "correction"), and the other with a mother's love (that of "mercy" and "consolation"): "the first curbs arrogance, the latter inspires trust; the first begets humility, the latter strengthens the faint-hearted; the first makes a person discreet, the latter devout. The first imbues us with fear of God, the latter tempers that fear with the joy of salvation....We are drawn when we are tested by temptations and trials; we run when inwardly suffused by consolation, breathing in the ointment-scented air."[107]

Accordingly, Bernard asks those who read his sermons on the *Song of Songs* to reflect those two sides of God. In their spiritual life, daily work, and ministries, leaders, he suggests, should offer consolation, a motherly side, to their followers, something that he and Benedict himself, as we recall, had to learn early in their own monastic careers when they were too hard on their fellow monks, not to mention themselves:

> Here is a point for the ear of those superiors who wish always to inspire fear in their communities and rarely promote their welfare. Learn, you who rule the earth. Learn that you must be mothers to those in your care, not masters; make an effort to arouse the response of love, not that of fear: and should there be occasion for severity, let it be paternal rather than tyrannical. Show affection as a mother would, correct like a father. Be gentle, avoid harshness, do not resort to blows....Why impose in addition your yoke on those whose burdens you ought rather to carry? Why will the young man, bitten by the serpent, shy away from the judgment of the priest, to whom he ought rather to run as to the bosom of a mother? If you are spiritual, instruct him in a spirit of gentleness, not forgetting that you may be tempted yourselves.[108]

At the same time, if gentleness does not work, Bernard recommends a more challenging expression of love. Drawing upon the story of the Good Samaritan, he states in another sermon that the wounds of the man whom the Good Samaritan saved "were healed not by oil alone but by wine and oil, to show that the spiritual physician must possess the wine of fervent zeal as well as the oil of gentleness, since he is called not only to console the timid but to correct the undisciplined. For if he sees that the wounded man, the sinner, rather than improving through the exhortations so gently addressed to him, rather disregards the kindness and becomes gradually more negligent, resting more securely in his sins, then, since the soothing oils have been tried in vain, the physician must use medicines with a more pungent efficacy. He must pour in the wine of repentance...."[109]

Here Bernard is advocating that those who seek to imitate the God in whose image they are made must at times express both a merciful, gentle, unconditional love and at other times a more challenging, confrontative, tough love. Bernard presumes that those who seek to identify themselves with monastic values, especially that of love, express both this "motherly" and "fatherly" side, incorporating into themselves their inherent masculine and feminine energies. In effect, he recommends that we become more androgynous.

The term "androgyny" comes from two Greek words: *andro* (male) and *gyne* (female), and usually refers to the interplay of masculine and feminine energies within the universe and the individual soul. Eastern religions refer to the Yin and Yang that make up a whole, and Carl Jung says in his writings, "Long before the physiologists demonstrated that by reason of our glandular structure there are both male and female elements in all of us, it was said that 'every man carries a woman within himself.' It is this female element in every male that I have called the 'anima.'"[110] The male element in every female Jung posited as the "animus." Jung believes that each of us, whatever our gender or sexual orientation, needs to come to name, accept, and integrate these masculine and feminine aspects of ourselves.

There are numerous allusions to this concept in medieval writings, especially those of the mystics. Bernard, in particular, seems to have been aware of its importance in ministry—as he shows in the frequent references he makes in his sermons on the *Song of Songs*. He also, it is worth noting, developed this concept in one of his last writings, mentioned earlier, his Life of St. Malachy, where he speaks of Malachy's paternal and maternal qualities: "He lived as though he were the one father of all. He cuddled them all and he protected them under the shelter of his wings, as a hen gathers her chickens. He did not distinguish sex, age, condition or person; he left no one out, embracing everyone in his merciful heart."[111]

Bernard, the New Monk

In 1153, Bernard was asked once more to act as mediator in an ecclesial dispute, one that took him from Clairvaux to Metz, Germany. He reluctantly accepted the invitation, but returned to the monastery exhausted from his labors. He died there, in the Valley of Light, on August 20. Before his death, his monks had grieved "inconsolably," we are told, asking him to never forget them, "you who have been father and mother to us...."[112]

Like Gregory the Great and numerous others, Bernard died under a cloud of controversy and disappointment, many people still blaming him for the crusade that had ended so tragically. Still, as the First Life says, "many people came from round about to pay their last respects" before his burial, "and the whole valley was full of weeping pilgrims come to make their farewells."[113] As a result of his own wishes, he was buried in the tunic in which Malachy had died—as Malachy had been buried in his habit. Bernard also had himself buried next to Malachy before the high altar of Clarivaux. Less than twenty-nine years later, on January 18, 1174, he was declared a saint, and almost seven hundred years later, on August 20, 1830, was given, on his feast day, the title of Doctor of the Church.

Bernard left a rich legacy, reflected not only in the numerous Cistercian daughter-houses that he had helped establish, but in the influence he had on an entire age. Surely one of the most notable of his effects was upon later Christian mystics as they turned to him for guidance in understanding their own experiences. He was the one who encouraged them, through his example, to pay attention to the movement of God in their hearts, to read not only from the scriptures but from "the book of experience" their lives offered. This emphasis on experience marks, according to Bernard McGinn, "a new and important shift in the development of Christian mysticism."[114] The message of the mystics, and of Bernard in particular, was about love: God's love for us, and our incompleteness unless we return that love. This was the message that was transmitted to the entire Middle Ages, and incorporated into the spiritualities and movements of such groups as the Franciscans and *Devotio Moderna,* and such saintly heroes as Julian of Norwich and Ignatius of Loyola. Though the monastic life may have originated with Antony's flight from the world, Bernard helped people see that the monastery was not a refuge from reality. Through his love and his calls for reform, he taught that no true monk or, really, any Christian can live for oneself alone; that an authentic spiritual life leads inevitably to a deeper immersion of oneself in the life of the Church and of the world. As William Yeomans says, "this is as much the conclusion of Bernard's life as it is of his doctrine."[115]

In many ways, Bernard of Clairvaux was a "new monk," not afraid of getting his hands dirty attempting to resolve the crises of his times both in the Church and in society; the prototype of later mystic reformers, such as Teresa of Avila and John of the Cross, who followed him. Although extremely frustrated at times, and rightly so, he shows how a person can work for transformation in the so-called "world," while maintaining the monk within, manifesting a love that is both unconditional and tender as well as challenging and "tough."

Conclusion

Let your light shine like a bright star in the western sky.

—Alcuin

David Knowles, the noted English historian of monasticism, once wrote that "the present must always learn from and be inspired by the vision of the past."[1] I have based this book on that insightful presupposition. It was inspired, as I suggested earlier, by a profound sense of the living presence of the past, and the belief that certain outstanding figures in the history of Christian monasticism are capable of acting today as spiritual mentors, teaching us about the need for recovering monastic values. If ever an age was in need of these values, it is ours. Prophetic figures from the past century with great foresight warned us of our present needs and increasingly dangerous predicament. Carl Jung, for one, described how modern society "abhors all inwardness" and how noise itself and our "technological gadgetry" contribute to addictive behaviors, slovenliness, superficiality, and, most perilously, "the spiritual disorientation of our time." "Most people are afraid of silence," he wrote to a Professor Oftinger more than fifty years ago, while "the need for noise is almost insatiable," protecting us "from painful reflection," while prolonging into later life "infantile dependence on the outside...."[2] Even earlier in the twentieth century, Aldous Huxley warned how our culture and economy are based upon keeping us perpetually distracted from the real issues of our lives:

> But it is upon fashions, cars, and gadgets, upon news and the advertising for which news exists, that our

> present industrial and economic system depends for its proper functioning. For...this system cannot work unless the demand for non-necessaries is not merely kept up, but continually expanded; and of course it cannot be kept up and expanded except by incessant appeals to greed, competitiveness and love of aimless distractions, which are the original sin of the mind; but never before today has an attempt been made to organize and exploit distractions, to make of them, because of their economic importance, the core and vital center of human life.[3]

The monastic figures from the past, examined here, however, teach a different approach to life, a different set of values. By turning to them as spiritual mentors, we have learned a great deal about discovering a more meaningful and ultimately happier way-of-living. Athanasius taught us about the value of sharing stories, and that one does not necessarily have to be a monk in a monastery to live out monastic values today. From the desert father Antony, we have learned of the values of silence and solitude and how they can foster discernment, the ability to begin to see differences between the right course of action—and the wrong. Hilary of Poitiers and Martin of Tours have taught us about the value of faith and its participative, communal dimension, while Augustine and Monica helped us see the importance of friendship and of recognizing a God often revealed in our passions and erotic side. We have also learned from Jerome, Paula, and Eustochium, of the need for qualified spiritual mentors and perhaps of becoming one ourselves, as Cassian and his friend, Germanus, taught us about the value of disclosing our secrets, and of becoming a leader who finds spiritual sustenance through dedication to inner work.

Others have added their own lessons through the example of their lives. Brigit's stories showed us how important compassion is in our work and ministries, while early Irish monasticism itself, with its "true monks" and "paramonastics," reveals the value of including laypeople in monastic communities as well as women in our churches' decision-making and leadership positions. As a result of his own busy-ness and anguish, Gregory the Great helped us recognize the importance of integrating contemplation in our daily lives and work, while Benedict and Scholastica taught us the values of stability and love. Finally, with his own emphasis on different types of loving and stages of mystical love, Bernard of Clairvaux recommended to us that we learn to read the "book of experience," the book of our lives, as well as the book of our hearts.

These are some of the lessons and values every "new monk" of the twenty-first century needs to identify and incorporate, making them part of his or her deeper Self. For the new monk who attempts to *both* develop an interior life *and* make a difference in the world today, these are not only *monastic* values, but *values of the soul*—and they apply to everyone, regardless of gender, occupation, material status, or place of residence. Within every human being there is a monastic archetype, a sacred energy, a contemplative dimension that must find expression in every generation. To identify the monk within, to begin to draw upon that archetypal energy, is to recognize every person's very human need to live simply, to pray often, and to choose well.

Of course, to begin to live this way will take time and effort, patience, courage, and persistence. As John Cassian says, "no virtue is perfected without effort," and all virtues are only "acquired over a long period" of time.[4] To begin to live this way presumes a dedication to developing an interior life, the interiority against which our culture today so vehemently fights. Cassian wisely suggests that we turn to "the inner man," what we might identify as "the true self." This true self for the Christian is symbolized by the "Christ within," and our dedication to becoming more "Christ-like," as the "Buddha within" is sought by followers of Buddha.[5] The famous monk who studied both Christian and Buddhist traditions, Thomas Merton, believed that incorporating monastic values enables "the old superficial self to be purged away" and permits "the gradual emergence of the true, secret self" when a Christian becomes united in "one Spirit" with Christ.[6] For both Christians and Buddhists, the "false self" is equated with being directed by ego, power, material possessions, or "inordinate" desires, while the emergence of the "true self" depends upon the growth of such virtues as compassion, generosity, hospitality, forgiveness, love.

Beginning with Antony the ascetic and ending with Bernard the lover, what our study of monasticism reveals is that to affirm and nurture the growth of the true inner self a "new monk" must develop an *asceticism of loving*. This form of asceticism, so much needed today, presumes that to love well a person needs discipline, the setting of limits, the investment of time and energy in relationships and work that reflect at least some of the values discussed here. Such an asceticism of loving involves a commitment to growth in self-knowledge, self-discipline, and self-love, all based upon the profound conviction, so difficult at times to believe, that God created us for a purpose, that God loved us first. To discover this and make this a daily, *lived* experience, one must learn to listen to the heartbeat of God, as was recommended by numerous wisdom figures in this book.

Such listening, necessarily rooted in the pursuit of Truth, can help us begin to unmask our illusions, to live more in touch with true Reality. As we attempt to become more honest with ourselves and others, this listening provides us a mirror in which we can look into our own faces, as Augustine finally did. It can liberate us from our obsessions, addictions, and illusions; can help us find a greater degree of authentic freedom and true happiness. Listening can also help us develop qualities of hospitality, generosity, and forgiveness that will counteract those of rudeness, impatience, and violence so prevalent in today's world. Listening is ultimately a way of being in the world: being attentive, living mindfully, encouraging gentleness and compassion in all our encounters one day at a time.

To develop the "monk within," to make listening a daily discipline and practice, begins with the heart—that place, as Gregory the Great affirms in one of his homilies, where "the power of grace" enters and "the light of truth" pervades."[7] True listening, what he calls "contemplation," is rooted in the heart; it is all about listening to the heart, and surrendering it to God. It is the attempt, he says, to "fix the eye of the heart on the very ray of the unencompassed Light."[8] A more contemporary writer, Wayne Teasdale, reminds us that monasticism itself "has its origin in the hidden places of the heart."[9]

The "new monk" today, like the monks of old, is a person who searches not only his or her own heart, but seeks to listen intently to the deepest and most neglected voices, those from *within* as well as those of the marginalized and poor *outside.* Such a new monk adopts the posture of John, the beloved disciple, who rested his head on Jesus' chest, listening to the heartbeat of God. Such a person learns, through this posture, what Wilhelm Grimm narrates in one of his fairy tales: "One human heart goes out to another undeterred by what lies between";[10] and what Will Johnson associates with the Sufi poet Rumi: "the energies of the heart are like a mighty river."[11] Listening to the heart is really what contemplation itself is all about; the heart of contemplation truly is the heart, the place where one can experience light in the midst of darkness, a light that bears fruit.

Adopting such monastic values in our lives is not an escape from the world, but an entrance into it. We do not necessarily need to enter a monastery, but to carry its perspective and values into our world, wherever we go. As the desert mother Syncletica warned, "There are many who live in the mountains and behave as if they were in the town, and they are wasting their time. It is possible to be a solitary in one's mind while living in a crowd, and it is possible for one who is a solitary to live in the crowd of his [or her] own thoughts."[12] Everything depends, it seems, on the inner quiet one pursues by following the inclinations of the heart. By doing so, we too may experience transformation; with our hearts united with God's, we too might become light to our own time, as we integrate the "firey ecstasies of the heart."[13]

Fire and light are powerful images. All of the saints whose lives we have explored in this book have been touched by them, as we recall from the chapter titles themselves; all reflect the light from the East where Christian monasticism originated and to which every period of monks has been drawn. Athanasius's stories of Antony tell of the beam of light that came to the holy man at a time when he most needed encouragement in his struggle with demons; Martin and Hilary, because of their spiritual leadership, were perceived as "new rays of light" during their own time; Augustine and Monica's friendship itself was like "a kindling fire," while Jerome's personality was compared to "flashing lightning."

Light and fire are also evident in the other lives examined here. Cassian's and Germanus's inner fire, their enthusiasm and desire for holiness, were recognized by the monks they visited; Brigit was described as a "golden, sparkling flame," who helped bring to birth a new form of Christianity in her native land; Gregory recommended that true leaders shine like a "candle placed on a candlestick," while Benedict's monasticism was compared to a magnificent road "glittering with thousands of lights." Bernard's Clairvaux was compared to a "valley of light" that was responsible for a monastic renaissance in the twelfth century and beyond.

In retrospect, we can see that all of the saints studied here reveal a God of fire, a God of light, one that Moses discovered in his own time in the burning bush on Mount Sinai (cf. Exodus 3). As he was asked to take off his shoes before it because he was on sacred ground, so too are we invited to honor the light shed by these saintly heroes, incorporating as best we can the monastic values that they exemplify. From them we might learn what Abba Joseph taught when a fellow monk asked him what more he should do to be saved. Stretching out his hands to heaven, we are told, his fingers became like ten lamps of fire. Then he said to the monk: 'Why not be totally changed into fire?'"[14]

This desire to be changed, to experience transformation, to find union with God perhaps underlies every person's attraction to monastic values today. Such a desire, when listened to, sets us on a journey, a pilgrimage of the heart that can be described only as "mystical." As the contemporary writer Paul Wilkes says, "Monastic values are mystical values, and mystical values are profoundly human values for all those who seek a relationship with God."[15] By studying the history of monasticism and its great heroes we come to realize that, for the Christian, much of what we call "monastic" is purely and simply what being a follower of

Christ is all about, and that being a monk, whether inside monastic enclosures or outside "in the world," is simply becoming the sort of person everyone ought to be, a person who unites action and contemplation in the care of souls. Discovering and welcoming the monk in each of us, silent, solitary, yearning for God, our lives can begin to shine like bright stars in the western sky, as Alcuin, the great teacher and monk at Charlemagne's court, once said,[16] helping others to perceive, perhaps for the first time, the light and love of God.

Notes

Introduction

1. William Wordsworth, "Lines Composed a Few Miles Above Tintern Abbey, On Revisiting the Banks of the Wye During a Tour. July 13, 1798," in *Poems of William Wordsworth* (Norwalk, CT: The Easton Press, 1995), 196.

2. Edward Gibbon, *The History of the Decline and Fall of the Roman Empire,* Vol. IV (London: The Folio Society, 1987), 299.

3. Thomas Merton, *Contemplative Prayer* (New York: Image Books, 1996), 85.

4. See Robert E. Daggy, ed., *"Honorable Reader": Reflections on My Work* (New York: Crossroad, 1991), 85.

5. Thomas Merton, *The Seven Storey Mountain* (San Diego: Harcourt Brace Jovanovich, 1976), 419.

6. See especially John S. Dunne, *Love's Mind: An Essay on Contemplative Life* (Notre Dame, IN: University of Notre Dame, 1993), vii, x, and, concerning his own life, *A Journey with God in Time: A Spiritual Quest* (Notre Dame, IN: University of Notre Dame, 2003).

7. Kathleen Norris, *The Cloister Walk* (New York: Riverhead Books, 1996), xiii.

8. See Morris Berman, *The Twilight of American Culture* (New York: W. W. Norton & Co., 2000), 57, 53, 49, 88, 54, 178, 157, 158.

9. A. M. [Donald] Allchin, *The Living Presence of the Past* (New York: Seabury Press, 1981), 18, 97.

10. See my book, *Pilgrimage: Exploring a Great Spiritual Practice* (Notre Dame, IN: Sorin Books, 2004), for a description of the origins of my desire to travel as well as a brief ecumenical history of pilgrimage and its various dimensions.

11. Elizabeth Johnson, *Friends of God and Prophets: A Feminist Theological Reading of the Communion of Saints* (New York: Continuum, 1999), 13.

12. See Richard Kierckhefer, and George Bond, eds., *Sainthood: Its Manifestations in World Religions* (Berkeley, CA: University of California Press, 1988).

13. Thomas Merton, *The Last of the Fathers* (New York: A Harvest/HBJ Book, 1954), 27.

14. See Jean Leclercq, OSB, *The Love of Learning and the Desire for God: A Study of Monastic Culture* (New York: Fordham University Press, 1985), 108 and 34.

15. This is the opinion of Linda Kulzer, a Benedictine, who is commenting on the Benedictine lay oblate movement. See Linda Kulzer and Roberta Bondi, eds., *Benedict in the World: Portraits of Monastic Oblates* (Collegeville, MN: The Liturgical Press, 2002), 5.

16. See Tom Cashman, "Modern Communities—Celtic Traditions," *Anamchairde* Newsletter, vol. 6, no. 3, summer 2000.

17. See Dennis and Trisha Day, "Some Reflections on the Emergence of Cistercian Associations," *Cistercian Studies Quarterly*, vol. 35, no. 1 (2000), 93–112.

18. See Kulzer and Bondi, *Benedict in the World: Portraits of Monastic Oblates*, 6.

19. Jean Leclercq, OSB, *The Love of Learning and the Desire for God: A Study of Monastic Culture*, 89.

20. See Rita Knipe, *The Water of Life: A Jungian Journey through Hawaiian Myth* (Honolulu: University of Hawaii Press, 1989), 74.

21. T. S. Eliot, "Little Gidding," in *Four Quartets* (New York: Harcourt Brace and Jovanovich, 1971), 51.

Chapter One: Light from the East

1. Jean Leclercq, OSB, *The Love of Learning and the Desire for God: A Study of Monastic Culture* (New York: Fordham University Press, 1985), 98.

2. See Armand Veilleux, trans., *Pachomian Koinonia*, Vol. I (Kalamazoo, MI: Cistercian Publications, 1980), 46.

3. For an excellent discussion of Pachomius's leadership, see Philip Rousseau, *Pachomius: The Making of a Community of Fourth-Century Egypt* (Berkeley, CA: University of California Press, 1985), especially 104–118.

4. See Philip Amidon, trans., *The Church History of Rufinus of Aquileia* (Oxford: Oxford University Press, 1997), 71.

5. See Kevin Corrigan, trans., *The Life of Saint Macrina* (Toronto: Peregrina Publishing Co., 1995), 6–7, for a story about Basil when he returned, "monstrously conceited," from the school of rhetoric as a young man, and how he learned from his sister, Macrina, not only a love of philosophy, but, perhaps most importantly, some degree of humility.

6. *Ibid.*, 7.

7. *Ibid*, v.

8. See James Goehring, *Ascetics, Society, and the Desert: Studies in Early Egyptian Monasticism* (Harrisburg, PA: Trinity Press International, 1999), 24. For an excellent resource on early Christian women leaders, see Jean LaPorte, *The Role of Women in Early Christianity* (New York: The Edwin Mellen Press, 1982).

9. See George Gingras, trans., *Egeria: Diary of a Pilgrimage* (New York: Newman Press, 1970), 87.

10. Robert Gregg, trans., *Athanasius: The Life of Antony and the Letter to Marcellinus* (New York: Paulist Press, 1980), 42–43.

11. Leclercq, *The Love of Learning and the Desire for God*, 90.

12. Derwas Chitty, *The Desert a City* (Crestwood, NY: St. Vladimir's Seminary Press, 1966), 2.

13. Hilary and Gregory are quoted in Edward Gibbon, *The History of the Decline and Fall of the Roman Empire*, Vol. III (London: The Folio Society, 1987), 33–34, 66.

14. See R. P. C. Hanson, *The Search for the Christian Doctrine of God: The Arian Controversy, 318–381* (Edinburgh: T&T Clark, 2000), xix–xx.

15. See Stanley Burgess, *The Holy Spirit: Ancient Christian Traditions* (Peabody, MA: Hendrickson Publishers, 1984), especially 116–123, 133–144, and 167–179. Basil's writings resulted in his being called "The Doctor of the Holy Spirit."

16. Alexander Roberts, trans., "The Sacred History of Sulpitius Severus," in Philip Schaff and Henry Wace, eds., *A Select Library of Nicene and Post-Nicene Fathers of the Christian Church*, vol. XI (Grand Rapids, MI: Wm. B. Eerdmans, 1986), 116.

17. Edward Gibbon, *Decline and Fall of the Roman Empire*, Vol. III, 35.

18. See Philip Amidon, trans., *The Church History of Rufinus of Aquileia*, 38.

19. Philip Rousseau, *Ascetics, Authority, and the Church* (Oxford: Oxford University Press, 1978), 83, 63.

20. See F. A. Wright, trans., *Select Letters of St. Jerome* (Cambridge, MA: Harvard University Press, 1930), 209, 169, 119, 217.

21. See Samuel Rubensen, *The Letters of St. Antony: Monasticism and the Making of a Saint* (Minneapolis, MN: Fortress Press, 1995), 182–183.

22. See Gregory Nazianzus, "Oration 21," *Select Orations, Sermons, Letters; Dogmatic Treatises,* in Philip Schaff and Henry Wace, eds., *A Select Library of Nicene and Post-Nicene Fathers of the Christian Church* (Grand Rapids, MI: Wm. B. Eerdmans, 1955), 274–275.

23. See Laura Foreman, *Alexander, the Conqueror* (San Diego, CA: Tehabi Books, 2004), for an excellent biography and artistic prints on Alexander and his era.

24. See Robert Payne, *The Fathers of the Eastern Church* (New York: Dorset Press, 1989), 25.

25. Charles Kannengiesser, *Early Christian Spirituality* (Philadelphia, PA: Fortress Press, 1986), 8–9.

26. See Simon Wood, trans., *Clement of Alexandria: Christ the Educator* (New York: Fathers of the Church, Inc., 1954), x, xv–xvii.

27. See Bernard McGinn, *The Foundations of Mysticism* (New York: Crossroad, 1991), 102–108, and Patricia Cox, *Biography in Late Antiquity* (Berkeley, CA: University of California Press, 1983), 18, footnote #10.

28. Henri Crouzel, *Origen,* trans. A. S. Worrall (San Francisco: Harper & Row, 1989), xi.

29. See Bernard McGinn, *The Foundations of Mysticism,* p. 109, and Henri Crouzel, *Origen,* "The Works of Origen," 37–49.

30. See G. A. Williamson, trans., *Eusebius: The History of the Church from Christ to Constantine* (New York: Penguin Books, 1989), 183.

31. See Bernard McGinn, *The Foundations of Mysticism,* 117, 109.

32. W. H. C. Frend, *The Early Church: From the Beginnings to 461* (London: SCM Press Ltd., 1982), 189.

33. Philip Amidon, trans., *The Church History of Rufinus of Aquileia,* 26–27.

34. Charles Kannengiesser, "Athanasius," in Adrian Hastings, ed., *The Oxford Companion to Christian Thought* (Oxford: Oxford University Press, 2000), 47.

35. See Archibald Robertson, ed., "Select Writings and Letters of Athanasius, Bishop of Alexandria," in Philip Schaff and Henry Wace, eds., *A Select Library of Nicene and Post-Nicene Fathers,* Vol. IV (Grand Rapids, MI: Wm. Eerdmans, 1980), 4–30, and A Religious of CSMV, trans., *On the Incarnation* (Crestwood, NY: St. Vladimir's Seminary Press, 2003), especially 89–96.

36. Philip Amidon, trans., *The Church History of Rufinus of Aquileia,* 13.

37. See Archibald Robertson, ed., "Select Writings and Letters of Athanasius, Bishop of Alexandria," xxxvii.

38. See David Brakke, *Athanasius and Asceticism* (Baltimore, MD: Johns Hopkins University Press, 1995), 267.

39. See, for example, Norman Russell, trans., *The Lives of the Desert Fathers* (Kalamazoo, MI: Cistercian Publications, 1981), 3.

40. See Philip Amidon, trans., *The Church History of Rufinus of Aquileia*, 70, and Samuel Rubenson, *The Letters of St. Antony: Monasticism and the Making of a Saint* (Minneapolis, MN: Fortress Press, 1995), 183.

41. See Robert Gregg, trans., *Athanasius: the Life of Antony and the Letter to Marcellinus*, 30, 97.

42. Edward Gibbon, *The History of the Decline and Fall of the Roman Empire*, Vol. IV (London: The Folio Society, 1987), 291.

43. See Letter 127, in W. H. Fremantle, trans., "The Principal Works of St. Jerome," in Philip Schaff and Henry Wace, eds., *A Select Library of Nicene and Post-Nicene Fathers of the Christian Church*, Second Series, Vol. VI (Grand Rapids, MI: Wm. B. Eerdmans Publishing Company, 1989), 254–255.

44. Edward Gibbon, *The History of the Decline and Fall of the Roman Empire*, Vol. III, 56.

45. See Robert Meyer, trans., *Palladius: The Lausiac History* (New York: Newman Press, 1964), 144–145.

46. Archibald Robinson, ed., "Select Writings and Letters of Athanasius, Bishop of Alexandria," li.

47. Gregory Nazianzus, "Oration 21," *Select Orations, Sermons, Letters; Dogmatic Treatises*, in Philip Schaff and Henry Wace, eds., *A Select Library of Nicene and Post-Nicene Fathers of the Christian Church*, 276.

48. See Athanasius, Festal Letter #39, in Archibald Robinson, ed., "Select Writings and Letters of Athanasius, Bishop of Alexandria," 551–552.

49. Charles Kannengiesser, "Athanasius," 49.

50. A Religious of CSMV, trans., *On the Incarnation*, 21.

51. See Tim Vivian and Apostolos N. Athanassakis, trans., *The Life of Antony: The Coptic Life and The Greek Life* (Kalamazoo, MI: Cistercian Publications, 2003), lix, footnote 75.

52. Quoted in David Brakke, *Athanasius and Asceticism*, 14.

53. See Gregory Nazianzus, "Oration 21," in *Select Orations, Sermons, Letters; Dogmatic Treatises*, 270, 275.

Chapter Two: Hearts on Fire

1. See, for example, in Robert Gregg, trans., *Athanasius: The Life of Antony and the Letter to Marcellinus* (New York: Paulist Press, 1980), 90, when Athanasius says that among Christian rulers as well as Antony's numerous followers, "all asked to have him as a father."

2. *Ibid.*, 29.

3. See Gregory Nazianzus, "Oration 21," in *Select Orations, Sermons, Letters; Dogmatic Treatises*, in Philip Schaff and Henry Wace, eds., *A Select Library of Nicene and Post-Nicene Fathers of the Christian Church* (Grand Rapids, MI: Wm. B. Eerdmans, 1955), 270.

4. See Patricia Cox, *Biography in Late Antiquity* (Berkeley, CA: University of California Press, 1983), 17–44.

5. Robert Gregg, trans., *Athanasius: The Life of Antony and the Letter to Marcellinus*, 42.

6. See Porphyry's *Life of Pythagoras*, #35, where he refers to the Greek philosopher's "unchanging condition," and that "he was neither more elated by pleasure, nor dejected by grief," in Kenneth Sylvan Guthrie, trans., *The Pythagorean Sourcebook and Library* (Grand Rapids, MI: Phanes Press, 1987), 130.

7. Jerome himself specifically mentions Antony's "seven letters in Coptic," which he sent to "various monasteries" in his work, *Lives of Illustrious Men*, found in Philip Schaff and Henry Wace, eds., *A Select Library of Nicene and Post-Nicene Fathers of the Christian Church*, vol. III (Grand Rapids, MI: Wm. B. Eerdmans, 1996), 379. The letters themselves are found in Derwas Chitty, trans., *The Letters of St. Anthony* (Oxford: SLG Press, 1975).

8. For a full exploration of the history and theological content of Antony's letters, see Samuel Rubenson, *The Letters of St. Antony: Monasticism and the Making of a Saint* (Minneapolis, MN: Fortress Press, 1995). For a discussion of Antony's education and other early monks' social background, see especially 9–14, 116–125.

9. See Derwas Chitty, trans,. *The Letters of Saint Antony the Great* (Oxford: SLG Press, 1975), iv.

10. See chapter seven, "The Sayings of the Desert Fathers," in Samuel Rubenson, *The Letters of St. Antony: Monasticism and the Making of a Saint*, 145–162, for a full examination of the sayings attributed to Antony, and how reliable they reflect the historical Antony.

11. See Tim Vivian, "Introduction," in Tim Vivian and Apostolos Athanassakis, trans., *The Life of Antony: The Coptic Life and The Greek Life* (Kalamazoo, MI: Cistercian Publications, 2003), xxvi–xxvii.

12. See Patricia Cox, *Biography in Late Antiquity: A Quest for the Holy Man* (Berkeley, CA: University of California Press, 1983), for an excellent examination of the paradigms of "the divine sage" and "the holy man."

13. See Timothy Ware, *The Orthodox Church* (New York: Penguin Books, 1997), 39–40. Ware, an Orthodox bishop living in Oxford, England, specifically mentions Antony as "the earliest and most celebrated of the monastic startsy."

14. See Robert Gregg, trans., *Athanasius: The Life of Antony and the Letter to Marcellinus*, 30–32.

15. *Ibid.*, 32–33.

16. Jerome, of course, would be the exception. Not to be outdone by Athanasius's work, he wrote his own hagiography on the Life of a different desert father, Paul of Thebes, which attempted to show that he, Paul, was really "the First Hermit." See Carolinne White, trans., "Life of Paul of Thebes by Jerome," *Early Christian Lives* (New York: Penguin Books, 1998), 73–84.

17. See the excellent research of E. A. Judge, quoted in James Goehring, *Ascetics, Society, and the Desert: Studies in Early Egyptian Monasticism* (Harrisburg, PA: Trinity Press International, 199), 20–26. Peter Brown develops this concept of "the holy man" in Late Antiquity as reconciler and advisor to villagers in a number of his works; see, for example, his *Authority and the Sacred* (Cambridge University Press, 1995), especially 57–78.

18. Robert Gregg, trans., *Athanasius: The Life of Antony and the Letter to Marcellinus*, 33.

19. See, for example, Robert Johnson, a Jungian therapist, *Owning Your Own Shadow* (HarperSanFrancisco, 1991), 10–20, where he says, "We cannot make light without a corresponding darkness." He even alludes to St. Antony: "No one can escape the dark side of life, but we can pay out that dark side intelligently. St. Anthony paid for his beatific vision by night horrors—visions of evil parading before him. He bore the tension between these opposites and finally came to that superordinate insight that we can truly call sainthood." Johnson believes, as does Jung, that "the way to the Self is through the shadow." For an informative discussion on the shadow, see Connie Zweig and Jeremiah Abrams, eds., *Meeting the Shadow: the Hidden Power of the Dark Side of Human Nature* (New York: G. P. Putnam's Sons, 1993).

20. See Gerald Messadie, *A History of the Devil* (New York: Kodansha International, 1996), 169, 172.

21. Regarding the persistence of pagan beliefs and rituals long after the conversion of Constantine, see Ramsey MacMullen, *Christianity and Paganism in the Fourth to the Eighth Centuries* (New Haven, CT: Yale University Press, 1997).

22. Athanasius specifically alludes to pagans on pages 83–89, and 99, in Robert Gregg, trans., *Athanasius: The Life of Antony and the Letter to Marcellinus.* For one scholar's views on demons and paganism, see Placido Alvarez, "Demon Stories in the *Life of Antony* by Athanasius," *Cistercian Studies Quarterly,* Vol. XXIII, 1988:2, 101–118.

23. See Athanasius, "History of the Arians," #67, in Archibald Robertson, ed., "Select Writings and Letters of Athanasius, Bishop of Alexandria," in Philip Schaff and Henry Wace, eds., *A Select Library of Nicene and Post-Nicene Fathers,* Vol. IV (Grand Rapids, MI: Wm. Eerdmans, 1980), 295.

24. See, for example, Robert Gregg, trans., *Athanasius: The Life of Antony and the Letter to Marcellinus,* 135, footnote #14, and David Brakke, *Athanasius and Asceticism* (Baltimore, MD: Johns Hopkins University Press, 1995), 229–230.

25. See, for example, Robert Meyer, trans., *Palladius: the Lausiac History* (New York: Newman Press, 1964), 53–54, which tells of abba Nathaniel who encounters the devil in the "shape of a boy." Although the boy in this story is not described as black, the devious ways of the devil are still associated with the youth. In Celtic Christianity, despite the affirmation of deep emotional bonds between soul friends and their seeming lack of fear concerning such relationships, the devil is also portrayed as a black man in a number of sources. Besides the black-faced demons in the hagiography of St. Brendan's, and a depiction of Christ being tempted by a black devil in the *Book of Kells,* the same black figure appears in at least one other hagiography, the *Life of St. Samson of Dol.* See Thomas Taylor, trans., *The Life of St. Samson of Dol* (London: S.P.C.K., 1925), 67–70. Gregory the Great, bishop of Rome from 590 to 604, also includes in his *Dialogues* a story of a restless monk in one of the monasteries St. Benedict founded who was being tempted by a "black boy." See "Dialogue Two," in Odo John Zimmerman, trans., *Saint Gregory the Great: Dialogues* (New York: Fathers of the Church, Inc., 1959), 66–67.

26. See Armand Veilleux, trans., *Pachomian Koinonia,* Vol. II (Kalamazoo, MI: Cisterican Publications, 1982), 161–162.

27. See John Clarke, *Looking at Lovemaking: Constructions of Sexuality in Roman Art 100 BC–AD 250* (Berkeley, CA: University of California Press, 1998), 119–142.

28. Concerning black men as Saracens, see Jacques Le Goff, *The Medieval Imagination*, translated by Arthur Goldhammer (Chicago: University of Chicago Press, 1988), 49. According to John Boswell, *Christianity, Social Tolerance, and Homosexuality* (Chicago: University of Chicago Press, 1980), 194–195, "Although the Qur'an and early religious writings of Islam display mildly negative attitudes toward homosexuality, Islamic society has generally ignored these deprecations, and most Muslim cultures have treated homosexuality with indifference...." Although there are injunctions against homoerotic behavior in Islam, "in both Persia and Ottoman Turkey, men engaged in same-sex activities frequently but kept these activities secret so to allow them greater sexual freedom in private." See James Smalls, *Homosexuality in Art* (New York: Parkstone Press Ltd., n.d.), 134. Interpreting the black man as a Saracen, of course, would not apply to the *Life of Antony's* depiction, since historically Athanasius wrote before Islam had been born. Nevertheless, later readers certainly might interpret the figure as both an infidel and a homosexual.

29. See Benedicta Ward, *The Sayings of the Desert Fathers* (London: Mowbrays, 1975), 117. For an excellent article on the subject, see Peter Frost, "Attitudes toward Blacks in the Early Christian Era," *The Second Century*, 8, 1991: 1–11.

30. Robert Gregg, trans., *Athanasius: The Life of Antony and the Letter to Marcellinus*, 64.

31. See *ibid.*, 53, on illusions in the *Life of Antony*. In his letters, Antony says that discernment is the ability to recognize differences between good and evil, and "reality from unreality." See Derwas Chitty, trans,. *The Letters of St. Anthony*, 11.

32. See Marie-Louise von Franz, *Projection and Re-Collection in Jungian Psychology: Reflections of the Soul* (London: Open Court, 1980), especially 95–121, for an insightful discussion of these matters.

33. See Robert Gregg, trans., *Athanasius: The Life of Antony and the Letter to Marcellinus*, 70–71, 60.

34. Certain pagan philosophers, such as Porphyry (234–305 CE), engaged in these ascetic practices too. See Patricia Cox, *Biography in Late Antiquity: A Quest for the Holy Man*, 27–29. Again, this lifestyle of Antony would make him more appealing to some of Athanasius's potential converts: pagan philosophers.

35. The phrase "furnace of transformation" is found in Henri Nouwen, *The Way of the Heart: Desert Spirituality and Contemporary Ministry* (New York: Seabury Press, 1981), 25.

36. See Mary Forman, "Amma Syncletica—A Spirituality of Experience," in Margot King, ed., *On Pilgrimage: The Best of Vox Benedictina 1984–1993* (Winnipeg, Canada: Hignell Printing Ltd., 1994), 262–263.

37. See prints of Bosch's and Grunewald's "Temptations of Saint Anthony" in Rosa Giorgi, *Saints in Art* (Los Angeles, CA: The J. Paul Getty Trust, 2003), 34–35, 37.

38. Robert Gregg, trans., *Athanasius: The Life of Antony and the Letter to Marcellinus*, 39.

39. Armand Veilleux, trans., *Pachomian Koinonia*, Vol. I (Kalamazoo, MI: Cistercian Publications, 1980), 28.

40. For a full account of Augustine's conversion, see Rex Warner, trans., *The Confessions of St. Augustine* (New York: The New American Library, 1963), especially 173–183.

41. See Stephen McKenna, trans., *Porphyry: On the Life of Plotinus and the Arrangement of His Work* (Edmonds, WA: Holmes Publishing Group, 2001), 28. Again, this image of a shaft of light shows how Athanasius may have been highly influenced by the work of Porphyry and others.

42. Kieran Kavanaugh and Otilio Rodriguez, trans., *Teresa of Avila: The Interior Castle* (New York: Paulist Press, 1979), 13.

43. Robert Gregg, trans., *Athanasius: The Life of Antony and the Letter to Marcellinus*, 41–42.

44. See Stephen McKenna, trans., *Porphyry: On the Life of Plotinus and the Arrangement of His Work*, 14, 17.

45. For an excellent discussion of classical pagan philosophy in the context of living and dying well, see Jeremy Driscoll, trans., *Evagrius Ponticus: Ad Monachos* (New York: Newman Press, 2003), 200–214.

46. See Tim Vivian, trans., *Journeying into God: Seven Early Monastic Lives* (Minneapolis, MN: Fortress Press, 1996), 52.

47. See Patrick Fermor, *A Time to Keep Silence* (Pleasantville, NY: The Akadine Press, Inc., 1997), 68.

48. Robert Gregg, trans., *Athanasius: The Life of Antony and the Letter to Marcellinus*, 42–44.

49. See Louis Bouyer, *La Vie de S. Antoine* (Bellefontaine: Fontenelle, 1977), 116–117.

50. See Robert Gregg, trans., *Athanasius: The Life of Antony and the Letter to Marcellinus*, 43.

51. *Ibid.*, 44–58.

52. *Ibid.*, 57–60, 46.

53. Antony, Letter III, in Derwas Chitty, trans., *The Letters of Saint Antony the Great,* 11.

54. See Thich Nhat Hanh, *Living Buddha, Living Christ* (New York: Riverhead Books, 1995) for an exposition on "mindfulness" in Buddhist thought.

55. See Letter IV in Derwas Chitty, trans., *The Letters of Saint Antony the Great,* 12–13.

56. See Porphyry's *Life of Pythagoras,* #40, where he advises self-reflection "two times of the day: the one when we go to sleep, and the other when we awake," in Kenneth Sylvan Guthrie, trans., *The Pythagorean Sourcebook and Library,* 131.

57. Robert Gregg, trans., *Athanasius: The Life of Antony and the Letter to Marcellinus,* 72–73.

58. See Joseph Lienhard, "On 'Discernment of Spirits' in the Early Church," *Theological Studies,* 41, 1980, 507. A good exposition on the Ignatian "examen" can be found in Herbert Alphonso, *Discovering Your Personal Vocation: The Search for Meaning through the Spiritual Exercises* (New York: Paulist Press, 2001).

59. See Robert Gregg, trans., *Athanasius: The Life of Antony and the Letter to Marcellinus,* 97.

60. Bernard McGinn, *The Foundations of Mysticism* (New York: Crossroad, 1991), 135.

61. Benedicta Ward, trans., *The Sayings of the Desert Fathers,* 234.

62. Douglas Burton-Christie, *The Word in the Desert: Scripture and the Quest for Holiness in Early Christian Monasticism* (New York: Oxford University Press, 1993), 8.

63. Henri Nouwen, *The Way of the Heart,* 19.

64. Thomas Merton, *Thoughts in Solitude* (New York: Farrar, Straus, Giroux, 1958), 82.

Chapter Three: New Rays of Light

1. See Sulpicius Severus, "Life of St. Martin," in Bernard Peebles, trans., "Sulpicius Severus: Writings," *Fathers of the Church,* Vol. 7 (Washington, DC: Catholic University of America Press, 1949), 116–117.

2. Nora Chadwick, *Poetry and Letters in Early Christian Gaul* (London: Bowes & Bowes, 1955), 90.

3. Joseph Emmenegger, *The Functions of Faith and Reason in the Theology of Saint Hilary of Poitiers* (Washington, DC : Catholic University of America Press, 1947), 29.

4. See "St. Hilary, Bishop of Poitiers, Doctor of the Church," in Herbert Thurston and Donald Attwater, eds., *Butler's Lives of the Saints,* Vol. I (Westminster, MD: Christian Classics, 1987), 77.

5. Philip Amidon, trans., *The Church History of Rufinus of Aquileia* (New York: Oxford University Press, 1997), 38.

6. See P. G. Walsh, trans., *Cassiodorus: Explanation of the Psalms,* Vol. I (New York: Paulist Press, 1990), 34, and Bernard McGinn, *The Doctors of the Church* (New York: Crossroad Publishing Co., 1999), 6.

7. Sulpicius Severus, "Life of St. Martin," in Bernard Peebles, trans., "Sulpicius Severus: Writings," 109–110.

8. Rev. E. W. Watson, "The Life and Writings of St. Hilary of Poitiers," in Philip Schaff and Henry Wace, eds. *A Select Library of Nicene and Post-Nicene Fathers of the Christian Church,* Vol. IX (Grand Rapids, MI: Wm. B. Eerdmans, 1997), lvii.

9. See Nora Chadwick, *Poetry and Letters in Early Christian Gaul,* 95. She speaks of the "distrust" and "hostility of the Gaulist bishops" not only against monasticism in general, but against Martin in particular.

10. Robert Wilken, *The Spirit of Early Christian Thought* (New Haven, CT: Yale University Press, 2003), 7.

11. Marcus Borg, *The Heart of Christianity* (HarperSanFrancisco, 2003), 27.

12. Lewis Thorpe, trans., *Gregory of Tours: The History of the Franks* (New York: Penguin Books, 1974), 91.

13. See Nora Chadwick, *Poetry and Letters in Early Christian Gaul,* 93, and Clare Stancliffe, *St. Martin and His Hagiographer* (Oxford: Clarendon Press, 1983), 31.

14. Clare Stancliffe, *St. Martin and His Hagiographer,* 64–65 where Stancliffe discusses how Athanasius's *Life of Antony* and Jerome's saints' Lives inspired Sulpicius with the general idea of writing about Martin. "Of perhaps more fundamental importance for his influence upon Sulpicius is another fourth-century author, Hilary of Poitiers...." Stancliffe makes mention of specific works and passages of Hilary's which "Sulpicius was consciously echoing...."

15. See Sulpicius Severus, "Dialogues," especially the Second and Third which focus on Martin's life, in Bernard Peebles, trans., "Sulpicius Severus: Writings," especially 232, 216–217, 221.

16. Sulpicius Severus, "Life of St. Martin," in Bernard Peebles, trans., "Sulpicius Severus: Writings," 103.

17. Sulpicius Severus, "First Dialogue," in Bernard Peebles, trans., "Sulpicius Severus: Writings," 193.

18. See Sulpicius Severus, "Life of St. Martin," in Bernard Peebles, trans., "Sulpicius Severus: Writings," 105–106.

19. *Ibid.*,106–107.

20. *Ibid.*, 107–108.

21. See, for example, Bernard Peebles, trans., "Sulpicius Severus: Writings," 92, and 108, footnote 4, and Christopher Donaldson, *Martin of Tours* (Norwich, England: Canterbury Press, 1997), xviii.

22. Sulpicius Severus, "Life of St. Martin," in Bernard Peebles, trans., "Sulpicius Severus: Writings," 109–110.

23. See Christopher Donaldson, *Martin of Tours*, 43, and Clare Stancliffe, *St. Martin and His Hagiographer*, 22.

24. Nora Chadwick, *Poetry and Letters in Early Christian Gaul*, 116.

25. See Sulpicius Severus, "Life of St. Martin," in Bernard Peebles, trans., "Sulpicius Severus: Writings," 110.

26. *Ibid*,, 110–112.

27. Fortunatus's most famous hymn was "Pange Lingua." Helen Waddell describes him "as the first of the medieval poets," in her *Songs of the Wandering Scholars* (London: The Folio Society, 1982), 111. One of his most beautiful poems, innocuously entitled by Waddell, "Written on an island off the Breton coast," when it was, in fact, entitled, *"Ad Rucconem diaconum, modo presbyterum"* (115), is dedicated to his lover, a deacon by the name of Rucco who evidently lived in Paris. It was after his visit to St. Martin's tomb at Tours that Fortunatus decided to become a monk, a move that eventually led to his becoming bishop of Poitiers three or four years before his death. For his poems, see Judith George, trans., *Venantius Fortunatus: Personal and Political Poems* (Liverpool University Press, 1995). For more about him as a poet, see "The Poet as Visionary: Venantius Fortunatus's 'New Mantle' for Saint Martin," in Giselle de Nie, *Word, Image and Experience: Dynamics of Miracle and Self-Perception in Sixth-Century Gaul* (Burlington, VT: Ashgate Publishing Company, 2003), 49–83, and Brian Patrick McGuire, *Friendship and Community: The Monastic Experience 350–1250* (Kalamazoo, MI: Cistercian Publications, 1988), 98–100.

28. E. W. Watson, "The Life and Writings of St. Hilary of Poitiers," xlviii. For the *Life of Hilary* itself, see Venantius Fortunatus, *"Vita Sancti Hilarii,"* in B. Krusch, ed., *Monumenta Germaniae Historica,* Auctores Antiquissimi, 4:2 (Berlin, 1885), 1–11.

29. See "The Miracles of Hilary" by Fortunatus in Raymond Van Dam, *Saints and Their Miracles in Late Antique Gaul* (Princeton, NJ: Princeton University Press, 1993), 155–161.

30. R. P. C. Hanson says in his *The Search for the Christian Doctrine of God,* 459, that the autobiographical references may not be all that personal since "Hilary's language here is so much indebted to the themes and expressions of traditional rhetoric that we cannot trust it to give us autobiographical details." Considering how many of late antiquity's writers, pagan and Christian, relied on earlier classical works to frame and to express their own ideas and even theologies of history, Hilary would not be the first to use other persons' writings to express his.

31. See Stephen McKenna, trans., *Saint Hilary of Poitiers: The Trinity* (Washington, DC: Catholic University Press of America, 1954), 3–5.

32. *Ibid.*, 5.

33. *Ibid.*, 6–9.

34. *Ibid.*, 10–17.

35. Sulpicius Severus, "Life of St. Martin," in Bernard Peebles, trans., "Sulpicius Severus: Writings," 138.

36. See Christopher Donaldson, *Martin of Tours,* 67–68, regarding the election of clergy. Augustine's opinion on including lay people in any ordination is found in Sr. Mary Magdeleine Muller, trans., "Life of St. Augustine by Bishop Possidius," in Roy Deferrari, ed., *Early Christian Biographies* (Washington, DC: Catholic University of America Press, 1952), 99.

37. Hilary of Poitiers is quoted in Philip Rousseau, *Ascetics, Authority, and the Church* (Oxford: Oxford University Press, 1978), 86.

38. See P. Smulders, trans., *Hilary of Poitiers' Preface to His Opus Historicum* (New York: E. J. Brill, 1995), 35.

39. Some believe that Constantius was already dead when Hilary wrote his *Invective Against Constantius;* others think that he was still alive. See D. H. Williams, "A Reassessment of the Early Career and Exile of Hilary of Poitiers," *Journal of Ecclesastical History,* Vol. 42, no. 2, April 1991, 208.

40. See E. W. Watson, "The Life and Writings of St. Hilary of Poitiers," xxv–xxvi.

41. Sulpicius Severus, "Life of St. Martin," in Bernard Peebles, trans., "Sulpicius Severus: Writings," 129.

42. See Archibald Robertson, "Select Writings and Letters of Athanasius, Bishop of Alexandria," Philip Schaff and Henry Wace, eds., *Nicene and Post-Nicene Fathers of the Christian Church,* Vol. IV (Grand Rapids, MI: Wm. B. Eerdmans, reprinted 1980), 289.

43. Lionel Wickham, trans., *Hilary of Poitiers: Conflicts of Conscience and Law in the Fourth-century Church* (Liverpool University Press, 1997), xiii.

44. See Alexander Roberts, trans., "The Sacred History of Sulpitius Severus," in Philip Schaff and Henry Wace, eds., *A Select Library of Nicene and Post-Nicene Fathers,* Vol. XI (Grand Rapids, MI: Wm. B. Eerdmans Publishing Co., 1986), 117.

45. Hilary of Poitiers, *Against Valens and Ursacius,* in Lionel Wickham, trans., *Hilary of Poitiers: Conflicts of Conscience and Law in the Fourth-century Church,* 17.

46. Stephen McKenna, trans. *Saint Hilary of Poitiers: The Trinity* (Washington, DC: Catholic University of America Press, 1954), 402.

47. Hilary, "On the Councils," in E. W. Watson, "The Life and Writings of St. Hilary of Poitiers," p. 24.

48. Judith Herrin, *The Formation of Christendom* (Oxford: Basil Blackwell, 1987), 69.

49. Archibald Robertson, "Select Writings and Letters of Athanasius, Bishop of Alexandria," lvii.

50. Stephen McKenna, trans. *Saint Hilary of Poitiers: The Trinity,* 107.

51. See E. W. Watson, "The Life and Writings of St. Hilary of Poitiers," lix.

52. Hilary of Poitiers, *On the Trinity,* quoted in Stanley Burgess, *The Holy Spirit: Ancient Christian Traditions* (Peabody, MA: Hendrickson Publisher, 1984), 169.

53. Stephen McKenna, trans. *Saint Hilary of Poitiers: The Trinity,* 45–46.

54. *Ibid.,* 187–189.

55. *Ibid.,* 188, 46, 52.

56. Origen, *Commentary on John's Gospel,* quoted in G. A. Williamson, trans., *Eusebius: the History of the Church from Christ to Constantine* (New York: Penguin Books, 1989), 202.

57. See Bernard McGinn, *The Foundations of Mysticism* (New York: Crossroad, 1991), 122.

58. Hilary of Poitiers, quoted in Joseph Emmenegger, *The Functions of Faith and Reason in the Theology of Saint Hilary of Poitiers* (Washington, DC: Catholic University of American Press, 1947), 211–212.

59. Stephen McKenna, trans. *Saint Hilary of Poitiers: The Trinity,* 51–52.

60. Sulpicius Severus, "Sacred History," translated by Alexander Roberts, in Philip Schaff and Henry Wace, eds., *A Select Lilbrary of Nicene and Post-Nicene Fathers,* Vol. XI (Grand Rapids, MI: Wm. B. Eerdmans, reprinted 1986), 118.

61. Sulpicius Severus, "Life of St. Martin," in Bernard Peebles, trans., "Sulpicius Severus: Writings," 112.

62. Clare Stancliffe, *St. Martin and His Hagiographer,* 24.

63. Sulpicius Severus, "Life of St. Martin," in Bernard Peebles, trans., "Sulpicius Severus: Writings," 115.

64. *Ibid.*, 17.

65. Nora Chadwick, *Poetry and Letters in Early Christian Gaul*, 99.

66. Sulpicius Severus, "Life of St. Martin," in Bernard Peebles, trans., "Sulpicius Severus: Writings," 117–118.

67. See Sharon Farmer, *Communities of Saint Martin: Legend and Ritual in Medieval Tours* (Ithaca, NY: Cornell University Press, 1991), 19.

68. Sulpicius Severus, "Life of St. Martin," in Bernard Peebles, trans., "Sulpicius Severus: Writings," 132, 119.

69. *Ibid.*, 122.

70. Sulpicius Severus, "The Second Dialogue," in Bernard Peebles, trans., "Sulpicius Severus: Writings," 201.

71. Sulpicius Severus, "Letter to Bassula," in Bernard Peebles, trans., "Sulpicius Severus: Writings," 158.

72. See Sulpicius Severus, "Letter to Aurelius," in Bernard Peebles, trans., "Sulpicius Severus: Writings," 147–148.

73. See Peter Brown, *The Cult of the Saints* (Chicago: University of Chicago Press, 1981), 4.

74. Stephen McKenna, trans., *Saint Hilary of Poitiers: The Trinity*, xiii.

75. See Rev. E. W. Watson, "The Life and Writings of St. Hilary of Poitiers," lvi–lvii.

76. See Hilary of Poitiers, *Commentary on Matthew*, quoted in Manlio Simonetti, ed., *Ancient Christian Commentary on Scripture: Matthew 14–28* (Downers Grove, IL: InterVarsity Press, 2002), 100.

Chapter Four: Like a Kindling Fire

1. See *Conf.* VIII, 6, in Rex Warner, trans., *The Confessions of St. Augustine* (New York: New American Library, 1963), 170–172.

2. *Ibid.*, 173–183.

3. George Lawless, *Augustine of Hippo and his Monastic Rule* (Oxford: Clarendon Press, 1987), 161.

4. See Ludwig Schopp, trans., "The Happy Life," in Ludwig Schopp, ed., *Writings of Saint Augustine*, Vol. I (New York: CIMA Publishing Co., 1948), 37.

5. Thomas Gilligan, trans., "The Soliloquies," in Ludwig Schopp, ed., *Writings of Saint Augustine*, Vol. I, 370.

6. Tarisicius Van Bavel, *The Rule of Saint Augustine* (Garden City, NY: Image Books, 1986), 11.

7. Thomas Gilligan, trans., "The Soliloquies," 363.

8. See Sr. Mary Magdeleine Muller and Roy Deferrari, trans., "Life of St. Augustine by Bishop Possidius," in Roy Deferrari, ed., *Early Christian Biographies* (Washington, DC: Catholic University of America Press, 1952), 76. This hagiography is not like those of Sts. Antony's and Martin's. Possidius's seems more "historical" than "mythological"; there is, for example, only one miracle-story: a healing Augustine performed, reluctantly, shortly before his own death (see p. 111). Regarding the community at Thagaste, there is some controversy over whether it really was monastic, but I agree with Peter Brown, who describes "the group of like-minded enthusiasts" gathered around Augustine as a "monastery," and George Lawless, who says that he believes "Augustine's foundation at Thagaste was, indeed, his first monastery." See Peter Brown, *Augustine of Hippo: A Biography—a New Edition* (Berkeley, CA: University of California Press, 2000), 129), and George Lawless, Augustine of Hippo and His Monastic Rule, 46.

9. See Peter Brown, *Augustine of Hippo: A Biography*, 131.

10. George Lawless, *Augustine of Hippo and his Monastic Rule*, 44.

11. Jean Leclercq, OSB, *The Love of Learning and the Desire for God: A Study of Monastic Culture* (New York: Fordham University Press, 1985), 181.

12. Henry Chadwick, trans., *Saint Augustine: Confessions* (Oxford: Oxford Univerisity Press, 1991), ix.

13. Brian Patrick McGuire, *Friendship and Community: The Monastic Experience, 350–1250* (Kalamazoo, MI: Cisterican Publications, 1988), 41.

14. See *Conf.* IX, 12; in Rex Warner, trans., *The Confessions of St. Augustine*, 205.

15. See *Conf.* II, 1–2; Warner, *Confessions of St. Augustine*, 40–42.

16. *Conf.* III, 1; Warner, *Confessions of St. Augustine*, 52.

17. *Conf.* IV, 2; Warner, *Confessions of St. Augustine*, 70.

18. See Ludwig Schopp, trans., "The Happy Life," pp. 51 and 59, where Augustine refers to Adeodatus as the youngest of all his companions at Cassiciacum, and how he "promises great success, unless my love deceives me." It is also ironic that, considering his father's struggle with eros, it is Adeodatus, probably thirteen-years-old at the time, and surely struggling with his own emerging sexuality, who says to the group, "Whoever has a spirit free from uncleanness has God." For Augustine's other work, this one containing a dialogue between him and his son alone, see Peter King, trans., *Augustine: Against the Academicians and The Teacher* (Indianapolis: Hackett Publishing Co., 1995), 94–146.

19. *Conf.* VI, 16; Warner, *Confessions of St. Augustine*, 132–133.

20. According to Aristotle and others, there were three categories of friendships: one based upon utility; one on pleasure; and a third, more rare, upon virtue, the sharing of common goals and ideals. Even marriage relationships, because they were between two who were basically unequal, could not be identified with friendship—although Aristotle did admit that there might be a "kind of friendship" between the marriage partners if each was of good moral character. Thus the term for friendship, *amiticia,* for the most part, was not to be applied to relationships between men and women. See Elizabeth Clark, *Jerome, Chrysostom, and Friends* (New York: The Edwin Mellen Press, 1979), 37–40, for a discussion on Aristotle's theory of friendship.

21. *Conf.* III, 4; Warner, *Confessions of St. Augustine,* 56–57.

22. See "Laelius: On Friendship" in Michael Grant, trans., *Cicero: On the Good Life* (New York: Penguin Books, 1984), 175–227.

23. *Ibid.,* 226–227.

24. See "The Platonists" in Peter Brown, *Augustine of Hippo,* 79–92.

25. See Michael Grant, *Cicero: On the Good Life,* 49–116, for Cicero's *The Tusculans,* on the essentials for a happy life. As we recall, Augustine wrote *The Happy Life* in 386, the same year as his conversion in Milan and retreat at Cassiciacum.

26. See J. H. Baxter, trans., *St. Augustine: Select Letters* (Cambridge, MA: Harvard University Press, 1980), 491–499.

27. Augustine, *City of God,* 19: 8; see Vernon Bourke, ed., *The City of God* (Garden City, NY: Image Books, 1958), 447.

28. See *Conf.* IV, 1–3; Warner, *Confessions of St. Augustine,* 69–73.

29. See *Conf.* IV, 4; Warner, *Confessions of St. Augustine,* 73–74.

30. See Margaret Miles, *Desire and Delight: A New Reading of Augustine's Confessions* (New York: Crossroad, 1992), 73–74. Although Miles acknowledges that "male and female homoeroticism…is amply documented throughout the history of the West," she does state that it would be "anachronistic in the extreme to attempt to label Augustine's sexual orientation in twentieth-century terms that rely on socially constructed categories."

31. For a discussion of male sexuality in classical times, see David Halperin, *One Hundred Years of Homosexuality And Other Essays on Greek Love* (New York: Routledge, 1990), and Eva Cantarella, *Bisexuality in the Ancient World* (New Haven: Yale University, 1992). For a discussion on contemporary male sexuality, including bisexuality, see Joel Ryce-Menuhin, *Naked and Erect: Male Sexuality and Feeling* (Wilmette, IL: Chiron Publications, 1996).

32. See Robert Fagles, trans., *Homer: The Iliad* (New York: Viking Penguin, 1990), 470.

33. *Conf.* IV, 4; Warner, *Confessions of St. Augustine,* 73.

34. *Ibid.,* 74–75.

35. See "The Buddha" by Michael Carrithers in Keith Thomas, ed., *Founders of Faith* (Oxford: Oxford University Press, 1986), 1–85, and N. K. Sandars, trans., *The Epic of Gilgamesh* (Baltimore, MD: Penguin Books, 1972).

36. See *Conf.* IV, 5–7; Warner, *Confessions of St. Augustine,* 75–77.

37. See *Conf.* IV, 8; Warner, *Confessions of St. Augustine,* 77–78.

38. *Conf.* V, 13; Warner, *Confessions of St. Augustine,* 108. For a discussion on Ambrose, see George Saint-Laurent's "Augustine's Hero-Sage-Holy Man: Ambrose of Milan" in *Word and Spirit: St. Augustine* (Petersham, MA: St. Bede's Publications, 1987), 22–34.

39. *Conf.* VI, 6; Warner, *Confessions of St. Augustine,* 120.

40. *Conf.* VI, 7; Warner, *Confessions of St. Augustine,* 121.

41. *Conf.* VI, 10; Warner, *Confessions of St. Augustine,* 126–127.

42. See *Conf.* IX, 4; Warner, *Confessions of St. Augustine,* 189, and Baxter, *St. Augustine: Select Letters,* 57.

43. See *Conf.* IV, 3: Warner, *Confessions of St. Augustine,* 73.

44. *Conf.* VI, 10; Warner, *Confessions of St. Augustine,* 127.

45. See Raymond Canning, trans., *The Rule of Saint Augustine* (Garden City, NY: Image Books, 1986), 11.

46. See *Conf.* VIII, 7, 12; Warner, *Confessions of St. Augustine,* 173, 183.

47. *Conf.* IX, 6; Warner, *Confessions of St. Augustine,* 193–194.

48. See Kenneth Mackenzie, trans., *Dante Alighieri's The Divine Comedy* (London: The Folio Society, 1979). In *Paradise,* Canto 32, pp. 452–453, Dante refers to Beatrice, his guide who has brought him to heaven, and her turning from him to God:

"...and though she seemed to be
So far away, she smiled and looked at me,
And turned once more to the eternal Fount."

C. S. Lewis uses the same phrase (in Italian) at the conclusion of his book, *A Grief Observed* (New York: Seabury Press, 1973), 60, when he describes the death of his wife: "How wicked it would be, if we could, to call the dead back! She said not to me but to the chaplain, 'I am at peace with God.' She smiled, but not at me. *Poi si torno all' eterna fontana.*"

49. *Conf.* IX, 3; Warner, *Confessions of St. Augustine,* 187–188.

50. See *Conf.* X, 8 (Warner, *Confessions of St. Augustine,* 218), for Augustine's reference to that harbor of memory, and *Conf.* IV, 14 (Warner, 84), when Augustine states that "man himself is a great deep." The writings of Carl Jung, especially his autobiography, *Memories, Dreams, Reflections* (New York: Vintage Books, 1961), offer many insights into the mysterious depths of the soul, which, he says, contain unconscious memories, including "ancestral."

51. See "Symposium" in Erich Segal, ed., *The Dialogues of Plato* (New York: Bantam Books, 1986), 233–286.

52. Letter quoted in Adele Fiske, "St. Augustine: Stages of Friendship," in *Friends and Friendship in the Monastic Tradition,* (Cuernavaca, Mexico: Centro Intercultural De Documentacion, 1970), 2/3. For Aelred of Rievaulx's understanding of friendship, see his classic, *Spiritual Friendship* (Kalamazoo, MI: Cistercian Publications, 1974).

53. Peter Brown, *Augustine of Hippo: A Biography,* 17.

54. See *Conf.* I, 6 (Warner, *Confessions of St. Augustine,* pp. 20–21); II, 3 (p. 13); III, 11 (pp. 66–67); V, 8 (p. 101); VI, 13 (p. 131).

55. *Conf.* IX, 10; Warner, *Confessions of St. Augustine,* 200–201.

56. *Conf.* IX, 12; Warner, *Confessions of St. Augustine,* 205.

57. See Henry Chadwick, *Augustine* (Oxford: Oxford University Press, 1986), 69.

58. See Augustine, *Against Academicians,* II, 2: 5, quoted in Peter Brown, *Augustine of Hippo: A Biography,* 97.

59. Augustine's earlier cold disdain for his father, possibly a result of his resentments at Patricius's affairs with other women, seems to dissipate when, after Monica's burial, he asks God to grant his parents peace and requests of the readers of his *Confessions* to remember both of his parents "with holy affection." See *Conf.* IX, 13; Warner, *Confessions of St. Augustine,* 209.

60. See *Conf.* VI, 14; Warner, *Confessions of St. Augustine,* 132. Romanianus was one of those who wanted to join Augustine in the community that was being planned in Milan. Augustine dedicated his *Against Academicians* and the *Concerning Religious Truth* to him, and possibly corresponded with him frequently, as can be seen in J. H. Baxter, *St. Augustine: Select Letters,* 3–17.

61. See *Conf.* V, 6;Warner, *Confessions of St. Augustine,* 96–99.

62. See *Conf.* VIII, 5; Warner, *Confessions of St. Augustine,* 167. Simplicianus succeeded Ambrose as bishop in Milan in 397.

63. *Conf.* V, 8; Warner, *Confessions of St. Augustine,* 102.

64. Carl Jung, *Collected Works,* Vol. 9, 1 (Princeton, NJ: Princeton University Press, 1969), 86–87.

65. There are numerous references in Augustine's correspondence to his work—and his lack of self-care, which led to poor health; see J. H. Baxter, trans., *St. Augustine: Select Letters*. In 410, for example, he addresses a letter to his "dearly beloved brethren, the clergy, and all the laity," written from the country, in which he laments that "in the weak state of my health I cannot adequately cope with all the attentions required from me by the members of Christ, whom love and fear of Him compel me to serve" (p. 213). In a letter written in 411 to Albina, daughter-in-law of the famous convert, Melania the Elder, Augustine is even more forthright concerning those duties: "God is my witness that it is only because of the service I owe to the love of my brethren and the fear of God that I put up with all the administration of the Church's business over which I am supposed to love the exercise of lordship, and that I have so little liking for it that I should wish to do without it, if it could be done without unfaithfulness to my office" (p. 241). And, in a letter to Lampadius, he asks for the man's prayers that God might give him leisure (p. 487).

66. For a discussion on Manichaean views on sexuality, see Elizabeth Clark, *St. Augustine on Marriage and Sexuality* (Washington, DC: Catholic University of America Press, 1996), 32–41.

67. See Vernon Bourke, ed., *The City of God,* 146 ff., for Augustine's discussion on Socrates, and in Book XIV, chapter 16 (pps. 315 ff.) of that work, of the "problem" of sexual passion, and how it is linked, for Augustine, with shame. Elizabeth Clark, in *St. Augustine on Marriage and Sexuality,* 5–6, states that as Augustine came to define his sexual ethics, he believed that the *only* justification for sexual intercourse was procreation, and that "any form of sexual activity which automatically ruled out the possibility of conception, such as anal or oral sex or same-sex relations, was to be condemned as 'against nature.'"

68. See C. S. Lewis, *The Four Loves* (Norwalk, CT: The Easton Press, 2002), 4. Throughout his book he uses the principle enunciated by Thomas A Kempis in *The Imitation of Christ;* how "the highest does not stand without the lowest."

69. See Adolf Guggenbuhl-Craig, *Power in the Helping Professions* (New York: Spring Publications, 1971).

70. See James Hillman, *Myth of Analysts* (Evanston, IL: Northwestern University Press, 1972), 141.

71. See Rosemary Haughton, *The Passionate God* (New York: Paulist Press, 1981), and *The Transformation of Man* (New York: Paulist Press, 1967).

72. See Joseph Campbell, *The Power of Myth* (New York: Doubleday, 1988), 89.

73. For Diotima's teachings on eros, see "Symposium" in Erich Segal, *The Dialogues of Plato*, 263–274.

74. T. S. Eliot, "Little Gidding," *The Complete Poems and Play, 1909–1950* (San Diego: Harcourt Brace Jovanovich, 1971), 139.

75. Sr. Mary Magdeleine Muller, and Roy Deferrari, trans., "Life of St. Augustine by Bishop Possidius," in Roy Deferrari, ed., *Early Christian Biographies*, 108.

76. See Vernon Bourke, ed., *St. Augustine: City of God* (Garden City, NY: Image Books, 1958), especially Book XIX, 427–482.

77. Augustine, Sermon 348, 2, quoted in Peter Brown, *Augustine of Hippo: A Biography*, 436.

78. See *Conf.* VIII, 12, X, 6, and X, 27; Warner, *Confessions of St. Augustine*, 183, 214, and 235.

79. See Tarisicius Van Bavel, *The Rule of Saint Augustine*, 12, 13, 16, 17, 22.

80. George Lawless, *Augustine of Hippo and His Monastic Rule*, 156.

81. See Tarisicius Van Bavel, *The Rule of Saint Augustine*, 3.

82. For the admonition in St. Benedict's Rule, see Timothy Fry, ed., *The Rule of Saint Benedict* (New York: Vintage Books, 1998), 3.

83. For Augustine's phrase, "ear of the heart," see Cuthbert Butler, *Western Mysticism* (New York: E. P. Dutton & Co., 1923), 30.

Chaper Five: Flashing Lightning

1. About seventeen to twenty letters that they addressed to each other have survived. For their content and commentary upon it, as well as a description of their relationship, see Carolinne White, *The Correspondence (394–419) Between Jerome and Augustine of Hippo* (Lewiston, NY: The Edwin Mellen Press, 1990), and Stephen Cannon, "The Jerome-Augustine Correspondence," in *Word and Spirit, a monastic review*, no. 9: St. Augustine (387–1987) (Petersham, MA: St. Bede's Publications, 1987), 35–45.

2. See Augustine, Letter 28, in Carolinne White, *The Correspondence (394–419) Between Jerome and Augustine of Hippo*, 65–70.

3. For all three hagiographies mentioned here, see Marie Liguoir Ewald, trans., in Roy J. Deferrari, ed., *Early Christian Biographies*

(Washington, DC: The Catholic University of America Press, 1981), pp. 217–297. On pp. 291–292, specific reference is made to the "inner monk" when the monk Malchus, after being taken captive by "Ishmaelites," speaks of "the monk whom I nearly lost in my own country I had found again in the desert" and how, at another time, "I...began to lament and sob for the monk I was on the point of losing."

4. Quoted in Jean Steinmann, *Saint Jerome and His Times* (Notre Dame, IN: Fides Publishers, 1959), 226.

5. See Jean Leclercq, *The Love of Learning and the Desire for God: A Study of Monastic Culture* (New York: Fordham University Press, 1961), 97.

6. Edward Kennard Rand, *Founders of the Middle Ages* (Cambridge: Harvard University Press, 1928), 125, calls Jerome one "of the foremost letter-writers of all ages," while Philip Rousseau, *Ascetics, Authority, and the Church in the Age of Jerome and Cassian* (Oxford: Oxford University Press, 1978), 99, states that Jerome's writings during his time comprise "the most significant corpus of ascetic literature in the West."

7. I agree with Stefan Rebenich, *Jerome* (New York: Routledge, 2002), and Eugene Rice, Jr., *Saint Jerome in the Renaissance* (Baltimore: Johns Hopkins University Press, 1988), who believe that it makes more sense to date Jerome's birth in the mid-340s CE than 331, as J. N. D. Kelly, *Jerome: His Life, Writings, and Controversies* (Peabody, MA: Hendrickson Publishers, 1998), suggests.

8. Jerome, quoted in Stefan Rebenich, *Jerome*, 2.

9. See Eugene Rice, Jr., *Saint Jerome in the Renaissance*, 204.

10. See Stefan Rebenich, *Jerome*, 7.

11. See Letter 22 in Charles C. Mierow, *The Letters of St. Jerome*, Vol. I (New York: Newman Press, 1963), 165–166.

12. Eugene Rice, Jr., *Saint Jerome in the Renaissance*, 6.

13. His passion for books was, in fact, considerable. As his biographer says, "One of his most enthusiastic extra-curricular pursuits, and one which was to remain with him throughout his life, was the building up of a library. This was to become his most precious possession, and he was later to confess that, when he abandoned everything else for the religious life, he could not bring himself to surrender 'the library which I had collected at Rome with immense zeal and labour.'" Even while Jerome was in the desert of Chalcis, he "brought his ever growing library with him (his cave must have been roomier than most), and evidently spent a great deal of time reading books...,and also having them copied." See J. N. D. Kelly, *Jerome: His Life, Writings, and Controversies*, 20, 48–49.

14. Letter 11, in Charles C. Mierow, *The Letters of St. Jerome,* Vol. I, 53.

15. Letter 12, in Charles C. Mierow, *The Letters of St. Jerome,* Vol. I, 55–56.

16. See Aemilius Lubeck, *Hieronymus quos nouerit scriptores et ex quibus hauserit* (Leipzig, 1872), for a listing of the references in Jerome's writings to Cicero's *Laelius: De Amicitia.*

17. See Letters 3 and 17, in Charles C. Mierow, *The Letters of St. Jerome,* Vol. I, 31, and 77.

18. Letter 105 in Carolinne White, *The Correspondence (394–419) Between Jerome and Augustine of Hippo,* 95.

19. Carolinne White discusses the classical origins of numerous Christian definitions of friendship in her excellent book, *Christian Friendship in the Fourth Century* (London: Cambridge University Press, 1992).

20. Letter 4 in Charles C. Mierow, *The Letters of St. Jerome,* Vol. I, 34.

21. Letter 5 in Charles C. Mierow, *The Letters of St. Jerome,* Vol. I, 37.

22. Letter 60 in F. A. Wright, trans., *Select Letters of St. Jerome* (Cambridge, MA: Harvard University Press, 1933), 309.

23. Letter 145 in W. H. Fremantle, trans., "The Principal Works of St. Jerome," in Philip Schaff and Henry Wace, eds., *A Select Library of Nicene and Post-Nicene Fathers of the Christian Church,* Second Series, Vol. VI (Grand Rapids, MI: Wm. B. Eerdmans Publishing Company, 1989), 288.

24. *Apologia contra Rufinum,* I, 30, quoted in Paul Monceaux, *St. Jerome: the Early Years* (London: Sheed & Ward, 1933), 13.

25. See Elizabeth Clark, *Jerome, Chrysostom, and Friends* (New York: The Dwin Mellen Press, 1979), 45.

26. J. N. D. Kelly, *Jerome: His Life, Writings, and Controversies,* 91.

27. See his letter 22, in Charles C. Mierow, *The Letters of St. Jerome,* Vol. I, 140, when Jerome laments what he had lost, and other references. See J. N. D. Kelly, *Jerome: His Life, Writings, and Controversies,* 21, where he discusses this.

28. See Charles C. Mierow, *The Letters of St. Jerome,* Vol. I, 140.

29. Jerome writes: "When one is old, the spark now and then glows among the burnt out ashes…." From his Commentary on Amos, II, prologue, quoted in J. N. D. Kelly, *Jerome: His Life, Writings, and Controversies,* 295.

30. Jerome is quoted in Boniface Ramsey, trans., *John Cassian: The Conferences* (New York: Paulist Press, 1997), 19.

31. See Letter 22 in Charles C. Mierow, *The Letters of St. Jerome,* Vol. I, 140. For a full discussion of Mary Magdalene and how she has been

identified, sometimes falsely, see Susan Haskins, *Mary Magdalen: Myth and Metaphor* (New York: Harcourt Brace & Co., 1993).

32. Charles C. Mierow, *The Letters of St. Jerome,* Vol. I, 149.

33. See "Laelius: On Friendship" in Michael Grant, trans., *Cicero: On the Good Life* (New York: Penguin Books, 1984), 191 and 197.

34. *Ibid.,* 203.

35. See Letter 45 in F. A. Wright, trans., *Select Letters of St. Jerome,* 181.

36. See James Hillman, *The Soul's Code: In Search of Character and Calling* (New York: Random House, 1996), 120–121.

37. Letter 127, in F. A. Wright, trans., *Select Letters of St. Jerome,* 439–467.

38. See Letter 27 in W. H. Fremantle, trans., "The Principal Works of St. Jerome," in Philip Schaff and Henry Wace, eds., *A Select Library of Nicene and Post-Nicene Fathers of the Christian Church,* Second Series, Vol. VI, 44.

39. *Ibid.,* Letter 45, 59.

40. *Ibid.,* Letter 108, 196.

41. *Ibid.,* Letter 45, 59.

42. *Ibid.,* Letter 108, 195–203.

43. *Ibid.,* Letter 99, 188.

44. See Letter 22, F. A. Wright, trans., *Select Letters of St. Jerome,* 159.

45. See Letter 108 in W. H. Fremantle, trans., "The Principal Works of St. Jerome," in Philip Schaff and Henry Wace, eds., *A Select Library of Nicene and Post-Nicene Fathers of the Christian Church,* Second Series, Vol. VI, 197.

46. See Letter 22 in Charles C. Mierow, *The Letters of St. Jerome,* Vol. I, 147–179.

47. Letter 151, quoted in J. N. D. Kelly, *Jerome: His Life, Writings, and Controversies,* 328.

48. See J. N. D. Kelly, *Jerome: His Life, Writings, and Controversies* (Peabody, MA: Hendrickson Publishers, 1998), 15.

49. See David Wiesen, *St. Jerome as a Satirist* (Ithaca, NY: Cornell University Press, 1964), 2, where the author states that St. Jerome "refers to himself on four occasions as a satirist in the larger sense of a penetrating and vituperative critic of human behavior," and in footnote 5, lists Letters 22, 32, and 50, "where Jerome specifically speaks of himself as a successor of Horace and Juvenal…."

50. From Jerome's "Commentary on the Epistle to the Galatians," quoted in Paul Monceaux, *St. Jerome: the Early Years* (London: Sheed & Ward, 1933), 38.

51. "Preface to Ezekiel," in W. H. Fremantle, trans., "The Principal Works of St. Jerome," in Philip Schaff and Henry Wace, eds., *A Select Library of Nicene and Post-Nicene Fathers of the Christian Church*, Second Series, Vol. VI, 500.

52. "Preface to Jeremiah," in W. H. Fremantle, trans., "The Principal Works of St. Jerome," in Philip Schaff and Henry Wace, eds., *A Select Library of Nicene and Post-Nicene Fathers of the Christian Church*, 499.

53. Postumianus, quoted in Sulpicius Severus, "First Dialogue," in Bernard Peebles, trans., "Sulpicius Severus: Writings," *Fathers of the Church*, Vol. 7 (Washington, DC: Catholic University of America Press, 1949), 172–173.

54. See Jean Steinmann, *Saint Jerome and His Times*, 355, for reference to Jerome as patron saint of both ill-tempered people and book-lovers.

55. Quoted in Eugene Rice, Jr., *Saint Jerome in the Renaissance*, 99.

56. For a full discussion of the meaning of Durer's famous woodprint, see Eugene Rice, Jr., *Saint Jerome in the Renaissance*, 39–41, 111–113.

57. Stefan Rebenich, *Jerome*, 59.

58. See Eugene Rice, Jr., *Saint Jerome in the Renaissance*, 47.

59. See "Life Paul of Thebes by Jerome," in Carolinne White, trans., *Early Christian Lives* (New York: Penguin Books, 1998), 73–84.

60. See Luther's comments in Eugene Rice, Jr., *Saint Jerome in the Renaissance*, 138–139. The Christian humanist, Erasmus, however, loved Jerome and was the first to establish a reliable canon of Jerome's authentic letters and treatises, while also writing the first biography of him, Rice says, which was "free of chronological confusion and legendary elaboration" (p. 124).

61. Whitley Stokes, trans., *The Martyrology of Oengus the Culdee* (London, 1905), 197.

62. See Eugene Rice, Jr., *Saint Jerome in the Renaissance*, 96–97.

63. See Letters 52 and 107 in F. A. Wright, trans., *Select Letters of St. Jerome*, 203 and 363.

64. See Nora Chadwick, *Poetry and Letters in Early Christian Gaul* (London: Bowes & Bowes, 1954), 21, where she says: "Both Paula and Eustochium already had a good knowledge of Greek, to which they now added that of Hebrew also. We owe much of Jerome's work on Holy Scripture to their trained help and devotion and to the stimulus which they gave him."

65. See Letter 127 in W. H. Fremantle, trans., "The Principal Works of St. Jerome," in Philip Schaff and Henry Wace, eds., *A Select Library of*

Nicene and Post-Nicene Fathers of the Christian Church, Second Series, Vol. VI, 255.

66. See Stefan Rebenich, *Jerome*, 53.

Chapter Six: A Kind of Fire

1. Cassian, Conl 11.4; Boniface Ramsey, *John Cassian: The Conferences* (New York: Paulist Press, 1997), 410, and Cassian, Inst 5: 24; Edgar Gibson, trans., "The Institutes of John Cassian," in P. Schaff and H. Wace, eds., *Nicene and Post-Nicene Fathers of the Christian Church*, Vol. XI (Grand Rapids, MI: Wm. B. Eerdmans, 1986), 242.

2. Colm Luibheid, trans., *John Cassian: Conferences* (New York: Paulist Press, 1985), 143. For this passage, in particular, I prefer Luibheid's translation to Ramsey's.

3. Cassian, Conl 1.23; Ramsey, *John Cassian: The Conferences*, 63–64.

4. Cassian, Conl 1.1; Ramsey, *Conferences*, 37.

5. Columba Stewart, in his book, *Cassian the Monk* (New York: Oxford University Press, 1998), 3, describes Cassian's "elusiveness," and states that "the chronology of major events in his life or his writings rests on deduction rather than solid evidence." Nothing at all is known about the early life of Germanus. Only Cassian's own references to him give us intimations of what sort of person he was. Stewart says on pp. 13–14 that the writer Palladius mentions Germanus briefly in his work, *Dialogue on the Life of John Chrysostom*.

6. Bernard McGinn, in *The Presence of God: A History of Western Christian Mysticism*, Vol. 1 (New York: Crossroad, 1991), x, describes Cassian as one of the three "founding fathers" of Western mysticism (along with Ambrose and Augustine), and goes on to state on p. 218 that Cassian's writings "were the most important links between Eastern and Western monasticism for over a millennium."

7. Owen Chadwick, *John Cassian* (London: Cambridge University Press, 1968), 162.

8. Gibson, "Institutes," 199.

9. For references to desert women, see Thomas Merton, *The Wisdom of the Desert* (New York: A New Directions Book, 1960), 32 & 55; Helen Waddell, trans., *The Desert Fathers* (Ann Arbor: University of Michigan Press, 1972), 66, 68, 85, 95, 103, 110, 126–127; and Elizabeth Bryson Bongie, trans., *The Life of Blessed Syncletica by Pseudo-Athanasius* (Toronto, Ontario: Peregrina Publishing Co., 1996); and Laura Swan, *The Forgotten Desert Mothers* (New York: Paulist Press, 2001).

10. See Robert Meyer, trans., *Palladius: The Lausiac History* (New York: Newman Press, 1964), 17.

11. See Benedicta Ward in *Harlots of the Desert* (London: Mowbray & Co., 1987) for early hagiographies of desert women.

12. See Cassian, Inst 5.24; Gibson, "Institutes," 242.

13. Cassian, Inst 2.3; Gibson, "Institutes," 206.

14. See, for example, Mk. 8:14–21 where Jesus warns his followers to avoid the influence and spirit of the Pharisees.

15. Cassian, Inst 12.13; Gibson, "Institutes," 283.

16. Cassian, Conl 2.13; Ramsey, *Conferences,* 98; Luibheid, *Conferences,* 71.

17. Cassian, Inst 2.3; Gibson, "Institutes," 206.

18. Benedicta Ward, *The Sayings of the Desert Fathers* (Kalamazoo, MI: Cistercian, 1984), 176.

19. Cassian, Inst 4; Gibson, "Institutes," 219 ff.

20. See Eugen Herrigel, *The Method of Zen* (New York: Vintage Books, 1974), 34–35, about what he calls "testing time."

21. Cassian, Inst 4; Gibson, "Institutes," 221 ff.

22. Cassian, Inst 10.22; Gibson, "Institutes," 274.

23. Cassian, Inst 5.41; Gibson, "Institutes," 233.

24. Cassian, Inst 4.24–25; Gibson, "Institutes," 226–227.

25. Cassian, Inst 10.25; Gibson, "Institutes," 275.

26. Cassian, Conl 2.5; Ramsey, *Conferences,* 87–88.

27. Cassian, Inst 4.9; Gibson, "Institutes," 221.

28. Cassian, Inst 12.28; Gibson, "Institutes," 289.

29. Cassian, Inst 5.39; Gibson, "Institutes," 232.

30. Cassian, Inst 4. 9; Gibson, "Institutes," 221.

31. Cassian, Conl 2.4; Ramsey, *Conferences,* 87.

32. Robert Gregg, trans., *Athanasius: The Life of Antony and the Letter to Marcellinus* (New York: Paulist Press, 1980), Ch. 16 in the "Life," 43.

33. Helen Waddell in her book, *The Desert Fathers,* p. 21, describes Cassian's Conferences as a "case book" in itself "of spiritual direction."

34. Today, in a society that has come to acknowledge the great diversity of addictive behaviors, most of us would appreciate the terminology concerning "sicknesses of the soul." We would, however, be much more reticent in associating "passion" with sin or "passions" with "disordered behavior" alone. Rosemary Haughton, for example, in her book, *The Passionate God* (New York: Paulist Press, 1981), speaks against such associations, declaring how the incarnation makes holy all materiality and bodiliness, and how sexual passion itself can lead us to

greater maturity and self-giving. Still, from the perspective of Cassian and other desert Christians, if a person is to experience "tranquility," or as they called it, "purity of heart," one must discipline or contain one's passions, and certainly name those behaviors that cause harm to oneself and others. For a discussion on "purity of heart," see Columba Stewart, *Cassian the Monk,* 43–47, and for one on passions as "disordered tendencies," see John Eudes Bamberger, trans., *Evagrius Ponticus: The Praktikos, Chapters on Prayer* (Kalamazoo, MI: Cistercian Publications, 1981), lxxvii–lxxxii.

35. See Joseph Colleran, trans., *St. Augustine: The Greatness of the Soul* (New York: Newman Press, 1978), in which Augustine describes the "seven levels" of the soul and states that the soul's "proper abode" and "homeland" is God.

36. Cassian, Inst 5.2; Gibson, "Institutes," 234.

37. Cassian, Inst 4.41; Gibson, "Institutes," 232. Cassian was not the first to recommend "contraries" as a way of curing spiritual disease. See Sr. Monica Wagner, trans., *Saint Basil: Ascetical Works* (New York: Fathers of the Church, Inc., 1950), 328–329, where Basil states in his "Long Rules," #51, that "the cure of those afflicted by evil passions should be effected according to the method used by physicians"; that is, a religious superior should "wage war upon their malady by setting up a counter-irritant to the vice, curing the infirmity of soul by drastic measures, if need be." See also Robert Meyer, trans., *Palladius: The Lausiac History,* 85, where Palladius says in #25 that "diseases are cured by their opposites." Christians seem to have embraced this wisdom from their pagan Roman culture, which had a common saying: *contraria contrariis curantur* (opposites are cured by opposites). See Peter Jones and Keith Sidwell, *Reading Latin* (New York: Cambridge University Press, 1986), 255. According to Oliver Davies, in his *Celtic Spirituality* (New York: Paulist Press, 1999), 39, this belief originated in Greek medical theory.

38. Cassian, Inst 7.13; Gibson, "Institutes," 252.

39. See Robert Meyer, trans., *Palladius: The Lausiac History,* 81–83.

40. Cassian, Inst 5.2; Gibson, "Institutes," 234.

41. For further information on the Celtic soul-friend tradition and its influence on the evolution of the sacrament of penance in the West, see O. D. Watkins, *A History of Penance,* Vols. I & II (London: Longmans, Green and Co., 1920), especially Vol. II on the "Keltic System." Other sources on the topic of the *anamchara* include Kenneth Leech, *Soul Friend: The Practice of Christian Spirituality* (New York: Harper & Row, 1977), and my own works, *The Celtic Soul Friend: A Trusted Guide for*

Today (Notre Dame, IN: Ave Maria Press, 2002), and *Stories of the Celtic Soul Friends: Their Meaning for Today* (New York: Paulist Press, 2004).

42. Cassian, Conl 1.22; Ramsey, *Conferences*, 63.

43. Cassian, Conl 2.11; Ramsey, *Conferences*, 91–93.

44. See Edward Sellner, "What Alcoholics Anonymous Can Teach Us About Reconciliation," *Worship*, Vol. 64, no. 4, July, 1990, 331–348, for a full discussion of AA's history and practice connected with Steps Four and Five; also *Step Five: Telling My Story* (Center City, MN: Hazelden Press, 1992).

45. Cassian, Conl 2.13; Ramsey, *Conferences*, 98.

46. Cassian, Inst 11.17; Gibson, "Institutes," 279.

47. Cassian, Inst 5.12; Gibson, "Institutes," 238.

48. See Mircea Eliade, *Rites and Symbols of Initiation* (New York: Harper Torchbooks, 1958), p. 4, on the importance of initiation for the regeneration of the entire community. Another excellent resource on initiation is Louis Mahdi, Steven Foster, and Meredith Little, eds., Betwixt and *Between: Patterns of Masculine and Feminine Initiation* (LaSalle, IL: Open Court, 1988).

49. Diarmuid O'Murchu, *Reclaiming Spirituality* (New York: Crossroad Publishing Co., 1997), 7.

50. See Edward Sellner, "Living and Ministering on the Edge: Marginality and Lay Leadership," *Chicago Studies*, Nov. 1994, vol. 33, no. 3: 267–283.

51. Cassian, Inst 2.9; Bonifice Ramsey, trans., *John Cassian: The Institutes* (New York: Newman Press, 2000), 43.

52. Cassian, Conl, Preface; Ramsey, *Conferences*, 30.

53. For a discussion of a desert Christian's developing a "single eye" and "purity of heart," see Norman Russell, trans., *The Lives of the Desert Fathers* (Kalamazoo, MI: Cistercian Publications, 1980), 30–37.

54. According to William Harmless, in *Desert Christians: An Introduction to the Literature of Early Monasticism* (Oxford: Oxford University Press, 2004), p. 384, Cassian's "vision" is that a "true monk is the single-hearted, one whose focus comes from staring death in the face—and beyond that, life with God."

55. Cassian, Inst 5.30; Gibson, "Institutes," 244.

56. See Benedicta Ward, trans., *The Sayings of the Desert Fathers*, 175.

57. See Edward Sellner, *Mentoring: the Ministry of Spiritual Kinship* (Cambridge, MA: Cowley Publications, 2002), which discusses various mentoring roles and the difference between "ordinary" mentors and "spiritual" mentors. While both types share in many of the same func-

tions, spiritual mentors are more explicitly concerned with a person's vocational discernment and relationship with God.

58. See Cassian, Inst 5.4; Gibson, "Institutes," 234–235.

59. Thomas Merton, *The Wisdom of the Desert*, 55.

60. See Nora Chadwick, *Poetry and Letters in Early Christian Gaul* (London: Bowes & Bowes, 1955), 230–233, where she compares and contrasts Cassian's and Sulpicius Severus's dialogues.

61. Cassian, Inst 12.8; Gibson, "Institutes," 282.

62. Cassian, Conl 16.3; Ramsey, *Conferences*, 558.

63. Owen Chadwick, "Introduction," in Colm Luibheid, trans., *John Cassian: Conferences* (New York: Paulist Press, 1985), 11.

64. Cuthbert Butler, *Benedictine Monachism* (New York: Longmans, Green and Co., 1919), 46, 111–112.

65. William Harmless, *Desert Christians: An Introduction to the Literature of Early Monasticism* (Oxford: Oxford University Press, 2004), 373.

66. See Owen Chadwick, *John Cassian*, footnote #1, 149, for references to Cassian and his influence in the Celtic Church—from the writings of Columban to the Anonymous *Life of St. Cuthbert* to the studies by John Ryan and Louis Gougaud.

Chapter Seven: Golden Sparkling Flame

1. See Christina Harrington, *Women in a Celtic Church: Ireland 450–1150* (Oxford: Oxford University Press, 2002), 72, where the author says "it looks very much as though the Irish continued to be selective in adopting patristic, English, and Continental [theological] notions, especially those which treated holy women." Harrington's book, while taking a revisionist and critical view of earlier scholars who have written on Celtic history and spirituality, especially regarding women in the Celtic Church, ends up affirming and even expanding upon the important ecclesial leadership roles women held in the Irish Church. Due to "Irish monasticism's pastoral outlook," women were engaged in a variety of ministries, she says, and lived "in a wide variety of places": not only at double monasteries and "laity-serving nunneries, but also at male monasteries, important churches, hermitages, and those local churches providing the eucharist for the local populace" (see pp. 129–130).

2. John Ryan, *Irish Monasticism: Origins and Early Development* (Dublin, 1931), 167.

3. For a full discussion of the influence of the desert elders upon Celtic Christianity, see my book, *The Celtic Soul Friend* (Notre Dame, IN: Ave Maria Press, 2002), especially chapter two, "Desert Mentoring and Secrets of the Heart."

4. See Julia Smith, "Celtic Asceticism and Carolingian Authority in Early Medieval Brittany," in W. J. Shields, ed., *Monks, Hermits and the Ascetic Tradition* (Oxford: Blackwell, 1985), 59.

5. See Richard Sharpe, "Some Problems Concerning the Organization of the Church in Early Medieval Ireland," *Peritia*, vol. 3, 1984: 230–270.

6. For a discussion of this scholarly debate over the question of ecclesial structure and authority in Ireland, see Colman Etchingham, *Church Oranization in Ireland, A.D. 650–1000* (Maynooth, Ireland: Laigin Publications, 1999), especially pp. 12–46.

7. Bernard McGinn, *The Growth of Mysticism* (New York: Crossroad, 1994), 86.

8. T. M. Charles-Edwards, in his book, *Early Christian Ireland* (Cambridge: Cambridge University Press, 2000), 251, 259, states that "by the 630s there is clear evidence that certain monastic churches were gaining a predominant position in the Irish Church…[and] bishops at least shared power with the heads of the greater monasteries….Good evidence exists, therefore, for two claims…: both that the Irish Church was episcopal and that it was peculiarly monastic in that the authority of abbots might override that of bishops."

9. See Edward Sellner, *The Celtic Soul Friend*, 108.

10. See Colman Etchingham, *Church Oranization in Ireland, A.D. 650–1000*, 319, 362, 465, and chapter seven, "Repentance, 'Paramonasticism' and the Elective Christian Elite," pp. 290–318.

11. From Brigit's hagiography by Cogitosus, found in J. P. Migne, *Patrologia Latina*, LXXII, cols. 777–790, translated by George Rochefort and Edward Sellner.

12. See Christina Harrington, *Women in a Celtic Church: Ireland 450–1150* (Oxford: Oxford University Press, 2002), 99, who says that "the significance of both sexes worshipping together in a single church can hardly be overemphasized in any examination of attitudes to gender in this era."

13. See A.W. Haddan and W. Stubbs, eds., *Councils and Ecclesiastical Documents Relating to Great Britain and Ireland* (Oxford: Clarendon Press, 1873), Vol. II, pt. 1, 292–293.

14. See "Ultan's Hymn," quoted in Whitley Stokes, trans., "Life of Brigit," *Lives of Saints from the Book of Lismore* (Oxford: Clarendon Press, 1890), 199.

15. Gerald of Wales, *The History and Topography of Ireland* (New York: Penguin Books, 1982), 81–82.

16. See Walter Berschin, "Radegundis and Brigit," in John Carey, Maire Herbert, and Padraig O Riain, eds., *Saints and Scholars: Studies in Irish Hagiography* (Dublin: Four Courts Press, 2001), 74. The author suggests that Cogitosus, the hagiographer of St. Brigit, may have known the work of Venantius Fortunatus, "the first medieval biographer to write a whole series" of hagiographies, including that of St. Radegundis and, as we saw in chapter three, of St. Hilary himself.

17. Padraic Colum, quoted in Mary Pollard, *In Search of St. Brigid, Foundress of Kildare* (Armagh, Northern Ireland: Trimprint Ltd., 1988), 13.

18. See Rita Minehan, *Rekindling the Flame: A Pilgrimage in the Footsteps of Brigid of Kildare* (Kildare, Ireland: Donovan Printing Ltd., 1999), 14–15, for a description of the relighting in 1993 of St. Brigit's fire.

19. While some historians such as John Ryan presuppose that we have a great deal of information on the historical St. Brigit, contemporary historians are more skeptical. See Professor Kim McCone, "An Introduction to Early Irish Saints' Lives," *The Maynooth Review*, Vol. 11, December, 1984, 26–59. He states on p. 46 that "if there was a historical Brigit, we have absolutely no reliable information about her." My position, as is apparent here, lies somewhere between the two positions. I agree with Myra Ulhfelder, trans., in *The Dialogues of Gregory the Great: Book Two, Saint Benedict* (New York: The Bobbs-Merrill Co., 1967), xviii, regarding the criterion of historicity, although I am more inclined to believe that legends actually reveal *something* about the historical life of a saint, while Ulhfelder stresses how the lives reveal "the thoughts, standards, and beliefs of a period" in which the saint lived.

20. Donncha O'Haodha, *Bethu Brigte* (Dublin: Dublin Institute for Advanced Studies, 1978), xxv.

21. For an excellent description of the Celts' religion and mythology, see Nora Chadwick, *The Celts* (New York: Pelican Books, 1970), especially chapter six.

22. Charles Squire, *Celtic Myth and Legend, Poetry and Romance* (Newcastle Publishing Co., 1975), 56.

23. Katherine Scherman, *The Flowering of Ireland* (Boston: Little, Brown, and Co., 1981), 53.

24. Barry Cunliffe, The Celtic World (New York: McGraw-Hill Book Co., 1979), 70. See my book, *Wisdom of the Celtic Saints: Revised and Expanded Edition* (St. Paul, MN: Bog Walk Press, 2006), 49–52, for a description of the meaning behind various numbers that the Celts considered especially potent.

25. See Thomas Merton, *The Wisdom of the Desert* (New York: New Directions, 1960), 55.

26. Richard Rolle, *The Fire of Love* (Baltimore, MD: Penguin, 1972), 52 and 56.

27. T. S. Eliot, "Little Gidding," *The Complete Poems and Plays, 1909–1950* (San Diego: Harcourt Brace Jovanovich, 1971), 145.

28. See Carl Jung, *Modern Man in Search of a Soul* (New York: A Harvest Book, 1933), and for his reference to fire and light symbols in the legends of the saints, see *Symbols of Transformation* (Princeton, NJ: Princeton University Press, 1956), 106 ff.

29. See R. A. S. Macalister, quoted in James Kenney, *The Sources for the Early History of Ireland: Ecclesiastical* (Dublin: Irish University Press Lmt., 1920), 358, and W. D. Killen, *The Ecclesiastical History of Ireland*, Vol. I (London: Macmillan & Co., 1975), 28–29.

30. See James Kenney, "IV. Cell-Dara (Kildare) and St. Brigit," *The Sources for the Early History of Ireland: Ecclesiastical*, 356–364, for a full discussion of legends and early lives.

31. While I have written extensively about the Celtic *anamchara*, or soul-friend, it is interesting to note that Joseph Falaky Nagy, in "The Reproductions of Irish Saints," p. 282, in John Carey, Maire Herbert, and Padraig O Riain, eds., *Saints and Scholars: Studies in Irish Hagiography*, also states that "the Irish saint is often presented in the Lives as a paradigmatic 'soul-friend'...."

32. Whitley Stokes, "Life of Brigit," *Lives of Saints from the Book of Lismore*, 195. When necessary, the quotations from the Book of Lismore have been slightly "modernized" so that his translation does not seem so archaic.

33. Antony, for example, goes into the desert alone to fight with demons; Martin maintains his anchorite lifestyle even after becoming bishop of Tours; Benedict, a contemporary of Brigit, lives his early adult life in a cave and rolls in nettles and thorns to fight the temptations of the flesh; and even Patrick to some degree, as he relates in his *Confessio*, spends his adolescence alone on a mountaintop in Ireland shepherding sheep.

34. Quoted in Pollard, *In Search of St. Brigid, Foundress of Kildare*, 20.

35. See Brigit's hagiography by Cogitosus, found in J. P. Migne, *Patrologia Latina,* LXXII, cols. 777–790.

36. Kenney, *The Sources for the Early History of Ireland: Ecclesiastical,* 357.

37. Liminality is a state in which a person striving for maturity and wisdom crosses a threshold into the unknown, and in meeting various obstacles as well as helping spirits along the way, returns home "as master of two worlds" with blessings that are shared with the community. For an explanation of this phenomenon, see Joseph Campbell, *The Hero with a Thousand Faces* (Princeton, NJ: Princeton University Press, 1968), as well as his *Primitive Mythology: the Masks of God* (New York: Penguin Books, 1987), especially Chapter Ten, "Mythological Thresholds of the Neolithic," 384–460, in which Brigit is discussed briefly. I discuss liminality as it pertains to the emergence of leadership in my article, "Living and Ministering on the Edge: Marginality and Lay Leadership," *Chicago Studies,* November, 1994, vol. 33, no. 3: 267–283.

38. Whitley Stokes, "Life of Brigit," *Lives of Saints from the Book of Lismore,* 183.

39. *Ibid.,* 184.

40. Whitley Stokes, "Life of Brigit," 185.

41. *Ibid.,* 187–188.

42. *Ibid.,* 192.

43. *Ibid.,* 194. A worthy complaint, no doubt.

44. *Ibid.,* 191.

45. *Ibid.,* 189.

46. *Ibid.,* 194.

47. *Ibid.,* 189.

48. *Ibid.,* 197.

49. *Ibid.,* 199–200.

50. See Peter Brown, "Potentia," *The Cult of the Saints* (Chicago: University of Chicago Press, 1981), 106–127. Brown states that the paradigm of a saint's power was his or her ability to heal—a major characteristic of Brigit's ministry.

51. Whitley Stokes, "Life of Brigit," 197–198.

52. T. S. Eliot, "Little Gidding," 139

53. John Ryan, *Irish Monasticism,* 183.

54. Donncha O'Haodha, *Bethu Brigte,* 24.

55. Carl Jung, "The Problem of the Attitude-Type," *Two Essays on Analytical Psychology, Collected Works,* Vol. 7, par. 78.

56. See Margaret Deanesly, *A History of the Medieval Church: 590–1500* (London: Methuen & Co. Ltd., 1925), 16.

Chapter Eight: A Candle in the Darkness

1. See Columban, "Letter I," in G. S. M. Walker, ed., *Sancti Columbani Opera* (Dublin: The Dublin Institute for Advanced Studies, 1970), 2–13. Columban wrote the pope, hoping to advise him on certain pastoral issues, especially the timing of Easter, and telling him that he had read his book, *Pastoral Care,* which Columban describes as a "work sweeter than honey." A story, found in a fifteenth-century manuscript, also attests to Gregory's popularity with the Irish. According to this apocryphal story, an Irish pilgrim went to Rome and remained there, marrying a Roman woman who became pregnant with Gregory the Great, "Gregory of the Gael," as he was called. When Gregory himself was about to die, he "gave instructions that, when the breath had left his body the empty corpse should be enclosed in a coffin with his name legibly inscribed thereon, and that the coffin should be committed to the Tiber. So it was done," and the coffin eventually made its way to the Aran islands where it found burial, "an Irishman in Irish earth. In witness of which fact one of the sounds of Aran has the name of Gregory Sound to this day." See Robin Flower, *The Western Island* (Oxford: Oxford University Press, 1944), 33–34.

2. See Bertram Colgrave, trans., *The Earliest Life of Gregory the Great* (Cambridge: Cambridge University Press, 1985), 19. For a full discussion of Alcuin regarding his monastic leadership and his friendships, see Brian Patrick McGuire, *Friendship and Community: The Monastic Experience 350–1250* (Kalamazoo, MI: Cistercian Publications, 1988), 116–127.

3. See Bertram Colgrave and R. A. B. Mynors, eds., *Bede's Ecclesiastical History of the English People* (Oxford: Oxford at the Clarendon Press, 1981), 123 and 69. Bede devoted one of his longest chapters (Book II, chapter one) to an account of his life. The popularity of Gregory in England is confirmed not only by Bede but by his contemporary Aldhelm and by many writers and chroniclers who followed them. There were altars dedicated to Gregory at Canterbury, York, and Whitby, and at the latter monastery the earliest surviving Life of Gregory was written by an anonymous monk. See Bertram Colgrave, trans., *The Earliest Life of Gregory the Great.*

4. There are numerous references to the Lombards in Gregory's correspondence and in his *Dialogues*: "...wild hordes of Lombards

unleashed from their own native land descended on us. The population of Italy, which had grown vast, like a rich harvest of grain, was cut down to wither away. Cities were sacked, fortifications overthrown, churches burned, monasteries and cloisters destroyed. Farms were abandoned, and the countryside, uncultivated became a wilderness. The land was no longer occupied by its owners, and wild beasts roamed the fields where so many people had once made their homes." See Odo John Zimmerman, trans., *Saint Gregory the Great: Dialogues* (New York: Fathers of the Church, Inc., 1959), 186.

5. F. Homes Dudden, *Gregory the Great: His Place in History and Thought,* Vol. I (London: Longmans, Green, and Co., 1905), 52.

6. Dom Jean Leclercq, "From St. Gregory to St. Bernard," in Dom Jean Leclercq, Dom Francois Vandenbroucke, and Louis Bouyer, *The Spirituality of the Middle Ages* (New York: The Seabury Press, 1968), 30, 3–4.

7. See Bernard McGinn, *The Growth of Mysticism* (New York: Crossroad, 1994), 35–36.

8. See Epistle CVI, Book IX, "To Syagrius, Aetherius, Virgilius, and Desiderius, Bishops," in Rev. James Barmby, trans., "Selected Epistles of Gregory the Great (Books IX-XVI)," in Philip Schaff and Henry Wace, eds., *A Select Library of Nicene and Post-Nicene Fathers of the Christian Church,* Vol. XIII (Grand Rapids, MI: Wm. B. Eerdmans Publishing Co., reprinted 1989), 25.

9. F. Homes Dudden, *Gregory the Great: His Place in History and Thought,* Vol. I, 8.

10. His great-great-grandfather, Felix III, was bishop of Rome from 483 to 492. See Odo John Zimmerman, trans., *Saint Gregory the Great: Dialogues,* p. 211, where Gregory describes his ancestor appearing to his aunt in a vision.

11. Quoted in R. A. Markus, *Gregory the Great and His World* (Cambridge, UK: Cambridge University Press, 1997), 9.

12. Rex Warner, trans., *The Confessions of St. Augustine* (New York: A Mentor Book, 1963), 173.

13. Peter Brown, *The Rise of Western Christendom* (Oxford: Blackwell Publishing, 1996), 201.

14. See Odo John Zimmerman, trans., *Saint Gregory: Dialogues,* 172–173.

15. See Henry Davis, trans., *St. Gregory the Great: Pastoral Care,* III: 12; 120–126. Gregory states that "bodily affliction" is a "great gift," and one way of learning patience with it is to consider the suffering of Christ which he patiently bore.

16. See F. Homes Dudden, *Gregory the Great: His Place in History and Thought,* Vol. I, 118.

17. See Peter Brown, *The Rise of Western Christendom,* 201.

18. Charles Kannengiesser, "Boethius, Cassiodorus, Gregory the Great," in G. R. Evans, ed., *The Medieval Theologians* (Oxford: Blackwell Publishers, 2001), 31.

19. Gregory the Great, "Homilies on Ezechiel," quoted in F. Homes Dudden, *Gregory the Great: His Place in History and Thought,* Vol. I, 119.

20. Odo John Zimmerman, trans., *Saint Gregory: Dialogues,* 3–4.

21. See Cuthbert Butler, *Western Mysticism* (New York: E. P. Dutton & Co., 1923), 109–115, regarding Gregory's associations with the experience of contemplation.

22. Odo John Zimmerman, trans., *Saint Gregory: Dialogues,* 105.

23. Gregory the Great, quoted in Butler, *Western Mysticism,* 102, and in McGinn, *The Growth of Mysticism,* 74.

24. See Butler, *Western Mysticism,* 108.

25. From *Morals on Job,* quoted in Butler, *Western Mysticism,* 224.

26. See Butler, *Western Mysticism,* 110, 114.

27. See Odo John Zimmerman, trans., *Saint Gregory: Dialogues,* III:36, pp. 177–178, and IV:58, pp. 270–272.

28. See, for example, Augustine in his first work, "The Happy Life," where he says "I threw off all ballast and brought my ship, shattered and leaking though it was, to the desired resting place," in Ludwig Schoff, trans., *Writings of Saint Augustine,* Vol. I (New York: Cima Publishing, 1948), 48.

29. See Gregory the Great, Epistle V, Book I, "To Theoctista, Sister of the Emperor," translated by Rev. James Barmby, from "Register of the Epistles of Saint Gregory the Great," in Philip Schaff and Henry Wace, eds., *A Select Library of Nicene and Post-Nicene Fathers of the Christian Church,* Vol. XII (Grand Rapids, MI: Wm. B. Eerdmans Publishing Co., reprinted 1989), 75.

30. From Gregory's "Introduction" to his *Morals on Job,* quoted in Rev. James Barmby, "Prolegomena," xvi, in Philip Schaff and Henry Wace, eds., *A Select Library of Nicene and Post-Nicene Fathers of the Christian Church,* Vol. XII.

31. Gregory the Great, *Morals on Job* 28:33, quoted in Butler, *Western Mysticism,* 221–222.

32. *Idem,* "Homilies on Ezechiel" II: 2.11, quoted in Markus, *Gregory the Great and His World,* 24–25.

33. *Idem, Morals on Job* 23:37, quoted in Butler, *Western Mysticism,* 231.

34. Lewis Thorpe, trans., *Gregory of Tours: The History of the Franks* (New York: Penguin Books, 1988), 544.

35. Gregory the Great, Epistle I, Book I, "To All the Bishops of Sicily," translated by Rev. James Barmby, from "Register of the Epistles of Saint Gregory the Great," 73.

36. See Henry Davis, trans., *St. Gregory the Great: Pastoral Care* (New York: Newman Press, 1950), 159.

37. See Gregory the Great, Epistle XXII, Book XIII, "To Rusticiana, Patrician Lady," p. 97, and Epistle XLII, Book XIII, "To Eulogius, Patriarch of Alexandria," 102, in Rev. James Barmby, trans., "Selected Epistles of Gregory the Great (Books IX–XVI)," in Philip Schaff and Henry Wace, eds., *A Select Library of Nicene and Post-Nicene Fathers of the Christian Church,* Vol. XIII.

38. While I agree with Conrad Leyser when he says "the tension he [Gregory] expressed between contemplative inquiry and the fulfillment of administrative duty was a creative rather than a debilitating force," I disagree with him that this conflict "did not reside in the soul." I believe it did, especially when one considers why Gregory chose to become a monk in the first place: because his public duties were distracting him from what he came to see at that time as his primary vocation, contemplation and prayer. See Conrad Leyser, "Expertise and Authority in Gregory the Great: The Social Function of Peritia," in John Cavadini, ed., *Gregory the Great: A Symposium* (Notre Dame, IN: University of Notre Dame Press, 1995), 39–40.

39. See Gregory the Great, Epistle V, Book I, "To Theoctista, Sister of the Emperor," translated by Rev. James Barmby, from "Register of the Epistles of Saint Gregory the Great," 74–76.

40. See Odo John Zimmerman, *Saint Gregory the Great: Dialogues,* 60–61.

41. See Gregory the Great, Epistle XLI, Book II, "To Castorius, Bishop," translated by Rev. James Barmby, from "Register of the Epistles of Saint Gregory the Great," 112. In this letter, Gregory relates how an abbot from the monastery of Sts. Andrew and Thomas, in the city of Ariminum, informed him that "the monks have suffered many prejudices and annoyances from prelates." He then forbids "by the authority of the blessed Peter, Prince of the apostles, in whose stead we preside over this Roman Church, that any bishop or secular person hereafter presume in any way to devise occasions of interfering with regard to the

revenues, property or writings of monasteries, or of the cells or villas thereto appertaining...."

42. See Charles Kannengiesser, "Boethius, Cassiodorus, Gregory the Great," 33.

43. See Dudden, *Gregory the Great: His Place in History and Thought,* Vol. I, 277. There are numerous references in Gregory's correspondence to his practice of giving relics away, as well as his refusal to do so when he thought a request unwarranted.

44. See Gregory the Great, Epistle XIII, "To Serenus, Bishop of Marseilles," in Rev. James Barmby, trans., "Selected Epistles of Gregory the Great (Books IX–XVI)," in Philip Schaff and Henry Wace, eds., *A Select Library of Nicene and Post-Nicene Fathers of the Christian Church,* 53–54.

45. See Celia Chazelle, "Memory, Instruction, Worship: 'Influence on Early Medieval Doctrines of the Artistic Image,'" in John C. Cavadini, ed., *Gregory the Great: A Symposium,* 187.

46. See Gregory the Great, Epistle I, Book I, "To All the Bishops of Sicily," translated by Rev. James Barmby, from "Register of the Epistles of Saint Gregory the Great," 73.

47. See *The Rule of St. Benedict,* especially chapter two on "the qualities of the abbot" whose primary task is "the guidance of souls."

48. Thomas Aquinas, quoted in Maria Lichtman, "Teaching and the Contemplative Life," *Christian Spirituality Bulletin,* Vol. 6, no. 2, Fall 1998: 14.

49. Odo John Zimmerman, trans., *Saint Gregory the Great: Dialogues,* 6.

50. F. Homes Dudden, *Gregory the Great: His Place in History and Thought,* Vol. I, 254–255.

51. *Dialogues* I:10, quoted in *Gregory the Great: His Place in History and Thought,* Vol. I, 339. I prefer this translation to the one found in Zimmerman, trans., *Saint Gregory the Great: Dialogues,* p. 48, "I could not very well continue listening to his accounts, much as I always enjoy doing so."

52. Gregory the Great, Epistle XV, Book X, "To Clementina, Patrician," in Rev. James Barmby, trans., *Selected Epistles of Gregory the Great (Books IX–XVI)*, 43.

53. Gregory the Great, Epistle XII, Book XI, "To Conon, Abbot of Lerins," in Rev. James Barmby, trans., "Selected Epistles of Gregory the Great (Books IX–XVI)," 53.

54. R. A. Markus, *Gregory the Great and His World,* 204.

55. See Henry Davis, trans., *St. Gregory the Great: Pastoral Care,* 26–27.

56. *Ibid.,* 40, 45,73–74.

57. *Ibid.,* 234, 82.

58. *Ibid.,* 35–37.

59. Though some today question whether Gregory actually wrote the *Dialogues,* I tend to agree with Gregorian scholars, F. Homes Dudden, R. A. Markus, and Bernard McGinn, all of whom presume he did. Whether he actually did or not, I see much of Gregory's life, thought, and values reflected in its contents. There are numerous allusions to Gregory's own ecclesial career and monastic associates in his dialogues, to friends whom he knew (and to whom he addressed his letters).

60. See Bernard Peebles, trans., "Sulpicius Severus: Writings," in *The Fathers of the Church,* Vol. 7 (Washington, DC: Catholic University of America Press, 1949), 89, where Peebles says: "Sulpicius's use of the dialogue-form as a vehicle for biography is striking and altogether effective. The similar procedure followed in the *Dialogues* of St. Gregory the Great is almost certainly based on Sulpicius's example."

61. See Odo John Zimmerman, *Saint Gregory the Great: Dialogues,* 3.

62. James J. O'Donnell, "The Holiness of Gregory," in John C. Cavadini, ed., *Gregory the Great: A Symposium,* 70.

63. See Epistle XVIII, Book I, "To Peter the Subdeacon," in Rev. James Barmby, from "Register of the Epistles of Saint Gregory the Great," in Philip Schaff and Henry Wace, eds., *A Select Library of Nicene and Post-Nicene Fathers of the Christian Church,* Vol. XII, 79.

64. *Ibid.,* 91, Epistle XLIV.

65. *Ibid.,* 95, Epistle LVI.

66. *Ibid.,* 92, Epistle XLIV.

67. See Odo John Zimmerman, *Saint Gregory the Great: Dialogues,* 3–4.

68. *Ibid.,* 5.

69. *Ibid.,* 204, 207, 213, 234, 236, 239, 261, 264, 267.

70. *Ibid.,* 233.

71. See Odo John Zimmerman, *Saint Gregory the Great: Dialogues,* 189.

72. Gregory the Great, Epistle CXXI, Book IX, "To Leander, Bishop of Seville," in Rev. James Barmby, trans., "Selected Epistles of Gregory the Great (Books IX–XVI)," 34. Leander was an intimate friend of Gregory's. Even though Gregory never saw him again after leaving Constantinople, he wrote Leander that "the image of your countenance is impressed forever on my innermost heart."

73. See Bertram Colgrave and R. A. B. Mynors, eds., *Bede's Ecclesiastical History of the English People,* 123. Bede the Venerable devoted one of his longest chapters to an account of Gregory's life.

74. Jeffrey Richards, *Consul of God: The Life and Times of Gregory the Great* (London: Routledge & Kegan Paul, 1980), 260.

75. Odo John Zimmerman, *Saint Gregory the Great: Dialogues,* 258–259.

Chaper Nine: The Glittering Road to Paradise

1. William Harmless, *Desert Christians: An Introduction to the Literature of Early Monasticism* (Oxford: Oxford University Press, 2004), 373.

2. F. Homes Dudden, *Gregory the Great,* Vol. II (London: Longmans, Green, and Co., 1905), 78, 174.

3. Cuthbert Butler, *Benedictine Monachism: Studies in Benedictine Life and Rule* (London: Longmans, Green and Co., 1919), 26.

4. Justin McCann, *Saint Benedict* (London: Sheed and Ward, 1937), 112.

5. *Ibid.,* p. 11, and D. H. Turner, "This Little Rule for Beginners," in the British Library Board, *The Benedictines in Britain* (London: The British Library, 1980), 16.

6. Jean Leclercq, *The Love of Learning and the Desire for God: A Study of Monastic Culture* (New York: Fordham University Press, 1961), 11.

7. See D. H. Turner, "This Little Rule for Beginners," in the British Library Board, *The Benedictines in Britain,* 15.

8. See Rule of St. Benedict, chapter one, in Timothy Fry, ed., *The Rule of Saint Benedict* (New York: Vintage Books, 1998), 8.

9. Cuthbert Butler, *Benedictine Monachism,* 27–28.

10. Odo John Zimmerman, trans., *Saint Gregory the Great: Dialogues* (New York: Fathers of the Church, Inc., 1959), 108.

11. *Ibid.,* 55–56.

12. R. A. Markus, *Gregory the Great and His World* (Cambridge, UK: Cambridge University Press, 1997), 68.

13. Terrence Kardong, *The Benedictines* (Wilmington, DE: Michael Glazier, 1988), 62.

14. Odo John Zimmerman, trans., *Saint Gregory the Great: Dialogues,* 72.

15. Bernard McGinn, "St. Benedict as the Steward of Creation," *The American Benedictine Review,* 39:2, June 1988, 162.

16. Odo John Zimmerman, trans., *Saint Gregory the Great: Dialogues,* 73.

17. *Ibid.*, 102.

18. See Justin McCann, *Saint Benedict,* p. 43. A beautiful children's book written by Kathleen Norris and illustrated by Tomie dePaola, *The Holy Twins: Benedict and Scholastica* (New York: G. P. Putnam's Sons, 2001), tells of the two saints' relationship.

19. Odo John Zimmerman, trans., *Saint Gregory the Great: Dialogues,* 55.

20. *Ibid.*, 55–56.

21. *Ibid.*, 57.

22. *Ibid.*, 59.

23. *Ibid.*, 60.

24. *Ibid.*, 60–61.

25. According to Odo John Zimmerman, the monastery that Benedict joined "is usually identified as Vicovaro." See his *Saint Gregory the Great: Dialogues,* 61.

26. *Ibid.*, 61–62.

27. *Ibid.*, 63.

28. *Ibid.*, 64.

29. *Ibid.*, 66.

30. See RB: prologue; Timothy Fry, ed., *The Rule of St. Benedict,* 5 & 3.

31. Odo John Zimmerman, *Saint Gregory the Great: Dialogues,* 67. According to Gregory, Benedict confronted the monk who, because of his obsessions, was missing his prayers, by striking him with his staff "for being so obstinate of heart." As a result of this rebuke, "from then on the monk remained quietly at prayer like the rest, without being bothered again by the tempter."

32. See "Bird" in J. E. Cirlot, *A Dictionary of Symbols* (New York: Philosophical Library, 1983), 26.

33. Odo John Zimmerman, *Saint Gregory the Great: Dialogues,* 71.

34. See Sulpicius Severus, "Life of St. Martin," in Bernard Peebles, trans., "Sulpicius Severus: Writings," *Fathers of the Church,* Vol. 7 (Washington, DC: Catholic University of America Press, 1949), 120–124.

35. Odo John Zimmerman, *Saint Gregory the Great: Dialogues,* 74.

36. Cuthbert Butler, *Benedictine Monachism,* 9.

37. See Odo John Zimmerman, *Saint Gregory the Great: Dialogues,* 75–101.

38. Columba Stewart, *Prayer and Community: The Benedictine Tradition* (Maryknoll, NY: Orbis Books, 1998), 26.

39. See Odo John Zimmerman, *Saint Gregory the Great: Dialogues*, 102.

40. *Ibid.*, 102–103.

41. See Mircea Eliade, *Shamanism: Archaic Techniques of Ecstasy* (Princeton University Press, 1974), 420.

42. See "Rain" and "Thunderbolt" in J. E. Cirlot, *A Dictionary of Symbols*, 271–272, and 342.

43. Odo John Zimmerman, *Saint Gregory the Great: Dialogues*, 103.

44. *Ibid.*, 103–104.

45. Odo Casel, "Benedict, Man of the Spirit," in *Monastic Studies*, no. 11, Advent 1975 (Pine City, NY: Mount Saviour Monastery), 164.

46. See Justin McCann, *Saint Benedict*, 43.

47. Odo John Zimmerman, *Saint Gregory the Great: Dialogues*, 104.

48. *Ibid.*, 104–108.

49. Bernard McGinn, *The Growth of Mysticism* (New York: Crossroad, 1994), 27.

50. See, for example, Benedict's Rule, chapter 60, "The Admission of Priests to the Monastery," where he advises his followers that if any priest asks to be received into the monastery, "do not agree too quickly," while advising the priest to be "subject to the discipline of the rule," and "give everyone an example of humility." See Timothy Fry, ed., *The Rule of Saint Benedict*, 58.

51. For a full discussion and translation of it, see Luke Eberle, trans., *The Rule of the Master* (Kalamazoo, MI: Cistercian Publications, 1977).

52. For the one hundred and sixty-three scriptural references, see Timothy Fry, ed., *The Rule of Saint Benedict*, 71–73.

53. *Ibid.*, 69.

54. David Knowles, "St. Benedict," in James Walsh, ed., *Spirituality Through the Centuries: Ascetics and Mystics of the Western Church* (London: Burns & Oates, n.d.), 63. For other writers' works, see Esther deWaal, *Seeking God: The Way of St. Benedict* (Collegeville, MN: Liturgical Press, 1984); *Living with Contradictions: Reflections on the Rule of St. Benedict* (San Francisco: Harper & Row, 1989); and Joan Chittister, *Wisdom Distilled from the Daily: Living the Rule of St. Benedict Today* (San Francisco: Harper & Row, 1990).

55. See Timothy Fry, ed., *The Rule of Saint Benedict*, 43–44, 53, and 30.

56. Owen Chadwick, ed., *Western Asceticism* (Philadelphia: Westminster Press, 1968), 27.

57. See Timothy Fry, ed., *The Rule of Saint Benedict*, 33, 35, 37, 51.

58. *Ibid.*, 3.
59. Cuthbert Butler, *Benedictine Monachism*, 30.
60. See Timothy Fry, ed., *The Rule of Saint Benedict,*, 28–29.
61. *Ibid.*, 37, 47–48.
62. *Ibid.*, 70.
63. See Terrence Kardong, *The Benedictines*, 28.
64. Timothy Fry, ed., *The Rule of Saint Benedict*, 5.
65. *Ibid.*, 3–20.
66. See Cuthbert Butler, *Benedictine Monachism*, 32, 123, 132–133.
67. See Timothy Fry, ed., *The Rule of Saint Benedict*, 7–8.
68. David Knowles, *Saints and Scholars: Twenty-five medieval portraits* (London: Cambridge University Press, 1962), 6.
69. See Timothy Fry, ed., *The Rule of Saint Benedict*, 14, 56, and 59.
70. I want to thank Rosemary Rader, O.S.B., of the Benedictine Priory in St. Paul, Minnesota, for this threefold understanding of stability from a talk she gave on that theme.
71. Thomas Merton, *The Wisdom of the Desert* (New York: A New Directions Book, 1960), 30.
72. John Eudes Bamberger, trans., *Evagrius Ponticus: The Praktikos & Chapters on Prayer* (Kalamazoo, MI: Cistercian Publications, 1981), 19.
73. See Ambrose Wathen, "*Conversatio* and Stability in the Rule of Benedict," in *Monastic Studies*, no. 11, Advent 1975, 6.
74. See Thich Nhat Hanh, *Living Buddha, Living Christ* (New York: Riverhead Books, 1995), 120–121. Benedictines and Buddhists today are continuing a dialogue on monasticism, perhaps initiated most dramatically by Thomas Merton in the late 1960s. For insight into that conversation, see Patrick Henry, ed., *Benedict's Dharma: Buddhists Reflect on the Rule of Saint Benedict* (New York: Riverhead Books, 2001).
75. Scott Russell Sanders, *Staying Put: Making a Home in a Restless World* (Boston, MA: Beacon Press, 1993), 121.
76. See Columba Stewart, *Prayer and Community: The Benedictine Tradition*, 71–77.
77. See Esther deWaal, *Seeking God: The Way of St. Benedict*, 55–65.
78. Timothy Fry, ed., *The Rule of Saint Benedict*, 12.
79. Peter the Deacon, quoted in Justin McCann, *Saint Benedict*, 216.
80. Peter Levi, *The Frontiers of Paradise: A Study of Monks and Monasteries* (London: Collins Harvill, 1988), 56–57.
81. Jean Leclercq, *The Love of Learning and the Desire for God: A Study of Monastic Culture*, 7.

Chapter Ten: Valley of Light

1. Bernard McGinn, *The Growth of Mysticism* (New York: Crossroad, 1994), xiii.

2. See Rolf Toman, ed., *The Art of Gothic* (Cologne, Germany: Konemann, 1998), 9–13, where Giovanni Santini, an Italian scholar, describes the universities as "new cathedrals" and Abbot Suger is identified as the "creator of Gothic." According to Toman, historians associate the new church architecture of the twelfth century with an "architecture of light." Suger, in his writings about the rebuilding of his abbey church, mentions the particular importance of light, developing an aesthetic of the ascent from the material world (i.e., the light from the windows and precious stones) toward the spiritual (the light of God). His views, in many ways, seem to reflect a neoplatonic philosophy of light.

3. Kenneth Clark, *Civilization: A Personal View* (New York: Harper & Row, 1969), 60.

4. Cuthbert Butler, *Benedictine Monachism* (New York: Longmans, Green and Co., 1919), 357–358.

5. *Ibid.*, 295–297, where Butler discusses the "prodigious length" of the Divine Office, manual labor, and the twelfth-century "reaction." For an excellent discussion of Gregorian and Cluniac Reform, see Christopher Bellitto, *Renewing Christianity: A History of Church Reform from Day One to Vatican II* (Mahwah, NJ: Paulist Press, 2001), 47–74. For a well-done history of Cluny and the important figures asssociated with it, see Edwin Mullins, *Cluny: In Search of God's Lost Empire* (New York: BlueBridge, 2006).

6. See Benedicta Ward, XVIII, "The Desert Myth," in *Signs and Wonders* (Hampshire, Great Britain: Ashgate Publishing, 1992), p. 186.

7. David Knowles, *Saints and Scholars: Twenty-five Medieval Portraits* (London: Cambridge University Press, 1962), 1.

8. Jean Leclercq, *The Love of Learning and the Desire for God: A Study of Monastic Culture* (New York: Fordham University Press, 1961), 106–107.

9. Bernard of Clairvaux, Letter 205, to Pope Eugenius III, in Bruno Scott James, trans., *The Letters of St. Bernard of Clairvaux* (London: Burns Oates, 1953), 280.

10. Thomas Merton, *The Last of the Fathers* (New York: A Harvest/HBJ Book, 1954), 29.

11. Bernard of Clairvaux, Letter 109 to Thomas, Provost of Beverley, in Bruno Scott James, trans., *The Letters of St. Bernard of Clairvaux*, 162.

12. Jean Leclercq, "General Introduction to the Works of Saint Bernard (1)," *Cistercian Studies Quarterly,* Vol. 40.1, 2005: 14.

13. See Timothy Fry, ed., *The Rule of Saint Benedict* (New York: Vintage Books, 1998), 5, and Etienne Gilson, "The Schools of Charity," in *The Mystical Theology of Saint Bernard* (London: Sheed and Ward, 1940), 200–202.

14. Jean Leclercq, *The Love of Learning and the Desire for God: A Study of Monastic Culture,* 107.

15. Benedicta Ward, XVIII, "The Desert Myth," in *Signs and Wonders,* 184.

16. See Etienne Gilson, *The Mystical Theology of Saint Bernard,* 10, where he says that "in *De Amicitia,* the men of the twelfth century found much they felt able to borrow; either as it stood or adapted to their needs." In the Cistercian monk Aelred of Rievaulx's major work, *Spiritual Friendship* (Kalamazoo, MI: Cistercian Publications, 1977), Cicero is referred to frequently, and his ideas on friendship are foundational for Aelred's Christian theology.

17. See Geoffrey Webb and Adrian Walker, trans., *St. Bernard of Clairvaux: The story of his Life as recorded in the Vita Prima Bernardi by certain of his contemporaries, William of St. Thierry, Arnold of Bonnevaux, Geoffrey and Philip of Clairvaux, and Odo of Deuil* (London: A.R. Morbray & Co., 1960), 16, 20–22. As described in this hagiography, Bernard is also *unlike* certain Irish saints such as St. Kevin who instead of jumping himself (as Bernard did) into the ice, cold water when tempted, pushed the temptress, Kathleen, into the lake at Glendalough!

18. Biographers disagree on the year of her death; see, for example, Watkin Williams, *Saint Bernard of Clairvaux* (Westminister, MD: The Newman Press, 1952), 7, who suggests the year 1106 or 1107, while Bruno S. James, *Saint Bernard of Clairvaux: An Essay in Biography* (New York: Harper & Brothers, 1957), 20, puts the year at 1104.

19. Geoffrey Webb and Adrian Walker, trans., *St. Bernard of Clairvaux...*, 18.

20. Bruno Scott James, *Saint Bernard of Clairvaux* (New York: Harper & Brothers Publishers, 1957), 20–21.

21. See Henri Daniel-Rops, *Bernard of Clairvaux: The Story of the Last of the Great Church Fathers* (New York: Hawthorn Books, 1964), 54. Daniel-Rops describes how in one famous painting, Murillo's "The Lactation of Saint Bernard," as well as a certain stained-glass window at Laines au Bois in the diocese of Troyes, France, "the great abbot is kneeling, arms widespread, gazing up at the Virgin Mary, who bares her

breast to quench the thirst of her servant as a mother does her child." A wonderful painting of the lactation can be seen in Madrid's Prado Museum. Thomas Merton, in his *The Last of the Fathers,* 86, says that "Saint Bernard is one of the greatest and most important theologians of Mary in the Catholic Church."

22. Bernard of Clairvaux, "Apology," chapter 4: 7, quoted in Bruno James, *Saint Bernard of Clairvaux,* 23.

23. Geoffrey Webb and Adrian Walker, trans., *St. Bernard of Clairvaux...,* 32.

24. See, for example, Ailbe Luddy, *Life and Teaching of St. Bernard* (Dublin: M. H. Gill & Son, 1937), 33.

25. See Martin Cawley, "Saint Stephen Harding: A Tribute for His 850th Anniversary, 1134–1984," in *Monasticism: A Historical Overview* (Still River, MA: St. Bede's Publications, 1984), 68–86.

26. Geoffrey Webb and Adrian Walker, trans., *St. Bernard of Clairvaux...,* 40.

27. *Ibid.,* 44.

28. *Ibid.,* 45.

29. *Ibid.,* 59–60.

30. *Ibid.,* 87.

31. Bruno Scott James, trans., *The Letters of St. Bernard of Clairvaux* (London: Burns Oates, 1953), x. Unfortunately, this chapter cannot adequately cover the relationship between Bernard and Abelard. The twelfth century saw the rise of scholasticism, a new approach to the study of theology that was more rational, systematic, and academic than the more traditional approach with theology grounded in spirituality. Although he had been preceded by John Scotus Erigena, an Irishman, in the ninth century, and Lanfranc and Anselm of Canterbury in the eleventh century, who are considered founders of this "new" approach, Abelard was scholasticism's leading exponent in the twelfth century—while Bernard was the chief exponent of the older approach The two men were bound to clash. See Leclercq, *The Love of Learning and the Desire for God,* 192 ff. For more information on Abelard, a Breton, see M. T. Clanchy, *Abelard: A Medieval Life* (Oxford: Blackwell Publishers, 1997), and James Burge, *Heloise and Abelard: A New Biography* (HarperSanFrancisco, 2003).

32. Geoffrey Webb and Adrian Walker, trans., *St. Bernard of Clairvaux: The story of his Life....,* 54–55.

33. *Ibid.,* 56.

34. See Watkin Williams, *Saint Bernard of Clairvaux,* 221–222, where he states that "it is probably to William that we owe in large measure the incentive which later led to the composition of the *Sermons on the Song of Songs.*" Ailbe Luddy also relates a story told by William about how he had received consolation when he was ill by visiting Bernard at Clairvaux; the two friends had "passed our time together nourishing our souls with conferences on subjects related to God," including Bernard's explanation of the Song of Songs. See Luddy, *Life and Teaching of St. Bernard,* 146–147.

35. Geoffrey Webb and Adrian Walker, trans., *St. Bernard of Clairvaux: The story of his Life...,* 58.

36. Bernard of Clairvaux, Letters 87, 88, and 89 to William of St. Thierry, in Bruno Scott James, trans., *The Letters of St. Bernard of Clairvaux,* 126–128.

37. Numerous scholars believe that William's abilities went unappreciated for centuries, lost in the shadow cast by Bernard's fame and William's own humility. Etienne Gilson and Jean Leclercq consider him one of the greatest theologians of the twelfth century. For more on the life and theology of William, see Jean Leclercq, "William of St. Thierry and Trinitarian Mysticism," in Jean Leclercq, Francois Vandenbrouck, and Louis Bouyer, *The Spirituality of the Middle Ages* (New York: Seabury Press, 1968), 200–205, and Etienne Gilson, "Notes on William of Saint-Thierry," Appendix V, in *The Mystical Theology of Saint Bernard* (New York: Sheed and Ward, 1940), 198–214. Essays on William, translated by Jerry Carfantan, can be found in *William, Abbot of St. Thierry: A Colloquium at the Abbey of St. Thierry* (Kalamazoo, MI: Cistercian Publications, 1987).

38. Bernard of Clairvaux, "From *On Consideration,*" in Pauline Matarasso, trans., *The Cistercian World: Monastic Writings of the Twelfth Century* (New York: Penguin Books, 1993), 87.

39. Coincidentally, these two, Rievaulx and Fountains, were the first to be suppressed by Henry VIII. For information on and beautiful photographs of all three, including a history of Cistercian abbeys, see David Robinson, ed., *The Cistercian Abbeys of Britain* (London: BT Batsford, 1998), and Jean-Francois Leroux-Dhys, *Cistercian Abbeys: History and Architecture* (Koln: Koneman, 1998). For another, older examination of Fountains alone, see Arthur Henderson, *Fountains Abbey: Then and Now* (London: Simpkin Marshall, LTD, 1936).

40. For a thorough discussion of Bernard's activity in setting up the daughter-houses, see chapter four, "The Daughters of Clairvaux," in Watkin Williams, *Saint Bernard of Clairvaux*, 60–95.

41. Bernard of Clairvaux, Letter 91, "To Oger, A Canon Regular," in Bruno Scott James, trans., *The Letters of St. Bernard of Clairvaux*, 135–136.

42. Geoffrey Webb and Adrian Walker, trans., *St. Bernard of Clairvaux*, 66.

43. Jean Leclercq, "Introduction," in Gillian R. Evans, trans., *Bernard of Clairvaux: Selected Works*, 17.

44. See Bernard of Clairvaux, "On Humility and Pride," in Gillian R. Evans, trans., *Bernard of Clairvaux: Selected Works*, 103–104, and 142–143.

45. See Bernard of Clairvaux, "On Humility and Pride," in G. R. Evans, trans., *Bernard of Clairvaux: Selected Works*, 140–141, and 104.

46. Jean Leclercq, "Introduction," in Gillian R. Evans, trans., *Bernard of Clairvaux*, 18.

47. See Jean Leclercq, "General Introduction to the Works of Saint Bernard (II)," *Cistercian Studies Quarterly*, Vol. 40.3, 2005: 244.

48. For the full text, see Bernard of Clairvaux, "On Loving God," in G. R. Evans, trans., *Bernard of Clairvaux: Selected Works*, 173–205.

49. Marie-Bernard Said, trans., *Homilies in Praise of the Blessed Virgin Mary by Bernard of Clairvaux* (Kalamazoo, MI: Cistercian Publications, 1993), 3.

50. Bernard of Clairvaux, "An Apology for Abbot William," in Pauline Matarasso, *The Cistercian World: Monastic Writings of the Twelfth Century*, 53–54.

51. *Ibid.*, 55.

52. *Ibid.*, 56–57.

53. For a full discussion of Suger's church and its treasures, see Erwin Panofsky, ed., *Abbot Suger on the Abbey Church of St.-Denis and Its Art Treasures* (Princeton, NJ: Princeton University Press, 1979).

54. See Bernard of Clairvaux, Letter 80, "To Suger, Abbot of St. Denis," in Bruno Scott James, trans., *The Letters of St. Bernard of Clairvaux*, 110–118.

55. *Ibid.*, Letter 411, "To Suger, Abbot of St. Denis," 480–481.

56. Jean Leclercq, "Introduction," in G. R. Evans, trans., *Bernard of Clairvaux: Selected Works*, 18.

57. See Geoffrey Webb and Adrian Walker, trans., *St. Bernard of Clairvaux: The story of his Life as recorded in the Vita Prima Bernardi*..., 77.

58. See Watkin Williams, *Saint Bernard of Clairvaux*, 106–107.

59. Geoffrey Webb and Adrian Walker, trans., *St. Bernard of Clairvaux: The story of his Life as recorded in the Vita Prima Bernardi…*, 79, 81.

60. Watkin Williams, *St. Bernard: The Man and His Message* (New York: Spiritual Books Associates, n.d.), 13.

61. Jean Leclercq explores what he calls Bernard's "personal charisma" in contrast to "functional" or "institutional" charisma in his "Toward a Sociological Interpretation of the Various Saint Bernards" in John Sommerfeldt, ed., *Bernardus Magister* (Spencer, MA: Cistercian Publications, 1992), especially 20–29.

62. Watkin Williams, *Studies in St, Bernard of Clairvaux* (London: Society for Promoting Christian Knowledge, 1927), 4.

63. See Bernard of Clairvaux, Letter 12, "To the Prior guy and Other Religious of the Grande Chartreuse," and Letter 19, "To Peter, Cardinal Deacon," in Bruno Scott James, trans., *The Letters of St. Bernard of Clairvaux*, 48, 54.

64. Bernard of Clairvaux, Letter 22, "To Matthew, the Legate," in Bruno Scott James, trans., *The Letters of St. Bernard of Clairvaux*, 56.

65. Bernard of Clairvaux, Letter 105, "To Master Walter of Chaumont," in Bruno Scott James, trans., *The Letters of St. Bernard of Clairvaux*, 153.

66. Bernard of Clairvaux, Letter 106, "To Romanus, a Subdeacon of the Curia at Rome," in Bruno Scott James, trans., *The Letters of St. Bernard of Clairvaux*, 154–155.

67. Bernard of Clairvaux, Letter 107, "To Henry Murdac," in Bruno Scott James, trans., *The Letters of St. Bernard of Clairvaux*, 156.

68. Bernard of Clairvaux, Letter 110, "To Thomas of Saint Omer," in Bruno Scott James, trans., *The Letters of St. Bernard of Clairvaux*, 167.

69. Bernard of Clairvaux, Letter 177, "To Aelred, Abbot of Rievaulx," in Bruno Scott James, trans., *The Letters of St. Bernard of Clairvaux*, 246–247.

70. Bernard of Clairvaux, Letter 108, "To Thomas, Provost of Beverley," in Bruno Scott James, trans., *The Letters of St. Bernard of Clairvaux*, 157.

71. Bernard of Clairvaux, Letters 119 and 120, "To Ermengarde, Formerly Countess of Brittany," in Bruno Scott James, trans., *The Letters of St. Bernard of Clairvaux*, 181–182.

72. Bernard of Clairvaux, Letter 390, "To Hildegarde, Abbess of Mont St. Rupert," in Bruno Scott James, trans., *The Letters of St. Bernard of Clairvaux*, 459–460. Bernard supported Hildegard, and even brought her writings to the pope, getting his approval of their authenticity. For

more about the famous Rhineland mystic, see Sabina Flanagan, *Hildegard of Bingen: A Visionary Life* (London: Routledge, 1989), and Fiona Maddocks, *Hildegard of Bingen, The Woman of Her Age* (New York: Image Books/Doubleday, 2001).

73. Bernard of Clairvaux, Letter 117, "To a Nun," in Bruno Scott James, trans., *The Letters of St. Bernard of Clairvaux*, 178–179.

74. Bernard of Clairvaux, Letter 118, "To a Nun of the Convent of St. Mary of Troyes," in Bruno Scott James, trans., *The Letters of St. Bernard of Clairvaux*, 180.

75. Bernard of Clairvaux, Letter 112, "To the Parents of the Aforementioned Geoffrey, to Console Them," in Bruno Scott James, trans., *The Letters of St. Bernard of Clairvaux*, 169.

76. "Absent abbot" is one of the kinder epithets. See Brian Patrick McGuire, *The Difficult Saint: Bernard of Clairvaux & His Tradition* (Kalamazoo, MI: Cistercian Publications, 1991), 27. Another writer, Dennis Tamburello, in his *Bernard of Clairvaux: Essential Writings* (New York: Crossroad Publishing, 2000), 27–36, suggests that Bernard was possibly gone about a third of his time during those years. I would agree with McGuire in concluding that his absence was much longer.

77. Bernard of Clairvaux, Letter 326, "To the Carthusian Prior of Portes," in Bruno Scott James, trans., *The Letters of St. Bernard of Clairvaux*, 402. A chimera was a mythical beast, a mixture of a lion, goat, and dragon.

78. See Brian Patrick McGuire, *The Difficult Saint*, 27–28.

79. See Stephen Clissold, *The Wisdom of the Spanish Mystics* (New York: New Directions Books, 1977), 85, and John Neihardt, chapter 20, "The Spirit Journey," in *Black Elk Speaks* (New York: Pocket Books, 1972), 190–194.

80. See Bernard of Clairvaux, Letters 144, 146, "To the Monks of Clairvaux," in Bruno Scott James, trans., *The Letters of St. Bernard of Clairvaux*, 212, 215.

81. Bernard of Clairvaux, quoted in Herbert Thurston and Donald Attwater, eds., *Butler's Lives of the Saints*, Vol. III (Westminster, MD: Christian Classics, 1987), 362.

82. Michael Casey, *Athirst for God* (Kalamazoo, MI: Cistercian Publications, 1988), 13.

83. Jean Leclercq, *Bernard of Clairvaux and the Cistercian Spirit* (Kalamazoo, MI: Cistercian Publications, 1976), 56–57.

84. See Watkin Williams' "Abelard," 289–313, in his book, *Saint Bernard of Clairvaux*, for a full account on the relationship between

Abelard and Bernard. For an excellent book on Abelard himself, see M. T. Clanchy's *Abelard: A Medieval Life* (Oxford: Blackwell Publishers, 1999).

85. For a look at the history and magnificent art and architecture of Vezelay, see Veronique Rouchon Mouilleron, *Vezelay: The Great Romanesque Church* (New York: Harry N. Abrams, Inc., n.d.).

86. This is how Brian P. McGuire describes Bernard in his book, *The Difficult Saint: Bernard of Clairvaux & His Tradition.*

87. Dennis Tamburello, *Bernard of Clairvaux: Essential Writings,* 27. Jean Leclercq also offers a good insight on Bernard and his times in "General Introduction to the Works of Saint Bernard (1)," *Cistercian Studies Quarterly,* Vol. 40.1, 2005: 24–25 when he says: "…he [Bernard] found himself torn between the demands of the Gospel—especially the beatitude about peacemakers…—and the culture to which he belonged, where violence played such a large role."

88. See trans., Robert Meyer, *Bernard of Clairvaux: The Life and Death of Saint Malachy the Irishman* (Kalamazoo, MI: Cistercian Publications, 1978), 33–34, for Bernard's hagiography, one that, while lauding the virtues of Malachy, is extremely critical of the native Irish, calling them a "good-for-nothing people," "steeped in barbarism," "Christian in name and pagan at heart."

89. For more on Bernard's and Malachy's relationship, see John Watt, *The Church in Medieval Ireland* (Dublin: Gill and Macmillan, 1972), 23, and Watkin Williams, *St. Bernard: the Man and His Message,* 43. For Bernard's correspondence with Malachy and the Irish, see Letters 383–386, in Bruno Scott James, trans., *The Letters of St. Bernard of Clairvaux,* 452–457.

90. See Jean Leclercq, "The Making of a Masterpiece," in Irene Edmonds, trans., *Bernard of Clairvaux: On the Song of Songs IV* (Kalamazoo, MI: Cistercian Publications, 1980), xi–xii, for a helpful chronological breakdown on when the sermons were most likely written.

91. *Ibid.,* sermon sixty-eight, 17.

92. *Ibid.,* sermon eighty-three, 184, and sermon seventy-nine, 143.

93. See Jean Leclercq, "General Introduction to the Works of Sain[illegible] Bernard (II)," *Cistercian Studies Quarterly,* Vol. 40.3, 2005: 244–24[illegible] where he states: "From among the Church Fathers he [Bernard] to[illegible] direct inspiration for his *Sermons on the Song of Songs* from Orig[illegible] homilies on that sacred book…." For insight into the great contribu[illegible] of Origen to the spiritual meaning of the *Song of Songs,* see R. P. La[illegible] trans., *Origen: The Song of Songs, Commentary and Homilies* (New[illegible] Newman Press, 1956).

94. See Kilian Walsh, trans., *Bernard of Clairvaux on the Song of Songs I* (Kalamazoo, MI: Cistercian Publications, 1981), 138.

95. Michael Casey, *Athirst for God,* 59.

96. Kilian Walsh, trans., *Bernard of Clairvaux on the Song of Songs II* (Kalamazoo, MI: Cistercian Publications, 1976), 38.

97. See in Kilian Walsh, trans., *Bernard of Clairvaux on the Song of Songs I,* p. x, and sermons two, three, and four, 8–24.

98. Kilian Walsh, trans., *Bernard of Clairvaux on the Song of Songs II,* 37.

99. Jean Leclercq, "General Introduction to the Works of Saint Bernard (III)," *Cistercian Studies Quarterly,* Vol. 40.4, 2005: 365–366.

100. Michael Casey, *Athirst for God,* 35.

101. See Irene Edmonds, trans., *Bernard of Clairvaux: On the Song of Songs IV,* 89–92.

102. See Etienne Gilson, *The Mystical Theology of Saint Bernard,* 21–25.

103. Kilian Walsh, trans., *Bernard of Clairvaux on the Song of Songs III* (Kalamazoo, MI: Cistercian Publications, 1979), 44.

104. See sermon eight in Kilian Walsh, trans., *Bernard of Clairvaux on the Song of Songs I,* 50.

105. Hildegard of Bingen, quoted in Bernard McGinn, *The Growth of Mysticism,* 336.

106. See Rolf Toman, ed., *The Art of Gothic,* 353. I would add that this famous depiction of Jesus with his beloved disciple seems to portray not only the union with God that a soul might experience, but also the value such writers as Bernard and Aelred gave to spiritual friendship, how it acted as vehicle to God, to union with God.

107. See Kilian Walsh, trans., *Bernard of Clairvaux on the Song of Songs* …rmon six, where he states that "mercy and judgment will be the …of my songs in the house of my pilgrimage," and sermon twenty- …*ernard of Clairvaux on the Song of Songs II,* 11–12.

…rmon twenty-three in *Bernard of Clairvaux on the Song of Songs*

…n forty-four in *Bernard of Clairvaux on the Song of Songs II,*

…*Man and His Symbols* (Garden City, NY: Doubleday &

…er, trans., *Bernard of Clairvaux: The Life and Death* …*man,* 109.

112. Geoffrey Webb and Adrian Walker, trans., *St. Bernard of Clairvaux: The story of his Life as recorded in the Vita Prima Bernardi...*, 124.

113. *Ibid.*, 126.

114. Bernard McGinn, *The Growth of Mysticism*, xiii.

115. William Yeomans, "St. Bernard of Clairvaux," in James Walsh, ed., *Spirituality Through the Centuries: Ascetics and Mystics of the Western Church* (London: Burns & Oates, n.d.), 120.

Conclusion

1. Dom David Knowles, *The Benedictines* (New York: Macmillan, 1930), 83.

2. Carl Jung, quoted in Meredith Sabini, ed., *The Earth Has Soul: The Nature Writings of C.S. Jung* (Berkeley, CA: North Atlantic Books, 2002), 158–161.

3. Aldous Huxley, "Distractions—I," in Christopher Isherwood, ed., *Vedanta for the Western World* (Hollywood, CA: Vedanta Press, 1946), 129.

4. See Boniface Ramsey, trans., *John Cassian: The Conferences* (New York: Paulist Press, 1997), 253, and *John Cassian: The Institutes* (New York: Paulist Press, 2000), 159.

5. See Thich Nhat Hanh, *Going Home: Jesus and Buddha as Brothers* (New York: Riverhead Books, 1999), 111.

6. See Thomas Merton, *Wisdom of the Desert* (New York: New Directions Publishing Corporation, 1970), 5–8.

7. David Hurst, trans., *Gregory the Great: Forty Gospel Homilies* (Kalamazoo, MI: Cistercian Publications, 1990), 37.

8. Gregory the Great, quoted in Cuthbert Butler, *Western Mysticism* (New York: E. P. Dutton & Co., 1923), 110.

9. Wayne Teasdale, *A Monk in the World: Cultivating a Spiritual Life* (Novato, CA: New World Library, 2002), xxviii.

10. Quoted in John Dunne, *A Journey with God in Time: A Spiritual Quest* (Notre Dame, IN: University of Notre Dame Press, 2003), 89.

11. See Will Johnson, *Rumi: Gazing at the Beloved* (Rochester, VT: Inner Traditions, 2003), 19.

12. Amma Syncletica, quoted in Benedicta Ward, trans., *The Sayings of the Desert Fathers* (London: Mowbray, 1983), 234.

13. See William Harmless, *Desert Christians* (Oxford: Oxford University Press, 2000), 398.

14. See Thomas Merton, *The Wisdom of the Desert*, 50.

15. Paul Wilkes, *Beyond the Walls: Monastic Wisdom for Everyday Life* (New York: Image Books, 2000), 68.

16. Alcuin, quoted in T. M. Charles-Edwards, *Early Christian Ireland* (Cambridge: Cambridge University Press, 2000), 599.